Complete Poems

BY CARL SANDBURG

ABRAHAM LINCOLN: THE PRAIRIE YEARS

ABRAHAM LINCOLN: THE WAR YEARS

MARY LINCOLN: WIFE AND WIDOW

STORM OVER THE LAND

LINCOLN COLLECTOR

THE PHOTOGRAPHS OF ABRAHAM LINCOLN
(with Frederick H. Meserve)

THE AMERICAN SONGBAG

THE CHICAGO RACE RIOTS

STEICHEN THE PHOTOGRAPHER

POTATO FACE

HOME FRONT MEMO

Novel

REMEMBRANCE ROCK

Poems

SMOKE AND STEEL

SLABS OF THE SUNBURNT WEST

CHICAGO POEMS   CORNHUSKERS

GOOD MORNING, AMERICA

SELECTED POEMS
(edited by Rebecca West)

THE PEOPLE, YES

COMPLETE POEMS

For Young Folks

ROOTABAGA STORIES   ROOTABAGA PIGEONS

ABE LINCOLN GROWS UP

EARLY MOON

Complete Poems
Carl Sandburg

HARCOURT, BRACE AND COMPANY, NEW YORK

Contents

CHICAGO POEMS

CHICAGO POEMS, *Continued*

CHICAGO POEMS, *Continued*

CORNHUSKERS

CORNHUSKERS, *Continued*

CORNHUSKERS, *Continued*

SMOKE AND STEEL

SMOKE AND STEEL, *Continued*

SMOKE AND STEEL, *Continued*

SMOKE AND STEEL, *Continued*

SLABS OF THE SUNBURNT WEST

GOOD MORNING, AMERICA

GOOD MORNING, AMERICA, *Continued*

GOOD MORNING, AMERICA, *Continued*

GOOD MORNING, AMERICA, *Continued*

THE PEOPLE, YES
Pages 439-617

NEW SECTION

NEW SECTION, *Continued*

NEW SECTION, *Continued*

Notes for a Preface

"FROM the age of six I had a mania for drawing the forms of things. By the time I was fifty I had published an infinity of designs: but all I have produced before the age of seventy is not worth taking into account. At seventy-three, I have learned a little about the real structure of nature, of animals, plants, trees, birds, fishes, and insects. In consequence, when I am eighty, I shall have made still more progress; at ninety I shall penetrate the mystery of things; at a hundred I shall certainly have reached a marvellous stage; and when I am a hundred and ten, everything I do, be it but a dot or a line, will be alive. I beg those who live as long as I to see if I do not keep my word. Written at the age of seventy-five by me, once Hokusai, today Gwako Rojin, the old man mad about drawing."—From Preface to *The Hundred Views of Fuji*.

1

The inexplicable is all around us. So is the incomprehensible. So is the unintelligible. Interviewing Babe Ruth in 1928 for the Chicago *Daily News*, I put it to him, "People come and ask what's your system for hitting home runs—that so?" "Yes," said the Babe, "and all I can tell 'em is I pick a good one and sock it. I get back to the dugout and they ask me what it was I hit and I tell 'em I don't know except it looked good."

Tyrus Raymond Cobb, who in twenty-four seasons played more games (3033), made more hits (4191), scored more runs (2244) and stole more bases (892) than any other player who ever wore spiked shoes—Ty Cobb at the end of one season got the question from sports writers, "We've watched you close this season and we find you've got eleven different ways of sliding to second. At what point between first and second do you decide which of those eleven ways you'll use?" Ty flashed, "I never think about it—I just slide!"

All around us the imponderable and the unfathomed—at these targets many a poet has shot his bullets of silver and scored a bull's-eye, or missed with dull pellets of paper.

Will Rogers, twirling his cowhand rope, insisted, "We are all ignorant but on different subjects." Picasso gives his slant as to his own ignorance related to that of others, "Why should I blame anybody else but myself if I cannot understand what I know nothing about?" And in Chicago we heard William Butler Yeats quote his father, "What can be explained is not poetry."

The Spanish poet Lorca saw one plain apple infinite as the sea. "The life of an apple when it is a delicate flower to the moment when, golden russet, it drops from the tree into the grass is as mysterious and as great as the perpetual rhythm of the tides. And a poet must know this." Lorca would instruct us: "The magic virtue of a poem consists in being always daemon-ridden so that it baptizes with dark water those who look at it. The daemon? Where is the daemon?"

I have known newspaper staffs where a saying ran, "The way to be a Star Reporter is to break all the rules." I heard Steinbeck say regarding *Of Mice and Men,* "I began with an equation and after that the story wrote itself." Paganini had a formula: toil, solitude, prayer. Steichen after World War I put in a year making a thousand photographs of a white cup and saucer, a quest in light and shadow. Maugham crosses up Forster on how to write a novel and both heave Walter Scott into the ash can. Shakespeare wrote a certain amount of trash—because his theater had to have a new play next Tuesday.

2

Readers of poetry—and writers of it—can harken to Thomas Babington Macaulay in 1825, "Perhaps no person can be a poet, or can even enjoy poetry, without a certain unsoundness of mind." Does he say that if you are perfectly sane, a respectable citizen with a well-ordered mind, you shouldn't try writing poetry or reading it? And if you are a little "off the beam" mentally you will get along better in the poetry world? Some would decide it is well he used the word "perhaps," which leaves it open to debate along with the American proverb, "Every family tree has its nut."

Many a father has held the viewpoint of Lord Chesterfield writing his son, "I do not find that God has made you a poet: and I am very glad that he has not." Sweeping ran the disgust of William Congreve in 1695, "Turn pimp, flatterer, quack, lawyer, parson, be chaplain to an atheist, . . . anything but poet; for a poet is worse, more servile, timorous and fawning, than any I have named."

"Opinions—how they do love their opinions!" I heard the Colorado poet Tom Ferril saying. "They imagine their every little idle opinion is a big idea."

We can find subtlety or fun in the Chicago surgeon Jake Buchbinder saying to Fanny Butcher, "I enjoy phony jewels as well as the real thing—if they are good fakes. I like make-believe pearls which are so real that they have to be taken to experts who can detect the true gleam. I like to see women wearing pendants from their ears made from reclaimed pop bottles—when I can't tell the difference."

3

Artist, beggarman or thief may take recourse to ancient Anglo-Saxon law. The accused in the dock hearing the question, "Are you guilty or not guilty?" had the privilege, if he so elected, to answer, "I stands mute."

Herein are somewhat more than 800 pieces written between the years 1910 and 1950. Seven books are now fastened and sealed into one book. How the pieces came to be written would make a long chapter in autobiography or a fair-sized book in itself. During the forty years of these writings came the First World War, the gay postwar prosperity years, the Great Depression, the Second World War, peace and the Cold War, global drama on a colossal scale.

Chicago Poems, in 1916, came first. Alice Corbin, an editor of the magazine *Poetry*, had urged the manuscript on Alfred Harcourt, then secretary of Henry Holt and Company, and his instigations brought the book into print. *Cornhuskers* followed in 1918. The third book, *Smoke and Steel*, came in 1920 under imprint of the new publishing house of Harcourt, Brace and Company, followed by *Slabs of the Sunburnt West* in 1922. The fifth book came in 1928, its title piece *Good Morning, America* being the Phi Beta Kappa poem at Harvard that year. The sixth came in 1936 titled *The People, Yes* and dedicated "to contributors dead and living." Affirmative of swarming and brawling Democracy, it attempts to give back to the people their own lingo.

Most of the pieces in the seventh, *New Section*, have herein their first publication between book covers, some having seen print in magazines and newspapers. This is true especially of those headed "War-Time," all but two of which appeared during the Second World War. If some of the pieces in this section seem to be not for this hour, they can, as with others in the earlier books, be passed by as annals, chronicles or punctuation points of a vanished period. Included in *New Section* are about forty pieces seeing print for the first time. This applies to all under the heading "Present Hour" and about half under "Sky Talk" which ends the book.

4

There are poets of the cloister and the quiet corner, of green fields and the earth serene in its changes. There are poets of streets and struggles, of dust and combat, of violence wanton or justified, of plain folk living close to a hard earth as in the great though neglected poem *Piers Plowman*. There have been poets whose themes wove through both of the foregoing approaches. John M. Synge presented a viewpoint in this era ever worth care and thought: ". . . When men lose their poetic feeling for ordinary life, and cannot write poetry of ordinary things, their exalted poetry is likely to lose its strength of exaltation, in the way men cease to build beautiful churches when they have lost happiness in building shops. Many of the older poets, such as Villon and Herrick and Burns, used the whole of their personal life as their material, and the verse written in this way was read by strong men, and thieves, and deacons, not by little cliques only."

Poetry and politics, the relation of the poets to society, to democracy, to monarchy, to dictatorships—we have here a theme whose classic is yet to be written. Some of its implications I tried for in my dedication of a book to the poet Stephen Vincent Benet:

"He knew the distinction between pure art and propaganda in the written or spoken word. He could sing to give men music, consolation, pleasure. He could intone chant or prayer pointing the need for men to act. He illustrated the code and creed of those writers who seek to widen the areas of freedom for all men, knowing that men of ideas vanish first when freedom vanishes. He saw that a writer's silence on living issues can in itself constitute a propaganda of conduct leading toward the deterioration or death of freedom. He wrote often hoping that men would act because of his words. He could have been Olympian, whimsical, seeking to be timeless amid bells of doom not to be put off."

5

There is a formal poetry perfect only in form, "all dressed up and nowhere to go." The number of syllables, the designated and required stresses of accent, the rhymes if wanted—they come off with the skill of a solved crossword puzzle. Yet its animation and connotation are less than that of "a dead mackerel in the moonshine," the latter even as an extinct form reporting that once it was a living fish aswim in bright waters.

A poet explains for us what for him is poetry by what he presents to us in his poems. A painter makes definitions of what for him is art by the kind of paintings his brush puts on canvas. An actor defines dramatic art as best he can by the way he plays his parts. The playwright in his offering of dramatic action and lines tells us what he regards as theater art. And so on down the line. The novelist explains his theory of creative literature by the stories and people in his books. There is no escape. There stands the work of the man, the woman, who wrought it. We go to it, read it, look at it, perhaps go back to it many a time and it is for each of us what we make of it. The creator of it can say it means this or that— or it means for you whatever you take it to mean. He can say it happened, it came into being and it now exists apart from him and nothing can be done about it.

Compact and charged with a curious Hoosier finality is the definition from George Ade: "A classic is a book that people refuse to let die."

6

Oliver Wendell Holmes, skilled rhymester, told a young poet: "When you write in prose you say what you mean. When you write in verse you say what you must." Having said this to the young man, Holmes bethought himself and then wrote, "I was thinking more especially of rhymed verse. Rhythm alone is a tether, and not a very long one. But rhymes are iron fetters; it is dragging a chain and ball to march under their incumbrance; it is a clog-dance you are figuring in when you execute your metrical *pas seul* . . . You want to say something about the heavenly bodies, and you have a beautiful line ending with the word stars . . . You cannot make any use of cars, I will suppose; you have no occasion to talk about scars; 'the red planet Mars' has been used already; Dibdin has said enough about the gallant tars; what is there left for you but bars? So you give up your trains of thought, capitulate to necessity, and manage to lug in some kind of allusion, in place or out of place, which will allow you to make use of bars. Can there be imagined a more certain process for breaking up all continuity of thought, than this miserable subjugation of intellect to the clink of well or ill matched syllables?"

The fact is ironic. A proficient and sometimes exquisite performer in rhymed verse goes out of his way to register the point that the more rhyme there is in poetry the more danger of its tricking the writer into something other than the urge in the beginning.

7

A well-done world history of poetry would tell us of the beginnings and the continuing tradition of blank verse, rhymed verse, ballads, ballades, sonnets, triolets, rondeaus, villanelles, the sestina, the pantoum, the hokku; also odes, elegiacs, idylls, lyrics, hymns, quatrains, couplets, ditties, limericks, and all the other forms. These are fixed, frozen, immutable; in a Japanese hokku you are allowed exactly seventeen syllables and if you try to make it in sixteen or eighteen you're out of luck. Such a history of poetry, however, might go a long way in research, chronicle, and discussion of a vital body of ancient and modern poems under the following (and more) heads:

1. Chants.
2. Psalms.
3. Gnomics.
4. Contemplations.
5. Proverbs.
6. Epitaphs.
7. Litanies.
8. Incidents of intensely concentrated action or utterance.

Under each of the above heads could be gathered a multitude of instances. There are "strict formalists in soup-and-fish" who would deny such instances being valid poetry. They can be confronted with a superb and passionate verse from the mouth of Oliver Cromwell: "My brethren, by the bowels of Christ I beseech you, bethink you that you may be mistaken." (Do we have here the cadenced utterance of passion?) Or we could cite the Union General in April of 1864, bemoaning blunders and corruption, "May God save my country—if there is a God—and if I have a country." Or a Michelangelo saying in 1509, "I have no friends of any kind and I do not want any," and forty years later writing, "I am always alone and I speak to no one."

We could add the Irish toast: "May the road to hell grow green waiting for you." We could copy from Olive Schreiner's diary: "I have such a longing for friendship, someone to talk to really. I wonder if it is all a delusion. Even any kind of love I want. Death is so near and I have loved so little." We could offer an epitaph from the novel *Remembrance Rock*:

> He was a practical man
> who lived dreamless.
> Now he sleeps here
> as he lived—dreamless.

Or we could draw from Justice Holmes: "I have always sought to guide the future—but it is very lonely sometimes trying to play God."

8

No two persons register precisely the same to a work of art. Mark Twain tells, as one version has it, of two men who for the first time laid eyes on the tumultuous and majestic Grand Canyon of Arizona. One cried out, "I'll be God damned!" The other fell to his knees in prayer. Mark contended their religious feelings were the same though the ritual was different.

After the first performance of Strauss's *Salome* in Berlin, the *Tageblatt's* music critic raved against it. Seeing Grieg in the lobby he asked the Norwegian composer, "What do you think of it?" The reply came cool as a cube of iced cucumber, "How can I tell you that? I have heard it only once."

Of Turner's painting, *The Slave Ship*, Ruskin wrote it was "perfect and immortal." The painter Inness declared, "It's claptrap." Thackeray was puzzled and neutral: "I don't know whether it's sublime or ridiculous."

Lincoln rated the Declaration of Independence an "immortal emblem," though Rufus Choate earlier held it to be a string of "glittering generalities." Choate it was who listened to Italian grand opera, hearing the words but not knowing what they were saying, and asking his daughter, "Interpret for me the libretto lest I dilate with the wrong emotion."

What is instinct? What is thought? Where is the absolute line between these two? Nobody knows—as yet. What is an Emotion as apart from an Idea? When are a Concept and a Feeling identical? Nobody knows—exactly—as yet. What is an ideational state of mind as set off from a reverie? When do the foregoing seemingly contrasted urges of blood and brain move into a confluence with an end result of Creative Art? They're working on it. If or when they filch this secret from the broad bosom of Mother Nature they will have solved the mystery of what for long has been termed Genius.

What is this borderland of dream and logic, of fantasy and reason, where the roots and tentacles of mind and personality float and drift into the sudden shaping of a flash resulting in a scheme, a form, a design, an invention, a machine, an image, a song, a symphony, a drama, a poem? There are those who believe they know—and those who hope they may yet know.

9

As years pass and experience writes new records in our mind life, we go back to some works of art we rejected in the early days and find values we missed. Work, love, laughter, pain, death, put impressions on us as time passes, and we brood over what has happened, praying it may be an "exalted brooding." Out of songs and scars and the mystery of personal development, we may get eyes that pick out intentions we had not seen before in people, in art, in books and poetry.

Naturally, too, the reverse happens. What we register to at one period of life, what we find gay and full of fine nourishment at one time, we may find later has lost interest for us. A few masterpieces last across the years. We usually discard some. A few masterpieces are enough. Why this is so we do not know. For each individual his new acquisitions and old discards are different.

Perhaps no wrong is done and no temple of human justice violated in pointing out that each authentic poet makes a style of his own. Sometimes this style is so clearly the poet's own that when he is imitated it is known who is imitated. Shakespeare, Villon, Li Po, Whitman—each sent forth his language and impress of thought and feeling from a different style of gargoyle spout. In the spacious highways of books major or minor, each poet is allowed the stride that will get him where he wants to go if, God help him, he can hit that stride and keep it.

10

At the age of six, as my fingers first found how to shape the alphabet, I decided to become a person of letters. At the age of ten I had scrawled letters on slates, on paper, on boxes and walls and I formed an ambition to become a sign-painter. At twenty I was an American soldier in Puerto Rico writing letters printed in the home town paper. At twenty-one I went to West Point, being a classmate of Douglas MacArthur and Ulysses S. Grant III—for two weeks—returning home after passing in spelling, geography, history, failing in arithmetic and grammar. At twenty-three I edited a college paper and wrote many a paragraph that after a lapse of fifty years still seems funny, the same applying to the college yearbook I edited the following year. Across several years I wrote many odd pieces— two slim books—not worth later reprint. In a six-year period came four books of poetry having a variety of faults, no other person more keenly aware of their accomplishments and shortcomings than myself. In the two books for children, in this period, are a few cornland tales that go on traveling, one about "The Two Skyscrapers Who Decided to Have a Child." At fifty I had published a two-volume biography and *The American Songbag*, and there was puzzlement as to whether I was a poet, a biographer, a wandering troubadour with a guitar, a midwest Hans Christian Andersen, or a historian of current events whose newspaper reporting was gathered into a book *The Chicago Race Riots*. At fifty-one I wrote America's first biography of a photographer. At sixty-one came a four-volume biography, bringing doctoral degrees at Harvard, Yale, New York University, Wesleyan, Lafayette, Lincoln Memorial, Syracuse, Rollins, Dartmouth—Augustana and Uppsala at Stockholm. I am still studying verbs and the mystery of how they connect nouns. I am more suspicious of adjectives than at any other time in all my born days. I have forgotten the meaning of twenty or thirty of my poems written thirty or forty years ago. I still favor several simple poems published long ago which continue to have an appeal for simple people. I have written by different methods and in a wide miscellany of moods and have seldom been afraid to travel in lands and seas where I met fresh scenes and new songs. All my life I have been trying to learn to read, to see and hear, and to write. At sixty-five I began my first novel, and the five years lacking a month I took to finish it, I was still traveling, still a seeker. I should like to think that as I go on writing there will be sentences truly alive, with verbs quivering, with nouns giving color and echoes. It could be, in the grace of God, I shall live to be eighty-nine, as did Hokusai, and speaking my farewell to earthly scenes, I might paraphrase: "If God had let me live five years longer I should have been a writer."

CHICAGO POEMS

Chicago Poems

CHICAGO

Hog Butcher for the World,
Tool Maker, Stacker of Wheat,
Player with Railroads and the Nation's Freight Handler;
Stormy, husky, brawling,
City of the Big Shoulders:

They tell me you are wicked and I believe them, for I have seen your
painted women under the gas lamps luring the farm boys.
And they tell me you are crooked and I answer: Yes, it is true I have seen
the gunman kill and go free to kill again.
And they tell me you are brutal and my reply is: On the faces of women
and children I have seen the marks of wanton hunger.
And having answered so I turn once more to those who sneer at this my
city, and I give them back the sneer and say to them:
Come and show me another city with lifted head singing so proud to be
alive and coarse and strong and cunning.
Flinging magnetic curses amid the toil of piling job on job, here is a tall
bold slugger set vivid against the little soft cities;
Fierce as a dog with tongue lapping for action, cunning as a savage pitted
against the wilderness,
    Bareheaded,
    Shoveling,
    Wrecking,
    Planning,
    Building, breaking, rebuilding,
Under the smoke, dust all over his mouth, laughing with white teeth,
Under the terrible burden of destiny laughing as a young man laughs,
Laughing even as an ignorant fighter laughs who has never lost a battle,

Bragging and laughing that under his wrist is the pulse, and under his ribs
the heart of the people,
Laughing!
Laughing the stormy, husky, brawling laughter of Youth, half-naked,
sweating, proud to be Hog Butcher, Tool Maker, Stacker of Wheat,
Player with Railroads and Freight Handler to the Nation.

SKETCH

THE shadows of the ships
Rock on the crest
In the low blue lustre
Of the tardy and the soft inrolling tide.

A long brown bar at the dip of the sky
Puts an arm of sand in the span of salt.

The lucid and endless wrinkles
Draw in, lapse and withdraw.
Wavelets crumble and white spent bubbles
Wash on the floor of the beach.

Rocking on the crest
In the low blue lustre
Are the shadows of the ships.

MASSES

AMONG the mountains I wandered and saw blue haze and red crag and
was amazed;
On the beach where the long push under the endless tide maneuvers, I
stood silent;
Under the stars on the prairie watching the Dipper slant over the horizon's
grass, I was full of thoughts.
Great men, pageants of war and labor, soldiers and workers, mothers lifting
their children—these all I touched, and felt the solemn thrill of them.
And then one day I got a true look at the Poor, millions of the Poor,

patient and toiling; more patient than crags, tides, and stars; innumerable, patient as the darkness of night—and all broken, humble ruins of nations.

LOST

DESOLATE and lone
All night long on the lake
Where fog trails and mist creeps,
The whistle of a boat
Calls and cries unendingly,
Like some lost child
In tears and trouble
Hunting the harbor's breast
And the harbor's eyes.

THE HARBOR

PASSING through huddled and ugly walls
By doorways where women
Looked from their hunger-deep eyes,
Haunted with shadows of hunger-hands,
Out from the huddled and ugly walls,
I came sudden, at the city's edge,
On a blue burst of lake,
Long lake waves breaking under the sun
On a spray-flung curve of shore;
And a fluttering storm of gulls,
Masses of great gray wings
And flying white bellies
Veering and wheeling free in the open.

THEY WILL SAY

OF my city the worst that men will ever say is this:
You took little children away from the sun and the dew,
And the glimmers that played in the grass under the great sky,
And the reckless rain; you put them between walls

To work, broken and smothered, for bread and wages,
To eat dust in their throats and die empty-hearted
For a little handful of pay on a few Saturday nights.

MILL-DOORS

You never come back.
I say good-by when I see you going in the doors,
The hopeless open doors that call and wait
And take you then for—how many cents a day?
How many cents for the sleepy eyes and fingers?

I say good-by because I know they tap your wrists,
In the dark, in the silence, day by day,
And all the blood of you drop by drop,
And you are old before you are young.
You never come back.

HALSTED STREET CAR

Come you, cartoonists,
Hang on a strap with me here
At seven o'clock in the morning
On a Halsted street car.

Take your pencils
And draw these faces.

Try with your pencils for these crooked faces,
That pig-sticker in one corner—his mouth—
That overall factory girl—her loose cheeks.

Find for your pencils
A way to mark your memory
Of tired empty faces.

After their night's sleep,
In the moist dawn

And cool daybreak,
Faces
Tired of wishes,
Empty of dreams.

CLARK STREET BRIDGE

Dust of the feet
And dust of the wheels,
Wagons and people going,
All day feet and wheels.

Now . . .
. . . Only stars and mist
A lonely policeman,
Two cabaret dancers,
Stars and mist again,
No more feet or wheels,
No more dust and wagons.

Voices of dollars
And drops of blood
. . . . .
Voices of broken hearts,
. . . Voices singing, singing,
. . . Silver voices, singing,
Softer than the stars,
Softer than the mist.

PASSERS-BY

Passers-by,
Out of your many faces
Flash memories to me
Now at the day end
Away from the sidewalks
Where your shoe soles traveled
And your voices rose and blent

To form the city's afternoon roar
Hindering an old silence.

Passers-by,
I remember lean ones among you,
Throats in the clutch of a hope,
Lips written over with strivings,
Mouths that kiss only for love,
Records of great wishes slept with,
    Held long
And prayed and toiled for:

    Yes,
Written on
Your mouths
And your throats
I read them
When you passed by.

THE WALKING MAN OF RODIN

LEGS hold a torso away from the earth.
And a regular high poem of legs is here.
Powers of bone and cord raise a belly and lungs
Out of ooze and over the loam where eyes look and ears hear
And arms have a chance to hammer and shoot and run motors.
    You make us
    Proud of our legs, old man.

And you left off the head here,
The skull found always crumbling neighbor of the ankles.

SUBWAY

Down between the walls of shadow
Where the iron laws insist,
    The hunger voices mock.

The worn wayfaring men
With the hunched and humble shoulders,
Throw their laughter into toil.

THE SHOVEL MAN

On the street
Slung on his shoulder is a handle half way across,
Tied in a big knot on the scoop of cast iron
Are the overalls faded from sun and rain in the ditches;
Spatter of dry clay sticking yellow on his left sleeve
And a flimsy shirt open at the throat,
I know him for a shovel man,
A dago working for a dollar six bits a day
And a dark-eyed woman in the old country dreams of him for one of the
world's ready men with a pair of fresh lips and a kiss better than
all the wild grapes that ever grew in Tuscany.

A TEAMSTER'S FAREWELL
Sobs En Route to a Penitentiary

Good-by now to the streets and the clash of wheels and locking hubs,
The sun coming on the brass buckles and harness knobs,
The muscles of the horses sliding under their heavy haunches,
Good-by now to the traffic policeman and his whistle,
The smash of the iron hoof on the stones,
All the crazy wonderful slamming roar of the street—
O God, there's noises I'm going to be hungry for.

FISH CRIER

I know a Jew fish crier down on Maxwell Street with a voice like a north
wind blowing over corn stubble in January.
He dangles herring before prospective customers evincing a joy identical
with that of Pavlowa dancing.

His face is that of a man terribly glad to be selling fish, terribly glad that
God made fish, and customers to whom he may call his wares from
a pushcart.

PICNIC BOAT

SUNDAY night and the park policemen tell each other it is dark as a
stack of black cats on Lake Michigan.
A big picnic boat comes home to Chicago from the peach farms of
Saugatuck.
Hundreds of electric bulbs break the night's darkness, a flock of red and
yellow birds with wings at a standstill.
Running along the deck-railings are festoons and leaping in curves are
loops of light from prow and stern to the tall smokestacks.
Over the hoarse crunch of waves at my pier comes a hoarse answer in
the rhythmic oompa of the brasses playing a Polish folk-song for the
home-comers.

HAPPINESS

I ASKED professors who teach the meaning of life to tell me what is hap-
piness.
And I went to famous executives who boss the work of thousands of men.
They all shook their heads and gave me a smile as though I was trying
to fool with them.
And then one Sunday afternoon I wandered out along the Desplaines
river
And I saw a crowd of Hungarians under the trees with their women and
children and a keg of beer and an accordion.

MUCKERS

TWENTY men stand watching the muckers.
    Stabbing the sides of the ditch
    Where clay gleams yellow,
    Driving the blades of their shovels
    Deeper and deeper for the new gas mains,
    Wiping sweat off their faces
        With red bandanas.

The muckers work on . . . pausing . . . to pull
Their boots out of suckholes where they slosh.

Of the twenty looking on
Ten murmur, "O, it's a hell of a job,"
Ten others, "Jesus, I wish I had the job."

BLACKLISTED

WHY shall I keep the old name?
What is a name anywhere anyway?
A name is a cheap thing all fathers and mothers leave each child:
A job is a job and I want to live, so
Why does God Almighty or anybody else care whether I take a new
    name to go by?

GRACELAND

TOMB of a millionaire,
A multi-millionaire, ladies and gentlemen,
Place of the dead where they spend every year
The usury of twenty-five thousand dollars
        For upkeep and flowers
To keep fresh the memory of the dead.
The merchant prince gone to dust
Commanded in his written will
Over the signed name of his last testament
Twenty-five thousand dollars be set aside
For roses, lilacs, hydrangeas, tulips,
For perfume and color, sweetness of remembrance
Around his last long home.

(A hundred cash girls want nickels to go to the movies tonight.
In the back stalls of a hundred saloons, women are at tables
Drinking with men or waiting for men jingling loose silver dollars in
    their pockets.
In a hundred furnished rooms is a girl who sells silk or dress goods or
    leather stuff for six dollars a week wages

And when she pulls on her stockings in the morning she is reckless
about God and the newspapers and the police, the talk of her home
town or the name people call her.)

CHILD OF THE ROMANS

THE dago shovelman sits by the railroad track
Eating a noon meal of bread and bologna.
    A train whirls by, and men and women at tables
    Alive with red roses and yellow jonquils,
    Eat steaks running with brown gravy,
    Strawberries and cream, eclairs and coffee.
The dago shovelman finishes the dry bread and bologna,
Washes it down with a dipper from the water-boy,
And goes back to the second half of a ten-hour day's work
Keeping the road-bed so the roses and jonquils
Shake hardly at all in the cut glass vases
Standing slender on the tables in the dining cars.

THE RIGHT TO GRIEF
To Certain Poets About to Die

TAKE your fill of intimate remorse, perfumed sorrow,
Over the dead child of a millionaire,
And the pity of Death refusing any check on the bank
Which the millionaire might order his secretary to scratch off
And get cashed.

  Very well,
You for your grief and I for mine.
Let me have a sorrow my own if I want to.

I shall cry over the dead child of a stockyards hunky.
His job is sweeping blood off the floor.
He gets a dollar seventy cents a day when he works
And it's many tubs of blood he shoves out with a broom day by day.

Now his three year old daughter
Is in a white coffin that cost him a week's wages.

Every Saturday night he will pay the undertaker fifty cents till the debt
    is wiped out.

The hunky and his wife and the kids
Cry over the pinched face almost at peace in the white box.
They remember it was scrawny and ran up high doctor bills.
They are glad it is gone for the rest of the family now will have more
    to eat and wear.

Yet before the majesty of Death they cry around the coffin
And wipe their eyes with red bandanas and sob when the priest says,
    "God have mercy on us all."

I have a right to feel my throat choke about this.
You take your grief and I mine—see?
Tomorrow there is no funeral and the hunky goes back to his job sweep-
    ing blood off the floor at a dollar seventy cents a day.
All he does all day long is keep on shoving hog blood ahead of him with
    a broom.

MAG

I wish to God I never saw you, Mag.
I wish you never quit your job and came along with me.
I wish we never bought a license and a white dress
For you to get married in the day we ran off to a minister
And told him we would love each other and take care of each other
Always and always long as the sun and the rain lasts anywhere.
Yes, I'm wishing now you lived somewhere away from here
And I was a bum on the bumpers a thousand miles away dead broke.
    I wish the kids had never come
    And rent and coal and clothes to pay for
    And a grocery man calling for cash,
    Every day cash for beans and prunes.
    I wish to God I never saw you, Mag.
    I wish to God the kids had never come.

ONION DAYS

Mrs. Gabrielle Giovannitti comes along Peoria Street every morning
at nine o'clock
With kindling wood piled on top of her head, her eyes looking straight
ahead to find the way for her old feet.
Her daughter-in-law, Mrs. Pietro Giovannitti, whose husband was killed
in a tunnel explosion through the negligence of a fellow-servant,
Works ten hours a day, sometimes twelve, picking onions for Jasper on
the Bowmanville road.
She takes a street car at half-past five in the morning, Mrs. Pietro Gio-
vannitti does,
And gets back from Jasper's with cash for her day's work, between nine
and ten o'clock at night.
Last week she got eight cents a box, Mrs. Pietro Giovannitti, picking
onions for Jasper,
But this week Jasper dropped the pay to six cents a box because so many
women and girls were answering the ads in the Daily News.
Jasper belongs to an Episcopal church in Ravenswood and on certain
Sundays
He enjoys chanting the Nicene creed with his daughters on each side of
him joining their voices with his.
If the preacher repeats old sermons of a Sunday, Jasper's mind wanders to
his 700-acre farm and how he can make it produce more efficiently
And sometimes he speculates on whether he could word an ad in the
Daily News so it would bring more women and girls out to his farm
and reduce operating costs.
Mrs. Pietro Giovannitti is far from desperate about life; her joy is in a
child she knows will arrive to her in three months.
And now while these are the pictures for today there are other pictures of
the Giovannitti people I could give you for tomorrow,
And how some of them go to the county agent on winter mornings with
their baskets for beans and cornmeal and molasses.
I listen to fellows saying here's good stuff for a novel or it might be
worked up into a good play.
I say there's no dramatist living can put old Mrs. Gabrielle Giovannitti
into a play with that kindling wood piled on top of her head coming
along Peoria Street nine o'clock in the morning.

POPULATION DRIFTS

New-mown hay smell and wind of the plain made her a woman whose
ribs had the power of the hills in them and her hands were tough
for work and there was passion for life in her womb.

She and her man crossed the ocean and the years that marked their faces
saw them haggling with landlords and grocers while six children
played on the stones and prowled in the garbage cans.

One child coughed its lungs away, two more have adenoids and can
neither talk nor run like their mother, one is in jail, two have jobs
in a box factory

And as they fold the pasteboard, they wonder what the wishing is and
the wistful glory in them that flutters faintly when the glimmer of
spring comes on the air or the green of summer turns brown:

They do not know it is the new-mown hay smell calling and the wind
of the plain praying for them to come back and take hold of life
again with tough hands and with passion.

CRIPPLE

Once when I saw a cripple
Gasping slowly his last days with the white plague,
Looking from hollow eyes, calling for air,
Desperately gesturing with wasted hands
In the dark and dust of a house down in a slum,
I said to myself
I would rather have been a tall sunflower
Living in a country garden
Lifting a golden-brown face to the summer,
Rain-washed and dew-misted,
Mixed with the poppies and ranking hollyhocks,
And wonderingly watching night after night
The clear silent processionals of stars.

A FENCE

Now the stone house on the lake front is finished and the workmen are
    beginning the fence.
The palings are made of iron bars with steel points that can stab the life
    out of any man who falls on them.
As a fence, it is a masterpiece, and will shut off the rabble and all vaga-
    bonds and hungry men and all wandering children looking for a
    place to play.
Passing through the bars and over the steel points will go nothing except
    Death and the Rain and Tomorrow.

ANNA IMROTH

Cross the hands over the breast here—so.
Straighten the legs a little more—so.
And call for the wagon to come and take her home.
Her mother will cry some and so will her sisters and brothers.
But all of the others got down and they are safe and this is the only one
    of the factory girls who wasn't lucky in making the jump when the
    fire broke.
It is the hand of God and the lack of fire escapes.

WORKING GIRLS

The working girls in the morning are going to work—long lines of them
    afoot amid the downtown stores and factories, thousands with little
    brick-shaped lunches wrapped in newspapers under their arms.
Each morning as I move through this river of young-woman life I feel a
    wonder about where it is all going, so many with a peach bloom of
    young years on them and laughter of red lips and memories in their
    eyes of dances the night before and plays and walks.
Green and gray streams run side by side in a river and so here are always
    the others, those who have been over the way, the women who know
    each one the end of life's gamble for her, the meaning and the clue,
    the how and the why of the dances and the arms that passed around
    their waists and the fingers that played in their hair.

Faces go by written over: "I know it all, I know where the bloom and
the laughter go and I have memories," and the feet of these move
slower and they have wisdom where the others have beauty.
So the green and the gray move in the early morning on the downtown
streets.

MAMIE

MAMIE beat her head against the bars of a little Indiana town and
dreamed of romance and big things off somewhere the way the rail-
road trains all ran.
She could see the smoke of the engines get lost down where the streaks
of steel flashed in the sun and when the newspapers came in on the
morning mail she knew there was a big Chicago far off, where all
the trains ran.
She got tired of the barber shop boys and the post office chatter and the
church gossip and the old pieces the band played on the Fourth of
July and Decoration Day
And sobbed at her fate and beat her head against the bars and was going
to kill herself
When the thought came to her that if she was going to die she might as
well die struggling for a clutch of romance among the streets of
Chicago.
She has a job now at six dollars a week in the basement of the Boston
Store
And even now she beats her head against the bars in the same old way
and wonders if there is a bigger place the railroads run to from Chi-
cago where maybe there is
　　　　　romance
　　　　　and big things
　　　　　and real dreams
　　　　　that never go smash.

PERSONALITY

Musings of a Police Reporter in the Identification Bureau

You have loved forty women, but you have only one thumb.

You have led a hundred secret lives, but you mark only one thumb.

You go round the world and fight in a thousand wars and win all the world's honors, but when you come back home the print of the one thumb your mother gave you is the same print of thumb you had in the old home when your mother kissed you and said good-by.

Out of the whirling womb of time come millions of men and their feet crowd the earth and they cut one another's throats for room to stand and among them all are not two thumbs alike.

Somewhere is a Great God of Thumbs who can tell the inside story of this.

CUMULATIVES

Storms have beaten on this point of land
And ships gone to wreck here
   and the passers-by remember it
   with talk on the deck at night
   as they near it.

Fists have beaten on the face of this old prize-fighter
And his battles have held the sporting pages
   and on the street they indicate him with their
   right forefinger as one who once wore
   a championship belt.

A hundred stories have been published and a thousand rumored
About why this tall dark man has divorced two beautiful young women
And married a third who resembles the first two
   and they shake their heads and say, "There he goes,"
   when he passes by in sunny weather or in rain
   along the city streets.

TO CERTAIN JOURNEYMEN

Undertakers, hearse drivers, grave diggers,
I speak to you as one not afraid of your business.

You handle dust going to a long country,
You know the secret behind your job is the same whether you lower the
    coffin with modern, automatic machinery, well-oiled and noiseless,
    or whether the body is laid in by naked hands and then covered by
    the shovels.

Your day's work is done with laughter many days of the year,
And you earn a living by those who say good-by today in thin whispers.

CHAMFORT

There's Chamfort. He's a sample.
Locked himself in his library with a gun,
Shot off his nose and shot out his right eye.
And this Chamfort knew how to write
And thousands read his books on how to live,
But he himself didn't know
How to die by force of his own hand—see?
They found him a red pool on the carpet
Cool as an April forenoon,
Talking and talking gay maxims and grim epigrams.
Well, he wore bandages over his nose and right eye,
Drank coffee and chatted many years
With men and women who loved him
Because he laughed and daily dared Death:
"Come and take me."

LIMITED

I AM riding on a limited express, one of the crack trains of the nation.
Hurtling across the prairie into blue haze and dark air go fifteen all-steel
  coaches holding a thousand people.
(All the coaches shall be scrap and rust and all the men and women
  laughing in the diners and sleepers shall pass to ashes.)
I ask a man in the smoker where he is going and he answers: "Omaha."

THE HAS-BEEN

A STONE face higher than six horses stood five thousand years gazing at
  the world seeming to clutch a secret.
A boy passes and throws a niggerhead that chips off the end of the nose
  from the stone face; he lets fly a mud ball that spatters the right eye
  and cheek of the old looker-on.
The boy laughs and goes whistling "ee-ee-ee ee-ee-ee." The stone face
  stands silent, seeming to clutch a secret.

IN A BACK ALLEY

REMEMBRANCE for a great man is this.
The newsies are pitching pennies.
And on the copper disk is the man's face.
Dead lover of boys, what do you ask for now?

A COIN

YOUR western heads here cast on money,
You are the two that fade away together,
    Partners in the mist.

Lunging buffalo shoulder,
Lean Indian face,
We who come after where you are gone
Salute your forms on the new nickel.

You are
To us:
The past.

Runners
On the prairie:
Good-by.

DYNAMITER

I SAT with a dynamiter at supper in a German saloon eating steak and
  onions.
And he laughed and told stories of his wife and children and the cause of
  labor and the working class.
It was laughter of an unshakable man knowing life to be a rich and red-
  blooded thing.
Yes, his laugh rang like the call of gray birds filled with a glory of joy
  ramming their winged flight through a rain storm.
His name was in many newspapers as an enemy of the nation and few
  keepers of churches or schools would open their doors to him.
Over the steak and onions not a word was said of his deep days and
  nights as a dynamiter.
Only I always remember him as a lover of life, a lover of children, a lover
  of all free, reckless laughter everywhere—lover of red hearts and red
  blood the world over.

ICE HANDLER

I KNOW an ice handler who wears a flannel shirt with pearl buttons the
  size of a dollar,
And he lugs a hundred-pound hunk into a saloon icebox, helps himself
  to cold ham and rye bread,
Tells the bartender it's hotter than yesterday and will be hotter yet
  tomorrow, by Jesus,
And is on his way with his head in the air and a hard pair of fists.
He spends a dollar or so every Saturday night on a two hundred pound
  woman who washes dishes in the Hotel Morrison.
He remembers when the union was organized he broke the noses of two

scabs and loosened the nuts so the wheels came off six different wagons one morning, and he came around and watched the ice melt in the street.

All he was sorry for was one of the scabs bit him on the knuckles of the right hand so they bled when he came around to the saloon to tell the boys about it.

JACK

JACK was a swarthy, swaggering son-of-a-gun.

He worked thirty years on the railroad, ten hours a day, and his hands were tougher than sole leather.

He married a tough woman and they had eight children and the woman died and the children grew up and went away and wrote the old man every two years.

He died in the poorhouse sitting on a bench in the sun telling reminiscences to other old men whose women were dead and children scattered.

There was joy on his face when he died as there was joy on his face when he lived—he was a swarthy, swaggering son-of-a-gun.

FELLOW CITIZENS

I DRANK musty ale at the Illinois Athletic Club with the millionaire manufacturer of Green River butter one night

And his face had the shining light of an old-time Quaker, he spoke of a beautiful daughter, and I knew he had a peace and a happiness up his sleeve somewhere.

Then I heard Jim Kirch make a speech to the Advertising Association on the trade resources of South America.

And the way he lighted a three-for-a-nickel stogie and cocked it at an angle regardless of the manners of our best people,

I knew he had a clutch on a real happiness even though some of the reporters on his newspaper say he is the living double of Jack London's Sea Wolf.

In the mayor's office the mayor himself told me he was happy though it is a hard job to satisfy all the office-seekers and eat all the dinners he is asked to eat.

Down in Gilpin Place, near Hull House, was a man with his jaw wrapped
    for a bad toothache,
And he had it all over the butter millionaire, Jim Kirch and the mayor
    when it came to happiness.
He is a maker of accordions and guitars and not only makes them from
    start to finish, but plays them after he makes them.
And he had a guitar of mahogany with a walnut bottom he offered for
    seven dollars and a half if I wanted it,
And another just like it, only smaller, for six dollars, though he never
    mentioned the price till I asked him,
And he stated the price in a sorry way, as though the music and the
    make of an instrument count for a million times more than the
    price in money.
I thought he had a real soul and knew a lot about God.
There was light in his eyes of one who has conquered sorrow in so far as
    sorrow is conquerable or worth conquering.
Anyway he is the only Chicago citizen I was jealous of that day.
He played a dance they play in some parts of Italy when the harvest of
    grapes is over and the wine presses are ready for work.

NIGGER

I AM the nigger.
Singer of songs,
Dancer . . .
Softer than fluff of cotton . . .
Harder than dark earth
Roads beaten in the sun
By the bare feet of slaves . . .
Foam of teeth . . . breaking crash of laughter . . .
Red love of the blood of woman,
White love of the tumbling pickaninnies . . .
Lazy love of the banjo thrum . . .
Sweated and driven for the harvest-wage,
Loud laughter with hands like hams,
Fists toughened on the handles,
Smiling the slumber dreams of old jungles,
Crazy as the sun and dew and dripping, heaving life of the jungle,

Brooding and muttering with memories of shackles:
> I am the nigger.
> Look at me.
> I am the nigger.

TWO NEIGHBORS

Faces of two eternities keep looking at me.
One is Omar Khayam and the red stuff
>> wherein men forget yesterday and tomorrow
>> and remember only the voices and songs,
>> the stories, newspapers and fights of today.
One is Louis Cornaro and a slim trick
>> of slow, short meals across slow, short years,
>> letting Death open the door only in slow, short inches.
I have a neighbor who swears by Omar.
I have a neighbor who swears by Cornaro.
>>>>>>> Both are happy.
Faces of two eternities keep looking at me.
>>>>>>>> Let them look.

STYLE

Style—go ahead talking about style.
You can tell where a man gets his style just
>> as you can tell where Pavlowa got her legs
>> or Ty Cobb his batting eye.

> Go on talking.
Only don't take my style away.
>> It's my face.
>> Maybe no good
>>> but anyway, my face.
I talk with it, I sing with it, I see, taste and feel with it, I know why I
> want to keep it.

Kill my style
>>> and you break Pavlowa's legs,
>>> and you blind Ty Cobb's batting eye.

TO BEACHEY, 1912

RIDING against the east,
A veering, steady shadow
Purrs the motor-call
Of the man-bird
Ready with the death-laughter
In his throat
And in his heart always
The love of the big blue beyond.

Only a man,
A far fleck of shadow on the east
Sitting at ease
With his hands on a wheel
And around him the large gray wings.
Hold him, great soft wings,
Keep and deal kindly, O wings,
With the cool, calm shadow at the wheel.

UNDER A HAT RIM

WHILE the hum and the hurry
Of passing footfalls
Beat in my ear like the restless surf
Of a wind-blown sea,
A soul came to me
Out of the look on a face.

Eyes like a lake
Where a storm-wind roams
Caught me from under
The rim of a hat.
    I thought of a midsea wreck
    and bruised fingers clinging
    to a broken state-room door.

IN A BREATH
To the Williamson Brothers

HIGH noon. White sun flashes on the Michigan Avenue asphalt. Drum of hoofs and whirr of motors. Women trapesing along in flimsy clothes catching play of sun-fire to their skin and eyes.

Inside the playhouse are movies from under the sea. From the heat of pavements and the dust of sidewalks, passers-by go in a breath to be witnesses of large cool sponges, large cool fishes, large cool valleys and ridges of coral spread silent in the soak of the ocean floor thousands of years.

A naked swimmer dives. A knife in his right hand shoots a streak at the throat of a shark. The tail of the shark lashes. One swing would kill the swimmer. . . . Soon the knife goes into the soft underneck of the veering fish. . . . Its mouthful of teeth, each tooth a dagger itself, set row on row, glistens when the shuddering, yawning cadaver is hauled up by the brothers of the swimmer.

Outside in the street is the murmur and singing of life in the sun— horses, motors, women trapesing along in flimsy clothes, play of sun- fire in their blood.

BATH

A MAN saw the whole world as a grinning skull and cross-bones. The rose flesh of life shriveled from all faces. Nothing counts. Everything is a fake. Dust to dust and ashes to ashes and then an old darkness and a useless silence. So he saw it all. Then he went to a Mischa Elman concert. Two hours waves of sound beat on his eardrums. Music washed something or other inside him. Music broke down and rebuilt something or other in his head and heart. He joined in five encores for the young Russian Jew with the fiddle. When he got outside his heels hit the sidewalk a new way. He was the same man in the same world as before. Only there was a singing fire and a climb of roses everlastingly over the world he looked on.

BRONZES

I

THE bronze General Grant riding a bronze horse in Lincoln Park
Shrivels in the sun by day when the motor cars whirr by in long proces-
   sions going somewhere to keep appointments for dinner and matineés
   and buying and selling
Though in the dusk and nightfall when high waves are piling
On the slabs of the promenade along the lake shore near by
I have seen the general dare the combers come closer
And make to ride his bronze horse out into the hoofs and guns of the
   storm.

II

I cross Lincoln Park on a winter night when the snow is falling.
Lincoln in bronze stands among the white lines of snow, his bronze
   forehead meeting soft echoes of the newsies crying forty thousand
   men are dead along the Yser, his bronze ears listening to the mum-
   bled roar of the city at his bronze feet.
A lithe Indian on a bronze pony, Shakespeare seated with long legs in
   bronze, Garibaldi in a bronze cape, they hold places in the cold,
   lonely snow tonight on their pedestals and so they will hold them
   past midnight and into the dawn.

DUNES

WHAT do we see here in the sand dunes of the white moon alone with
   our thoughts, Bill,
Alone with our dreams, Bill, soft as the women tying scarves around their
   heads dancing,
Alone with a picture and a picture coming one after the other of all the
   dead,
The dead more than all these grains of sand one by one piled here in the
   moon,
Piled against the sky-line taking shapes like the hand of the wind wanted,
What do we see here, Bill, outside of what the wise men beat their
   heads on,
Outside of what the poets cry for and the soldiers drive on headlong and
   leave their skulls in the sun for—what, Bill?

ON THE WAY

LITTLE one, you have been buzzing in the books,
Flittering in the newspapers and drinking beer with lawyers
And amid the educated men of the clubs you have been getting an earful
    of speech from trained tongues.
Take an earful from me once, go with me on a hike
Along sand stretches on the great inland sea here
And while the eastern breeze blows on us and the restless surge
Of the lake waves on the breakwater breaks with an ever fresh monotone,
Let us ask ourselves: What is truth? what do you or I know?
How much do the wisest of the world's men know about where the
    massed human procession is going?

You have heard the mob laughed at?
I ask you: Is not the mob rough as the mountains are rough?
And all things human rise from the mob and relapse and rise again as
    rain to the sea?

READY TO KILL

TEN minutes now I have been looking at this.
I have gone by here before and wondered about it.
This is a bronze memorial of a famous general
Riding horseback with a flag and a sword and a revolver on him.
I want to smash the whole thing into a pile of junk to be hauled away to
    the scrap yard.
I put it straight to you,
After the farmer, the miner, the shop man, the factory hand, the fireman
    and the teamster,
Have all been remembered with bronze memorials,
Shaping them cn the job of getting all of us
Something to eat and something to wear,
When they stack a few silhouettes
        Against the sky
        Here in the park,

And show the real huskies that are doing the work of the world, and
    feeding people instead of butchering them,
Then maybe I will stand here
And look easy at this general of the army holding a flag in the air,
And riding like hell on horseback
Ready to kill anybody that gets in his way,
Ready to run the red blood and slush the bowels of men all over the
    sweet new grass of the prairie.

TO A CONTEMPORARY BUNKSHOOTER

You come along . . . tearing your shirt . . . yelling about Jesus.
    Where do you get that stuff?
    What do you know about Jesus?
Jesus had a way of talking soft and outside of a few bankers and higher-
    ups among the con men of Jerusalem everybody liked to have this
    Jesus around because he never made any fake passes and everything
    he said went and he helped the sick and gave the people hope.

You come along squirting words at us, shaking your fist and calling us
    all dam fools so fierce the froth slobbers over your lips . . . always
    blabbing we're all going to hell straight off and you know all
    about it.

I've read Jesus' words. I know what he said. You don't throw any scare
    into me. I've got your number. I know how much you know about
    Jesus.
He never came near clean people or dirty people but they felt cleaner
    because he came along. It was your crowd of bankers and business
    men and lawyers hired the sluggers and murderers who put Jesus out
    of the running.

I say the same bunch backing you nailed the nails into the hands of this
    Jesus of Nazareth. He had lined up against him the same crooks and
    strong-arm men now lined up with you paying your way.

This Jesus was good to look at, smelled good, listened good. He threw
    out something fresh and beautiful from the skin of his body and the
    touch of his hands wherever he passed along.

You slimy bunkshooter, you put a smut on every human blossom in reach
of your rotten breath belching about hell-fire and hiccupping about
this Man who lived a clean life in Galilee.

When are you going to quit making the carpenters build emergency
hospitals for women and girls driven crazy with wrecked nerves from
your gibberish about Jesus—I put it to you again: Where do you get
that stuff; what do you know about Jesus?

Go ahead and bust all the chairs you want to. Smash a whole wagon
load of furniture at every performance. Turn sixty somersaults and
stand on your nutty head. If it wasn't for the way you scare the
women and kids I'd feel sorry for you and pass the hat.
I like to watch a good four-flusher work, but not when he starts people
puking and calling for the doctors.
I like a man that's got nerve and can pull off a great original performance,
but you—you're only a bug-house peddler of second-hand gospel—
you're only shoving out a phoney imitation of the goods this Jesus
wanted free as air and sunlight.

You tell people living in shanties Jesus is going to fix it up all right with
them by giving them mansions in the skies after they're dead and the
worms have eaten 'em.
You tell $6 a week department store girls all they need is Jesus; you take
a steel trust wop, dead without having lived, gray and shrunken at
forty years of age, and you tell him to look at Jesus on the cross and
he'll be all right.
You tell poor people they don't need any more money on payday and
even if it's fierce to be out of a job, Jesus'll fix that up all right, all
right—all they gotta do is take Jesus the way you say.
I'm telling you Jesus wouldn't stand for the stuff you're handing out. Jesus
played it different. The bankers and lawyers of Jerusalem got their
sluggers and murderers to go after Jesus just because Jesus wouldn't
play their game. He didn't sit in with the big thieves.

I don't want a lot of gab from a bunkshooter in my religion.
I won't take my religion from any man who never works except with his
mouth and never cherishes any memory except the face of the
woman on the American silver dollar.

I ask you to come through and show me where you're pouring out the blood of your life.

I've been to this suburb of Jerusalem they call Golgotha, where they nailed Him, and I know if the story is straight it was real blood ran from His hands and the nail-holes, and it was real blood spurted in red drops where the spear of the Roman soldier rammed in between the ribs of this Jesus of Nazareth.

SKYSCRAPER

By day the skyscraper looms in the smoke and sun and has a soul.

Prairie and valley, streets of the city, pour people into it and they mingle among its twenty floors and are poured out again back to the streets, prairies and valleys.

It is the men and women, boys and girls so poured in and out all day that give the building a soul of dreams and thoughts and memories.

(Dumped in the sea or fixed in a desert, who would care for the building or speak its name or ask a policeman the way to it?)

Elevators slide on their cables and tubes catch letters and parcels and iron pipes carry gas and water in and sewage out.

Wires climb with secrets, carry light and carry words, and tell terrors and profits and loves—curses of men grappling plans of business and questions of women in plots of love.

Hour by hour the caissons reach down to the rock of the earth and hold the building to a turning planet.

Hour by hour the girders play as ribs and reach out and hold together the stone walls and floors.

Hour by hour the hand of the mason and the stuff of the mortar clinch the pieces and parts to the shape an architect voted.

Hour by hour the sun and the rain, the air and the rust, and the press of time running into centuries, play on the building inside and out and use it.

Men who sunk the pilings and mixed the mortar are laid in graves where the wind whistles a wild song without words

And so are men who strung the wires and fixed the pipes and tubes and those who saw it rise floor by floor.

Souls of them all are here, even the hod carrier begging at back doors hundreds of miles away and the bricklayer who went to state's prison for shooting another man while drunk.

(One man fell from a girder and broke his neck at the end of a straight plunge—he is here—his soul has gone into the stones of the building.)

On the office doors from tier to tier—hundreds of names and each name standing for a face written across with a dead child, a passionate lover, a driving ambition for a million dollar business or a lobster's ease of life.

Behind the signs on the doors they work and the walls tell nothing from room to room.

Ten-dollar-a-week stenographers take letters from corporation officers, lawyers, efficiency engineers, and tons of letters go bundled from the building to all ends of the earth.

Smiles and tears of each office girl go into the soul of the building just the same as the master-men who rule the building.

Hands of clocks turn to noon hours and each floor empties its men and women who go away and eat and come back to work.

Toward the end of the afternoon all work slackens and all jobs go slower as the people feel day closing on them.

One by one the floors are emptied. . . . The uniformed elevator men are gone. Pails clang. . . . Scrubbers work, talking in foreign tongues. Broom and water and mop clean from the floors human dust and spit, and machine grime of the day.

Spelled in electric fire on the roof are words telling miles of houses and people where to buy a thing for money. The sign speaks till midnight.

Darkness on the hallways. Voices echo. Silence holds. . . . Watchmen walk slow from floor to floor and try the doors. Revolvers bulge from their hip pockets. . . . Steel safes stand in corners. Money is stacked in them.

A young watchman leans at a window and sees the lights of barges butting their way across a harbor, nets of red and white lanterns in a railroad yard, and a span of glooms splashed with lines of white and blurs of crosses and clusters over the sleeping city.

By night the skyscraper looms in the smoke and the stars and has a soul.

Handfuls

FOG

THE fog comes
on little cat feet.

It sits looking
over harbor and city
on silent haunches
and then moves on.

POOL

OUT of the fire
Came a man sunken
To less than cinders,
A tea-cup of ashes or so.
And I,
The gold in the house,
Writhed into a stiff pool.

JAN KUBELIK

YOUR bow swept over a string, and a long low note quivered to the air.
(A mother of Bohemia sobs over a new child perfect learning to suck
 milk.)

Your bow ran fast over all the high strings fluttering and wild.
(All the girls in Bohemia are laughing on a Sunday afternoon in the hills
 with their lovers.)

CHOOSE

THE single clenched fist lifted and ready,
Or the open asking hand held out and waiting.
Choose:
For we meet by one or the other.

CRIMSON

CRIMSON is the slow smolder of the cigar end I hold,
Gray is the ash that stiffens and covers all silent the fire.
(A great man I know is dead and while he lies in his coffin a gone flame
    I sit here in cumbering shadows and smoke and watch my thoughts
    come and go.)

WHITELIGHT

YOUR whitelight flashes the frost tonight
Moon of the purple and silent west.
Remember me one of your lovers of dreams.

FLUX

SAND of the sea runs red
Where the sunset reaches and quivers.
Sand of the sea runs yellow
Where the moon slants and wavers.

KIN

BROTHER, I am fire
Surging under the ocean floor.
I shall never meet you, brother—
Not for years, anyhow;

Maybe thousands of years, brother.
Then I will warm you,
Hold you close, wrap you in circles,
Use you and change you—
Maybe thousands of years, brother.

WHITE SHOULDERS

YOUR white shoulders
    I remember
And your shrug of laughter.

    Low laughter
    Shaken slow
From your white shoulders.

LOSSES

I HAVE love
And a child,
A banjo
And shadows.
(Losses of God,
All will go
And one day
We will hold
Only the shadows.)

TROTHS

YELLOW dust on a bumble
    bee's wing,
Grey lights in a woman's
    asking eyes,
Red ruins in the changing
    sunset embers:

I take you and pile high
the memories.
Death will break her claws
on some I keep.

War Poems
(1914-1915)

KILLERS

I AM singing to you
Soft as a man with a dead child speaks;
Hard as a man in handcuffs,
Held where he cannot move:

Under the sun
Are sixteen million men,
Chosen for shining teeth,
Sharp eyes, hard legs,
And a running of young warm blood in their wrists.

And a red juice runs on the green grass;
And a red juice soaks the dark soil.
And the sixteen million are killing . . . and killing and killing.

I never forget them day or night:
They beat on my head for memory of them;
They pound on my heart and I cry back to them,
To their homes and women, dreams and games.

I wake in the night and smell the trenches,
And hear the low stir of sleepers in lines—
Sixteen million sleepers and pickets in the dark:
Some of them long sleepers for always,
Some of them tumbling to sleep tomorrow for always,
Fixed in the drag of the world's heartbreak,
Eating and drinking, toiling . . . on a long job of killing.
  Sixteen million men.

AMONG THE RED GUNS

*After waking at dawn one morning when the wind sang low among dry
leaves in an elm*

Among the red guns,
In the hearts of soldiers
Running free blood
In the long, long campaign:
  Dreams go on.

Among the leather saddles,
In the heads of soldiers
Heavy in the wracks and kills
Of all straight fighting:
  Dreams go on.

Among the hot muzzles,
In the hands of soldiers
Brought from flesh-folds of women—
Soft amid the blood and crying—
In all your hearts and heads
Among the guns and saddles and muzzles:

  Dreams,
Dreams go on,
Out of the dead on their backs,
Broken and no use any more:
Dreams of the way and the end go on.

IRON

GUNS,
Long, steel guns,
Pointed from the war ships
In the name of the war god.
Straight, shining, polished guns,
Clambered over with jackies in white blouses,
Glory of tan faces, tousled hair, white teeth,
Laughing lithe jackies in white blouses,
Sitting on the guns singing war songs, war chanties.

Shovels,
Broad, iron shovels,
Scooping out oblong vaults,
Loosening turf and leveling sod.

I ask you
To witness—
The shovel is brother to the gun.

MURMURINGS IN A FIELD HOSPITAL

[*They picked him up in the grass where he had lain two days in the rain
with a piece of shrapnel in his lungs.*]

COME to me only with playthings now . . .
A picture of a singing woman with blue eyes
Standing at a fence of hollyhocks, poppies and sunflowers . . .
Or an old man I remember sitting with children telling stories
Of days that never happened anywhere in the world . . .

No more iron cold and real to handle,
Shaped for a drive straight ahead.
Bring me only beautiful useless things.
Only old home things touched at sunset in the quiet . . .
And at the window one day in summer
Yellow of the new crock of butter
Stood against the red of new climbing roses . . .
And the world was all playthings.

STATISTICS

NAPOLEON shifted,
Restless in the old sarcophagus
And murmured to a watchguard:
"Who goes there?"
"Twenty-one million men,
Soldiers, armies, guns,
Twenty-one million
Afoot, horseback,
In the air,
Under the sea."
And Napoleon turned to his sleep:
"It is not my world answering;
It is some dreamer who knows not
The world I marched in
From Calais to Moscow."
And he slept on
In the old sarcophagus
While the aëroplanes
Droned their motors
Between Napoleon's mausoleum
And the cool night stars.

FIGHT

RED drips from my chin where I have been eating.
Not all the blood, nowhere near all, is wiped off my mouth.

Clots of red mess my hair
And the tiger, the buffalo, know how.

I was a killer.
        Yes, I am a killer.

I come from killing.
        I go to more.

I drive red joy ahead of me from killing.
Red gluts and red hungers run in the smears and juices of my inside bones:
The child cries for a suck mother and I cry for war.

BUTTONS

I HAVE been watching the war map slammed up for advertising in front
 of the newspaper office.
Buttons—red and yellow buttons—blue and black buttons—are shoved
 back and forth across the map.

A laughing young man, sunny with freckles,
Climbs a ladder, yells a joke to somebody in the crowd,
And then fixes a yellow button one inch west
And follows the yellow button with a black button one inch west.

(Ten thousand men and boys twist on their bodies in a red soak along a
 river edge,
Gasping of wounds, calling for water, some rattling death in their throats.)
Who would guess what it cost to move two buttons one inch on the war
 map here in front of the newspaper office where the freckle-faced
 young man is laughing to us?

AND THEY OBEY

SMASH down the cities.
Knock the walls to pieces.
Break the factories and cathedrals, warehouses and homes
Into loose piles of stone and lumber and black burnt wood:
 You are the soldiers and we command you.

Build up the cities.
Set up the walls again.
Put together once more the factories and cathedrals, warehouses and homes
Into buildings for life and labor:
 You are workmen and citizens all: We command you.

JAWS

Seven nations stood with their hands on the jaws of death.
It was the first week in August, Nineteen Hundred Fourteen.
I was listening, you were listening, the whole world was listening,
And all of us heard a Voice murmuring:
        "I am the way and the light,
        He that believeth on me
        Shall not perish
        But shall have everlasting life."
Seven nations listening heard the Voice and answered:
        "O Hell!"
The jaws of death began clicking and they go on clicking:
        "O Hell!"

SALVAGE

Guns on the battle lines have pounded now a year between Brussels and
    Paris.
And, William Morris, when I read your old chapter on the great arches
    and naves and little whimsical corners of the Churches of Northern
    France—Brr-rr!
I'm glad you're a dead man, William Morris, I'm glad you're down in the
    damp and mouldy, only a memory instead of a living man—I'm glad
    you're gone.
You never lied to us, William Morris, you loved the shape of those stones
    piled and carved for you to dream over and wonder because workmen
    got joy of life into them,
Workmen in aprons singing while they hammered, and praying, and put-
    ting their songs and prayers into the walls and roofs, the bastions and
    cornerstones and gargoyles—all their children and kisses of women
    and wheat and roses growing.
I say, William Morris, I'm glad you're gone, I'm glad you're a dead man.
Guns on the battle lines have pounded a year now between Brussels and
    Paris.

WARS

In the old wars drum of hoofs and the beat of shod feet.
In the new wars hum of motors and the tread of rubber tires.
In the wars to come silent wheels and whirr of rods not yet dreamed out
   in the heads of men.

In the old wars clutches of short swords and jabs into faces with spears.
In the new wars long-range guns and smashed walls, guns running a spit
   of metal and men falling in tens and twenties.
In the wars to come new silent deaths, new silent hurlers not yet dreamed
   out in the heads of men.

In the old wars kings quarreling and thousands of men following.
In the new wars kings quarreling and millions of men following.
In the wars to come kings kicked under the dust and millions of men fol-
   lowing great causes not yet dreamed out in the heads of men.

The Road and the End

THE ROAD AND THE END

I SHALL foot it
Down the roadway in the dusk,
Where shapes of hunger wander
And the fugitives of pain go by.
I shall foot it
In the silence of the morning,
See the night slur into dawn,
Hear the slow great winds arise

Where tall trees flank the way
And shoulder toward the sky.

The broken boulders by the road
Shall not commemorate my ruin.
Regret shall be the gravel under foot.
I shall watch for
Slim birds swift of wing
That go where wind and ranks of thunder
Drive the wild processionals of rain.

The dust of the traveled road
Shall touch my hands and face.

CHOICES

THEY offer you many things,
    I a few.
Moonlight on the play of fountains at night
With water sparkling a drowsy monotone,
Bare-shouldered, smiling women and talk
And a cross-play of loves and adulteries
And a fear of death
              and a remembering of regrets:
All this they offer you.
I come with:
    salt and bread
    a terrible job of work
    and tireless war;
Come and have now:
    hunger
    danger
    and hate.

GRAVES

I DREAMED one man stood against a thousand,
One man damned as a wrongheaded fool.
One year and another he walked the streets,

And a thousand shrugs and hoots
Met him in the shoulders and mouths he passed.

    He died alone
And only the undertaker came to his funeral.

Flowers grow over his grave anod in the wind,
And over the graves of the thousand, too,
The flowers grow anod in the wind.

    Flowers and the wind,
Flowers anod over the graves of the dead,
Petals of red, leaves of yellow, streaks of white,
Masses of purple sagging . . .
I love you and your great way of forgetting.

AZTEC MASK

I WANTED a man's face looking into the jaws and throat of life
With something proud on his face, so proud no smash of the jaws,
No gulp of the throat leaves the face in the end
With anything else than the old proud look:
        Even to the finish, dumped in the dust,
        Lost among the used-up cinders,
        This face, men would say, is a flash,
        Is laid on bones taken from the ribs of the earth,
        Ready for the hammers of changing, changing years,
        Ready for the sleeping, sleeping years of silence.
        Ready for the dust and fire and wind.
I wanted this face and I saw it today in an Aztec mask.
A cry out of storm and dark, a red yell and a purple prayer,
A beaten shape of ashes
           waiting the sunrise or night,
           something or nothing,
           proud-mouthed,
           proud-eyed gambler.

MOMUS

Momus is the name men give your face,
The brag of its tone, like a long low steamboat whistle
Finding a way mid mist on a shoreland,
Where gray rocks let the salt water shatter spray
  Against horizons purple, silent.

  Yes, Momus,
Men have flung your face in bronze
To gaze in gargoyle downward on a street-whirl of folk.
They were artists did this, shaped your sad mouth,
Gave you a tall forehead slanted with calm, broad wisdom;
All your lips to the corners and your cheeks to the high bones
Thrown over and through with a smile that forever wishes and wishes,
    purple, silent, fled from all the iron things of life, evaded like a sought
    bandit, gone into dreams, by God.

I wonder, Momus,
Whether shadows of the dead sit somewhere and look with deep laughter
On men who play in terrible earnest the old, known, solemn repetitions
    of history.
A droning monotone soft as sea laughter hovers from your kindliness of
    bronze,
You give me the human ease of a mountain peak, purple, silent;
Granite shoulders heaving above the earth curves,
Careless eye-witness of the spawning tides of men and women
Swarming always in a drift of millions to the dust of toil, the salt of tears,
And blood drops of undiminishing war.

THE ANSWER

You have spoken the answer.
A child searches far sometimes
Into the red dust
            On a dark rose leaf
And so you have gone far
            For the answer is:
                    Silence.

In the republic
Of the winking stars
                and spent cataclysms
Sure we are it is off there the answer is hidden and folded over,
Sleeping in the sun, careless whether it is Sunday or any other day of the
    week,

Knowing silence will bring all one way or another.

Have we not seen
Purple of the pansy
            out of the mulch
            and mold
            crawl
            into a dusk
            of velvet?
            blur of yellow?
Almost we thought from nowhere but it was the silence,
            the future,
            working.

TO A DEAD MAN

Over the dead line we have called to you
To come across with a word to us,
Some beaten whisper of what happens
Where you are over the dead line
Deaf to our calls and voiceless.

The flickering shadows have not answered
Nor your lips sent a signal
Whether love talks and roses grow
And the sun breaks at morning
Splattering the sea with crimson.

UNDER

I

I AM the undertow
Washing tides of power
Battering the pillars
Under your things of high law.

II

I am a sleepless
Slowfaring eater,
Maker of rust and rot
In your bastioned fastenings,
Caissons deep.

III

I am the Law
Older than you
And your builders proud.

I am deaf
In all days
Whether you
Say "Yes" or "No."

I am the crumbler:
Tomorrow.

A SPHINX

CLOSE-MOUTHED you sat five thousand years and never let out a whisper.
Processions came by, marchers, asking questions you answered with gray
    eyes never blinking, shut lips never talking.
Not one croak of anything you know has come from your cat crouch of
    ages.
I am one of those who know all you know and I keep my questions: I
    know the answers you hold.

WHO AM I?

My head knocks against the stars.
My feet are on the hilltops.
My finger-tips are in the valleys and shores of universal life.
Down in the sounding foam of primal things I reach my hands and play
    with pebbles of destiny.
I have been to hell and back many times.
I know all about heaven, for I have talked with God.
I dabble in the blood and guts of the terrible.
I know the passionate seizure of beauty
And the marvelous rebellion of man at all signs reading "Keep Off."

My name is Truth and I am the most elusive captive in the universe.

OUR PRAYER OF THANKS

For the gladness here where the sun is shining at evening on the weeds at
    the river,
    Our prayer of thanks.

For the laughter of children who tumble barefooted and bareheaded in
    the summer grass,
    Our prayer of thanks.

For the sunset and the stars, the women and the white arms that hold us,
    Our prayer of thanks.

    God,
If you are deaf and blind, if this is all lost to you,
God, if the dead in their coffins amid the silver handles on the edge of
    town, or the reckless dead of war days thrown unknown in pits, if
    these dead are forever deaf and blind and lost,
    Our prayer of thanks.

    God,
The game is all your way, the secrets and the signals and the system; and
    so for the break of the game and the first play and the last.
    Our prayer of thanks.

Fogs and Fires

AT A WINDOW

GIVE me hunger,
O you gods that sit and give
The world its orders.
Give me hunger, pain and want,
Shut me out with shame and failure
From your doors of gold and fame,
Give me your shabbiest, weariest hunger!

But leave me a little love,
A voice to speak to me in the day end,
A hand to touch me in the dark room
Breaking the long loneliness.
In the dusk of day-shapes
Blurring the sunset,
One little wandering, western star
Thrust out from the changing shores of shadow.
Let me go to the window,
Watch there the day-shapes of dusk
And wait and know the coming
Of a little love.

UNDER THE HARVEST MOON

UNDER the harvest moon,
When the soft silver
Drips shimmering
Over the garden nights,

Death, the gray mocker,
Comes and whispers to you
As a beautiful friend
Who remembers.

Under the summer roses
When the flagrant crimson
Lurks in the dusk
Of the wild red leaves,
Love, with little hands,
Comes and touches you
With a thousand memories,
And asks you
Beautiful, unanswerable questions.

THE GREAT HUNT

I CANNOT tell you now;
    When the wind's drive and whirl
    Blow me along no longer,
    And the wind's a whisper at last—
Maybe I'll tell you then—
              some other time.

    When the rose's flash to the sunset
    Reels to the rack and the twist,
    And the rose is a red bygone,
    When the face I love is going
    And the gate to the end shall clang,
    And it's no use to beckon or say, "So long"—
Maybe I'll tell you then—
              some other time.

I never knew any more beautiful than you:
    I have hunted you under my thoughts,
    I have broken down under the wind
    And into the roses looking for you.
    I shall never find any
              greater than you.

MONOTONE

THE monotone of the rain is beautiful,
And the sudden rise and slow relapse
Of the long multitudinous rain.

The sun on the hills is beautiful,
Or a captured sunset sea-flung,
Bannered with fire and gold.

A face I know is beautiful—
With fire and gold of sky and sea,
And the peace of long warm rain.

JOY

LET a joy keep you.
Reach out your hands
And take it when it runs by,
As the Apache dancer
Clutches his woman.
I have seen them
Live long and laugh loud,
Sent on singing, singing,
Smashed to the heart
Under the ribs
With a terrible love.
Joy always,
Joy everywhere—
Let joy kill you!
Keep away from the little deaths.

SHIRT

I REMEMBER once I ran after you and tagged the fluttering shirt of you in
the wind.
Once many days ago I drank a glassful of something and the picture of
you shivered and slid on top of the stuff.
And again it was nobody else but you I heard in the singing voice of a care-
less humming woman.
One night when I sat with chums telling stories at a bonfire flickering red
embers, in a language its own talking to a spread of white stars:
      It was you that slunk laughing
      in the clumsy staggering shadows.
Broken answers of remembrance let me know you are alive with a peering
phantom face behind a doorway somewhere in the city's push and fury
Or under a pack of moss and leaves waiting in silence under a twist of
oaken arms ready as ever to run away again when I tag the fluttering
shirt of you.

AZTEC

     You came from the Aztecs
     With a copper on your fore-arms
     Tawnier than a sunset
     Saying good-by to an even river.

     And I said, you remember,
     Those fore-arms of yours
     Were finer than bronzes
     And you were glad.

         It was tears
     And a path west
         and a home-going
         when I asked
     Why there were scars of worn gold
     Where a man's ring was fixed once

On your third finger.
          And I call you
To come back
          before the days are longer.

TWO

MEMORY of you is . . . a blue spear of flower.
I cannot remember the name of it.
Alongside a bold dripping poppy is fire and silk.
                    And they cover you.

BACK YARD

SHINE on, O moon of summer.
Shine to the leaves of grass, catalpa and oak,
All silver under your rain tonight.

An Italian boy is sending songs to you tonight from an accordion.
A Polish boy is out with his best girl; they marry next month; tonight they
     are throwing you kisses.

An old man next door is dreaming over a sheen that sits in a cherry tree
     in his back yard.

The clocks say I must go—I stay here sitting on the back porch drinking
     white thoughts you rain down.

     Shine on, O moon,
Shake out more and more silver changes.

ON THE BREAKWATER

ON the breakwater in the summer dark, a man and a girl are sitting,
She across his knee and they are looking face into face
Talking to each other without words, singing rhythms in silence to each
     other.

A funnel of white ranges the blue dusk from an outgoing boat,
Playing its searchlight, puzzled, abrupt, over a streak of green,
And two on the breakwater keep their silence, she on his knee.

MASK

FLING your red scarf faster and faster, dancer.
It is summer and the sun loves a million green leaves, masses of green.
Your red scarf flashes across them calling and a-calling.
The silk and flare of it is a great soprano leading a chorus
Carried along in a rouse of voices reaching for the heart of the world.
Your toes are singing to meet the song of your arms:

Let the red scarf go swifter.
Summer and the sun command you.

PEARL FOG

OPEN the door now.
Go roll up the collar of your coat
To walk in the changing scarf of mist.

Tell your sins here to the pearl fog
And know for once a deepening night
Strange as the half-meanings
Alurk in a wise woman's mousey eyes.

Yes, tell your sins
And know how careless a pearl fog is
Of the laws you have broken.

I SANG

I SANG to you and the moon
But only the moon remembers.
I sang

O reckless free-hearted
    free-throated rhythms,
Even the moon remembers them
  And is kind to me.

FOLLIES

SHAKEN,
 The blossoms of lilac,
 And shattered,
 The atoms of purple.
Green dip the leaves,
 Darker the bark,
Longer the shadows.

Sheer lines of poplar
Shimmer with masses of silver
And down in a garden old with years
And broken walls of ruin and story,
Roses rise with red rain-memories.
  May!
 In the open world
The sun comes and finds your face,
 Remembering all.

JUNE

PAULA is digging and shaping the loam of a salvia,
 Scarlet Chinese talker of summer.
Two petals of crabapple blossom blow fallen in Paula's hair,
 And fluff of white from a cottonwood.

NOCTURNE IN A DESERTED BRICKYARD

STUFF of the moon
Runs on the lapping sand
Out to the longest shadows.

Under the curving willows,
And round the creep of the wave line,
Fluxions of yellow and dusk on the waters
Make a wide dreaming pansy of an old pond in the night.

HYDRANGEAS

DRAGOONS, I tell you the white hydrangeas turn rust and go soon.
Already mid-September a line of brown runs over them.
One sunset after another tracks the faces, the petals.
Waiting, they look over the fence for what way they go.

THEME IN YELLOW

I SPOT the hills
With yellow balls in autumn.
I light the prairie cornfields
Orange and tawny gold clusters
And I am called pumpkins.
On the last of October
When dusk is fallen
Children join hands
And circle round me
Singing ghost songs
And love to the harvest moon;
I am a jack-o'-lantern
With terrible teeth
And the children know
I am fooling.

BETWEEN TWO HILLS

BETWEEN two hills
The old town stands.
The houses loom
And the roofs and trees
And the dusk and the dark,

The damp and the dew
Are there.

The prayers are said
And the people rest
For sleep is there
And the touch of dreams
Is over all.

LAST ANSWERS

I WROTE a poem on the mist
And a woman asked me what I meant by it.
I had thought till then only of the beauty of the mist, how pearl and
    gray of it mix and reel,
And change the drab shanties with lighted lamps at evening into points
    of mystery quivering with color.

  I answered:
The whole world was mist once long ago and some day it will all go back
    to mist,
Our skulls and lungs are more water than bone and tissue
And all poets love dust and mist because all the last answers
Go running back to dust and mist.

WINDOW

NIGHT from a railroad car window
Is a great, dark, soft thing
Broken across with slashes of light.

YOUNG SEA

THE sea is never still.
It pounds on the shore
Restless as a young heart,
Hunting.

The sea speaks
And only the stormy hearts
Know what it says:
It is the face
     of a rough mother speaking.

The sea is young.
One storm cleans all the hoar
And loosens the age of it.
I hear it laughing, reckless.

They love the sea,
Men who ride on it
And know they will die
Under the salt of it.

Let only the young come,
  Says the sea.
Let them kiss my face
  And hear me.
I am the last word
  And I tell
Where storms and stars come from.

BONES

SLING me under the sea.
Pack me down in the salt and wet.
No farmer's plow shall touch my bones.
No Hamlet hold my jaws and speak
How jokes are gone and empty is my mouth.
Long, green-eyed scavengers shall pick my eyes,
Purple fish play hide-and-seek,
And I shall be song of thunder, crash of sea,
Down on the floors of salt and wet.
    Sling me . . . under the sea.

PALS

TAKE a hold now
On the silver handles here,
Six silver handles,
One for each of his old pals.

Take hold
And lift him down the stairs,
Put him on the rollers
Over the floor of the hearse.

Take him on the last haul,
To the cold straight house,
The level even house,
To the last house of all.

The dead say nothing
And the dead know much
And the dead hold under their tongues
A locked-up story.

CHILD

THE young child, Christ, is straight and wise
And asks questions of the old men, questions
Found under running water for all children
And found under shadows thrown on still waters
By tall trees looking downward, old and gnarled.
Found to the eyes of children alone, untold,
Singing a low song in the loneliness.
And the young child, Christ, goes on asking
And the old men answer nothing and only know love
For the young child. Christ, straight and wise.

POPPIES

She loves blood-red poppies for a garden to walk in.
In a loose white gown she walks
                    and a new child tugs at cords in her body.
Her head to the west at evening when the dew is creeping,
A shudder of gladness runs in her bones and torsal fiber:
She loves blood-red poppies for a garden to walk in.

CHILD MOON

The child's wonder
At the old moon
Comes back nightly.
She points her finger
To the far silent yellow thing
Shining through the branches
Filtering on the leaves a golden sand,
Crying with her little tongue, "See the moon!"
And in her bed fading to sleep
With babblings of the moon on her little mouth.

MARGARET

Many birds and the beating of wings
Make a flinging reckless hum
In the early morning at the rocks
Above the blue pool
Where the gray shadows swim lazy.

In your blue eyes, O reckless child,
I saw today many little wild wishes,
Eager as the great morning.

Shadows

POEMS DONE ON A LATE NIGHT CAR

I. CHICKENS

I AM The Great White Way of the city:
When you ask what is my desire, I answer:
"Girls fresh as country wild flowers,
With young faces tired of the cows and barns,
Eager in their eyes as the dawn to find my mysteries,
Slender supple girls with shapely legs,
Lure in the arch of their little shoulders
And wisdom from the prairies to cry only softly at the ashes of my mysteries."

II. USED UP

*Lines based on certain regrets that come with rumination upon the
painted faces of women on North Clark Street, Chicago*

Roses,
Red roses,
Crushed
In the rain and wind
Like mouths of women
Beaten by the fists of
Men using them.
  O little roses
  And broken leaves
  And petal wisps:
You that so flung your crimson
  To the sun
Only yesterday.

III. HOME

Here is a thing my heart wishes the world had more of:
I heard it in the air of one night when I listened
To a mother singing softly to a child restless and angry in the darkness.

IT IS MUCH

WOMEN of night life amid the lights
Where the line of your full, round throats
Matches in gleam the glint of your eyes
And the ring of your heart-deep laughter:
    It is much to be warm and sure of tomorrow.

Women of night life along the shadows,
Lean at your throats and skulking the walls,
Gaunt as a bitch worn to the bone,
Under the paint of your smiling faces:
    It is much to be warm and sure of tomorrow.

TRAFFICKER

AMONG the shadows where two streets cross,
A woman lurks in the dark and waits
To move on when a policeman heaves in view.
Smiling a broken smile from a face
Painted over haggard bones and desperate eyes,
All night she offers passers-by what they will
Of her beauty wasted, body faded, claims gone,
And no takers.

HARRISON STREET COURT

I HEARD a woman's lips
Speaking to a companion
Say these words:

"A woman what hustles
Never keeps nothin'
For all her hustlin'.
Somebody always gets
What she goes on the street for.
If it ain't a pimp
It's a bull what gets it.
I been hustlin' now
Till I ain't much good any more.
I got nothin' to show for it.
Some man got it all,
Every night's hustlin' I ever did."

SOILED DOVE

LET us be honest; the lady was not a harlot until she married a corporation
lawyer who picked her from a Ziegfeld chorus.

Before then she never took anybody's money and paid for her silk
stockings out of what she earned singing and dancing.

She loved one man and he loved six women and the game was changing
her looks, calling for more and more massage money and high coin
for the beauty doctors.

Now she drives a long, underslung motor car all by herself, reads in the
day's papers what her husband is doing to the inter-state commerce
commission, requires a larger corsage from year to year, and wonders
sometimes how one man is coming along with six women.

JUNGHEIMER'S

IN western fields of corn and northern timber lands,
    They talk about me, a saloon with a soul,
    The soft red lights, the long curving bar,
    The leather seats and dim corners,
    Tall brass spittoons, a nigger cutting ham,
And the painting of a woman half-dressed thrown reckless across a bed
    after a night of booze and riots.

GONE

EVERYBODY loved Chick Lorimer in our town.
        Far off
     Everybody loved her.
So we all love a wild girl keeping a hold
      On a dream she wants.
Nobody knows now where Chick Lorimer went.
Nobody knows why she packed her trunk . . . a few old things
And is gone,
         Gone with her little chin
         Thrust ahead of her
         And her soft hair blowing careless
         From under a wide hat,
Dancer, singer, a laughing passionate lover.

Were there ten men or a hundred hunting Chick?
Were there five men or fifty with aching hearts?
      Everybody loved Chick Lorimer.
      Nobody knows where she's gone.

Other Days
(1900-1910)

DREAMS IN THE DUSK

DREAMS in the dusk,
Only dreams closing the day
And with the day's close going back
To the gray things, the dark things,
The far, deep things of dreamland.

Dreams, only dreams in the dusk,
Only the old remembered pictures
Of lost days when the day's loss
Wrote in tears the heart's loss.

Tears and loss and broken dreams
May find your heart at dusk.

DOCKS

STROLLING along
By the teeming docks,
I watch the ships put out.
Black ships that heave and lunge
And move like mastodons
Arising from lethargic sleep.

The fathomed harbor
Calls them not nor dares
Them to a strain of action,
But outward, on and outward,

Sounding low-reverberating calls,
Shaggy in the half-lit distance,
They pass the pointed headland,
View the wide, far-lifting wilderness
And leap with cumulative speed
To test the challenge of the sea.

Plunging,
Doggedly onward plunging,
Into salt and mist and foam and sun.

ALL DAY LONG

ALL day long in fog and wind,
The waves have flung their beating crests
Against the palisades of adamant.
    My boy, he went to sea, long and long ago,
    Curls of brown were slipping underneath his cap,
    He looked at me from blue and steely eyes;
    Natty, straight and true, he stepped away,
    My boy, he went to sea.
All day long in fog and wind,
The waves have flung their beating crests
Against the palisades of adamant.

WAITING

TODAY I will let the old boat stand
Where the sweep of the harbor tide comes in
To the pulse of a far, deep-steady sway.
And I will rest and dream and sit on the deck
    Watching the world go by
And take my pay for many hard days gone I remember.

I will choose what clouds I like
In the great white fleets that wander the blue
As I lie on my back or loaf at the rail.
And I will listen as the veering winds kiss me and fold me
And put on my brow the touch of the world's great will.

Daybreak will hear the heart of the boat beat,
　Engine throb and piston play
In the quiver and leap at call of life.
Tomorrow we move in the gaps and heights
On changing floors of unlevel seas
And no man shall stop us and no man follow
For ours is the quest of an unknown shore
And we are husky and lusty and shouting-gay.

FROM THE SHORE

A LONE gray bird,
Dim-dipping, far-flying,
Alone in the shadows and grandeurs and tumults
Of night and the sea
And the stars and storms.

Out over the darkness it wavers and hovers,
Out into the gloom it swings and batters,
Out into the wind and the rain and the vast,
Out into the pit of a great black world,
Where fogs are at battle, sky-driven, sea-blown,
Love of mist and rapture of flight,
Glories of chance and hazards of death
On its eager and palpitant wings.

Out into the deep of the great dark world,
Beyond the long borders where foam and drift
Of the sundering waves are lost and gone
On the tides that plunge and rear and crumble.

UPLANDS IN MAY

WONDER as of old things
Fresh and fair come back
Hangs over pasture and road.
Lush in the lowland grasses rise
And upland beckons to upland.
The great strong hills are humble.

DREAM GIRL

You will come one day in a waver of love,
Tender as dew, impetuous as rain,
The tan of the sun will be on your skin,
The purr of the breeze in your murmuring speech,
You will pose with a hill-flower grace.

You will come, with your slim, expressive arms,
A poise of the head no sculptor has caught
And nuances spoken with shoulder and neck,
Your face in a pass-and-repass of moods
As many as skies in delicate change
Of cloud and blue and flimmering sun.

Yet,
You may not come, O girl of a dream,
We may but pass as the world goes by
And take from a look of eyes into eyes,
A film of hope and a memoried day.

PLOWBOY

AFTER the last red sunset glimmer,
Black on the line of a low hill rise,
Formed into moving shadows, I saw
A plowboy and two horses lined against the gray,
Plowing in the dusk the last furrow.
The turf had a gleam of brown,
And smell of soil was in the air,
And, cool and moist, a haze of April.

I shall remember you long,
Plowboy and horses against the sky in shadow.
I shall remember you and the picture
You made for me,
Turning the turf in the dusk
And haze of an April gloaming.

BROADWAY

I SHALL never forget you, Broadway
Your golden and calling lights.

I'll remember you long,
Tall-walled river of rush and play.

Hearts that know you hate you
And lips that have given you laughter
Have gone to their ashes of life and its roses,
Cursing the dreams that were lost
In the dust of your harsh and trampled stones.

OLD WOMAN

THE owl-car clatters along, dogged by the echo
From building and battered paving-stone;
The headlight scoffs at the mist
And fixes its yellow rays in the cold slow rain;
Against a pane I press my forehead
And drowsily look on the walls and sidewalks.

The headlight finds the way
And life is gone from the wet and the welter—
Only an old woman, bloated, disheveled and bleared
Far-wandered waif of other days,
Huddles for sleep in a doorway,
Homeless.

NOON HOUR

SHE sits in the dust at the walls
   And makes cigars,
Bending at the bench
With fingers wage-anxious,
Changing her sweat for the day's pay.

Now the noon hour has come,
And she leans with her bare arms
On the window-sill over the river,
Leans and feels at her throat
Cool-moving things out of the free open ways:

At her throat and eyes and nostrils
The touch and the blowing cool
Of great free ways beyond the walls.

'BOES

I WAITED today for a freight train to pass.
Cattle cars with steers butting their horns against the bars, went by.
And a half a dozen hoboes stood on bumpers between cars.
Well, the cattle are respectable, I thought.
Every steer has its transportation paid for by the farmer sending it to
   market,
While the hoboes are law-breakers in riding a railroad train without a
   ticket.
It reminded me of ten days I spent in the Allegheny County jail in
   Pittsburgh.
I got ten days even though I was a veteran of the Spanish-American war.
Cooped in the same cell with me was an old man, a bricklayer and a
   booze-fighter.
But it just happened he, too, was a veteran soldier, and he had fought
   to preserve the Union and free the niggers.
We were three in all, the other being a Lithuanian who got drunk on
   payday at the steel works and got to fighting a policeman;
All the clothes he had was a shirt, pants and shoes—somebody got his
   hat and coat and what money he had left over when he got drunk.

UNDER A TELEPHONE POLE

I AM a copper wire slung in the air,
Slim against the sun I make not even a clear line of shadow.
Night and day I keep singing—humming and thrumming:

It is love and war and money; it is the fighting and the tears, the work
    and want,
Death and laughter of men and women passing through me, carrier of
    your speech,
In the rain and the wet dripping, in the dawn and the shine drying,
            A copper wire.

I AM THE PEOPLE, THE MOB

I AM the people—the mob—the crowd—the mass.
Do you know that all the great work of the world is done through me?
I am the workingman, the inventor, the maker of the world's food and
    clothes.
I am the audience that witnesses history. The Napoleons come from me
    and the Lincolns. They die. And then I send forth more Napoleons
    and Lincolns.
I am the seed ground. I am a prairie that will stand for much plowing.
    Terrible storms pass over me. I forget. The best of me is sucked out
    and wasted. I forget. Everything but Death comes to me and makes
    me work and give up what I have. And I forget.
Sometimes I growl, shake myself and spatter a few red drops for history
    to remember. Then—I forget.
When I, the People, learn to remember, when I, the People, use the
    lessons of yesterday and no longer forget who robbed me last year,
    who played me for a fool—then there will be no speaker in all the
    world say the name: "The People," with any fleck of a sneer in his
    voice or any far-off smile of derision.
The mob—the crowd—the mass—will arrive then.

GOVERNMENT

THE Government—I heard about the Government and I went out to find
    it. I said I would look closely at it when I saw it.
Then I saw a policeman dragging a drunken man to the calaboose. It
    was the Government in action.
I saw a ward alderman slip into an office one morning and talk with a
    judge. Later in the day the judge dismissed a case against a pickpocket

who was a live ward worker for the alderman. Again I saw this was the Government, doing things.

I saw militiamen level their rifles at a crowd of workingmen who were trying to get other workingmen to stay away from a shop where there was a strike on. Government in action.

Everywhere I saw that Government is a thing made of men, that Government has blood and bones, it is many mouths whispering into many ears, sending telegrams, aiming rifles, writing orders, saying "yes" and "no."

Government dies as the men who form it die and are laid away in their graves and the new Government that comes after is human, made of heartbeats of blood, ambitions, lusts, and money running through it all, money paid and money taken, and money covered up and spoken of with hushed voices.

A Government is just as secret and mysterious and sensitive as any human sinner carrying a load of germs, traditions and corpuscles handed down from fathers and mothers away back.

LANGUAGES

THERE are no handles upon a language
Whereby men take hold of it
And mark it with signs for its remembrance.
It is a river, this language,
Once in a thousand years
Breaking a new course
Changing its way to the ocean.
It is mountain effluvia
Moving to valleys
And from nation to nation
Crossing borders and mixing.
Languages die like rivers.
Words wrapped round your tongue today
And broken to shape of thought
Between your teeth and lips speaking
Now and today
Shall be faded hieroglyphics

Ten thousand years from now.
Sing—and singing—remember
Your song dies and changes
And is not here tomorrow
Any more than the wind
Blowing ten thousand years ago.

LETTERS TO DEAD IMAGISTS

EMILY DICKINSON:
You gave us the bumblebee who has a soul,
The everlasting traveler among the hollyhocks,
And how God plays around a back yard garden.

STEVIE CRANE:
War is kind and we never knew the kindness of war till you came;
Nor the black riders and clashes of spear and shield out of the sea,
Nor the mumblings and shots that rise from dreams on call.

SHEEP

THOUSANDS of sheep, soft-footed, black-nosed sheep—one by one going up the hill and over the fence—one by one four-footed pattering up and over—one by one wiggling their stub tails as they take the short jump and go over—one by one silently unless for the multitudinous drumming of their hoofs as they move on and go over—thousands and thousands of them in the gray haze of evening just after sundown—one by one slanting in a long line to pass over the hill—

I am the slow, long-legged Sleepyman and I love you sheep in Persia, California, Argentina, Australia, or Spain—you are the thoughts that help me when I, the Sleepyman, lay my hands on the eyelids of the children of the world at eight o'clock every night—you thousands and thousands of sheep in a procession of dusk making an endless multitudinous drumming on the hills with your hoofs.

THE RED SON

I LOVE your faces I saw the many years
I drank your milk and filled my mouth
With your home talk, slept in your house
And was one of you.
     But a fire burns in my heart.
Under the ribs where pulses thud
And flitting between bones of skull
Is the push, the endless mysterious command,
    Saying:
"I leave you behind—
You for the little hills and the years all alike,
You with your patient cows and old houses
Protected from the rain,
I am going away and I never come back to you;
Crags and high rough places call me,
Great places of death
Where men go empty handed
And pass over smiling
To the star-drift on the horizon rim.
My last whisper shall be alone, unknown;
I shall go to the city and fight against it,
And make it give me passwords
Of luck and love, women worth dying for,
And money.
    I go where you wist not of
    Nor I nor any man nor woman.
    I only know I go to storms
    Grappling against things wet and naked."
There is no pity of it and no blame.
None of us is in the wrong.
After all it is only this:
    You for the little hills and I go away.

THE MIST

I AM the mist, the impalpable mist,
Back of the thing you seek.
My arms are long,
Long as the reach of time and space.

Some toil and toil, believing,
Looking now and again on my face,
Catching a vital, olden glory.

But no one passes me,
I tangle and snare them all.
I am the cause of the Sphinx,
The voiceless, baffled, patient Sphinx.

I was at the first of things,
I will be at the last.
      I am the primal mist
      And no man passes me;
      My long impalpable arms
      Bar them all.

THE JUNK MAN

I AM glad God saw Death
And gave Death a job taking care of all who are tired of living:

When all the wheels in a clock are worn and slow and the connections
    loose
And the clock goes on ticking and telling the wrong time from hour to
    hour
And people around the house joke about what a bum clock it is,
How glad the clock is when the big Junk Man drives his wagon
Up to the house and puts his arms around the clock and says:
      "You don't belong here,

You gotta come
Along with me,"
How glad the clock is then, when it feels the arms of the Junk Man close
   around it and carry it away.

SILVER NAILS

A MAN was crucified. He came to the city a stranger, was accused, and nailed to a cross. He lingered hanging. Laughed at the crowd. "The nails are iron," he said. "You are cheap. In my country when we crucify we use silver nails . . ." So he went jeering. They did not understand him at first. Later they talked about him in changed voices in the saloons, bowling alleys, and churches. It came over them every man is crucified only once in his life and the law of humanity dictates silver nails be used for the job. A statue was erected to him in a public square. Not having gathered his name when he was among them, they wrote him as John Silvernail on the statue.

GYPSY

I ASKED a gypsy pal
To imitate an old image
And speak old wisdom.
She drew in her chin,
Made her neck and head
The top piece of a Nile obelisk
   and said:
Snatch off the gag from thy mouth, child,
And be free to keep silence.
Tell no man anything for no man listens,
Yet hold thy lips ready to speak.

CORNHUSKERS

TO

JANET AND MARGARET

Cornhuskers

PRAIRIE

I was born on the prairie and the milk of its wheat, the red of its clover,
the eyes of its women, gave me a song and a slogan.

Here the water went down, the icebergs slid with gravel, the gaps and
the valleys hissed, and the black loam came, and the yellow sandy
loam.
Here between the sheds of the Rocky Mountains and the Appalachians,
here now a morning star fixes a fire sign over the timber claims and
cow pastures, the corn belt, the cotton belt, the cattle ranches.
Here the gray geese go five hundred miles and back with a wind under
their wings honking the cry for a new home.
Here I know I will hanker after nothing so much as one more sunrise or a
sky moon of fire doubled to a river moon of water.

The prairie sings to me in the forenoon and I know in the night I rest easy
in the prairie arms, on the prairie heart.

. . .

> After the sunburn of the day
> handling a pitchfork at a hayrack,
> after the eggs and biscuit and coffee,
> the pearl-gray haystacks
> in the gloaming
> are cool prayers
> to the harvest hands.

In the city among the walls the overland passenger train is choked and
the pistons hiss and the wheels curse.

On the prairie the overland flits on phantom wheels and the sky and
    the soil between them muffle the pistons and cheer the wheels.

. . .

I am here when the cities are gone.
I am here before the cities come.
I nourished the lonely men on horses.
I will keep the laughing men who ride iron.
I am dust of men.

The running water babbled to the deer, the cottontail, the gopher.
You came in wagons, making streets and schools,
Kin of the ax and rifle, kin of the plow and horse,
Singing *Yankee Doodle, Old Dan Tucker, Turkey in the Straw,*
You in the coonskin cap at a log house door hearing a lone wolf howl,
You at a sod house door reading the blizzards and chinooks let loose
    from Medicine Hat,
I am dust of your dust, as I am brother and mother
To the copper faces, the worker in flint and clay,
The singing women and their sons a thousand years ago
Marching single file the timber and the plain.

I hold the dust of these amid changing stars.
I last while old wars are fought, while peace broods mother-like,
While new wars arise and the fresh killings of young men.
I fed the boys who went to France in great dark days.
Appomattox is a beautiful word to me and so is Valley Forge and the
    Marne and Verdun,
I who have seen the red births and the red deaths
Of sons and daughters, I take peace or war, I say nothing and wait.

Have you seen a red sunset drip over one of my cornfields, the shore of
    night stars, the wave lines of dawn up a wheat valley?
Have you heard my threshing crews yelling in the chaff of a strawpile
    and the running wheat of the wagonboards, my cornhuskers, my
    harvest hands hauling crops, singing dreams of women, worlds,
    horizons?

. . .

    Rivers cut a path on flat lands.
    The mountains stand up.

The salt oceans press in
And push on the coast lines.
The sun, the wind, bring rain
And I know what the rainbow writes across the east or
    west in a half-circle:
A love-letter pledge to come again.

. . .

Towns on the Soo Line,
Towns on the Big Muddy,
Laugh at each other for cubs
And tease as children.

Omaha and Kansas City, Minneapolis and St. Paul, sisters in a house
    together, throwing slang, growing up.
Towns in the Ozarks, Dakota wheat towns, Wichita, Peoria, Buffalo, sis-
    ters throwing slang, growing up.

. . .

Out of prairie-brown grass crossed with a streamer of wigwam smoke—
    out of a smoke pillar, a blue promise—out of wild ducks woven in
    greens and purples—
Here I saw a city rise and say to the peoples round the world: Listen, I am
    strong, I know what I want.
Out of log houses and stumps—canoes stripped from tree-sides—flat-
    boats coaxed with an ax from the timber claims—in the years when
    the red and the white men met—the houses and streets rose.

A thousand red men cried and went away to new places for corn and
    women: a million white men came and put up skyscrapers, threw
    out rails and wires, feelers to the salt sea: now the smokestacks bite
    the skyline with stub teeth.

In an early year the call of a wild duck woven in greens and purples:
    now the riveter's chatter, the police patrol, the song-whistle of the
    steamboat.

To a man across a thousand years I offer a handshake.
I say to him: Brother, make the story short, for the stretch of a thou-
    sand years is short.

. . .

What brothers these in the dark?
What eaves of skyscrapers against a smoke moon?
These chimneys shaking on the lumber shanties
When the coal boats plow by on the river—
The hunched shoulders of the grain elevators—
The flame sprockets of the sheet steel mills
And the men in the rolling mills with their shirts off
Playing their flesh arms against the twisting wrists of steel:
          what brothers these
          in the dark
          of a thousand years?

                    . . .

A headlight searches a snowstorm.
A funnel of white light shoots from over the pilot of the Pioneer Lim-
     ited crossing Wisconsin.

In the morning hours, in the dawn,
The sun puts out the stars of the sky
And the headlight of the Limited train.

The fireman waves his hand to a country school teacher on a bobsled.
A boy, yellow hair, red scarf and mittens, on the bobsled, in his lunch
     box a pork chop sandwich and a V of gooseberry pie.

The horses fathom a snow to their knees.
Snow hats are on the rolling prairie hills.
The Mississippi bluffs wear snow hats.

                    . . .

Keep your hogs on changing corn and mashes of grain,
     O farmerman.
     Cram their insides till they waddle on short legs
     Under the drums of bellies, hams of fat.
     Kill your hogs with a knife slit under the ear.
     Hack them with cleavers.
     Hang them with hooks in the hind legs.

                    . . .

A wagonload of radishes on a summer morning.
Sprinkles of dew on the crimson-purple balls.

The farmer on the seat dangles the reins on the rumps of dapple-gray
    horses.
The farmer's daughter with a basket of eggs dreams of a new hat to
    wear to the county fair.

      . . .

On the left- and right-hand side of the road,
         Marching corn—
I saw it knee high weeks ago—now it is head high—tassels of red silk
    creep at the ends of the ears.

      . . .

I am the prairie, mother of men, waiting.
They are mine, the threshing crews eating beefsteak, the farmboys driv-
    ing steers to the railroad cattle pens.
They are mine, the crowds of people at a Fourth of July basket picnic,
    listening to a lawyer read the Declaration of Independence, watch-
    ing the pinwheels and Roman candles at night, the young men and
    women two by two hunting the bypaths and kissing-bridges.
They are mine, the horses looking over a fence in the frost of late Octo-
    ber saying good morning to the horses hauling wagons of rutabaga
    to market.
They are mine, the old zigzag rail fences, the new barbwire.

      . . .

The cornhuskers wear leather on their hands.
There is no let-up to the wind.
Blue bandanas are knotted at the ruddy chins.

Falltime and winter apples take on the smolder of the five-o'clock No-
    vember sunset: falltime, leaves, bonfires, stubble, the old things go,
    and the earth is grizzled.
The land and the people hold memories, even among the anthills and
    the angleworms, among the toads and woodroaches—among grave-
    stone writings rubbed out by the rain—they keep old things that
    never grow old.

The frost loosens cornhusks.
The sun, the rain, the wind
         loosen cornhusks.
The men and women are helpers.

They are all cornhuskers together.
I see them late in the western evening
          in a smoke-red dust.

. . .

The phantom of a yellow rooster flaunting a scarlet comb, on top of a
     dung pile crying hallelujah to the streaks of daylight,
The phantom of an old hunting dog nosing in the underbrush for musk-
     rats, barking at a coon in a treetop at midnight, chewing a bone,
     chasing his tail round a corncrib,
The phantom of an old workhorse taking the steel point of a plow
     across a forty-acre field in spring, hitched to a harrow in summer,
     hitched to a wagon among cornshocks in fall,
These phantoms come into the talk and wonder of people on the front
     porch of a farmhouse late summer nights.
"The shapes that are gone are here," said an old man with a cob pipe
     in his teeth one night in Kansas with a hot wind on the alfalfa.

. . .

Look at six eggs
In a mockingbird's nest.

Listen to six mockingbirds
Flinging follies of O-be-joyful
Over the marshes and uplands.

Look at songs
Hidden in eggs.

. . .

When the morning sun is on the trumpet-vine blossoms, sing at the
     kitchen pans: Shout All Over God's Heaven.
When the rain slants on the potato hills and the sun plays a silver shaft
     on the last shower, sing to the bush at the backyard fence: Mighty
     Lak a Rose.
When the icy sleet pounds on the storm windows and the house lifts
     to a great breath, sing for the outside hills: The Ole Sheep Done
     Know the Road, the Young Lambs Must Find the Way.

. . .

Spring slips back with a girl face calling always: "Any new songs for
     me? Any new songs?"

O prairie girl, be lonely, singing, dreaming, waiting—your lover comes—
    your child comes—the years creep with toes of April rain on new-
    turned sod.
O prairie girl, whoever leaves you only crimson poppies to talk with,
    whoever puts a good-by kiss on your lips and never comes back—
There is a song deep as the falltime redhaws, long as the layer of black
    loam we go to, the shine of the morning star over the corn belt,
    the wave line of dawn up a wheat valley.

. . .

O prairie mother, I am one of your boys.
I have loved the prairie as a man with a heart shot full of pain over love.
Here I know I will hanker after nothing so much as one more sunrise
    or a sky moon of fire doubled to a river moon of water.

. . .

I speak of new cities and new people.
I tell you the past is a bucket of ashes.
I tell you yesterday is a wind gone down,
    a sun dropped in the west.
I tell you there is nothing in the world
    only an ocean of tomorrows,
    a sky of tomorrows.

I am a brother of the cornhuskers who say
    at sundown:
        Tomorrow is a day.

RIVER ROADS

LET the crows go by hawking their caw and caw.
They have been swimming in midnights of coal mines somewhere.
Let 'em hawk their caw and caw.

Let the woodpecker drum and drum on a hickory stump.
He has been swimming in red and blue pools somewhere hundreds of
    years
And the blue has gone to his wings and the red has gone to his head.
Let his red head drum and drum.

Let the dark pools hold the birds in a looking-glass.
And if the pool wishes, let it shiver to the blur of many wings, old swimmers from old places.

Let the redwing streak a line of vermilion on the green wood lines.
And the mist along the river fix its purple in lines of a woman's shawl on lazy shoulders.

PRAIRIE WATERS BY NIGHT

CHATTER of birds two by two raises a night song joining a litany of running water—sheer waters showing the russet of old stones remembering many rains.

And the long willows drowse on the shoulders of the running water, and sleep from much music; joined songs of day-end, feathery throats and stony waters, in a choir chanting new psalms.

It is too much for the long willows when low laughter of a red moon comes down; and the willows drowse and sleep on the shoulders of the running water.

EARLY MOON

THE baby moon, a canoe, a silver papoose canoe, sails and sails in the Indian west.
A ring of silver foxes, a mist of silver foxes, sit and sit around the Indian moon.
One yellow star for a runner, and rows of blue stars for more runners, keep a line of watchers.
O foxes, baby moon, runners, you are the panel of memory, fire-white writing tonight of the Red Man's dreams.
Who squats, legs crossed and arms folded, matching its look against the moon-face, the star-faces, of the West?
Who are the Mississippi Valley ghosts, of copper foreheads, riding wiry ponies in the night?—no bridles, love-arms on the pony necks, riding in the night a long old trail?
Why do they always come back when the silver foxes sit around the early moon, a silver papoose, in the Indian west?

LAUGHING CORN

THERE was a high majestic fooling
Day before yesterday in the yellow corn.

And day after tomorrow in the yellow corn
There will be high majestic fooling.

The ears ripen in late summer
And come on with a conquering laughter,
Come on with a high and conquering laughter.

The long-tailed blackbirds are hoarse.
One of the smaller blackbirds chitters on a stalk
And a spot of red is on its shoulder
And I never heard its name in my life.

Some of the ears are bursting.
A white juice works inside.
Cornsilk creeps in the end and dangles in the wind.
Always—I never knew it any other way—
The wind and the corn talk things over together.
And the rain and the corn and the sun and the corn
Talk things over together.

Over the road is the farmhouse.
The siding is white and a green blind is slung loose.
It will not be fixed till the corn is husked.
The farmer and his wife talk things over together.

AUTUMN MOVEMENT

I CRIED over beautiful things knowing no beautiful thing lasts.

The field of cornflower yellow is a scarf at the neck of the copper sun-
burned woman, the mother of the year, the taker of seeds.

The northwest wind comes and the yellow is torn full of holes, new beautiful things come in the first spit of snow on the northwest wind, and the old things go, not one lasts.

FALLTIME

GOLD of a ripe oat straw, gold of a southwest moon,
Canada thistle blue and flimmering larkspur blue,
Tomatoes shining in the October sun with red hearts,
Shining five and six in a row on a wooden fence,
Why do you keep wishes on your faces all day long,
Wishes like women with half-forgotten lovers going to new cities?
What is there for you in the birds, the birds, the birds, crying down on the
    north wind in September, acres of birds spotting the air going south?
Is there something finished? And some new beginning on the way?

ILLINOIS FARMER

BURY this old Illinois farmer with respect.
He slept the Illinois nights of his life after days of work in Illinois corn-
fields.
Now he goes on a long sleep.
The wind he listened to in the cornsilk and the tassels, the wind that
    combed his red beard zero mornings when the snow lay white on the
    yellow ears in the bushel basket at the corncrib,
The same wind will now blow over the place here where his hands must
    dream of Illinois corn.

HITS AND RUNS

I REMEMBER the Chillicothe ball players grappling the Rock Island ball
    players in a sixteen-inning game ended by darkness.
And the shoulders of the Chillicothe players were a red smoke against the
    sundown and the shoulders of the Rock Island players were a yellow
    smoke against the sundown.
And the umpire's voice was hoarse calling balls and strikes and outs and
    the umpire's throat fought in the dust for a song.

VILLAGE IN LATE SUMMER

LIPS half-willing in a doorway.
Lips half-singing at a window.
Eyes half-dreaming in the walls.
Feet half-dancing in a kitchen.
Even the clocks half-yawn the hours
And the farmers make half-answers.

BLIZZARD NOTES

I DON'T blame the kettle drums—they are hungry.
And the snare drums—I know what they want—they are empty too.
And the harring booming bass drums—they are hungriest of all.

. . .

The howling spears of the Northwest die down.
The lullabies of the Southwest get a chance, a mother song.
A cradle moon rides out of a torn hole in the ragbag top of the sky.

SUNSET FROM OMAHA HOTEL WINDOW

INTO the blue river hills
The red sun runners go
And the long sand changes
And today is a goner
And today is not worth haggling over.

    Here in Omaha
    The gloaming is bitter
    As in Chicago
    Or Kenosha.

The long sand changes.
Today is a goner.
Time knocks in another brass nail.
Another yellow plunger shoots the dark.

Constellations
Wheeling over Omaha
As in Chicago
Or Kenosha.

The long sand is gone
　　　　and all the talk is stars.
They circle in a dome over Nebraska.

STILL LIFE

Cool your heels on the rail of an observation car.

Let the engineer open her up for ninety miles an hour.

Take in the prairie right and left, rolling land and new hay crops, swaths of new hay laid in the sun.

A gray village flecks by and the horses hitched in front of the post office never blink an eye.

A barnyard and fifteen Holstein cows, dabs of white on a black wall map, never blink an eye.

A signalman in a tower, the outpost of Kansas City, keeps his place at a window with the serenity of a bronze statue on a dark night when lovers pass whispering.

BAND CONCERT

Band concert public square Nebraska city. Flowing and circling dresses, summer-white dresses. Faces, flesh tints flung like sprays of cherry blossoms. And gigglers, God knows, gigglers, rivaling the pony whinnies of the Livery Stable Blues.

Cowboy rags and nigger rags. And boys driving sorrel horses hurl a cornfield laughter at the girls in dresses, summer-white dresses. Amid the cornet staccato and the tuba oompa, gigglers, God knows, gigglers daffy with life's razzle dazzle.

Slow good-night melodies and Home Sweet Home. And the snare drummer bookkeeper in a hardware store nods hello to the daughter of a railroad conductor—a giggler, God knows, a giggler—and the summer-white dresses filter fanwise out of the public square.

The crushed strawberries of ice cream soda places, the night wind in cottonwoods and willows, the lattice shadows of doorsteps and porches, these know more of the story.

THREE PIECES ON THE SMOKE OF AUTUMN

SMOKE of autumn is on it all.
The streamers loosen and travel.
The red west is stopped with a gray haze.
They fill the ash trees, they wrap the oaks,
They make a long-tailed rider
In the pocket of the first, the earliest evening star.

. . .

Three muskrats swim west on the Desplaines River.

There is a sheet of red ember glow on the river; it is dusk; and the muskrats one by one go on patrol routes west.

Around each slippery padding rat, a fan of ripples; in the silence of dusk a faint wash of ripples, the padding of the rats going west, in a dark and shivering river gold.

(A newspaper in my pocket says the Germans pierce the Italian line; I have letters from poets and sculptors in Greenwich Village; I have letters from an ambulance man in France and an I. W. W. man in Vladivostok.)

I lean on an ash and watch the lights fall, the red ember glow, and three muskrats swim west in a fan of ripples on a sheet of river gold.

. . .

Better the blue silence and the gray west,
The autumn mist on the river,
And not any hate and not any love,
And not anything at all of the keen and the deep:

Only the peace of a dog head on a barn floor,
And the new corn shoveled in bushels
And the pumpkins brought from the corn rows,
Umber lights of the dark,
Umber lanterns of the loam dark.

Here a dog head dreams.
Not any hate, not any love.
Not anything but dreams.
Brother of dusk and umber.

LOCALITIES

WAGON WHEEL GAP is a place I never saw
And Red Horse Gulch and the chutes of Cripple Creek.

Red-shirted miners picking in the sluices,
Gamblers with red neckties in the night streets,
The fly-by-night towns of Bull Frog and Skiddoo,
The night-cool limestone white of Death Valley,
The straight drop of eight hundred feet
From a shelf road in the Hasiampa Valley:
Men and places they are I never saw.

I have seen three White Horse taverns,
One in Illinois, one in Pennsylvania,
One in a timber-hid road of Wisconsin.

I bought cheese and crackers
Between sun showers in a place called White Pigeon
Nestling with a blacksmith shop, a post office,
And a berry-crate factory, where four roads cross.

On the Pecatonica River near Freeport
I have seen boys run barefoot in the leaves
Throwing clubs at the walnut trees
In the yellow-and-gold of autumn,
And there was a brown mash dry on the inside of their hands.

On the Cedar Fork Creek of Knox County
I know how the fingers of late October
Loosen the hazel nuts.
I know the brown eyes of half-open hulls.
I knows boys named Lindquist, Swanson, Hildebrand.
I remember their cries when the nuts were ripe.
And some are in machine shops; some are in the navy;
And some are not on payrolls anywhere.
Their mothers are through waiting for them to come home.

CABOOSE THOUGHTS

It's going to come out all right—do you know?
The sun, the birds, the grass—they know.
They get along—and we'll get along.

Some days will be rainy and you will sit waiting
And the letter you wait for won't come,
And I will sit watching the sky tear off gray and gray
And the letter I wait for won't come.

There will be ac-ci-dents.
I know ac-ci-dents are coming.
Smash-ups, signals wrong, washouts, trestles rotten,
Red and yellow ac-ci-dents.
But somehow and somewhere the end of the run
The train gets put together again
And the caboose and the green tail lights
Fade down the right of way like a new white hope.

I never heard a mockingbird in Kentucky
Spilling its heart in the morning.

I never saw the snow on Chimborazo.
It's a high white Mexican hat, I hear.

I never had supper with Abe Lincoln.
Nor a dish of soup with Jim Hill.

But I've been around.
I know some of the boys here who can go a little.
I know girls good for a burst of speed any time.

I heard Williams and Walker
Before Walker died in the bughouse.

I knew a mandolin player
Working in a barber shop in an Indiana town,
And he thought he had a million dollars.

I knew a hotel girl in Des Moines.
She had eyes; I saw her and said to myself
The sun rises and the sun sets in her eyes.
I was her steady and her heart went pit-a-pat.
We took away the money for a prize waltz at a Brotherhood dance.
She had eyes; she was safe as the bridge over the Mississippi at Burlington;
     I married her.

Last summer we took the cushions going west.
Pike's Peak is a big old stone, believe me.
It's fastened down; something you can count on.

It's going to come out all right—do you know?
The sun, the birds, the grass—they know.
They get along—and we'll get along.

ALIX

The mare Alix breaks the world's trotting record one day. I see her heels
     flash down the dust of an Illinois race track on a summer afternoon.
     I see the timekeepers put their heads together over stop-watches, and
     call to the grand stand a split second is clipped off the old world's
     record and a new world's record fixed.

I see the mare Alix led away by men in undershirts and streaked faces.
     Dripping Alix in foam of white on the harness and shafts. And the
     men in undershirts kiss her ears and rub her nose, and tie blankets on
     her, and take her away to have the sweat sponged.

I see the grand stand jammed with prairie people yelling themselves hoarse.
Almost the grand stand and the crowd of thousands are one pair of
legs and one voice standing up and yelling hurrah.

I see the driver of Alix and the owner smothered in a fury of handshakes,
a mob of caresses. I see the wives of the driver and owner smothered
in a crush of white summer dresses and parasols.
Hours later, at sundown, gray dew creeping on the sod and sheds, I see
Alix again:

> Dark, shining-velvet Alix,
> Night-sky Alix in a gray blanket,
> Led back and forth by a nigger.
> Velvet and night-eyed Alix
> With slim legs of steel.

And I want to rub my nose against the nose of the mare Alix.

POTATO BLOSSOM SONGS AND JIGS

> RUM tiddy um,
> tiddy um,
> tiddy um tum tum.

My knees are loose-like, my feet want to sling their selves.
I feel like tickling you under the chin—honey—and a-asking: Why Does a
Chicken Cross the Road?
When the hens are a-laying eggs, and the roosters pluck-pluck-put-akut
and you—honey—put new potatoes and gravy on the table, and there
ain't too much rain or too little:

> Say, why do I feel so gabby?
> Why do I want to holler all over the place?

. . .

Do you remember I held empty hands to you
and I said all is yours
the handfuls of nothing?

. . .

I ask you for white blossoms.
I bring a concertina after sunset under the apple trees.
I bring out "The Spanish Cavalier" and "In the Gloaming, O My Darling."

The orchard here is near and home-like.

The oats in the valley run a mile.

Between are the green and marching potato vines.

The lightning bugs go criss-cross carrying a zigzag of fire: the potato bugs
are asleep under their stiff and yellow-striped wings: here romance
stutters to the western stars, "Excuse . . . me . . ."

. . .

Old foundations of rotten wood.

An old barn done-for and out of the wormholes ten-legged roaches shook
up and scared by sunlight.

So a pickax digs a long tooth with a short memory.

Fire can not eat this rubbish till it has lain in the sun.

. . .

The story lags.

The story has no connections.

The story is nothing but a lot of banjo plinka planka plunks.

The roan horse is young and will learn: the roan horse buckles into harness
and feels the foam on the collar at the end of a haul: the roan horse
points four legs to the sky and rolls in the red clover: the roan horse
has a rusty jag of hair between the ears hanging to a white star be-
tween the eyes.

. . .

In Burlington long ago

And later again in Ashtabula

I said to myself:

I wonder how far Ophelia went with Hamlet.

What else was there Shakespeare never told?

There must have been something.

If I go bugs I want to do it like Ophelia.

There was class to the way she went out of her head.

. . .

Does a famous poet eat watermelon?

Excuse me, ask me something easy.

I have seen farmhands with their faces in fried catfish on a Monday morn-
ing.

And the Japanese, two-legged like us,
The Japanese bring slices of watermelon into pictures.
The black seeds make oval polka dots on the pink meat.

Why do I always think of niggers and buck-and-wing dancing whenever
I see watermelon?

Summer mornings on the docks I walk among bushel peach baskets piled
ten feet high.
Summer mornings I smell new wood and the river wind along with
peaches.
I listen to the steamboat whistle hong-honging, hong-honging across the
town.
And once I saw a teameo straddling a street with a hay-rack load of melons.

. . .

Niggers play banjos because they want to.
The explanation is easy.

It is the same as why people pay fifty cents for tickets to a policemen's
masquerade ball or a grocers-and-butchers' picnic with a fat man's
foot race.
It is the same as why boys buy a nickel's worth of peanuts and eat them
and then buy another nickel's worth.
Newsboys shooting craps in a back alley have a fugitive understanding of
the scientific principle involved.
The jockey in a yellow satin shirt and scarlet boots, riding a sorrel pony at
the county fair, has a grasp of the theory.
It is the same as why boys go running lickety-split
away from a school-room geography lesson
in April when the crawfishes come out
and the young frogs are calling
and the pussywillows and the cat-tails
know something about geography themselves.

. . .

I ask you for white blossoms.
I offer you memories and people.
I offer you a fire zigzag over the green and marching vines.
I bring a concertina after supper under the home-like apple trees.

I make up songs about things to look at:
>potato blossoms in summer night mist filling the garden with white spots;
>a cavalryman's yellow silk handkerchief stuck in a flannel pocket over the left side of the shirt, over the ventricles of blood, over the pumps of the heart.

Bring a concertina after sunset under the apple trees.
Let romance stutter to the western stars, "Excuse . . . me . . ."

LOAM

IN the loam we sleep,
In the cool moist loam,
To the lull of years that pass
And the break of stars,

From the loam, then,
The soft warm loam,
    We rise:
To shape of rose leaf,
Of face and shoulder.

We stand, then,
    To a whiff of life,
Lifted to the silver of the sun
Over and out of the loam
    A day.

MANITOBA CHILDE ROLAND

LAST night a January wind was ripping at the shingles over our house and whistling a wolf song under the eaves.

I sat in a leather rocker and read to a six-year-old girl the Browning poem, *Childe Roland to the Dark Tower Came.*

And her eyes had the haze of autumn hills and it was beautiful to her and she could not understand.

A man is crossing a big prairie, says the poem, and nothing happens—and he goes on and on—and it's all lonesome and empty and nobody home.

And he goes on and on—and nothing happens—and he comes on a horse's skull, dry bones of a dead horse—and you know more than ever it's all lonesome and empty and nobody home.

And the man raises a horn to his lips and blows—he fixes a proud neck and forehead toward the empty sky and the empty land—and blows one last wonder-cry.

And as the shuttling automatic memory of man clicks off its results willy-nilly and inevitable as the snick of a mouse-trap or the trajectory of a 42-centimeter projectile,

I flash to the form of a man to his hips in snow drifts of Manitoba and Minnesota—in the sled derby run from Winnipeg to Minneapolis.

He is beaten in the race the first day out of Winnipeg—the lead dog is eaten by four team mates—and the man goes on and on—running while the other racers ride—running while the other racers sleep—

Lost in a blizzard twenty-four hours, repeating a circle of travel hour after hour—fighting the dogs who dig holes in the snow and whimper for sleep—pushing on—running and walking five hundred miles to the end of the race—almost a winner—one toe frozen, feet blistered and frost-bitten.

And I know why a thousand young men of the Northwest meet him in the finishing miles and yell cheers—I know why judges of the race call him a winner and give him a special prize even though he is a loser.

I know he kept under his shirt and around his thudding heart amid the blizzards of five hundred miles that one last wonder-cry of Childe Roland—and I told the six-year-old girl all about it.

And while the January wind was ripping at the shingles and whistling
a wolf song under the eaves, her eyes had the haze of autumn hills
and it was beautiful to her and she could not understand.

WILDERNESS

THERE is a wolf in me . . . fangs pointed for tearing gashes . . . a red
tongue for raw meat . . . and the hot lapping of blood—I keep this
wolf because the wilderness gave it to me and the wilderness will
not let it go.

There is a fox in me . . . a silver-gray fox . . . I sniff and guess . . . I
pick things out of the wind and air . . . I nose in the dark night and
take sleepers and eat them and hide the feathers . . . I circle and
loop and double-cross.

There is a hog in me . . . a snout and a belly . . . a machinery for
eating and grunting . . . a machinery for sleeping satisfied in the
sun—I got this too from the wilderness and the wilderness will not
let it go.

There is a fish in me . . . I know I came from salt-blue water-gates . . .
I scurried with shoals of herring . . . I blew waterspouts with por-
poises . . . before land was . . . before the water went down . . .
before Noah . . . before the first chapter of Genesis.

There is a baboon in me . . . clambering-clawed . . . dog-faced . . .
yawping a galoot's hunger . . . hairy under the armpits . . . here
are the hawk-eyed hankering men . . . here are the blonde and blue-
eyed women . . . here they hide curled asleep waiting . . . ready to
snarl and kill . . . ready to sing and give milk . . . waiting—I keep
the baboon because the wilderness says so.

There is an eagle in me and a mockingbird . . . and the eagle flies among
the Rocky Mountains of my dreams and fights among the Sierra
crags of what I want . . . and the mockingbird warbles in the early
forenoon before the dew is gone, warbles in the underbrush of my
Chattanoogas of hope, gushes over the blue Ozark foothills of my
wishes—And I got the eagle and the mockingbird from the wilderness.

O, I got a zoo, I got a menagerie, inside my ribs, under my bony head, under my red-valve heart—and I got something else: it is a man-child heart, a woman-child heart: it is a father and mother and lover: it came from God-Knows-Where: it is going to God-Knows-Where—For I am the keeper of the zoo: I say yes and no: I sing and kill and work: I am a pal of the world: I came from the wilderness.

Persons Half Known

CHICAGO POET

I SALUTED a nobody.
I saw him in a looking-glass.
He smiled—so did I.
He crumpled the skin on his forehead,
    frowning—so did I.
Everything I did he did.
I said, "Hello, I know you."
And I was a liar to say so.

Ah, this looking-glass man!
Liar, fool, dreamer, play-actor,
Soldier, dusty drinker of dust—
Ah! he will go with me
Down the dark stairway
When nobody else is looking,
When everybody else is gone.

He locks his elbow in mine,
I lose all—but not him.

FIRE-LOGS

NANCY HANKS dreams by the fire;
Dreams, and the logs sputter,
And the yellow tongues climb.
Red lines lick their way in flickers.
Oh, sputter, logs.
      Oh, dream, Nancy.
Time now for a beautiful child.
Time now for a tall man to come.

REPETITIONS

THEY are crying salt tears
Over the beautiful beloved body
Of Inez Milholland,
Because they are glad she lived,
Because she loved open-armed,
Throwing love for a cheap thing
Belonging to everybody—
Cheap as sunlight,
And morning air.

ADELAIDE CRAPSEY

AMONG the bumblebees in red-top hay, a freckled field of brown-eyed
    Susans dripping yellow leaves in July,
      I read your heart in a book.

And your mouth of blue pansy—I know somewhere I have seen it rain-
    shattered.

And I have seen a woman with her head flung between her naked knees,
    and her head held there listening to the sea, the great naked sea
    shouldering a load of salt.

And the blue pansy mouth sang to the sea:
>   *Mother of God, I'm so little a thing,*
>   *Let me sing longer,*
>   *Only a little longer.*

And the sea shouldered its salt in long gray combers hauling new shapes
   on the beach sand.

YOUNG BULLFROGS

JIMMY WIMBLEDON listened a first week in June.
Ditches along prairie roads of Northern Illinois
Filled the arch of night with young bullfrog songs.
Infinite mathematical metronomic croaks rose and spoke,
Rose and sang, rose in a choir of puzzles.
They made his head ache with riddles of music.
They rested his head with beaten cadence.
Jimmy Wimbledon listened.

MEMOIR OF A PROUD BOY

HE lived on the wings of storm.
The ashes are in Chihuahua.

Out of Ludlow and coal towns in Colorado
Sprang a vengeance of Slav miners, Italians, Scots, Cornishmen, Yanks
Killings ran under the spoken commands of this boy
With eighty men and rifles on a hogback mountain.

They killed swearing to remember
The shot and charred wives and children
In the burnt camp of Ludlow,
And Louis Tikas, the laughing Greek,
Plugged with a bullet, clubbed with a gun butt.

As a home war
It held the nation a week

And one or two million men stood together
And swore by the retribution of steel.

It was all accidental.
He lived flecking lint off coat lapels
Of men he talked with.
He kissed the miners' babies
And wrote a Denver paper
Of picket silhouettes on a mountain line.

He had no mother but Mother Jones
Crying from a jail window of Trinidad:
"All I want is room enough to stand
And shake my fist at the enemies of the human race."

Named by a grand jury as a murderer
He went to Chihuahua, forgot his old Scotch name,
Smoked cheroots with Pancho Villa
And wrote letters of Villa as a rock of the people.

How can I tell how Don Magregor went?

Three riders emptied lead into him.
He lay on the main street of an inland town.
A boy sat near all day throwing stones
To keep pigs away.

The Villa men buried him in a pit
With twenty Carranzistas.

There is drama in that point . . .
. . . the boy and the pigs.
Griffith would make a movie of it to fetch sobs.
Victor Herbert would have the drums whirr
In a weave with a high fiddle-string's single clamor.

"And the muchacho sat there all day throwing stones
To keep the pigs away," wrote Gibbons to the *Tribune*.

Somewhere in Chihuahua or Colorado
Is a leather bag of poems and short stories.

BILBEA

(From tablet writing, Babylonian excavations of 4th millennium B.C.)

Bilbea, I was in Babylon on Saturday night.
I saw nothing of you anywhere.
I was at the old place and the other girls were there, but no Bilbea.

Have you gone to another house? or city?
Why don't you write?
I was sorry. I walked home half-sick.

Tell me how it goes.
Send me some kind of a letter.
And take care of yourself.

SOUTHERN PACIFIC

Huntington sleeps in a house six feet long.
Huntington dreams of railroads he built and owned.
Huntington dreams of ten thousand men saying: Yes, sir.

Blithery sleeps in a house six feet long.
Blithery dreams of rails and ties he laid.
Blithery dreams of saying to Huntington: Yes, sir.

Huntington,
Blithery, sleep in houses six feet long.

WASHERWOMAN

The washerwoman is a member of the Salvation Army.
And over the tub of suds rubbing underwear clean
She sings that Jesus will wash her sins away
And the red wrongs she has done God and man
Shall be white as driven snow.
Rubbing underwear she sings of the Last Great Washday.

PORTRAIT OF A MOTORCAR

It's a lean car . . . a long-legged dog of a car . . . a gray-ghost eagle
   car.
The feet of it eat the dirt of a road . . . the wings of it eat the hills.
Danny the driver dreams of it when he sees women in red skirts and red
   sox in his sleep.
It is in Danny's life and runs in the blood of him . . . a lean gray-ghost
   car.

GIRL IN A CAGE

Here in a cage the dollars come down.
To the click of a tube the dollars tumble.
And out of a mouth the dollars run.

I finger the dollars,
Paper and silver,
Thousands a day.

Some days it's fun
            to finger the dollars.
Some days . . .
         the dollars keep on
         in a sob or a whisper:
A flame of rose in the hair,
A flame of silk at the throat.

BUFFALO BILL

Boy heart of Johnny Jones—aching today?
Aching, and Buffalo Bill in town?
Buffalo Bill and ponies, cowboys, Indians?

Some of us know
All about it, Johnny Jones.

Buffalo Bill is a slanting look of the eyes,
  A slanting look under a hat on a horse.
He sits on a horse and a passing look is fixed
  On Johnny Jones, you and me, barelegged,
A slanting, passing, careless look under a hat on a horse.

Go clickety-clack, O pony hoofs along the street.
Come on and slant your eyes again, O Buffalo Bill.
Give us again the ache of our boy hearts.
Fill us again with the red love of prairies, dark nights, lonely wagons, and
    the crack-crack of rifles sputtering flashes into an ambush.

SIXTEEN MONTHS

On the lips of the child Janet float changing dreams.
It is a thin spiral of blue smoke,
A morning campfire at a mountain lake.

On the lips of the child Janet,
Wisps of haze on ten miles of corn,
Young light blue calls to young light gold of morning.

CHILD MARGARET

The child Margaret begins to write numbers on a Saturday morning, the
    first numbers formed under her wishing child fingers.
All the numbers come well-born, shaped in figures assertive for a frieze
    in a child's room.
Both 1 and 7 are straightforward, military, filled with lunge and
    attack, erect in shoulder-straps.
The 6 and 9 salute as dancing sisters, elder and younger, and 2
    is a trapeze actor swinging to handclaps.
All the numbers are well-born, only 3 has a hump on its back and 8
    is knock-kneed.
The child Margaret kisses all once and gives two kisses to 3 and 8.
(Each number is a bran-new rag doll. . . . O in the wishing fingers . . .
    millions of rag dolls, millions and millions of new rag dolls!!)

SINGING NIGGER

Your bony head, Jazbo, O dock walloper,
Those grappling hooks, those wheelbarrow handlers,
The dome and the wings of you, nigger,
The red roof and the door of you,
I know where your songs came from.
I know why God listens to your, "Walk All Over God's Heaven."
I heard you shooting craps, "My baby's going to have a new dress."
I heard you in the cinders, "I'm going to live anyhow until I die."
I saw five of you with a can of beer on a summer night and I listened to
    the five of you harmonizing six ways to sing, "Way Down Yonder
    in the Cornfield."
I went away asking where I come from.

Leather Leggings

LEATHER LEGGINGS

They have taken the ball of earth
    and made it a little thing.

They were held to the land and horses;
    they were held to the little seas.
They have changed and shaped and welded;
    they have broken the old tools and made
    new ones; they are ranging the white
    scarves of cloudland; they are bumping
    the sunken bells of the Carthaginians
    and Phœnicians:

they are handling
the strongest sea
as a thing to be handled.

The earth was a call that mocked;
    it is belted with wires and meshed with
    steel; from Pittsburgh to Vladivostok is
    an iron ride on a moving house; from
    Jerusalem to Tokyo is a reckoned span;
    and they talk at night in the storm and
    salt, the wind and the war.

They have counted the miles to the Sun
    and Canopus; they have weighed a small
    blue star that comes in the southeast
    corner of the sky on a foretold errand.
We shall search the sea again.
We shall search the stars again.
There are no bars across the way.
There is no end to the plan and the clue,
    the hunt and the thirst.
The motors are drumming, the leather leggings
    and the leather coats wait:
                Under the sea
                and out to the stars
                we go.

PRAYERS OF STEEL

Lay me on an anvil, O God.
Beat me and hammer me into a crowbar.
Let me pry loose old walls.
Let me lift and loosen old foundations.

Lay me on an anvil, O God.
Beat me and hammer me into a steel spike.
Drive me into the girders that hold a skyscraper together.

Take red-hot rivets and fasten me into the central girders.
Let me be the great nail holding a skyscraper through blue nights into white stars.

ALWAYS THE MOB

JESUS emptied the devils of one man into forty hogs and the hogs took the edge of a high rock and dropped off and down into the sea: a mob.

The sheep on the hills of Australia, blundering four-footed in the sunset mist to the dark, they go one way, they hunt one sleep, they find one pocket of grass for all.

Karnak? Pyramids? Sphinx paws tall as a coolie? Tombs kept for kings and sacred cows? A mob.

Young roast pigs and naked dancing girls of Belshazzar, the room where a thousand sat guzzling when a hand wrote: Mene, mene, tekel, upharsin? A mob.

The honeycomb of green that won the sun as the Hanging Gardens of Nineveh, flew to its shape at the hands of a mob that followed the fingers of Nebuchadnezzar: a mob of one hand and one plan.

Stones of a circle of hills at Athens, staircases of a mountain in Peru, scattered clans of marble dragons in China: each a mob on the rim of a sunrise: hammers and wagons have them now.

Locks and gates of Panama? The Union Pacific crossing deserts and tunneling mountains? The Woolworth on land and the *Titanic* at sea? Lighthouses blinking a coast line from Labrador to Key West? Pig-iron bars piled on a barge whistling in a fog off Sheboygan? A mob: hammers and wagons have them tomorrow.

The mob? A typhoon tearing loose an island from thousand-year moorings and bastions, shooting a volcanic ash with a fire tongue that licks up cities and peoples. Layers of worms eating rocks and forming loam and valley floors for potatoes, wheat, watermelons.

The mob? A jag of lightning, a geyser, a gravel mass loosening . . .

The mob . . . kills or builds . . . the mob is Attila or Genghis Khan,
the mob is Napoleon, Lincoln.

I am born in the mob—I die in the mob—the same goes for you—I don't
care who you are.

I cross the sheets of fire in No Man's Land for you, my brother—I slip a
steel tooth into your throat, you my brother—I die for you and I
kill you—It is a twisted and gnarled thing, a crimson wool:

> One more arch of stars,
> In the night of our mist,
> In the night of our tears.

JABBERERS

I RISE out of my depths with my language.
You rise out of your depths with your language.

Two tongues from the depths,
Alike only as a yellow cat and a green parrot are alike,
Fling their staccato tantalizations
Into a wildcat jabber
Over a gossamer web of unanswerables.

The second and the third silence,
Even the hundredth silence,
Is better than no silence at all
(Maybe this is a jabber too—are we at it again, you and I?)

I rise out of my depths with my language.
You rise out of your depths with your language.

One thing there is much of; the name men call it by is time; into this gulf
our syllabic pronunciamentos empty by the way rockets of fire curve
and are gone on the night sky; into this gulf the jabberings go as the
shower at a scissors grinder's wheel. . . .

CARTOON

I AM making a Cartoon of a Woman. She is the People. She is the Great
  Dirty Mother.
And Many Children hang on her Apron, crawl at her Feet, snuggle at her
  Breasts.

INTERIOR

In the cool of the night time
The clocks pick off the points
And the mainsprings loosen.
They will need winding.
One of these days . . .
            they will need winding.

Rabelais in red boards,
Walt Whitman in green,
Hugo in ten-cent paper covers,
Here they stand on shelves
In the cool of the night time
And there is nothing . . .
To be said against them . . .
Or for them . . .
In the cool of the night time
And the clocks.

A man in pigeon-gray pajamas.
The open window begins at his feet
And goes taller than his head.
Eight feet high is the pattern.

Moon and mist make an oblong layout.
Silver at the man's bare feet.
He swings one foot in a moon silver.
And it costs nothing.

One more day of bread and work.
One more day . . . so much rags . . .

The man barefoot in moon silver
Mutters "You" and "You"
To things hidden
In the cool of the night time,
In Rabelais, Whitman, Hugo,
In an oblong of moon mist.

Out from the window . . . prairielands.
Moon mist whitens a golf ground.
Whiter yet is a limestone quarry.
The crickets keep on chirring.

Switch engines of the Great Western
Sidetrack box cars, make up trains
For Weehawken, Oskaloosa, Saskatchewan;
The cattle, the coal, the corn, must go
In the night . . . on the prairielands.

Chuff-chuff go the pulses.
They beat in the cool of the night time.
Chuff-chuff and chuff-chuff . . .
These heartbeats travel the night a mile
And touch the moon silver at the window
And the bones of the man.
It costs nothing.

Rabelais in red ʰ   ds,
Whitman ⁱ   ꞯen,
Hugo iⁿ   ꞓñ-cent paper covers,
Here ; ꞷy stand on shelves
In the cool of the night time
And the clocks.

STREET WINDOW

THE pawn-shop man knows hunger,
And how far hunger has eaten the heart
Of one who comes with an old keepsake.
Here are wedding rings and baby bracelets,

Scarf pins and shoe buckles, jeweled garters,
Old-fashioned knives with inlaid handles,
Watches of old gold and silver,
Old coins worn with finger-marks.
They tell stories.

PALLADIUMS

In the newspaper office—who are the spooks?
Who wears the mythic coat invisible?

Who pussyfoots from desk to desk
                    with a speaking forefinger?
Who gumshoes amid the copy paper
                    with a whispering thumb?

Speak softly—the sacred cows may hear.
Speak easy—the sacred cows must be fed.

CLOCKS

Here is a face that says half-past seven the same way whether a murder or
    a wedding goes on, whether a funeral or a picnic crowd passes.
A tall one I know at the end of a hallway broods in shadows and is watch-
    ing booze eat out the insides of the man of the house; it has seen five
    hopes go in five years: one woman, one child, and three dreams.
A little one carried in a leather box by an actress rides with her to hotels
    and is under her pillow in a sleeping-car between one-night stands.
One hoists a phiz over a railroad station; it points numbers to people a
    quarter-mile away who believe it when other clocks fail.
And of course . . . there are wrist watches over the pulses of airmen eager
    to go to France. . . .

LEGENDS

CLOWNS DYING

FIVE circus clowns dying this year, morning newspapers told their lives,
   how each one horizontal in a last gesture of hands arranged by an
   undertaker, shook thousands into convulsions of laughter from behind
   rouge-red lips and powder-white face.

STEAMBOAT BILL

When the boilers of the *Robert E. Lee* exploded, a steamboat winner of
   many races on the Mississippi went to the bottom of the river and
   never again saw the wharves of Natchez and New Orleans.
And a legend lives on that two gamblers were blown toward the sky and
   during their journey laid bets on which of the two would go higher
   and which would be first to set foot on the turf of the earth again.

FOOT AND MOUTH PLAGUE

When the mysterious foot and mouth epidemic ravaged the cattle of
   Illinois, Mrs. Hector Smith wept bitterly over the government killing
   forty of her soft-eyed Jersey cows; through the newspapers she wept
   over her loss for millions of readers in the Great Northwest.

SEVENS

The lady who has had seven lawful husbands has written seven years for
   a famous newspaper telling how to find love and keep it: seven thou-
   sand hungry girls in the Mississippi Valley have read the instructions
   seven years and found neither illicit loves nor lawful husbands.

PROFITEER

I who saw ten strong young men die anonymously, I who saw ten old
   mothers hand over their sons to the nation anonymously, I who saw
   ten thousand touch the sunlit silver finalities of undistinguished hu-
   man glory—why do I sneeze sardonically at a bronze drinking foun-
   tain named after one who participated in the war vicariously and
   bought ten farms?

PSALM OF THOSE WHO GO FORTH BEFORE DAYLIGHT

THE policeman buys shoes slow and careful; the teamster buys gloves slow and careful; they take care of their feet and hands; they live on their feet and hands.

The milkman never argues; he works alone and no one speaks to him; the city is asleep when he is on the job; he puts a bottle on six hundred porches and calls it a day's work; he climbs two hundred wooden stairways; two horses are company for him; he never argues.

The rolling-mill men and the sheet-steel men are brothers of cinders; they empty cinders out of their shoes after the day's work; they ask their wives to fix burnt holes in the knees of their trousers; their necks and ears are covered with a smut; they scour their necks and ears; they are brothers of cinders.

HORSES AND MEN IN RAIN

LET us sit by a hissing steam radiator a winter's day, gray wind pattering frozen raindrops on the window,
And let us talk about milk wagon drivers and grocery delivery boys.

Let us keep our feet in wool slippers and mix hot punches—and talk about mail carriers and messenger boys slipping along the icy sidewalks.
Let us write of olden, golden days and hunters of the Holy Grail and men called "knights" riding horses in the rain, in the cold frozen rain for ladies they loved.

A roustabout hunched on a coal wagon goes by, icicles drip on his hat rim, sheets of ice wrapping the hunks of coal, the caravanserai a gray blur in slant of rain.
Let us nudge the steam radiator with our wool slippers and write poems of Launcelot, the hero, and Roland, the hero, and all the olden golden men who rode horses in the rain.

QUESTIONNAIRE

HAVE I told any man to be a liar for my sake?

Have I sold ice to the poor in summer and coal to the poor in winter for
the sake of daughters who nursed brindle bull terriers and led with
a leash their dogs clothed in plaid wool jackets?

Have I given any man an earful too much of my talk—or asked any man
to take a snootful of booze on my account?

Have I put wool in my own ears when men tried to tell me what was good
for me? Have I been a bum listener?

Have I taken dollars from the living and the unborn while I made speeches
on the retributions that shadow the heels of the dishonest?

Have I done any good under cover? Or have I always put it in the show
windows and the newspapers?

NEAR KEOKUK

THIRTY-TWO Greeks are dipping their feet in a creek.
Sloshing their bare feet in a cool flow of clear water.
All one midsummer day ten hours the Greeks
          stand in leather shoes shoveling gravel.
Now they hold their toes and ankles
          to the drift of running water.
Then they go to the bunk cars
          and eat mulligan and prune sauce,
Smoke one or two pipefuls, look at the stars,
          tell smutty stories
About men and women they have known,
          countries they have seen,
Railroads they have built—
          and then the deep sleep of children.

SLANTS AT BUFFALO, NEW YORK

A FOREFINGER of stone, dreamed by a sculptor, points to the sky.
It says: This way! this way!

Four lions snore in stone at the corner of the shaft.
They too are the dream of a sculptor.
They too say: This way! this way!

The street cars swing at a curve.
The middle-class passengers witness low life.
The car windows frame low life all day in pictures.

Two Italian cellar delicatessens
                    sell red and green peppers.
The Florida bananas furnish a burst of yellow.
The lettuce and the cabbage give a green.

Boys play marbles in the cinders.
The boys' hands need washing.
The boys are glad; they fight among each other.

A plank bridge leaps the Lehigh Valley railroad.
Then acres of steel rails, freight cars, smoke,
And then . . . the blue lake shore
. . . Erie with Norse blue eyes . . . and the white sun.

FLAT LANDS

FLAT lands on the end of town where real estate men are crying new sub-
    divisions,
The sunsets pour blood and fire over you hundreds and hundreds of nights,
    flat lands—blood and fire of sunsets thousands of years have been
    pouring over you.
And the stars follow the sunsets. One gold star. A shower of blue stars.
    Blurs of white and gray stars. Vast marching processions of stars arch-
    ing over you flat lands where frogs sob this April night.
"Lots for Sale—Easy Terms" run letters painted on a board—and the stars
    wheel onward, the frogs sob this April night.

LAWYER

WHEN the jury files in to deliver a verdict after weeks of direct and cross
examinations, hot clashes of lawyers and cool decisions of the judge,
There are points of high silence—twiddling of thumbs is at an end—bailiffs
near cuspidors take fresh chews of tobacco and wait—and the clock
has a chance for its ticking to be heard.
A lawyer for the defense clears his throat and holds himself ready if the
word is "Guilty" to enter motion for a new trial, speaking in a soft
voice, speaking in a voice slightly colored with bitter wrongs mingled
with monumental patience, speaking with mythic Atlas shoulders of
many preposterous, unjust circumstances.

THREE BALLS

JABOWSKY'S place is on a side street and only the rain washes the dusty
three balls.
When I passed the window a month ago, there rested in proud isolation:
A family bible with hasps of brass twisted off, a wooden clock with pendu-
lum gone,
And a porcelain crucifix with the glaze nicked where the left elbow of
Jesus is represented.
I passed today and they were all there, resting in proud isolation, the clock
and the crucifix saying no more and no less than before, and a yellow
cat sleeping in a patch of sun alongside the family bible with the
hasps off.
Only the rain washes the dusty three balls in front of Jabowsky's place on
a side street.

CHICKS

THE chick in the egg picks at the shell, cracks open one oval world, and
enters another oval world.

"Cheep . . . cheep . . . cheep" is the salutation of the newcomer, the
emigrant, the casual at the gates of the new world.

"Cheep . . . cheep" . . . from oval to oval, sunset to sunset, star to star.

It is at the door of this house, this teeny weeny eggshell exit, it is here
    men say a riddle and jeer each other: who are you? where do you go
    from here?

(In the academies many books, at the circus many sacks of peanuts, at the
    club rooms many cigar butts.)

"Cheep . . . cheep" . . . from oval to oval, sunset to sunset, star to star.

HUMDRUM

If I had a million lives to live
    and a million deaths to die
    in a million humdrum worlds,
I'd like to change my name
    and have a new house number to go by
    each and every time I died
    and started life all over again.

I wouldn't want the same name every time
    and the same old house number always,
    dying a million deaths,
    dying one by one a million times:
    —would you?
             or you?
                  or you?

JOLIET

On the one hand the steel works.
On the other hand the penitentiary.
Santa Fé trains and Alton trains
Between smokestacks on the west
And gray walls on the east.
And Lockport down the river.

Part of the valley is God's.
And part is man's.

The river course laid out
A thousand years ago.
The canals ten years back.

The sun on two canals and one river
Makes three stripes of silver
Or copper and gold
Or shattered sunflower leaves.
     Talons of an iceberg
     Scraped out this valley.
     Claws of an avalanche loosed here.

KNUCKS

In Abraham Lincoln's city,
Where they remember his lawyer's shingle,
The place where they brought him
Wrapped in battle flags,
Wrapped in the smoke of memories
From Tallahassee to the Yukon,
The place now where the shaft of his tomb
Points white against the blue prairie dome,
In Abraham Lincoln's city . . . I saw knucks
In the window of Mister Fischman's second-hand store
On Second Street.

I went in and asked, "How much?"
"Thirty cents apiece," answered Mister Fischman.
And taking a box of new ones off a shelf
He filled anew the box in the showcase
And said incidentally, most casually
And incidentally:
"I sell a carload a month of these."

I slipped my fingers into a set of knucks,
Cast-iron knucks molded in a foundry pattern,
And there came to me a set of thoughts like these:
Mister Fischman is for Abe and the "malice to none" stuff,

And the street car strikers and the strike-breakers,
And the sluggers, gunmen, detectives, policemen,
Judges, utility heads, newspapers, priests, lawyers,
They are all for Abe and the "malice to none" stuff.

I started for the door.
"Maybe you want a lighter pair,"
Came Mister Fischman's voice.
I opened the door . . . and the voice again:
"You are a funny customer."

Wrapped in battle flags,
Wrapped in the smoke of memories,
This is the place they brought him,
This is Abraham Lincoln's home town.

TESTAMENT

I GIVE the undertakers permission to haul my body
to the graveyard and to lay away all, the head, the
feet, the hands, all: I know there is something left
over they can not put away.

Let the nanny goats and the billy goats of the shanty
people eat the clover over my grave   and if any yellow
hair or any blue smoke of flowers is good enough to grow
over me   let the dirty-fisted children of the shanty
people pick these flowers.

I have had my chance to live with the people who have
too much and the people who have too little and I chose
one of the two and I have told no man why.

Haunts

VALLEY SONG

Your eyes and the valley are memories.
Your eyes fire and the valley a bowl.
It was here a moonrise crept over the timberline.
It was here we turned the coffee cups upside down.
And your eyes and the moon swept the valley.

I will see you again tomorrow.
I will see you again in a million years.
I will never know your dark eyes again.
These are three ghosts I keep.
These are three sumach-red dogs I run with.

All of it wraps and knots to a riddle:
I have the moon, the timberline, and you.
All three are gone—and I keep all three.

IN TALL GRASS

Bees and a honeycomb in the dried head of a horse in a pasture corner—
    a skull in the tall grass and a buzz and a buzz of the yellow honey-
    hunters.

And I ask no better a winding sheet
                (over the earth and under the sun).

Let the bees go honey-hunting with yellow blur of wings in the dome of
    my head, in the rumbling, singing arch of my skull.

Let there be wings and yellow dust and the drone of dreams of honey—
who loses and remembers?—who keeps and forgets?

In a blue sheen of moon over the bones and under the hanging honey-
comb the bees come home and the bees sleep.

UPSTAIRS

I TOO have a garret of old playthings.
I have tin soldiers with broken arms upstairs.
I have a wagon and the wheels gone upstairs.
I have guns and a drum, a jumping-jack and a magic lantern.
And dust is on them and I never look at them upstairs.
I too have a garret of old playthings.

MONOSYLLABIC

LET me be monosyllabic today, O Lord.
Yesterday I loosed a snarl of words on a fool,
      on a child.
Today, let me be monosyllabic . . . a crony of old men
      who wash sunlight in their fingers and
      enjoy slow-pacing clocks.

FILMS

I HAVE kept all, not one is thrown away, not one given to the ragman, not
    one thrust in a corner with a "P-f-f."
The red ones and the blue, the long ones in stripes, and each of the little
    black and white checkered ones.
Keep them: I tell my heart: keep them another year, another ten years:
    they will be wanted again.
They came once, they came easy, they came like a first white flurry of
    snow in late October,
Like any sudden, presumptuous, beautiful thing, and they were cheap at
    the price, cheap like snow.

Here a red one and there a long one in yellow stripes,
O there shall be no ragman have these yet a year, yet ten years.

KREISLER

SELL me a violin, mister, of old mysterious wood.
Sell me a fiddle that has kissed dark nights on the forehead where men
kiss sisters they love.
Sell me dried wood that has ached with passion clutching the knees and
arms of a storm.
Sell me horsehair and rosin that has sucked at the breasts of the morning
sun for milk.
Sell me something crushed in the heartsblood of pain readier than ever
for one more song.

THE SEA HOLD

THE sea is large.
The sea hold on a leg of land in the Chesapeake hugs an early sunset and
a last morning star over the oyster beds and the late clam boats of
lonely men.
Five white houses on a half-mile strip of land . . . five white dice rolled
from a tube.

Not so long ago . . . the sea was large . . .
And today the sea has lost nothing . . . it keeps all.

I am a loon about the sea.
I make so many sea songs, I cry so many sea cries, I forget so many sea
songs and sea cries.

I am a loon about the sea.
So are five men I had a fish fry with once in a tar-paper shack trembling
in a sand storm.
The sea knows more about them than they know themselves.
They know only how the sea hugs and will not let go.

The sea is large.
The sea must know more than any of us.

GOLDWING MOTH

A GOLDWING moth is between the scissors and the ink bottle on the desk.
Last night it flew hundreds of circles around a glass bulb and a flame wire.
The wings are a soft gold; it is the gold of illuminated initials in manu-
scripts of the medieval monks.

LOIN CLOTH

BODY of Jesus taken down from the cross
Carved in ivory by a lover of Christ,
It is a child's handful you are here,
The breadth of a man's finger,
And this ivory loin cloth
Speaks an interspersal in the day's work,
The carver's prayer and whim
And Christ-love.

HEMLOCK AND CEDAR

THIN sheets of blue smoke among white slabs . . . near the shingle mill
. . . winter morning.
Falling of a dry leaf might be heard . . . circular steel tears through a
log.
Slope of woodland . . . brown . . . soft . . . tinge of blue such as pansy
eyes.
Farther, field fires . . . funnel of yellow smoke . . . spellings of other
yellow in corn stubble.
Bobsled on a down-hill road . . . February snow mud . . . horses steam-
ing . . . Oscar the driver sings ragtime under a spot of red seen a
mile . . . the red wool yarn of Oscar's stocking cap is seen from the
shingle mill to the ridge of hemlock and cedar.

SUMMER SHIRT SALE

THE summer shirt sale of a downtown haberdasher is glorified in a show-window slang: everybody understands the language: red dots, yellow circles, blue anchors, and dove-brown hooks, these perform explosions in color: stripes and checks fight for the possession of front lines and salients: detectives, newsies, teameoes, niggers, all stop, look, and listen: the shirt sale and the show window kick at the street with a noise joyous as a clog dancer: the ensemble is a challenge to the ghost who walks on paydays.

MEDALLION

THE brass medallion profile of your face I keep always.
It is not jingling with loose change in my pockets.
It is not stuck up in a show place on the office wall.
I carry it in a special secret pocket in the day
And it is under my pillow at night.
The brass came from a long ways off: it was up against hell and high water,
      fire and flood, before the face was put on it.
It is the side of a head; a woman wishes; a woman waits; a woman swears
      behind silent lips that the sea will bring home what is gone.

BRICKLAYER LOVE

I THOUGHT of killing myself because I am only a bricklayer and you a
      woman who loves the man who runs a drug store.

I don't care like I used to; I lay bricks straighter than I used to and I sing
      slower handling the trowel afternoons.

When the sun is in my eyes and the ladders are shaky and the mortar
      boards go wrong, I think of you.

ASHURNATSIRPAL III
(From Babylonian tablet, 4,000 years Before Christ)

THREE walls around the town of Tela when I came.
They expected everything of those walls;
Nobody in the town came out to kiss my feet.

I knocked the walls down, killed three thousand soldiers,
Took away cattle and sheep, took all the loot in sight,
And burned special captives.

Some of the soldiers—I cut off hands and feet.
Others—I cut off ears and fingers.
Some—I put out the eyes.
I made a pyramid of heads.
I strung heads on trees circling the town.

When I got through with it
There wasn't much left of the town of Tela.

MAMMY HUMS

THIS is the song I rested with:
The right shoulder of a strong man I leaned on.
The face of the rain that drizzled on the short neck of a canal boat.
The eyes of a child who slept while death went over and under.
The petals of peony pink that fluttered in a shot of wind come and gone.

This is the song I rested with:
Head, heels, and fingers rocked to the nigger mammy humming of it, to
    the mile-off steamboat landing whistle of it.

The murmurs run with bees' wings
                in a late summer sun.
They go and come with white surf
                slamming on a beach all day.

Get this.
And then you may sleep with a late afternoon slumber sun.
Then you may slip your head in an elbow knowing nothing—only sleep.
If so you sleep in the house of our song,
If so you sleep under the apple trees of our song,
Then the face of sleep must be the one face you were looking for.

BRINGERS

COVER me over
In dusk and dust and dreams.

Cover me over
And leave me alone.

Cover me over,
You tireless, great.

Hear me and cover me,
Bringers of dusk and dust and dreams.

CRIMSON RAMBLER

Now that a crimson rambler
    begins to crawl over the house
    of our two lives—

Now that a red curve
    winds across the shingles—

Now that hands
    washed in early sunrises
    climb and spill scarlet
    on a white lattice weave—

Now that a loop of blood
    is written on our roof
    and reaching around a chimney—

How are the two lives of this house
    to keep strong hands and strong hearts?

HAUNTS

THERE are places I go when I am strong.
One is a marsh pool where I used to go
            with a long-ear hound-dog.
One is a wild crabapple tree; I was there
        a moonlight night with a girl.
The dog is gone; the girl is gone; I go to these
        places when there is no other place to go.

HAVE ME

HAVE me in the blue and the sun.
Have me on the open sea and the mountains.

When I go into the grass of the sea floor, I will go alone.
This is where I came from—the chlorine and the salt are blood and bones.
It is here the nostrils rush the air to the lungs. It is here oxygen clamors
    to be let in.
And here in the root grass of the sea floor I will go alone.

Love goes far. Here love ends.
Have me in the blue and the sun.

FIRE DREAMS
(*Written to be read aloud, if so be, Thanksgiving Day*)

I REMEMBER here by the fire,
In the flickering reds and saffrons,
They came in a ramshackle tub,
Pilgrims in tall hats,
Pilgrims of iron jaws,
Drifting by weeks on beaten seas,
And the random chapters say
They were glad and sang to God.

And so
Since the iron-jawed men sat down
And said, "Thanks, O God,"
For life and soup and a little less
Than a hobo handout today,
Since gray winds blew gray patterns of sleet on Plymouth Rock,
Since the iron-jawed men sang "Thanks, O God,"
You and I, O Child of the West,
Remember more than ever
November and the hunter's moon,
November and the yellow-spotted hills.

And so
In the name of the iron-jawed men
I will stand up and say yes till the finish is come and gone.
God of all broken hearts, empty hands, sleeping soldiers,
God of all star-flung beaches of night sky,
I and my love-child stand up together today and sing: "Thanks, O
    God."

BABY FACE

WHITE MOON comes in on a baby face.
The shafts across her bed are flimmering.

Out on the land White Moon shines,
Shines and glimmers against gnarled shadows,
All silver to slow twisted shadows
Falling across the long road that runs from the house.

Keep a little of your beauty
And some of your flimmering silver
For her by the window tonight
Where you come in, White Moon.

THE YEAR

I

A STORM of white petals,
Buds throwing open baby fists
Into hands of broad flowers.

II

Red roses running upward,
Clambering to the clutches of life
Soaked in crimson.

III

Rabbles of tattered leaves
Holding golden flimsy hopes
Against the tramplings
Into the pits and gullies.

IV

Hoarfrost and silence:
Only the muffling
Of winds dark and lonesome—
Great lullabies to the long sleepers.

DRUMNOTES *

DAYS of the dead men, Danny.
Drum for the dead, drum on your
    remembering heart.

Jaurès, a great love-heart of France,
    a slug of lead in the red valves.
Kitchener of Khartoum, tall, cold, proud,
    a shark's mouthful.
Franz Josef, the old man of forty haunted
    kingdoms, in a tomb with the Hapsburg
    fathers, moths eating a green uniform
    to tatters, worms taking all and leaving
    only bones and gold buttons, bones and
    iron crosses.
Jack London, Jim Riley, Verhaeren, riders to
    the republic of dreams.

Days of the dead, Danny.
Drum on your remembering heart.

* Copyright, Dodd, Mead & Co.

MOONSET

Leaves of poplars pick Japanese prints against the west.
Moon sand on the canal doubles the changing pictures.
         The moon's good-by ends pictures.
The west is empty. All else is empty. No moon-talk at all now.
         Only dark listening to dark.

GARDEN WIRELESS

How many feet ran with sunlight, water, and air?

What little devils shaken of laughter, cramming their little ribs with
    chuckles,

Fixed this lone red tulip, a woman's mouth of passion kisses, a nun's
    mouth of sweet thinking, here topping a straight line of green, a pillar
    stem?

Who hurled this bomb of red caresses?—nodding balloon-film shooting its
    wireless every fraction of a second these June days:
                 Love me before I die;
                 Love me—love me now.

HANDFULS

         Blossoms of babies
         Blinking their stories
         Come soft
         On the dusk and the babble;
         Little red gamblers,
         Handfuls that slept in the dust.

         Summers of rain,
         Winters of drift,
         Tell off the years;

And they go back
Who came soft—
Back to the sod,
To silence and dust;
Gray gamblers,
    Handfuls again.

COOL TOMBS

WHEN Abraham Lincoln was shoveled into the tombs, he forgot the copperheads and the assassin . . . in the dust, in the cool tombs.

And Ulysses Grant lost all thought of con men and Wall Street, cash and collateral turned ashes . . . in the dust, in the cool tombs.

Pocahontas' body, lovely as a poplar, sweet as a red haw in November or a pawpaw in May, did she wonder? does she remember? . . . in the dust, in the cool tombs?

Take any streetful of people buying clothes and groceries, cheering a hero or throwing confetti and blowing tin horns . . . tell me if the lovers are losers . . . tell me if any get more than the lovers . . . in the dust . . . in the cool tombs.

Shenandoah

SHENANDOAH

In the Shenandoah Valley, one rider gray and one rider blue, and the sun
on the riders wondering.

Piled in the Shenandoah, riders blue and riders gray, piled with shovels,
one and another, dust in the Shenandoah taking them quicker than
mothers take children done with play.

The blue nobody remembers, the gray nobody remembers, it's all old and
old nowadays in the Shenandoah.

. . .

And all is young, a butter of dandelions slung on the turf, climbing blue
flowers of the wishing woodlands wondering: a midnight purple violet
claims the sun among old heads, among old dreams of repeating heads
of a rider blue and a rider gray in the Shenandoah.

NEW FEET

Empty battlefields keep their phantoms.
Grass crawls over old gun wheels
And a nodding Canada thistle flings a purple
Into the summer's southwest wind,
Wrapping a root in the rust of a bayonet,
Reaching a blossom in rust of shrapnel.

OLD OSAWATOMIE

John Brown's body under the morning stars.
Six feet of dust under the morning stars.
And a panorama of war performs itself
Over the six-foot stage of circling armies.
Room for Gettysburg, Wilderness, Chickamauga,
On a six-foot stage of dust.

GRASS

Pile the bodies high at Austerlitz and Waterloo.
Shovel them under and let me work—
         I am the grass; I cover all.

And pile them high at Gettysburg
And pile them high at Ypres and Verdun.
Shovel them under and let me work.
Two years, ten years, and passengers ask the conductor:
         What place is this?
         Where are we now?

         I am the grass.
         Let me work.

FLANDERS

Flanders, the name of a place, a country of people,
Spells itself with letters, is written in books.

"Where is Flanders?" was asked one time,
Flanders known only to those who lived there
And milked cows and made cheese and spoke the home language.

"Where is Flanders?" was asked.
And the slang adepts shot the reply: Search me.

A few thousand people milking cows, raising radishes,
On a land of salt grass and dunes, sand-swept with a sea-breath on it:
This was Flanders, the unknown, the quiet,
The place where cows hunted lush cuds of green on lowlands,
And the raw-boned plowmen took horses with long shanks
Out in the dawn to the sea-breath.

Flanders sat slow-spoken amid slow-swung windmills,
Slow-circling windmill arms turning north or west,
Turning to talk to the swaggering winds, the childish winds,
So Flanders sat with the heart of a kitchen girl
Washing wooden bowls in the winter sun by a window.

GARGOYLE

I SAW a mouth jeering. A smile of melted red iron ran over it. Its laugh was
    full of nails rattling. It was a child's dream of a mouth.
A fist hit the mouth: knuckles of gun-metal driven by an electric wrist
    and shoulder. It was a child's dream of an arm.
The fist hit the mouth over and over, again and again. The mouth bled
    melted iron, and laughed its laughter of nails rattling.
And I saw the more the fist pounded the more the mouth laughed. The
    fist is pounding and pounding, and the mouth answering.

OLD TIMERS

I AM an ancient reluctant conscript.

On the soup wagons of Xerxes I was a cleaner of pans.

On the march of Miltiades' phalanx I had a haft and head;
I had a bristling gleaming spear-handle.

Red-headed Cæsar picked me for a teamster.
He said, "Go to work, you Tuscan bastard,
Rome calls for a man who can drive horses."

The units of conquest led by Charles the Twelfth,
The whirling whimsical Napoleonic columns:
They saw me one of the horseshoers.

I trimmed the feet of a white horse Bonaparte swept the night stars with.

Lincoln said, "Get into the game; your nation takes you."
And I drove a wagon and team and I had my arm shot off
At Spotsylvania Court House.

I am an ancient reluctant conscript.

HOUSE

Two Swede families live downstairs and an Irish policeman upstairs, and
    an old soldier, Uncle Joe.
Two Swede boys go upstairs and see Joe. His wife is dead, his only son
    is dead, and his two daughters in Missouri and Texas don't want him
    around.
The boys and Uncle Joe crack walnuts with a hammer on the bottom of
    a flatiron while the January wind howls and the zero air weaves laces
    on the window glass.
Joe tells the Swede boys all about Chickamauga and Chattanooga, how
    the Union soldiers crept in rain somewhere a dark night and ran for-
    ward and killed many Rebels, took flags, held a hill, and won a victory
    told about in the histories in school.
Joe takes a piece of carpenter's chalk, draws lines on the floor and piles
    stove wood to show where six regiments were slaughtered climbing a
    slope.
"Here they went" and "Here they went," says Joe, and the January wind
    howls and the zero air weaves laces on the window glass.
The two Swede boys go downstairs with a big blur of guns, men, and hills
    in their heads. They eat herring and potatoes and tell the family war
    is a wonder and soldiers are a wonder.
One breaks out with a cry at supper: I wish we had a war now and I could
    be a soldier.

JOHN ERICSSON DAY MEMORIAL, 1918

INTO the gulf and the pit of the dark night, the cold night, there is a man
goes into the dark and the cold and when he comes back to his people
he brings fire in his hands and they remember him in the years after-
ward as the fire bringer—they remember or forget—the man whose
head kept singing to the want of his home, the want of his people.

For this man there is no name thought of—he has broken from jungles
and the old oxen and the old wagons—circled the earth with ships—
belted the earth with steel—swung with wings and a drumming motor
in the high blue sky—shot his words on a wireless way through shat-
tering sea storms:—out from the night and out from the jungles his
head keeps singing—there is no road for him but on and on.

Against the sea bastions and the land bastions, against the great air pockets
of stars and atoms, he points a finger, finds a release clutch, touches a
button no man knew before.

The soldier with a smoking gun and a gas mask—the workshop man under
the smokestacks and the blueprints—these two are brothers of the
handshake never forgotten—for these two we give the salt tears of
our eyes, the salute of red roses, the flame-won scarlet of poppies.

For the soldier who gives all, for the workshop man who gives all, for
these the red bar is on the flag—the red bar is the heart's-blood of the
mother who gave him, the land that gave him.

The gray foam and the great wheels of war go by and take all—and the
years give mist and ashes—and our feet stand at these, the memory
places of the known and the unknown, and our hands give a flame-
won poppy—our hands touch the red bar of a flag for the sake of those
who gave—and gave all.

REMEMBERED WOMEN

For a woman's face remembered as a spot of quick light on the flat land
    of dark night,
For this memory of one mouth and a forehead they go on in the gray
    rain and the mud, they go on among the boots and guns.
The horizon ahead is a thousand fang flashes, it is a row of teeth that bite
    on the flanks of night, the horizon sings of a new kill and a big kill.
The horizon behind is a wall of dark etched with a memory, fixed with a
    woman's face—they fight on and on, boots in the mud and heads in
    the gray rain—for the women they hate and the women they love—
    for the women they left behind, they fight on.

OUT OF WHITE LIPS

Out of white lips a question: Shall seven million dead ask for their blood
    a little land for the living wives and children, a little land for the
    living brothers and sisters?

Out of white lips:—Shall they have only air that sweeps round the earth
    for breath of their nostrils and no footing on the dirt of the earth for
    their battle-drabbed, battle-soaked shoes?

Out of white lips:—Is the red in the flag the blood of a free man on a
    piece of land his own or is it the red of a sheep slit in the throat for
    mutton?

Out of white lips a white pain murmurs: Who shall have land? Him who
    has stood ankle deep in the blood of his comrades, in the red trenches
    dug in the land?

MEMOIR

Papa Joffre, the shoulders of him wide as the land of France.

We look on the shoulders filling the stage of the Chicago Auditorium.

A fat mayor has spoken much English and the mud of his speech is crossed with quicksilver hisses elusive and rapid from floor and gallery.

A neat governor speaks English and the listeners ring chimes to his clear thoughts.

Joffre speaks a few words in French; this is a voice of the long firing line that runs from the salt sea dunes of Flanders to the white spear crags of the Swiss mountains.

This is the man on whose yes and no has hung the death of battalions and brigades; this man speaks of the tricolor of his country now melted in a great resolve with the starred bunting of Lincoln and Washington.

This is the hero of the Marne, massive, irreckonable; he lets tears roll down his cheek; they trickle a wet salt off his chin onto the blue coat.

There is a play of American hands and voices equal to sea-breakers and a lift of white sun on a stony beach.

A MILLION YOUNG WORKMEN, 1915

A MILLION young workmen straight and strong lay stiff on the grass and roads,
And the million are now under soil and their rottening flesh will in the years feed roots of blood-red roses.
Yes, this million of young workmen slaughtered one another and never saw their red hands.
And oh, it would have been a great job of killing and a new and beautiful thing under the sun if the million knew why they hacked and tore each other to death.
The kings are grinning, the kaiser and the czar—they are alive riding in leather-seated motor cars, and they have their women and roses for ease, and they eat fresh poached eggs for breakfast, new butter on toast, sitting in tall water-tight houses reading the news of war.
I dreamed a million ghosts of the young workmen rose in their shirts all soaked in crimson . . . and yelled:
God damn the grinning kings, God damn the kaiser and the czar.

[CHICAGO, 1915]

SMOKE

I sɪт in a chair and read the newspapers.

Millions of men go to war, acres of them are buried, guns and ships
broken, cities burned, villages sent up in smoke, and children where
cows are killed off amid hoarse barbecues vanish like finger-rings of
smoke in a north wind.

I sit in a chair and read the newspapers.

A TALL MAN

Tʜᴇ mouth of this man is a gaunt strong mouth.
The head of this man is a gaunt strong head.

The jaws of this man are bone of the Rocky Mountains, the Appa-
lachians.
The eyes of this man are chlorine of two sobbing oceans,
Foam, salt, green, wind, the changing unknown.
The neck of this man is pith of buffalo prairie, old longing and new
beckoning of corn belt or cotton belt,
Either a proud Sequoia trunk of the wilderness
Or huddling lumber of a sawmill waiting to be a roof.

Brother mystery to man and mob mystery,
Brother cryptic to lifted cryptic hands,
He is night and abyss, he is white sky of sun, he is the head of the people.
The heart of him the red drops of the people,
The wish of him the steady gray-eagle crag-hunting flights of the people.

Humble dust of a wheel-worn road,
Slashed sod under the iron-shining plow,
These of service in him, these and many cities, many borders, many
wrangles between Alaska and the Isthmus, between the Isthmus and
the Horn, and east and west of Omaha, and east and west of Paris,
Berlin, Petrograd.

The blood in his right wrist and the blood in his left wrist run with the
   right wrist wisdom of the many and the left wrist wisdom of the
   many.
It is the many he knows, the gaunt strong hunger of the many.

THE FOUR BROTHERS
Notes for War Songs (November, 1917)

MAKE war songs out of these;
Make chants that repeat and weave.
Make rhythms up to the ragtime chatter of the machine guns;
Make slow-booming psalms up to the boom of the big guns.
Make a marching song of swinging arms and swinging legs,
        Going along,
        Going along,
On the roads from San Antonio to Athens, from Seattle to Bagdad—
The boys and men in winding lines of khaki, the circling squares of
   bayonet points.

Cowpunchers, cornhuskers, shopmen, ready in khaki;
Ballplayers, lumberjacks, ironworkers, ready in khaki;
A million, ten million, singing, "I am ready."
This the sun looks on between two seaboards,
In the land of Lincoln, in the land of Grant and Lee.

I heard one say, "I am ready to be killed."
I heard another say, "I am ready to be killed."
O sunburned clear-eyed boys!
I stand on sidewalks and you go by with drums and guns and bugles,
        You—and the flag!
And my heart tightens, a fist of something feels my throat
        When you go by,
You on the kaiser hunt, you and your faces saying, "I am ready to be
   killed."

They are hunting death,
Death for the one-armed mastoid kaiser.
They are after a Hohenzollern head:
There is no man-hunt of men remembered like this.

The four big brothers are out to kill.
France, Russia, Britain, America—
The four republics are sworn brothers to kill the kaiser.

Yes, this is the great man-hunt;
And the sun has never seen till now
Such a line of toothed and tusked man-killers,
In the blue of the upper sky,
In the green of the undersea,
In the red of winter dawns.
Eating to kill,
Sleeping to kill,
Asked by their mothers to kill,
Wished by four-fifths of the world to kill—
To cut the kaiser's throat,
To hack the kaiser's head,
To hang the kaiser on a high-horizon gibbet.

And is it nothing else than this?
Three times ten million men thirsting the blood
Of a half-cracked one-armed child of the German kings?
Three times ten million men asking the blood
Of a child born with his head wrong-shaped,
The blood of rotted kings in his veins?
If this were all, O God,
I would go to the far timbers
And look on the gray wolves
Tearing the throats of moose:
I would ask a wilder drunk of blood.

Look! It is four brothers in joined hands together.
        The people of bleeding France,
        The people of bleeding Russia,
        The people of Britain, the people of America—
These are the four brothers, these are the four republics.

At first I said it in anger as one who clenches his fist in wrath to fling
        his knuckles into the face of some one taunting;
Now I say it calmly as one who has thought it over and over again at
        night, among the mountains, by the sea-combers in storm.

I say now, by God, only fighters today will save the world, nothing but
    fighters will keep alive the names of those who left red prints of
    bleeding feet at Valley Forge in Christmas snow.
On the cross of Jesus, the sword of Napoleon, the skull of Shakespeare,
    the pen of Tom Jefferson, the ashes of Abraham Lincoln, or any sign
    of the red and running life poured out by the mothers of the world,
By the God of morning glories climbing blue the doors of quiet homes,
    by the God of tall hollyhocks laughing glad to children in peaceful
    valleys, by the God of new mothers wishing peace to sit at windows
    nursing babies,
I swear only reckless men, ready to throw away their lives by hunger,
    deprivation, desperate clinging to a single purpose imperturbable and
    undaunted, men with the primitive guts of rebellion,
Only fighters gaunt with the red brand of labor's sorrow on their brows
    and labor's terrible pride in their blood, men with souls asking
    danger—only these will save and keep the four big brothers.

Good-night is the word, good-night to the kings, to the czars,
        Good-night to the kaiser.
The breakdown and the fade-away begins.
The shadow of a great broom, ready to sweep out the trash, is here.

One finger is raised that counts the czar,
The ghost who beckoned men who come no more—
The czar gone to the winds on God's great dustpan,
The czar a pinch of nothing,
The last of the gibbering Romanoffs.

Out and good-night—
The ghosts of the summer palaces
And the ghosts of the winter palaces!
Out and out, good-night to the kings, the czars, the kaisers.

Another finger will speak,
And the kaiser, the ghost who gestures a hundred million sleeping-
    waking ghosts,
The kaiser will go onto God's great dustpan—
The last of the gibbering Hohenzollerns.
Look! God pities this trash, God waits with a broom and a dustpan,
God knows a finger will speak and count them out.

It is written in the stars;
It is spoken on the walls;
It clicks in the fire-white zigzag of the Atlantic wireless;
It mutters in the bastions of thousand-mile continents;
It sings in a whistle on the midnight winds from Walla Walla to Meso-
    potamia:
Out and good-night.

The millions slow in khaki,
The millions learning *Turkey in the Straw* and *John Brown's Body*,
The millions remembering windrows of dead at Gettysburg, Chicka-
    mauga, and Spotsylvania Court House,
The millions dreaming of the morning star of Appomattox,
The millions easy and calm with guns and steel, planes and prows:
        There is a hammering, drumming hell to come.
        The killing gangs are on the way.

God takes one year for a job.
God takes ten years or a million.
God knows when a doom is written.
God knows this job will be done and the words spoken:
Out and good-night.
        The red tubes will run,
        And the great price be paid,
        And the homes empty,
        And the wives wishing,
        And the mothers wishing.
There is only one way now, only the way of the red tubes and the great
    price.

        Well . . .
Maybe the morning sun is a five-cent yellow balloon,
And the evening stars the joke of a God gone crazy.
Maybe the mothers of the world,
And the life that pours from their torsal folds—
Maybe it's all a lie sworn by liars,
And a God with a cackling laughter says:
"I, the Almighty God,
I have made all this,
I have made it for kaisers, czars, and kings."

Three times ten million men say: No.
Three times ten million men say:
     God is a God of the People.
And the God who made the world
     And fixed the morning sun,
     And flung the evening stars,
     And shaped the baby hands of life,
This is the God of the Four Brothers;
This is the God of bleeding France and bleeding Russia;
This is the God of the people of Britain and America.

The graves from the Irish Sea to the Caucasus peaks are ten times a
    million.
The stubs and stumps of arms and legs, the eyesockets empty, the crip-
    ples, ten times a million.
The crimson thumb-print of this anathema is on the door panels of a
    hundred million homes.
Cows gone, mothers on sick-beds, children cry a hunger and no milk
    comes in the noon-time or at night.
The death-yells of it all, the torn throats of men in ditches calling for
    water, the shadows and the hacking lungs in dugouts, the steel
    paws that clutch and squeeze a scarlet drain day by day—the storm
    of it is hell.
But look! child! the storm is blowing for a clean air.

Look! the four brothers march
And hurl their big shoulders
And swear the job shall be done.

Out of the wild finger-writing north and south, east and west, over the
    blood-crossed, blood-dusty ball of earth,
Out of it all a God who knows is sweeping clean,
Out of it all a God who sees and pierces through, is breaking and clean-
    ing out an old thousand years, is making ready for a new thousand
    years.
The four brothers shall be five and more.

Under the chimneys of the winter-time the children of the world shall
    sing new songs.
Among the rocking restless cradles the mothers of the world shall sing
    new sleepy-time songs.

SMOKE AND STEEL

Smoke Nights

SMOKE AND STEEL

Smoke of the fields in spring is one,
Smoke of the leaves in autumn another.
Smoke of a steel-mill roof or a battleship funnel,
They all go up in a line with a smokestack,
Or they twist . . . in the slow twist . . . of the wind.

If the north wind comes they run to the south.
If the west wind comes they run to the east.
     By this sign
     all smokes
     know each other.
Smoke of the fields in spring and leaves in autumn,
Smoke of the finished steel, chilled and blue,
By the oath of work they swear: "I know you."

Hunted and hissed from the center
Deep down long ago when God made us over,
Deep down are the cinders we came from—
You and I and our heads of smoke.

       . . . .

Some of the smokes God dropped on the job
Cross on the sky and count our years
And sing in the secrets of our numbers;
Sing their dawns and sing their evenings,
Sing an old log-fire song:
     You may put the damper up,
     You may put the damper down,
     The smoke goes up the chimney just the same.

Smoke of a city sunset skyline,
Smoke of a country dusk horizon—
    They cross on the sky and count our years.

     . . . .

Smoke of a brick-red dust
    Winds on a spiral
    Out of the stacks
For a hidden and glimpsing moon.
This, said the bar-iron shed to the blooming mill,
This is the slang of coal and steel.
The day-gang hands it to the night-gang,
The night-gang hands it back.

Stammer at the slang of this—
Let us understand half of it.
    In the rolling mills and sheet mills,
    In the harr and boom of the blast fires,
    The smoke changes its shadow
    And men change their shadow;
    A nigger, a wop, a bohunk changes.

    A bar of steel—it is only
Smoke at the heart of it, smoke and the blood of a man.
A runner of fire ran in it, ran out, ran somewhere else,
And left—smoke and the blood of a man
And the finished steel, chilled and blue.
So fire runs in, runs out, runs somewhere else again,
And the bar of steel is a gun, a wheel, a nail, a shovel,
A rudder under the sea, a steering-gear in the sky;
And always dark in the heart and through it,
    Smoke and the blood of a man.
Pittsburgh, Youngstown, Gary—they make their steel with men.

In the blood of men and the ink of chimneys
The smoke nights write their oaths:
Smoke into steel and blood into steel;
Homestead, Braddock, Birmingham, they make their steel with men.
Smoke and blood is the mix of steel.

The birdmen drone
in the blue; it is steel
a motor sings and zooms.

. . . .

Steel barbwire around The Works.

Steel guns in the holsters of the guards at the gates of The Works.

Steel ore-boats bring the loads clawed from the earth by steel, lifted and
lugged by arms of steel, sung on its way by the clanking clam-shells.

The runners now, the handlers now, are steel; they dig and clutch and
haul; they hoist their automatic knuckles from job to job; they are
steel making steel.

Fire and dust and air fight in the furnaces; the pour is timed, the billets
wriggle; the clinkers are dumped:

Liners on the sea, skyscrapers on the land; diving steel in the sea, climb-
ing steel in the sky.

. . . .

Finders in the dark, you Steve with a dinner bucket, you Steve clumping
in the dusk on the sidewalks with an evening paper for the woman
and kids, you Steve with your head wondering where we all end up—

Finders in the dark, Steve: I hook my arm in cinder sleeves; we go down
the street together; it is all the same to us; you Steve and the rest
of us end on the same stars; we all wear a hat in hell together, in
hell or heaven.

Smoke nights now, Steve.
Smoke, smoke, lost in the sieves of yesterday;
Dumped again to the scoops and hooks today.
Smoke like the clocks and whistles, always.
Smoke nights now.
Tomorrow something else.

. . . .

Luck moons come and go:
Five men swim in a pot of red steel.
Their bones are kneaded into the bread of steel:
Their bones are knocked into coils and anvils
And the sucking plungers of sea-fighting turbines.
Look for them in the woven frame of a wireless station.
So ghosts hide in steel like heavy-armed men in mirrors.

Peepers, skulkers—they shadow-dance in laughing tombs.
They are always there and they never answer.

One of them said: "I like my job, the company is good to me, America
    is a wonderful country."
One: "Jesus, my bones ache; the company is a liar; this is a free country,
    like hell."
One: "I got a girl, a peach; we save up and go on a farm and raise pigs
    and be the boss ourselves."
And the others were roughneck singers a long ways from home.
Look for them back of a steel vault door.

        They laugh at the cost.
        They lift the birdmen into the blue.
        It is steel a motor sings and zooms.

In the subway plugs and drums,
In the slow hydraulic drills, in gumbo or gravel,
Under dynamo shafts in the webs of armature spiders.
They shadow-dance and laugh at the cost.
         . . . .

The ovens light a red dome.
Spools of fire wind and wind.
Quadrangles of crimson sputter.
The lashes of dying maroon let down.
Fire and wind wash out the slag.
Forever the slag gets washed in fire and wind.
The anthem learned by the steel is:
        Do this or go hungry.
Look for our rust on a plow.
Listen to us in a threshing-engine razz.
Look at our job in the running wagon wheat.
         . . . .

Fire and wind wash at the slag.
Box-cars, clocks, steam-shovels, churns, pistons, boilers, scissors—
Oh, the sleeping slag from the mountains, the slag-heavy pig-iron will go
    down many roads.
Men will stab and shoot with it, and make butter and tunnel rivers, and
    mow hay in swaths, and slit hogs and skin beeves, and steer air-
    planes across North America, Europe, Asia, round the world.

Hacked from a hard rock country, broken and baked in mills and smelters,
    the rusty dust waits
Till the clean hard weave of its atoms cripples and blunts the drills chew-
    ing a hole in it.
The steel of its plinths and flanges is reckoned, O God, in one-millionth
    of an inch.

       . . . .

Once when I saw the curves of fire, the rough scarf women dancing,
Dancing out of the flues and smokestacks—flying hair of fire, flying feet
    upside down;
Buckets and baskets of fire exploding and chortling, fire running wild out
    of the steady and fastened ovens;
Sparks cracking a harr-harr-huff from a solar-plexus of rock-ribs of the
    earth taking a laugh for themselves;
Ears and noses of fire, gibbering gorilla arms of fire, gold mud-pies, gold
    bird-wings, red jackets riding purple mules, scarlet autocrats tumbling
    from the humps of camels, assassinated czars straddling vermilion
    balloons;
I saw then the fires flash one by one: good-by: then smoke, smoke;
And in the screens the great sisters of night and cool stars, sitting women
    arranging their hair,
Waiting in the sky, waiting with slow easy eyes, waiting and half-
    murmuring:
      "Since you know all
      and I know nothing,
      tell me what I dreamed last night."

       . . . .

Pearl cobwebs in the windy rain,
in only a flicker of wind,
are caught and lost and never known again.

A pool of moonshine comes and waits,
but never waits long: the wind picks up
loose gold like this and is gone.

A bar of steel sleeps and looks slant-eyed
on the pearl cobwebs, the pools of moonshine;
sleeps slant-eyed a million years,
sleeps with a coat of rust, a vest of moths,
a shirt of gathering sod and loam.

The wind never bothers . . . a bar of steel.
The wind picks only . . . pearl cobwebs . . . pools of moonshine.

FIVE TOWNS ON THE B. AND O.

By day . . . tireless smokestacks . . . hungry smoky shanties hanging to
    the slopes . . . crooning:
    We get by, that's all.
By night . . . all lit up . . . fire-gold bars, fire-gold flues . . . and the
    shanties shaking in clumsy shadows . . . almost the hills shaking
    . . . all crooning: By God, we're going to find out or know why.

WORK GANGS

Box cars run by a mile long.
And I wonder what they say to each other
When they stop a mile long on a sidetrack.
    Maybe their chatter goes:
I came from Fargo with a load of wheat up to the danger line.
I came from Omaha with a load of shorthorns and they splintered my
    boards.
I came from Detroit heavy with a load of flivvers.
I carried apples from the Hood River last year and this year bunches of
    bananas from Florida; they look for me with watermelons from Mis-
    sissippi next year.

Hammers and shovels of work gangs sleep in shop corners
when the dark stars come on the sky and the night watchmen walk and
    look.

Then the hammer heads talk to the handles,
then the scoops of the shovels talk,
how the day's work nicked and trimmed them,
how they swung and lifted all day,
how the hands of the work gangs smelled of hope.
In the night of the dark stars
when the curve of the sky is a work gang handle,
in the night on the mile long sidetracks,

in the night where the hammers and shovels sleep in corners,
the night watchmen stuff their pipes with dreams—
and sometimes they doze and don't care for nothin',
and sometimes they search their heads for meanings, stories, stars.
    The stuff of it runs like this:
A long way we come; a long way to go; long rests and long deep sniffs for
    our lungs on the way.
Sleep is a belonging of all; even if all songs are old songs and the singing
    heart is snuffed out like a switchman's lantern with the oil gone,
    even if we forget our names and houses in the finish, the secret of
    sleep is left us, sleep belongs to all, sleep is the first and last and
    best of all.

People singing; people with song mouths connecting with song hearts;
    people who must sing or die; people whose song hearts break if there
    is no song mouth; these are my people.

PENNSYLVANIA

I HAVE been in Pennsylvania,
In the Monongahela and the Hocking Valleys.

In the blue Susquehanna
On a Saturday morning
I saw the mounted constabulary go by,
I saw boys playing marbles.
Spring and the hills laughed.

And in places
Along the Appalachian chain,
I saw steel arms handling coal and iron,
And I saw the white-cauliflower faces
Of miners' wives waiting for the men to come home from the day's work.

I made color studies in crimson and violet
Over the dust and domes of culm at sunset.

WHIRLS

NEITHER rose leaves gathered in a jar—respectably in Boston—these—nor drops of Christ blood for a chalice—decently in Philadelphia or Baltimore.

Cinders—these—hissing in a marl and lime of Chicago—also these—the howling of northwest winds across North and South Dakota—or the spatter of winter spray on sea rocks of Kamchatka.

People Who Must

PEOPLE WHO MUST

I PAINTED on the roof of a skyscraper.
I painted a long while and called it a day's work.
The people on a corner swarmed and the traffic cop's whistle never let up all afternoon.
They were the same as bugs, many bugs on their way—
Those people on the go or at a standstill;
And the traffic cop a spot of blue, a splinter of brass,
Where the black tides ran around him
And he kept the street. I painted a long while
And called it a day's work.

ALLEY RATS

THEY were calling certain styles of whiskers by the name of "lilacs."
And another manner of beard assumed in their chatter a verbal guise
Of "mutton chops," "galways," "feather dusters."

Metaphors such as these sprang from their lips while other street cries
Sprang from sparrows finding scattered oats among interstices of the curb.
Ah-hah these metaphors—and Ah-hah these boys—among the police they
    were known
As the Dirty Dozen and their names took the front pages of newspapers
And two of them croaked on the same day at a "necktie party" . . . if
    we employ the metaphors of their lips.

ELEVENTH AVENUE RACKET

    THERE is something terrible
    about a hurdy-gurdy,
    a gypsy man and woman,
    and a monkey in red flannel
    all stopping in front of a big house
    with a sign "For Rent" on the door
    and the blinds hanging loose
    and nobody home.
    I never saw this.
    I hope to God I never will.

    Whoop-de-doodle-de-doo.
    Hoodle-de-harr-de-hum.
Nobody home? Everybody home.
    Whoop-de-doodle-de-doo.
Mamie Riley married Jimmy Higgins last night: Eddie Jones died of
    whooping cough: George Hacks got a job on the police force: the
    Rosenheims bought a brass bed: Lena Hart giggled at a jackie: a
    pushcart man called tomaytoes, tomaytoes.
    Whoop-de-doodle-de-doo.
    Hoodle-de-harr-de-hum.
        Nobody home? Everybody home.

HOME FIRES

IN a Yiddish eating place on Rivington Street . . . faces . . . coffee
　　spots . . . children kicking at the night stars with bare toes from
　　bare buttocks.
They know it is September on Rivington when the red tomaytoes cram
　　the pushcarts,
Here the children snozzle at milk bottles, children who have never seen
　　a cow.
Here the stranger wonders how so many people remember where they
　　keep home fires.

HATS

　　　　HATS, where do you belong?
　　　　　　what is under you?

On the rim of a skyscraper's forehead
I looked down and saw: hats: fifty thousand hats:
Swarming with a noise of bees and sheep, cattle and waterfalls,
Stopping with a silence of sea grass, a silence of prairie corn.
　　　　　Hats: tell me your high hopes.

THEY ALL WANT TO PLAY HAMLET

THEY all want to play Hamlet.
They have not exactly seen their fathers killed
Nor their mothers in a frame-up to kill,
Nor an Ophelia dying with a dust gagging the heart,
Not exactly the spinning circles of singing golden spiders,
Not exactly this have they got at nor the meaning of flowers—O flowers,
　　flowers slung by a dancing girl—in the saddest play the inkfish,
　　Shakespeare, ever wrote;
Yet they all want to play Hamlet because it is sad like all actors are sad
　　and to stand by an open grave with a joker's skull in the hand and

then to say over slow and say over slow wise, keen, beautiful words
   masking a heart that's breaking, breaking,
This is something that calls and calls to their blood.
They are acting when they talk about it and they know it is acting to be
   particular about it and yet: They all want to play Hamlet.

THE MAYOR OF GARY

I ASKED the Mayor of Gary about the 12-hour day and the 7-day week.
And the Mayor of Gary answered more workmen steal time on the job in
   Gary than any other place in the United States.
"Go into the plants and you will see men sitting around doing nothing—
   machinery does everything," said the Mayor of Gary when I asked
   him about the 12-hour day and the 7-day week.
And he wore cool cream pants, the Mayor of Gary, and white shoes, and
   a barber had fixed him up with a shampoo and a shave and he was
   easy and imperturbable though the government weather bureau ther-
   mometer said 96 and children were soaking their heads at bubbling
   fountains on the street corners.
And I said good-by to the Mayor of Gary and I went out from the city
   hall and turned the corner into Broadway.
And I saw workmen wearing leather shoes scruffed with fire and cinders,
   and pitted with little holes from running molten steel,
And some had bunches of specialized muscles around their shoulder blades
   hard as pig iron, muscles of their forearms were sheet steel and they
   looked to me like men who had been somewhere.

[GARY, INDIANA, 1915]

OMAHA

RED barns and red heifers spot the green
grass circles around Omaha—the farmers
haul tanks of cream and wagon loads of
cheese.

Shale hogbacks across the river at Council
Bluffs—and shanties hang by an eyelash to
the hill slants back around Omaha.

A span of steel ties up the kin of Iowa and
Nebraska across the yellow, big-hoofed Missouri
River.

Omaha, the roughneck, feeds armies,
Eats and swears from a dirty face.
Omaha works to get the world a breakfast.

GALOOTS

GALOOTS, you hairy, hankering,
Snousle on the bones you eat, chew at the gristle and lick the last of it.
Grab off the bones in the paws of other galoots—hook your claws in their
    sleazy mouths—snap and run.
If long-necks sit on their rumps and sing wild cries to the winter moon,
    chasing their tails to the flickers of foolish stars . . . let 'em howl.
Galoots fat with too much, galoots lean with too little, galoot millions and
    millions, snousle and snicker on, plug your exhausts, hunt your snacks
    of fat and lean, grab off yours.

CRABAPPLE BLOSSOMS

SOMEBODY's little girl—how easy to make a sob story over who she was once
    and who she is now.
Somebody's little girl—she played once under a crabapple tree in June and
    the blossoms fell on the dark hair.

It was somewhere on the Erie line and the town was Salamanca or Painted
    Post or Horse's Head.
And out of her hair she shook the blossoms and went into the house and
    her mother washed her face and her mother had an ache in her heart
    at a rebel voice, "I don't want to."

Somebody's little girl—forty little girls of somebodies splashed in red tights
    forming horseshoes, arches, pyramids—forty little show girls, ponies,
    squabs.
How easy a sob story over who she once was and who she is now—and
    how the crabapple blossoms fell on her dark hair in June.

Let the lights of Broadway spangle and splatter—and the taxis hustle the
crowds away when the show is over and the street goes dark.
Let the girls wash off the paint and go for their midnight sandwiches—
let 'em dream in the morning sun, late in the morning, long after the
morning papers and the milk wagons—
Let 'em dream long as they want to . . . of June somewhere on the Erie
line . . . and crabapple blossoms.

REAL ESTATE NEWS

ARMOUR AVENUE was the name of this street and door signs on empty
houses read "The Silver Dollar," "Swede Annie" and the Christian
names of madams such as "Myrtle" and "Jenny."
Scrap iron, rags and bottles fill the front rooms hither and yon and signs
in Yiddish say Abe Kaplan & Co. are running junk shops in whore
houses of former times.
The segregated district, the Tenderloin, is here no more; the red-lights are
gone; the ring of shovels handling scrap iron replaces the banging of
pianos and the bawling songs of pimps.

[CHICAGO, 1915]

MANUAL SYSTEM

MARY has a thingamajig clamped on her ears
And sits all day taking plugs out and sticking plugs in.
Flashes and flashes—voices and voices
calling for ears to pour words in
Faces at the ends of wires asking for other faces
at the ends of other wires:
All day taking plugs out and sticking plugs in,
Mary has a thingamajig clamped on her ears.

STRIPES

POLICEMAN in front of a bank 3 A.M. . . . . lonely.
Policeman State and Madison . . . high noon . . . mobs . . . cars . . .
parcels . . . lonely.

Woman in suburbs . . . keeping night watch on a sleeping typhoid patient . . . only a clock to talk to . . . lonesome.

Woman selling gloves . . . bargain day department store . . . furious crazy-work of many hands slipping in and out of gloves . . . lonesome.

HONKY TONK IN CLEVELAND, OHIO

It's a jazz affair, drum crashes and cornet razzes.
The trombone pony neighs and the tuba jackass snorts.
The banjo tickles and titters too awful.
The chippies talk about the funnies in the papers.
 The cartoonists weep in their beer.
 Ship riveters talk with their feet
 To the feet of floozies under the tables.
A quartet of white hopes mourn with interspersed snickers:
 "I got the blues.
 I got the blues.
 I got the blues."
And . . . as we said earlier:
 The cartoonists weep in their beer.

CRAPSHOOTERS

Somebody loses whenever somebody wins.
This was known to the Chaldeans long ago.
And more: somebody wins whenever somebody loses.
This too was in the savvy of the Chaldeans.

They take it heaven's hereafter is an eternity of crap games where they try their wrists years and years and no police come with a wagon; the game goes on forever.
The spots on the dice are the music signs of the songs of heaven here.
God is Luck: Luck is God: we are all bones the High Thrower rolled: some are two spots, some double sixes.

The myths are Phoebe, Little Joe, Big Dick.
Hope runs high with a: Huh, seven—huh, come seven
This too was in the savvy of the Chaldeans.

SOUP

I saw a famous man eating soup.
I say he was lifting a fat broth
Into his mouth with a spoon.
His name was in the newspapers that day
Spelled out in tall black headlines
And thousands of people were talking about him.

When I saw him,
He sat bending his head over a plate
Putting soup in his mouth with a spoon.

CLINTON SOUTH OF POLK

I wander down on Clinton street south of Polk
And listen to the voices of Italian children quarreling.
It is a cataract of coloratura
And I could sleep to their musical threats and accusations.

BLUE ISLAND INTERSECTION

Six street ends come together here.
They feed people and wagons into the center.
In and out all day horses with thoughts of nose-bags,
Men with shovels, women with baskets and baby buggies.
Six ends of streets and no sleep for them all day.
The people and wagons come and go, out and in.
Triangles of banks and drug stores watch.
The policemen whistle, the trolley cars bump:
Wheels, wheels, feet, feet, all day.

In the false dawn when the chickens blink
And the east shakes a lazy baby toe at tomorrow,
And the east fixes a pink half-eye this way,
In the time when only one milk wagon crosses
These three streets, these six street ends,
It is the sleep time and they rest.
The triangle banks and drug stores rest.
The policeman is gone, his star and gun sleep.
The owl car blutters along in a sleep-walk.

RED-HEADED RESTAURANT CASHIER

SHAKE back your hair, O red-headed girl.
Let go your laughter and keep your two proud freckles on your chin.
Somewhere is a man looking for a red-headed girl and some day maybe
    he will look into your eyes for a restaurant cashier and find a lover,
    maybe.
Around and around go ten thousand men hunting a red-headed girl with
    two freckles on her chin.
I have seen them hunting, hunting.
        Shake back your hair; let go your laughter.

BOY AND FATHER

THE boy Alexander understands his father to be a famous lawyer.
The leather law books of Alexander's father fill a room like hay in a barn.
Alexander has asked his father to let him build a house like bricklayers
    build, a house with walls and roofs made of big leather law books.

        The rain beats on the windows
        And the raindrops run down the window glass
        And the raindrops slide off the green blinds down the siding.
The boy Alexander dreams of Napoleon in John C. Abbott's history,
    Napoleon the grand and lonely man wronged, Napoleon in his life
    wronged and in his memory wronged.
The boy Alexander dreams of the cat Alice saw, the cat fading off into
    the dark and leaving the teeth of its Cheshire smile lighting the
    gloom.

Buffaloes, blizzards, way down in Texas, in the panhandle of Texas snug-
gling close to New Mexico,
These creep into Alexander's dreaming by the window when his father
talks with strange men about land down in Deaf Smith County.
Alexander's father tells the strange men: Five years ago we ran a Ford out
on the prairie and chased antelopes.

Only once or twice in a long while has Alexander heard his father say
"my first wife" so-and-so and such-and-such.
A few times softly the father has told Alexander, "Your mother . . . was
a beautiful woman . . . but we won't talk about her."
Always Alexander listens with a keen listen when he hears his father men-
tion "my first wife" or "Alexander's mother."

Alexander's father smokes a cigar and the Episcopal rector smokes a cigar
and the words come often: mystery of life, mystery of life.
These two come into Alexander's head blurry and gray while the rain
beats on the windows and the raindrops run down the window glass
and the raindrops slide off the green blinds and down the siding.
These and: There is a God, there must be a God, how can there be rain
or sun unless there is a God?

So from the wrongs of Napoleon and the Cheshire cat smile on to the
buffaloes and blizzards of Texas and on to his mother and to God, so
the blurry gray rain dreams of Alexander have gone on five minutes,
maybe ten, keeping slow easy time to the raindrops on the window
glass and the raindrops sliding off the green blinds and down the
siding.

CLEAN CURTAINS

New neighbors came to the corner house at Congress and Green streets.

The look of their clean white curtains was the same as the rim of a nun's
bonnet.

One way was an oyster pail factory, one way they made candy, one way
paper boxes, strawboard cartons.

The warehouse trucks shook the dust of the ways loose and the wheels
  whirled dust—there was dust of hoof and wagon wheel and rubber
  tire—dust of police and fire wagons—dust of the winds that circled
  at midnights and noon listening to no prayers.

"O mother, I know the heart of you," I sang passing the rim of a nun's
  bonnet—O white curtains—and people clean as the prayers of Jesus
  here in the faded ramshackle at Congress and Green.

Dust and the thundering trucks won—the barrages of the street wheels
  and the lawless wind took their way—was it five weeks or six the little
  mother, the new neighbors, battled and then took away the white
  prayers in the windows?

CRIMSON CHANGES PEOPLE

Did I see a crucifix in your eyes
and nails and Roman soldiers
and a dusk Golgotha?

Did I see Mary, the changed woman,
washing the feet of all men,
clean as new grass
when the old grass burns?

Did I see moths in your eyes, lost moths,
with a flutter of wings that meant:
we can never come again.

Did I see No Man's Land in your eyes
and men with lost faces, lost loves,
and you among the stubs crying?

Did I see you in the red death jazz of war
losing moths among lost faces,
speaking to the stubs who asked you
to speak of songs and God and dancing,
of bananas, northern lights or Jesus,
any hummingbird of thought whatever
flying away from the red death jazz of war?

Did I see your hand make a useless gesture
trying to say with a code of five fingers
something the tongue only stutters?
did I see a dusk Golgotha?

NEIGHBORS

On Forty-first Street
near Eighth Avenue
a frame house wobbles.

If houses went on crutches
this house would be
one of the cripples.

A sign on the house:
Church of the Living God
And Rescue Home for Orphan Children.

From a Greek coffee house
Across the street
A cabalistic jargon
Jabbers back.
    And men at tables
    Spill Peloponnesian syllables
    And speak of shovels for street work.
    And the new embankments of the Erie Railroad
    At Painted Post, Horse's Head, Salamanca.

CAHOOTS

Play it across the table.
What if we steal this city blind?
If they want any thing let 'em nail it down.

Harness bulls, dicks, front office men,
And the high goats up on the bench,
Ain't they all in cahoots?

Ain't it fifty-fifty all down the line,
Petemen, dips, boosters, stick-ups and guns—
          what's to hinder?

          Go fifty-fifty.
If they nail you call in a mouthpiece.
Fix it, you gazump, you slant-head, fix it.
          Feed 'em. . . .

Nothin' ever sticks to my fingers, nah, nah,
          nothin' like that,
But there ain't no law we got to wear mittens—
          huh—is there?
Mittens, that's a good one—mittens!
There oughta be a law everybody wear mittens.

BLUE MAROONS

"You slut," he flung at her.
It was more than a hundred times
He had thrown it into her face
And by this time it meant nothing to her.
She said to herself upstairs sweeping,
"Clocks are to tell time with, pitchers
Hold milk, spoons dip out gravy, and a
Coffee pot keeps the respect of those
Who drink coffee—I am a woman whose
Husband gives her a kiss once for ten
Times he throws it in my face, 'You slut.'
If I go to a small town and him along
Or if I go to a big city and him along,
What of it? Am I better off?" She swept
The upstairs and came downstairs to fix
Dinner for the family.

THE HANGMAN AT HOME

WHAT does the hangman think about
When he goes home at night from work?
When he sits down with his wife and
Children for a cup of coffee and a
Plate of ham and eggs, do they ask
Him if it was a good day's work
And everything went well or do they
Stay off some topics and talk about
The weather, baseball, politics
And the comic strips in the papers
And the movies? Do they look at his
Hands when he reaches for the coffee
Or the ham and eggs? If the little
Ones say, Daddy, play horse, here's
A rope—does he answer like a joke:
I seen enough rope for today?
Or does his face light up like a
Bonfire of joy and does he say:
It's a good and dandy world we live
In. And if a white face moon looks
In through a window where a baby girl
Sleeps and the moon-gleams mix with
Baby ears and baby hair—the hangman—
How does he act then? It must be easy
For him. Anything is easy for a hangman,
I guess.

MAN, THE MAN-HUNTER

I SAW Man, the man-hunter,
Hunting with a torch in one hand
And a kerosene can in the other,
Hunting with guns, ropes, shackles.

I listened
And the high cry rang,
The high cry of Man, the man-hunter:
We'll get you yet,   you   sbxyzch!

I listened later.
The high cry rang:
Kill him!   kill him!   the sbxyzch!

In the morning the sun saw
Two butts of something, a smoking rump,
And a warning in charred wood:
                         Well, we got him,
                    the   sbxyzch.

THE SINS OF KALAMAZOO

THE sins of Kalamazoo are neither scarlet nor crimson.
The sins of Kalamazoo are a convict gray, a dishwater drab.
And the people who sin the sins of Kalamazoo are neither scarlet nor
     crimson.
They run to drabs and grays—and some of them sing they shall be washed
     whiter than snow—and some: We should worry.

Yes, Kalamazoo is a spot on the map
And the passenger trains stop there
And the factory smokestacks smoke
And the grocery stores are open Saturday nights
And the streets are free for citizens who vote
And inhabitants counted in the census.
Saturday night is the big night.
          Listen with your ears on a Saturday night in Kalamazoo
          And say to yourself: I hear America, I hear, *what* do I hear?

Main street there runs through the middle of the town
And there is a dirty post office
And a dirty city hall
And a dirty railroad station

And the United States flag cries, cries the Stars and Stripes to the four
    winds on Lincoln's birthday and the Fourth of July.

Kalamazoo kisses a hand to something far off.
Kalamazoo calls to a long horizon, to a shivering silver angel, to a creeping
    mystic what-is-it.
"We're here because we're here," is the song of Kalamazoo.
"We don't know where we're going but we're on our way," are the words.
There are hound dogs of bronze on the public square, hound dogs looking
    far beyond the public square.

Sweethearts there in Kalamazoo
Go to the general delivery window of the post office
And speak their names and ask for letters
And ask again, "Are you sure there is nothing for me?
I wish you'd look again—there must be a letter for me."

And sweethearts go to the city hall
And tell their names and say, "We want a license."
And they go to an installment house and buy a bed on time and a clock
And the children grow up asking each other, "What can we do to kill
    time?"
They grow up and go to the railroad station and buy tickets for Texas,
    Pennsylvania, Alaska.
"Kalamazoo is all right," they say. "But I want to see the world."
And when they have looked the world over they come back saying it is all
    like Kalamazoo.

The trains come in from the east and hoot for the crossings,
And buzz away to the peach country and Chicago to the west
Or they come from the west and shoot on to the Battle Creek breakfast
    bazaars
And the speedbug heavens of Detroit.

"I hear America, I hear, what do I hear?"
Said a loafer lagging along on the sidewalks of Kalamazoo,
Lagging along and asking questions, reading signs.

Oh yes, there is a town named Kalamazoo,
A spot on the map where the trains hesitate.

I saw the sign of a five and ten cent store there
And the Standard Oil Company and the International Harvester
And a graveyard and a ball grounds
And a short order counter where a man can get a stack of wheats
And a pool hall where a rounder leered confidential like and said:
"Lookin' for a quiet game?"

The loafer lagged along and asked,
"Do you make guitars here?
Do you make boxes the singing wood winds ask to sleep in?
Do you rig up strings the singing wood winds sift over and sing low?"
The answer: "We manufacture musical instruments here."

Here I saw churches with steeples like hatpins,
Undertaking rooms with sample coffins in the show window
And signs everywhere satisfaction is guaranteed,
Shooting galleries where men kill imitation pigeons,
And there were doctors for the sick,
And lawyers for people waiting in jail,
And a dog catcher and a superintendent of streets,
And telephones, water-works, trolley cars,
And newspapers with a splatter of telegrams from sister cities of Kala-
    mazoo the round world over.

And the loafer lagging along said:
Kalamazoo, you ain't in a class by yourself;
I seen you before in a lot of places.
If you are nuts America is nuts.
        And lagging along he said bitterly:
        Before I came to Kalamazoo I was silent.
        Now I am gabby, God help me, I am gabby.

Kalamazoo, both of us will do a fadeaway.
I will be carried out feet first
And time and the rain will chew you to dust
And the winds blow you away.
And an old, old mother will lay a green moss cover on my bones
And a green moss cover on the stones of your post office and city hall.

   Best of all
I have loved your kiddies playing run-sheep-run
And cutting their initials on the ball ground fence.
They knew every time I fooled them who was fooled and how.

   Best of all
I have loved the red gold smoke of your sunsets;
I have loved a moon with a ring around it
Floating over your public square;
I have loved the white dawn frost of early winter silver
And purple over your railroad tracks and lumber yards.

   The wishing heart of you I loved, Kalamazoo.
   I sang bye-lo, bye-lo to your dreams.
I sang bye-lo to your hopes and songs.
I wished to God there were hound dogs of bronze on your public square,
Hound dogs with bronze paws looking to a long horizon with a shivering
  silver angel,
   a creeping mystic what-is-it.

Broken-Face Gargoyles

BROKEN-FACE GARGOYLES

ALL I can give you is broken-face gargoyles.
It is too early to sing and dance at funerals,
Though I can whisper to you I am looking for an undertaker humming
  a lullaby and throwing his feet in a swift and mystic buck-and-wing,
  now you see it and now you don't.

Fish to swim a pool in your garden flashing a speckled silver,
A basket of wine-saps filling your room with flame-dark for your eyes and
the tang of valley orchards for your nose,
Such a beautiful pail of fish, such a beautiful peck of apples, I cannot
bring you now.
It is too early and I am not footloose yet.

I shall come in the night when I come with a hammer and saw.
I shall come near your window, where you look out when your eyes open
in the morning,
And there I shall slam together bird-houses and bird-baths for wing-loose
wrens and hummers to live in, birds with yellow wing tips to blur
and buzz soft all summer,
So I shall make little fool homes with doors, always open doors for all
and each to run away when they want to.
I shall come just like that even though now it is early and I am not yet
footloose,
Even though I am still looking for an undertaker with a raw, wind-bitten
face and a dance in his feet.
I make a date with you (put it down) for six o'clock in the evening a
thousand years from now.

All I can give you now is broken-face gargoyles.
All I can give you now is a double gorilla head with two fish mouths and
four eagle eyes hooked on a street wall, spouting water and looking
two ways to the ends of the street for the new people, the young
strangers, coming, coming, always coming.

    It is early.
    I shall yet be footloose.

APRONS OF SILENCE

    MANY things I might have said today.
    And I kept my mouth shut.
    So many times I was asked
    To come and say the same things
    Everybody was saying, no end

To the yes-yes, yes-yes,
    me-too, me-too.

The aprons of silence covered me.
A wire and hatch held my tongue.
I spit nails into an abyss and listened.
I shut off the gabble of Jones, Johnson, Smith,
All whose names take pages in the city directory.

I fixed up a padded cell and lugged it around.
I locked myself in and nobody knew it.
Only the keeper and the kept in the hoosegow
Knew it—on the streets, in the post office,
On the cars, into the railroad station
Where the caller was calling, "All a-board,
All a-board for . . . Blaa-blaa . . . Blaa-blaa,
Blaa-blaa . . . and all points northwest . . . all a-board."
Here I took along my own hoosegow
And did business with my own thoughts.
Do you see? It must be the aprons of silence.

DEATH SNIPS PROUD MEN

DEATH is stronger than all the governments because the governments are
    men and men die and then death laughs: Now you see 'em, now you
    don't.

Death is stronger than all proud men and so death snips proud men on
    the nose, throws a pair of dice and says: Read 'em and weep.

Death sends a radiogram every day: When I want you I'll drop in—and
    then one day he comes with a master-key and lets himself in and says:
    We'll go now.

Death is a nurse mother with big arms: 'Twon't hurt you at all; it's your
    time now; you just need a long sleep, child; what have you had any-
    how better than sleep?

GOOD NIGHT

MANY ways to spell good night.

Fireworks at a pier on the Fourth of July
    spell it with red wheels and yellow spokes.
They fizz in the air, touch the water and quit.
Rockets make a trajectory of gold-and-blue
    and then go out.

Railroad trains at night spell with a smokestack mushrooming a white
    pillar.

Steamboats turn a curve in the Mississippi crying in a baritone that crosses
    lowland cottonfields to a razorback hill.

It is easy to spell good night.
             Many ways to spell good night.

SHIRT

    MY shirt is a token and symbol,
    more than a cover for sun and rain,
    my shirt is a signal,
    and a teller of souls.

    I can take off my shirt and tear it,
    and so make a ripping razzly noise,
    and the people will say,
    "Look at him tear his shirt."

    I can keep my shirt on.
    I can stick around and sing like a little bird
    and look 'em all in the eye and never be fazed.
        I can keep my shirt on.

JAZZ FANTASIA

Drum on your drums, batter on your banjoes,
sob on the long cool winding saxophones.
Go to it, O jazzmen.

Sling your knuckles on the bottoms of the happy
tin pans, let your trombones ooze, and go husha-
husha-hush with the slippery sand-paper.

Moan like an autumn wind high in the lonesome treetops, moan soft like
you wanted somebody terrible, cry like a racing car slipping away from a
motorcycle cop, bang-bang! you jazzmen, bang altogether drums, traps,
banjoes, horns, tin cans—make two people fight on the top of a stairway
and scratch each other's eyes in a clinch tumbling down the stairs.

Can the rough stuff . . . now a Mississippi steamboat pushes up the night
river with a hoo-hoo-hoo-oo . . . and the green lanterns calling to the high
soft stars . . . a red moon rides on the humps of the low river hills . . .
go to it, O jazzmen.

DO YOU WANT AFFIDAVITS?

There's a hole in the bottom of the sea.
      Do you want affidavits?
There's a man in the moon with money for you.
      Do you want affidavits?
There are ten dancing girls in a sea-chamber off Nantucket waiting for you.
There are tall candles in Timbuctoo burning penance for you.
There are—anything else?
Speak now—for now we stand amid the great wishing windows—and the
    law says we are free to be wishing all this week at the windows.
Shall I raise my right hand and swear to you in the monotone of a notary
    public? this is "the truth, the whole truth, and nothing but the truth."

"OLD-FASHIONED REQUITED LOVE"

I HAVE ransacked the encyclopedias
And slid my fingers among topics and titles
Looking for you.

And the answer comes slow.
There seems to be no answer.

I shall ask the next banana peddler the who and the why of it.

Or—the iceman with his iron tongs gripping a clear cube in summer sun-
light—maybe he will know.

PURPLE MARTINS

IF WE were such and so, the same as these,
maybe we too would be slingers and sliders,
tumbling half over in the water mirrors,
tumbling half over at the horse heads of the sun,
tumbling our purple numbers.

Twirl on, you and your satin blue.
Be water birds, be air birds.
Be these purple tumblers you are.

Dip and get away
From loops into slip-knots,
Write your own ciphers and figure eights.
It is your wooded island here in Lincoln park.
Everybody knows this belongs to you.

Five fat geese
Eat grass on a sod bank
And never count your slinging ciphers,
                                   your sliding figure eights,

A man on a green paint iron bench,
Slouches his feet and sniffs in a book,
And looks at you and your loops and slip-knots,
And looks at you and your sheaths of satin blue,
And slouches again and sniffs in the book,
And mumbles: It is an idle and a doctrinaire exploit.
Go on tumbling half over in the water mirrors.
Go on tumbling half over at the horse heads of the sun.
     Be water birds, be air birds.
     Be these purple tumblers you are.

BRASS KEYS

Joy . . . weaving two violet petals for a coat lapel . . .
painting on a slab of night sky a Christ face . . .
slipping new brass keys into rusty iron locks and
shouldering till at last the door gives and we are in
a new room . . . forever and ever violet petals, slabs,
the Christ face, brass keys and new rooms.

are we near or far? . . . is there anything else? . . . who comes back?
. . . and why does love ask nothing and give all? and why is love rare as
a tailed comet shaking guesses out of men at telescopes ten feet long? why
does the mystery sit with its chin on the lean forearm of women in gray
eyes and women in hazel eyes?

are any of these less proud, less important, than a cross-examining lawyer?
are any of these less perfect than the front page of a morning newspaper?

the answers are not computed and attested in the back of an arithmetic
for the verifications of the lazy

there is no authority in the phone book for us to call
and ask the why, the wherefore, and the howbeit
it's . . . a riddle . . . by God

PICK-OFFS

THE telescope picks off star dust
on the clean steel sky and sends it to me.

The telephone picks off my voice and
sends it cross country a thousand miles.

The eyes in my head pick off pages of
Napoleon memoirs . . . a rag handler,
a head of dreams walks in a sheet of
mist . . . the palace panels shut in no-
bodies drinking nothings out of silver
helmets . . . in the end we all come to a
rock island and the hold of the sea-walls.

MANUFACTURED GODS

THEY put up big wooden gods.
Then they burned the big wooden gods
And put up brass gods and
Changing their minds suddenly
Knocked down the brass gods and put up
A doughface god with gold earrings.
The poor mutts, the pathetic slant heads,
They didn't know a little tin god
Is as good as anything in the line of gods
Nor how a little tin god answers prayer
And makes rain and brings luck
The same as a big wooden god or a brass
God or a doughface god with golden
Earrings.

MASK

To have your face left overnight
Flung on a board by a crazy sculptor;
To have your face drop off a board

And fall to pieces on a floor
Lost among lumps all finger-marked
      —How now?

To be calm and level, placed high,
Looking among perfect women bathing
And among bareheaded long-armed men,
Corner dreams of a crazy sculptor,
And then to fall, drop clean off the board,
Four o'clock in the morning and not a dog
Nor a policeman anywhere—

    Hoo hoo!
had it been my laughing face
maybe I would laugh with you,
but my lover's face, the face I give
women and the moon and the sea!

Playthings of the Wind

FOUR PRELUDES ON PLAYTHINGS OF THE WIND

"The past is a bucket of ashes."

1

THE woman named Tomorrow
sits with a hairpin in her teeth
and takes her time
and does her hair the way she wants it
and fastens at last the last braid and coil
and puts the hairpin where it belongs

and turns and drawls: Well, what of it?
My grandmother, Yesterday, is gone.
What of it? Let the dead be dead.

2

The doors were cedar
and the panels strips of gold
and the girls were golden girls
and the panels read and the girls chanted:
      We are the greatest city,
      the greatest nation:
      nothing like us ever was.
The doors are twisted on broken hinges.
Sheets of rain swish through on the wind
      where the golden girls ran and the panels read:
      We are the greatest city,
      the greatest nation,
      nothing like us ever was.

3

It has happened before.
Strong men put up a city and got
      a nation together,
And paid singers to sing and women
      to warble: We are the greatest city,
            the greatest nation,
            nothing like us ever was.

And while the singers sang
and the strong men listened
and paid the singers well
and felt good about it all,
   there were rats and lizards who listened
   . . . and the only listeners left now
   . . . are . . . the rats . . . and the lizards.

And there are black crows
crying, "Caw, caw,"
bringing mud and sticks
building a nest

over the words carved
on the doors where the panels were cedar
and the strips on the panels were gold
and the golden girls came singing:
>We are the greatest city,
>the greatest nation:
>nothing like us ever was.

The only singers now are crows crying, "Caw, caw,"
And the sheets of rain whine in the wind and doorways.
And the only listeners now are . . . the rats . . . and the lizards.

4

The feet of the rats
scribble on the doorsills;
the hieroglyphs of the rat footprints
chatter the pedigrees of the rats
and babble of the blood
and gabble of the breed
of the grandfathers and the great-grandfathers
of the rats.

And the wind shifts
and the dust on a doorsill shifts
and even the writing of the rat footprints
tells us nothing, nothing at all
about the greatest city, the greatest nation
where the strong men listened
and the women warbled: Nothing like us ever was.

BROKEN TABERNACLES

HAVE I broken the smaller tabernacles, O Lord?
And in the destruction of these set up the greater and massive, the ever-
lasting tabernacles?
I know nothing today, what I have done and why, O Lord, only I have
broken and broken tabernacles.
They were beautiful in a way, these tabernacles torn down by strong
hands swearing—

They were beautiful—why did the hypocrites carve their own names on
the corner-stones? why did the hypocrites keep on singing their own
names in their long noses every Sunday in these tabernacles?
Who lays any blame here among the split corner-stones?

OSAWATOMIE

I DON'T know how he came,
shambling, dark, and strong.

He stood in the city and told men:
My people are fools, my people are young and strong, my people must
learn, my people are terrible workers and fighters.
Always he kept on asking: Where did that blood come from?

They said: You for the fool killer,
you for the booby hatch
and a necktie party.

They hauled him into jail.
They sneered at him and spit on him,
And he wrecked their jails,
Singing, "God damn your jails,"
And when he was most in jail
Crummy among the crazy in the dark
Then he was most of all out of jail
Shambling, dark, and strong,
Always asking: Where did that blood come from?
They laid hands on him
And the fool killers had a laugh
And the necktie party was a go, by God.
They laid hands on him and he was a goner.
They hammered him to pieces and he stood up.
They buried him and he walked out of the grave, by God,
Asking again: Where did that blood come from?

LONG GUNS

THEN came, Oscar, the time of the guns.
And there was no land for a man, no land for a country,
 Unless guns sprang up
 And spoke their language.
The how of running the world was all in guns.

The law of a God keeping sea and land apart,
The law of a child sucking milk,
The law of stars held together,
 They slept and worked in the heads of men
 Making twenty mile guns, sixty mile guns,
 Speaking their language
 Of no land for a man, no land for a country
Unless . . . guns . . . unless . . . guns.

There was a child wanted the moon shot off the sky,
 asking a long gun to get the moon,
 to conquer the insults of the moon,
 to conquer something, anything,
 to put it over and win the day,
To show them the running of the world was all in guns.
There was a child wanted the moon shot off the sky.
They dreamed . . . in the time of the guns . . . of guns.

DUSTY DOORS

 CHILD of the Aztec gods,
 how long must we listen here,
 how long before we go?

 The dust is deep on the lintels.
 The dust is dark on the doors.
 If the dreams shake our bones,
  what can we say or do?

Since early morning we waited.
Since early, early morning, child.
There must be dreams on the way now.
There must be a song for our bones.

The dust gets deeper and darker.
Do the doors and lintels shudder?
   How long must we listen here?
   How long before we go?

FLASH CRIMSON

I SHALL cry God to give me a broken foot.

I shall ask for a scar and a slashed nose.

I shall take the last and the worst.

I shall be eaten by gray creepers in a bunkhouse where no runners of the
   sun come and no dogs live.

And yet—of all "and yets" this is the bronze strongest—

I shall keep one thing better than all else; there is the blue steel of a great
   star of early evening in it; it lives longer than a broken foot or any
   scar.

The broken foot goes to a hole dug with a shovel or the bone of a nose
   may whiten on a hilltop—and yet—"and yet"—

There is one crimson pinch of ashes left after all; and none of the shifting
   winds that whip the grass and none of the pounding rains that beat
   the dust, know how to touch or find the flash of this crimson.

I cry God to give me a broken foot, a scar, or a lousy death.

I who have seen the flash of this crimson, I ask God for the last and worst.

THE LAWYERS KNOW TOO MUCH

THE lawyers, Bob, know too much.
They are chums of the books of old John Marshall.
They know it all, what a dead hand wrote,
A stiff dead hand and its knuckles crumbling,
The bones of the fingers a thin white ash.
    The lawyers know
    a dead man's thoughts too well.

In the heels of the higgling lawyers, Bob,
Too many slippery ifs and buts and howevers,
Too much hereinbefore provided whereas,
Too many doors to go in and out of.

    When the lawyers are through
    What is there left, Bob?
    Can a mouse nibble at it
    And find enough to fasten a tooth in?

    Why is there always a secret singing
    When a lawyer cashes in?
    Why does a hearse horse snicker
    Hauling a lawyer away?

The work of a bricklayer goes to the blue.
The knack of a mason outlasts a moon.
The hands of a plasterer hold a room together.
The land of a farmer wishes him back again.
    Singers of songs and dreamers of plays
    Build a house no wind blows over.
The lawyers—tell me why a hearse horse snickers hauling a lawyer's bones.

LOSERS

    IF I should pass the tomb of Jonah
    I would stop there and sit for a while;
    Because I was swallowed one time deep in the dark
    And came out alive after all.

If I pass the burial spot of Nero
I shall say to the wind, "Well, well!"—
I who have fiddled in a world on fire,
I who have done so many stunts not worth doing.

I am looking for the grave of Sinbad too.
I want to shake his ghost-hand and say,
"Neither of us died very early, did we?"

And the last sleeping-place of Nebuchadnezzar—
When I arrive there I shall tell the wind:
"You ate grass; I have eaten crow—
Who is better off now or next year?"

Jack Cade, John Brown, Jesse James,
There too I could sit down and stop for a while.
I think I could tell their headstones:
"God, let me remember all good losers."

I could ask people to throw ashes on their heads
In the name of that sergeant at Belleau Woods,
Walking into the drumfires, calling his men,
"Come on, you . . . Do you want to live forever?"

PLACES

Roses and gold
For you today,
And the flash of flying flags.

I will have
Ashes,
Dust in my hair,
Crushes of hoofs.

Your name
Fills the mouth
Of rich man and poor.

Women bring
Armfuls of flowers
And throw on you.

I go hungry
Down in dreams
And loneliness,
Across the rain
To slashed hills
Where men wait and hope for me.

THREES

I WAS a boy when I heard three red words
a thousand Frenchmen died in the streets
for: Liberty, Equality, Fraternity—I asked
why men die for words.

I was older; men with mustaches, sideburns,
lilacs, told me the high golden words are:
Mother, Home, and Heaven—other older men with
face decorations said: God, Duty, Immortality
—they sang these threes slow from deep lungs.

Years ticked off their say-so on the great clocks
of doom and damnation, soup and nuts: meteors flashed
their say-so: and out of great Russia came three
dusky syllables workmen took guns and went out to die
for: Bread, Peace, Land.

And I met a marine of the U. S. A., a leatherneck with a girl on his knee
for a memory in ports circling the earth and he said: Tell me how to say
three things and I always get by—gimme a plate of ham and eggs—how
much?—and—do you love me, kid?

THE LIARS
(*March*, 1919)

A LIAR goes in fine clothes.
A liar goes in rags.
A liar is a liar, clothes or no clothes.
A liar is a liar and lives on the lies he tells
          and dies in a life of lies.
And the stonecutters earn a living—with lies—
          on the tombs of liars.

A liar looks 'em in the eye
And lies to a woman,
Lies to a man, a pal, a child, a fool.
And he is an old liar; we know him many years back.

  A liar lies to nations.
  A liar lies to the people.
A liar takes the blood of the people
And drinks this blood with a laugh and a lie,
  A laugh in his neck,
  A lie in his mouth.
And this liar is an old one; we know him many years.
  He is straight as a dog's hind leg.
  He is straight as a corkscrew.
He is white as a black cat's foot at midnight.

The tongue of a man is tied on this,
On the liar who lies to nations,
The liar who lies to the people.
The tongue of a man is tied on this
And ends: To hell with 'em all.
          To hell with 'em all.

It's a song hard as a riveter's hammer,
  Hard as the sleep of a crummy hobo,
  Hard as the sleep of a lousy doughboy,
 Twisted as a shell-shock idiot's gibber.

The liars met where the doors were locked.
They said to each other: Now for war.
The liars fixed it and told 'em: Go.

Across their tables they fixed it up,
Behind their doors away from the mob.
And the guns did a job that nicked off millions.
The guns blew seven million off the map,
The guns sent seven million west.
Seven million shoving up the daisies.
Across their tables they fixed it up,
            The liars who lie to nations.

    And now
    Out of the butcher's job
    And the boneyard junk the maggots have cleaned,
    Where the jaws of skulls tell the jokes of war ghosts,
Out of this they are calling now: Let's go back where we were.
            Let us run the world again, us, us.
Where the doors are locked the liars say: Wait and we'll cash in again.

So I hear The People talk.
I hear them tell each other:
    Let the strong men be ready.
    Let the strong men watch.
    Let your wrists be cool and your head clear.
    Let the liars get their finish,
    The liars and their waiting game, waiting a day again
    To open the doors and tell us: War! get out to your war again.

So I hear The People tell each other:
    Look at today and tomorrow.
    Fix this clock that nicks off millions
    When The Liars say it's time.
    Take things in your own hands.
            To hell with 'em all,
    The liars who lie to nations,
    The liars who lie to The People.

PRAYER AFTER WORLD WAR

WANDERING oversea dreamer,
Hunting and hoarse, Oh daughter and mother,
Oh daughter of ashes and mother of blood,
Child of the hair let down, and tears,
Child of the cross in the south
And the star in the north,
Keeper of Egypt and Russia and France,
Keeper of England and Poland and Spain,
Make us a song for tomorrow.
Make us one new dream, us who forget,
Out of the storm let us have one star.

    Struggle, Oh anvils, and help her.
Weave with your wool, Oh winds and skies.
Let your iron and copper help,
        Oh dirt of the old dark earth.

Wandering oversea singer,
Singing of ashes and blood,
Child of the scars of fire,
    Make us one new dream, us who forget.
    Out of the storm let us have one star.

A. E. F.

THERE will be a rusty gun on the wall, sweetheart,
The rifle grooves curling with flakes of rust.
A spider will make a silver string nest in the
        darkest, warmest corner of it.
The trigger and the range-finder, they too will be rusty.
And no hands will polish the gun, and it will hang on the wall.
Forefingers and thumbs will point absently and casually toward it.
It will be spoken among half-forgotten, wished-to-be-forgotten things.
They will tell the spider: Go on, you're doing good work.

PENCILS

PENCILS
telling where the wind comes from
　　open a story.

　　Pencils
telling where the wind goes
　　end a story.

　　These eager pencils
　　come to a stop
　　. . . only . . . when the stars high over
　　come to a stop.

Out of cabalistic tomorrows
come cryptic babies calling life
a strong and a lovely thing.

I have seen neither these
nor the stars high over
come to a stop.

Neither these nor the sea horses
running with the clocks of the moon.
Nor even a shooting star
snatching a pencil of fire
writing a curve of gold and white.

Like you . . . I counted the shooting stars of a
winter night and my head was dizzy with all
of them calling one by one:
　　　　　　　　　Look for us again.

JUG

THE shale and water thrown together so-so first of all,
Then a potter's hand on the wheel and his fingers shaping the jug; out
    of the mud a mouth and a handle;
Slimpsy, loose and ready to fall at a touch, fire plays on it, slow fire coax-
    ing all the water out of the shale mix.
Dipped in glaze more fire plays on it till a molasses lava runs in waves,
    rises and retreats, a varnish of volcanoes.
Take it now; out of mud now here is a mouth and handle; out of this
    now mothers will pour milk and maple syrup and cider, vinegar, apple
    juice, and sorghum.
There is nothing proud about this; only one out of many; the potter's
    wheel slings them out and the fires harden them hours and hours
    thousands and thousands.
"Be good to me, put me down easy on the floors of the new concrete
    houses; I was poured out like a concrete house and baked in fire too."

AND THIS WILL BE ALL?

AND this will be all?
And the gates will never open again?
And the dust and the wind will play around the rusty door hinges and
    the songs of October moan, Why-oh, why-oh?

And you will look to the mountains
And the mountains will look to you
And you will wish you were a mountain
And the mountain will wish nothing at all?
      This will be all?
The gates will never-never open again?

The dust and the wind only
And the rusty door hinges and moaning October
And Why-oh, why-oh, in the moaning dry leaves,
      This will be all?

clover and bumblebees, all bluegrass, johnny-jump-ups, grassroots, springs of running water or rivers or lakes or high spreading trees or hazel bushes or sumach or thorn-apple branches or high in the air the bird nest with spotted blue eggs shaken in the roaming wind of the treetops—

    So it is scrawled here,
    "I direct and devise
    So and so and such and such,"
    And this is the last word.
    There is nothing more to it.

In a shanty out in the Wilderness, ghosts of tomorrow sit, waiting to come and go, to do their job.

They will go into the house of the Dead and take the shivering sheets of paper and make a bonfire and dance a deadman's dance over the hissing crisp.

In a slang their own the dancers out of the Wilderness will write a paper for the living to read and sign:

The dead need peace, the dead need sleep, let the dead have peace and sleep, let the papers of the Dead who fix the lives of the Living, let them be a hissing crisp and ashes, let the young men and the young women forever understand we are through and no longer take the say-so of the Dead;

Let the dead have honor from us with our thoughts of them and our thoughts of land and all appurtenances thereto and all deposits of oil and gold and coal and silver, and all pockets and repositories of gravel and diamonds, dung and permanganese, and all clover and bumblebees, all bluegrass, johnny-jump-ups, grassroots, springs of running water or rivers or lakes or high spreading trees or hazel bushes or sumach or thorn-apple branches or high in the air the bird nest with spotted blue eggs shaken in the roaming wind of the treetops.

And so, it is a shack of ghosts, a lean-to they have in the Wilderness, and they are waiting and they have learned strange songs how easy it is to wait and how anything comes to those who wait long enough and how most of all it is easy to wait for death, and waiting, dream of new cities.

Mist Forms

CALLS

BECAUSE I have called to you
as the flame flamingo calls,
or the want of a spotted hawk
is called—
            because in the dusk
the warblers shoot the running
waters of short songs to the
homecoming warblers—
                        because
the cry here is wing to wing
and song to song—

    I am waiting,
waiting with the flame flamingo,
the spotted hawk, the running water
warbler—
            waiting for you.

SEA-WASH

THE sea-wash never ends.
The sea-wash repeats, repeats.
Only old songs? Is that all the sea knows?
        Only the old strong songs?
        Is that all?
The sea-wash repeats, repeats.

SILVER WIND

Do you know how the dream looms? how if summer misses one of us
    the two of us miss summer—
Summer when the lungs of the earth take a long breath for the change
    to low contralto singing mornings when the green corn leaves first
    break through the black loam—
And another long breath for the silver soprano melody of the moon
    songs in the light nights when the earth is lighter than a feather,
    the iron mountains lighter than a goose down—
So I shall look for you in the light nights then, in the laughter of slats
    of silver under a hill hickory.
In the listening tops of the hickories, in the wind motions of the hickory
    shingle leaves, in the imitations of slow sea water on the shingle
    silver in the wind—
        I shall look for you.

EVENING WATERFALL

WHAT was the name you called me?—
And why did you go so soon?

The crows lift their caw on the wind,
And the wind changed and was lonely.

The warblers cry their sleepy-songs
Across the valley gloaming,
Across the cattle-horns of early stars.

Feathers and people in the crotch of a treetop
Throw an evening waterfall of sleepy-songs.

What was the name you called me?—
And why did you go so soon?

CRUCIBLE

HOT gold runs a winding stream on the inside of a green bowl.

Yellow trickles in a fan figure, scatters a line of skirmishers, spreads a
    chorus of dancing girls, performs blazing ochre evolutions, gathers
    the whole show into one stream, forgets the past and rolls on.

The sea-mist green of the bowl's bottom is a dark throat of sky crossed
    by quarreling forks of umber and ochre and yellow changing faces.

SUMMER STARS

BEND low again, night of summer stars.
So near you are, sky of summer stars,
So near, a long-arm man can pick off stars,
Pick off what he wants in the sky bowl,
So near you are, summer stars,
So near, strumming, strumming,
        So lazy and hum-strumming.

THROW ROSES

THROW roses on the sea where the dead went down.
        The roses speak to the sea,
        And the sea to the dead.
Throw roses, O lovers—
        Let the leaves wash on the salt in the sun.

JUST BEFORE APRIL CAME

THE snow-piles in dark places are gone.
Pools by the railroad tracks shine clear.
The gravel of all shallow places shines.
A white pigeon reels and somersaults.

Frogs plutter and squdge—and frogs beat
      the air with a recurring thin
      steel sliver of melody.
Crows go in fives and tens; they march their
      black feathers past a blue pool; they
      celebrate an old festival.
A spider is trying his webs, a pink bug sits
      on my hand washing his forelegs.
I might ask: Who are these people?

STARS, SONGS, FACES

GATHER the stars if you wish it so.
Gather the songs and keep them.
Gather the faces of women.
Gather for keeping years and years.
      And then . . .
Loosen your hands, let go and say good-by.
    Let the stars and songs go.
    Let the faces and years go.
    Loosen your hands and say good-by.

SANDPIPERS

TEN miles of flat land along the sea.
Sandland where the salt water kills the sweet potatoes.
Homes for sandpipers—the script of their feet is on the sea shingles—
    they write in the morning, it is gone at noon—they write at noon, it
    is gone at night.
Pity the land, the sea, the ten mile flats, pity anything but the sand-
    pipers' wire legs and feet.

THREE VIOLINS

THREE violins are trying their hearts.
The piece is MacDowell's Wild Rose.
    And the time of the wild rose

And the leaves of the wild rose
And the dew-shot eyes of the wild rose
Sing in the air over three violins.
Somebody like you was in the heart of MacDowell.
Somebody like you is in three violins.

THE WIND SINGS WELCOME IN EARLY SPRING
(For Paula)

THE grip of the ice is gone now.
The silvers chase purple.
The purples tag silver.
　　They let out their runners
Here where summer says to the lilies:
　　"Wish and be wistful,
Circle this wind-hunted, wind-sung water."

Come along always, come along now.
You for me, kiss me, pull me by the ear.
Push me along with the wind push.
Sing like the whinnying wind.
Sing like the hustling obstreperous wind.

Have you ever seen deeper purple . . .
　　this in my wild wind fingers?
Could you have more fun with a pony or a goat?
Have you seen such flicking heels before,
Silver jig heels on the purple sky rim?
　　Come along always, come along now.

TAWNY

THESE are the tawny days: your face comes back.

The grapes take on purple: the sunsets redden
early on the trellis.

The bashful mornings hurl gray mist on the stripes
of sunrise.

Creep, silver on the field, the frost is welcome.

Run on, yellow balls on the hills, and you tawny
pumpkin flowers, chasing your lines of orange.

Tawny days: and your face again.

SLIPPERY

THE six month child
Fresh from the tub
Wriggles in our hands.
This is our fish child.
Give her a nickname: Slippery.

HELGA

THE wishes on this child's mouth
Came like snow on marsh cranberries;
The tamarack kept something for her;
The wind is ready to help her shoes.
The north has loved her; she will be
A grandmother feeding geese on frosty
Mornings; she will understand
Early snow on the cranberries
Better and better then.

BABY TOES

THERE is a blue star, Janet,
Fifteen years' ride from us,
If we ride a hundred miles an hour.

There is a white star, Janet,
Forty years' ride from us,
If we ride a hundred miles an hour.

Shall we ride
To the blue star
Or the white star?

PEOPLE WITH PROUD CHINS

I TELL them where the wind comes from,
Where the music goes when the fiddle is in the box.

Kids—I saw one with a proud chin, a sleepyhead,
And the moonline creeping white on her pillow.
   I have seen their heads in the starlight
   And their proud chins marching in a mist of stars.

They are the only people I never lie to.
   I give them honest answers,
Answers shrewd as the circles of white on brown chestnuts.

WINTER MILK

THE milk-drops on your chin, Helga,
Must not interfere with the cranberry red of your cheeks
Nor the sky winter blue of your eyes.
Let your mammy keep hands off the chin.
This is a high holy spatter of white on the reds and blues.

Before the bottle was taken away,
Before you so proudly began today
Drinking your milk from the rim of a cup
They did not splash this high holy white on your chin.

There are dreams in your eyes, Helga.
Tall reaches of wind sweep the clear blue.
The winter is young yet, so young.
Only a little cupful of winter has touched your lips.
Drink on . . . milk with your lips . . . dreams with your eyes.

SLEEPYHEADS

Sleep is a maker of makers. Birds sleep. Feet cling to a perch. Look at the balance. Let the legs loosen, the backbone untwist, the head go heavy over, the whole works tumbles a done bird off the perch.

Fox cubs sleep. The pointed head curls round into hind legs and tail. It is a ball of red hair. It is a muff waiting. A wind might whisk it in the air across pastures and rivers, a cocoon, a pod of seeds. The snooze of the black nose is in a circle of red hair.

Old men sleep. In chimney corners, in rocking chairs, at wood stoves, steam radiators. They talk and forget and nod and are out of talk with closed eyes. Forgetting to live. Knowing the time has come useless for them to live. Old eagles and old dogs run and fly in the dreams.

Babies sleep. In flannels the papoose faces, the bambino noses, and dodo, dodo the song of many matushkas. Babies—a leaf on a tree in the spring sun. A nub of a new thing sucks the sap of a tree in the sun, yes a new thing, a what-is-it? A left hand stirs, an eyelid twitches, the milk in the belly bubbles and gets to be blood and a left hand and an eyelid. Sleep is a maker of makers.

SUMACH AND BIRDS

If you never came with a pigeon rainbow purple
Shining in the six o'clock September dusk:
If the red sumach on the autumn roads
Never danced on the flame of your eyelashes:
If the red-haws never burst in a million
Crimson fingertwists of your heartcrying:
If all this beauty of yours never crushed me
Then there are many flying acres of birds for me,
Many drumming gray wings going home I shall see,
Many crying voices riding the north wind.

WOMEN WASHING THEIR HAIR

THEY have painted and sung
the women washing their hair,
and the plaits and strands in the sun,
and the golden combs
and the combs of elephant tusks
and the combs of buffalo horn and hoof.

The sun has been good to women,
drying their heads of hair
as they stooped and shook their shoulders
and framed their faces with copper
and framed their eyes with dusk or chestnut.

The rain has been good to women.
If the rain should forget,
if the rain left off for a year—
the heads of women would wither,
the copper, the dusk and chestnuts, go.

They have painted and sung
the women washing their hair—
reckon the sun and rain in, too.

PEACH BLOSSOMS

WHAT cry of peach blossoms
      let loose on the air today
I heard with my face thrown
      in the pink-white of it all?
      in the red whisper of it all?

What man I heard saying:
      Christ, these are beautiful!

And Christ and Christ was in his mouth,
      over these peach blossoms?

HALF MOON IN A HIGH WIND

MONEY is nothing now, even if I had it,
O mooney moon, yellow half moon,
Up over the green pines and gray elms,
Up in the new blue.

     Streel, streel,
White lacey mist sheets of cloud,
Streel in the blowing of the wind,
Streel over the blue-and-moon sky,
Yellow gold half moon. It is light
On the snow; it is dark on the snow,
Streel, O lacey thin sheets, up in the new blue.

Come down, stay there, move on.
I want you, I don't, keep all.
There is no song to your singing.
I am hit deep, you drive far,
O mooney yellow half moon,
Steady, steady; or will you tip over?
Or will the wind and the streeling
Thin sheets only pass and move on
And leave you alone and lovely?
I want you, I don't, come down,
     Stay there, move on.
Money is nothing now, even if I had it.

REMORSE

THE horse's name was Remorse.
There were people said, "Gee, what a nag!"
And they were Edgar Allan Poe bugs and so
They called him Remorse.
          When he was a gelding
He flashed his heels to other ponies
And threw dust in the noses of other ponies

And won his first race and his second
And another and another and hardly ever
Came under the wire behind the other runners.

And so, Remorse, who is gone, was the hero of a play
By Henry Blossom, who is now gone.

What is there to a monicker? Call me anything.
A nut, a cheese, something that the cat brought in.
    Nick me with any old name.
Class me up for a fish, a gorilla, a slant head, an egg, a ham.
Only . . . slam me across the ears sometimes . . . and hunt for a white
    star
In my forehead and twist the bang of my forelock around it.
Make a wish for me. Maybe I will light out like a streak of wind.

RIVER MOONS

The double moon, one on the high backdrop of the west, one on the
    curve of the river face,
The sky moon of fire and the river moon of water, I am taking these
    home in a basket, hung on an elbow, such a teeny weeny elbow, in
    my head.
I saw them last night, a cradle moon, two horns of a moon, such an early
    hopeful moon, such a child's moon for all young hearts to make a
    picture of.
The river—I remember this like a picture—the river was the upper twist
    of a written question mark.
I know now it takes many many years to write a river, a twist of water
    asking a question.
And white stars moved when the moon moved, and one red star kept burn-
    ing, and the Big Dipper was almost overhead.

SAND SCRIBBLINGS

The wind stops, the wind begins.
The wind says stop, begin.

A sea shovel scrapes the sand floor.
The shovel changes, the floor changes.

The sandpipers, maybe they know.
Maybe a three-pointed foot can tell.
Maybe the fog moon they fly to, guesses.

The sandpipers cheep "Here" and get away.
Five of them fly and keep together flying.

Night hair of some sea woman
Curls on the sand when the sea leaves
The salt tide without a good-by.

Boxes on the beach are empty.
Shake 'em and the nails loosen.
They have been somewhere.

HOW YESTERDAY LOOKED

THE high horses of the sea broke their white riders
On the walls that held and counted the hours
The wind lasted.

Two landbirds looked on and the north and the east
Looked on and the wind poured cups of foam
And the evening began.

The old men in the shanties looked on and lit their
Pipes and the young men spoke of the girls
For a wild night like this.

The south and the west looked on and the moon came
When the wind went down and the sea was sorry
And the singing slow.

Ask how the sunset looked between the wind going
Down and the moon coming up and I would struggle
To tell the how of it.

I give you fire here, I give you water, I give you
The wind that blew them across and across,
The scooping, mixing wind.

PAULA

Nothing else in this song—only your face.
Nothing else here—only your drinking, night-gray eyes.

The pier runs into the lake straight as a rifle barrel.
I stand on the pier and sing how I know you mornings.
It is not your eyes, your face, I remember.
It is not your dancing, race-horse feet.
It is something else I remember you for on the pier mornings.

Your hands are sweeter than nut-brown bread when you touch me.
Your shoulder brushes my arm—a south-west wind crosses the pier.
I forget your hands and your shoulder and I say again:

Nothing else in this song—only your face.
Nothing else here—only your drinking, night-gray eyes.

LAUGHING BLUE STEEL

Two fishes swimming in the sea,
Two birds flying in the air,
Two chisels on an anvil—maybe.
Beaten, hammered, laughing blue steel to each other—maybe.
Sure I would rather be a chisel with you
                              than a fish.
Sure I would rather be a chisel with you
                              than a bird.
Take these two chisel-pals, O God.
Take 'em and beat 'em, hammer 'em,
                        hear 'em laugh.

THEY ASK EACH OTHER WHERE THEY CAME FROM

Am I the river your white birds fly over?
Are you the green valley my silver channels roam?
The two of us a bowl of blue sky day time

and a bowl of red stars night time?
Who picked you
out of the first great whirl of nothings
and threw you here?

HOW MUCH?

How much do you love me, a million bushels?
Oh, a lot more than that, Oh, a lot more.

And tomorrow maybe only half a bushel?
Tomorrow maybe not even a half a bushel.

And is this your heart arithmetic?
This is the way the wind measures the weather.

THROWBACKS

SOMEWHERE you and I remember we came.
Stairways from the sea and our heads dripping.
Ladders of dust and mud and our hair snarled.
Rags of drenching mist and our hands clawing, climbing.
You and I that snickered in the crotches and corners,
            in the gab of our first talking.
Red dabs of dawn summer mornings and the rain sliding off our shoulders
      summer afternoons.
Was it you and I yelled songs and songs in the nights
            of big yellow moons?

WIND SONG

LONG ago I learned how to sleep,
In an old apple orchard where the wind swept by counting its money and
      throwing it away,
In a wind-gaunt orchard where the limbs forked out and listened or never
      listened at all,

In a passel of trees where the branches trapped the wind into whistling,
   "Who, who are you?"
I slept with my head in an elbow on a summer afternoon and there I took
   a sleep lesson.
There I went away saying: I know why they sleep, I know how they trap
   the tricky winds.
Long ago I learned how to listen to the singing wind and how to forget
   and how to hear the deep whine,
Slapping and lapsing under the day blue and the night stars:
        Who, who are you?

       Who can ever forget
       listening to the wind go by
       counting its money
       and throwing it away?

THREE SPRING NOTATIONS ON BIPEDS

1

The down drop of the blackbird,
The wing catch of arrested flight,
The stop midway and then off:
   off for triangles, circles, loops
   of new hieroglyphs—
This is April's way: a woman:
"O yes, I'm here again and your heart
   knows I was coming."

2

White pigeons rush at the sun,
A marathon of wing feats is on:
"Who most loves danger? Who most loves
   wings? Who somersaults for God's sake
   in the name of wing power
   in the sun and blue
   on an April Thursday?"
So ten winged heads, ten winged feet,
   race their white forms over Elmhurst.

They go fast: once the ten together were
   a feather of foam bubble, a chrysanthemum
   whirl speaking to silver and azure.

                    3
The child is on my shoulders.
In the prairie moonlight the child's legs
   hang over my shoulders.
She sits on my neck and I hear her calling
   me a good horse.
She slides down—and into the moon silver of
   a prairie stream
She throws a stone and laughs at the clug-clug.

SANDHILL PEOPLE

I took away three pictures.
One was a white gull forming a half-mile arch from the pines toward Wau-
   kegan.
One was a whistle in the little sandhills, a bird crying either to the sunset
   gone or the dusk come.
One was three spotted waterbirds, zigzagging, cutting scrolls and jags,
   writing a bird Sanscrit of wing points, half over the sand, half over
   the water, a half-love for the sea, a half-love for the land.

I took away three thoughts.
One was a thing my people call "love," a shut-in river hunting the sea,
   breaking white falls between tall clefs of hill country.
One was a thing my people call "silence," the wind running over the
   butter faced sand-flowers, running over the sea, and never heard of
   again.
One was a thing my people call "death," neither a whistle in the little
   sandhills, nor a bird Sanscrit of wing points, yet a coat all the stars
   and seas have worn, yet a face the beach wears between sunset and
   dusk.

FAR ROCKAWAY NIGHT TILL MORNING

WHAT can we say of the night?
The fog night, the moon night,
       the fog moon night last night?

There swept out of the sea a song.
There swept out of the sea—
       torn white plungers.
There came on the coast wind drive
In the spit of a driven spray,
On the boom of foam and rollers,
The cry of midnight to morning:
      Hoi-a-loa.
      Hoi-a-loa.
      Hoi-a-loa.

Who has loved the night more than I have?
Who has loved the fog moon night last night
      more than I have?

Out of the sea that song
    —can I ever forget it?
Out of the sea those plungers
    —can I remember anything else?
Out of the midnight morning cry: Hoi-a-loa:
    —how can I hunt any other songs now?

HUMMINGBIRD WOMAN

WHY should I be wondering
How you would look in black velvet and yellow?
      in orange and green?
I who cannot remember whether it was a dash of blue
Or a whirr of red under your willow throat—
Why do I wonder how you would look in hummingbird feathers?

BUCKWHEAT

1

THERE was a late autumn cricket,
And two smoldering mountain sunsets
Under the valley roads of her eyes.

There was a late autumn cricket,
A hangover of summer song,
Scraping a tune
Of the late night clocks of summer,
In the late winter night fireglow,
This in a circle of black velvet at her neck.

2

In pansy eyes a flash, a thin rim of white light, a beach bonfire ten miles
across dunes, a speck of a fool star in night's half circle of velvet.

In the corner of the left arm a dimple, a mole, a forget-me-not, and it flut-
tered a hummingbird wing, a blur in the honey-red clover, in the
honey-white buckwheat.

BLUE RIDGE

BORN a million years ago you stay here a million years . . . watching the
women come and live and be laid away . . . you and they thin-gray
thin-dusk lovely.
So it goes: either the early morning lights are lovely or the early morning
star.
I am glad I have seen racehorses, women, mountains.

VALLEY SONG

THE sunset swept
To the valley's west, you remember.

The frost was on.
A star burnt blue.
We were warm, you remember,
And counted the rings on a moon.

The sunset swept
To the valley's west
And was gone in a big dark door of stars.

MIST FORMS

THE sheets of night mist travel a long valley.
I know why you came at sundown in a scarf mist.

What was it we touched asking nothing and asking all?
How many times can death come and pay back what we saw?

In the oath of the sod, the lips that swore,
In the oath of night mist, nothing and all,
A riddle is here no man tells, no woman.

PIGEON

THE flutter of blue pigeon's wings
Under a river bridge
Hunting a clean dry arch,
A corner for a sleep—
This flutters here in a woman's hand.

A singing sleep cry,
A drunken poignant two lines of song,
Somebody looking clean into yesterday

And remembering, or looking clean into
Tomorrow, and reading,—
This sings here as a woman's sleep cry sings.

Pigeon friend of mine,
Fly on, sing on.

CHASERS

THE sea at its worst drives a white foam up,
The same sea sometimes so easy and rocking with green mirrors.
So you were there when the white foam was up
And the salt spatter and the rack and the dulse—
You were done fingering these, and high, higher and higher
Your feet went and it was your voice went, "Hai, hai, hai,"
Up where the rocks let nothing live and the grass was gone,
Not even a hank nor a wisp of sea moss hoping.
Here your feet and your same singing, "Hai, hai, hai."

Was there anything else to answer than, "Hai, hai, hai"?
Did I go up those same crags yesterday and the day before
Scruffing my shoe leather and scraping the tough gnomic stuff
Of stones woven on a cold criss-cross so long ago?
Have I not sat there . . . watching the white foam up,
The hoarse white lines coming to curve, foam, slip back?
Didn't I learn then how the call comes, "Hai, hai, hai"?

HORSE FIDDLE

FIRST I would like to write for you a poem to be shouted in the teeth of
    a strong wind.
Next I would like to write one for you to sit on a hill and read down the
    river valley on a late summer afternoon, reading it in less than a whis-
    per to Jack on his soft wire legs learning to stand up and preach, Jack-
    in-the-pulpit.
As many poems as I have written to the moon and the streaming of the
    moon spinners of light, so many of the summer moon and the winter

moon I would like to shoot along to your ears for nothing, for a laugh, a song,

> for nothing at all,
> for one look from you,
> for your face turned away
> and your voice in one clutch
> half way between a tree-wind moan
> and a night-bird sob.

Believe nothing of it all, pay me nothing, open your window for the other singers and keep it shut for me.

The road I am on is a long road and I can go hungry again like I have gone hungry before.

What else have I done nearly all my life than go hungry and go on singing?

> Leave me with the hoot owl.
> I have slept in a blanket listening.
> He learned it, he must have learned it
> From two moons, the summer moon
> And the winter moon
> And the streaming of the moon spinners of light.

TIMBER WINGS

THERE was a wild pigeon came often to Hinkley's timber.

Gray wings that wrote their loops and triangles on the walnuts and the hazel.

> There was a wild pigeon.

There was a summer came year by year to Hinkley's timber.

Rainy months and sunny and pigeons calling and one pigeon best of all who came.

> There was a summer.

It is so long ago I saw this wild pigeon and listened.

It is so long ago I heard the summer song of the pigeon who told me why night comes, why death and stars come, why the whippoorwill remembers three notes only and always.

It is so long ago; it is like now and today; the gray-wing pigeon's way of
  telling it all, telling it to the walnuts and hazel, telling it to me.
    So there is memory.
    So there is a pigeon, a summer, a gray wing beating my shoulder.

NIGHT STUFF

Listen a while, the moon is a lovely woman, a lonely woman, lost in a
  silver dress, lost in a circus rider's silver dress.

Listen a while, the lake by night is a lonely woman, a lovely woman, circled
  with birches and pines mixing their green and white among stars shat-
  tered in spray clear nights.

I know the moon and the lake have twisted the roots under my heart the
  same as a lonely woman, a lovely woman, in a silver dress, in a circus
  rider's silver dress.

SPANISH

Fasten black eyes on me.
I ask nothing of you under the peach trees,
Fasten your black eyes in my gray
              with the spear of a storm.
The air under the peach blossoms is a haze of pink.

SHAG-BARK HICKORY

In the moonlight under a shag-bark hickory tree
Watching the yellow shadows melt in hoof-pools,
Listening to the yes and the no of a woman's hands,
I kept my guess why the night was glad.

The night was lit with a woman's eyes.
The night was crossed with a woman's hands,
The night kept humming an undersong.

THE SOUTH WIND SAYS SO

IF the oriole calls like last year
when the south wind sings in the oats,
if the leaves climb and climb on a bean pole
saying over a song learnt from the south wind,
if the crickets send up the same old lessons
found when the south wind keeps on coming,
we will get by, we will keep on coming,
we will get by, we will come along,
we will fix our hearts over,
the south wind says so.

Accomplished Facts

ACCOMPLISHED FACTS

EVERY year Emily Dickinson sent one friend
the first arbutus bud in her garden.

In a last will and testament Andrew Jackson
remembered a friend with the gift of George
Washington's pocket spy-glass.

Napoleon too, in a last testament, mentioned a silver
watch taken from the bedroom of Frederick the Great,
and passed along this trophy to a particular friend.

O. Henry took a blood carnation from his coat lapel
and handed it to a country girl starting work in a
bean bazaar, and scribbled: "Peach blossoms may or
may not stay pink in city dust."

So it goes. Some things we buy, some not.
Tom Jefferson was proud of his radishes, and Abe
Lincoln blacked his own boots, and Bismarck called
Berlin a wilderness of brick and newspapers.

So it goes. There are accomplished facts.
Ride, ride, ride on in the great new blimps—
Cross unheard-of oceans, circle the planet.
When you come back we may sit by five hollyhocks.
We might listen to boys fighting for marbles.
The grasshopper will look good to us.

So it goes . . .

GRIEG BEING DEAD

GRIEG being dead we may speak of him and his art.
Grieg being dead we can talk about whether he was any good or not.
Grieg being with Ibsen, Björnson, Lief Ericson and the rest,
Grieg being dead does not care a hell's hoot what we say.

Morning, Spring, Anitra's Dance,
He dreams them at the doors of new stars.

CHORDS

IN the morning, a Sunday morning, shadows of sea and adumbrants of
    rock in her eyes . . . horseback in leather boots and leather gauntlets
    by the sea.

In the evening, a Sunday evening, a rope of pearls on her white shoulders
    . . . and a speaking, brooding black velvet, relapsing to the voiceless

. . . battering Russian marches on a piano . . . drive of blizzards across Nebraska.

Yes, riding horseback on hills by the sea . . . sitting at the ivory keys in black velvet, a rope of pearls on white shoulders.

DOGHEADS

AMONG the grassroots
In the moonlight, who comes circling,
    red tongues and high noses?
Is one of 'em Buck and one of 'em
    White Fang?

In the moonlight, who are they, cross-legged,
    telling their stories over and over?
Is one of 'em Martin Eden and one of 'em Larsen
    the Wolf?

Let an epitaph read:
    He loved the straight eyes of dogs
    and the strong heads of men.

TRINITY PLACE

THE grave of Alexander Hamilton is in Trinity yard at the end of Wall Street.

The grave of Robert Fulton likewise is in Trinity yard where Wall Street stops.

And in this yard stenogs, bundle boys, scrubwomen, sit on the tombstones, and walk on the grass of graves, speaking of war and weather, of babies, wages and love.

An iron picket fence . . . and streaming thousands along Broadway sidewalks . . . straw hats, faces, legs . . . a singing, talking, hustling river . . . down the great street that ends with a Sea.

. . . easy is the sleep of Alexander Hamilton.
. . . easy is the sleep of Robert Fulton.
. . . easy are the great governments and the great steamboats.

PORTRAIT
(*For* S. A.)

To write one book in five years
or five books in one year,
to be the painter and the thing painted,
. . . where are we, bo?

Wait—get his number.
The barber shop handling is here
and the tweeds, the cheviot, the Scotch Mist,
and the flame orange scarf.

Yet there is more—he sleeps under bridges
with lonely crazy men; he sits in country
jails with bootleggers; he adopts the children
of broken-down burlesque actresses; he has
cried a heart of tears for Windy MacPherson's
father; he pencils wrists of lonely women.

Can a man sit at a desk in a skyscraper in Chicago
and be a harnessmaker in a corn town in Iowa
and feel the tall grass coming up in June
and the ache of the cottonwood trees
singing with the prairie wind?

POTOMAC RIVER MIST

ALL the policemen, saloonkeepers and efficiency experts in Toledo knew
    Bern Dailey; secretary ten years when Whitlock was mayor.
Pickpockets, yeggs, three card men, he knew them all and how they flit
    from zone to zone, birds of wind and weather, singers, fighters,
    scavengers.

The Washington monument pointed to a new moon for us and a gang
  from over the river sang ragtime to a ukulele.
The river mist marched up and down the Potomac, we hunted the fog-
  swept Lincoln Memorial, white as a blonde woman's arm.
We circled the city of Washington and came back home four o'clock in
  the morning, passing a sign: House Where Abraham Lincoln Died,
  Admission 25 Cents.

I got a letter from him in Sweden and I sent him a postcard from Norway
  . . . every newspaper from America ran news of "the flu."

The path of a night fog swept up the river to the Lincoln Memorial when
  I saw it again and alone at a winter's end, the marble in the mist
  white as a blonde woman's arm.

JACK LONDON AND O. HENRY

BOTH were jailbirds; no speechmakers at all;
speaking best with one foot on a brass rail;
a beer glass in the left hand and the right
hand employed for gestures.

And both were lights snuffed out . . . no warning
. . . no lingering:
Who knew the hearts of these boozefighters?

HIS OWN FACE HIDDEN

HOKUSAI's portrait of himself
Tells what his hat was like
And his arms and legs. The only faces
Are a river and a mountain
And two laughing farmers.

  The smile of Hokusai
  is under his hat.

CUPS OF COFFEE

THE haggard woman with a hacking cough and a deathless love whispers of white flowers . . . in your poem you pour like a cup of coffee, Gabriel.

The slim girl whose voice was lost in the waves of flesh piled on her bones . . . and the woman who sold to many men and saw her breasts shrivel . . . in two poems you pour these like a cup of coffee, Francois.

The woman whose lips are a thread of scarlet, the woman whose feet take hold on hell, the woman who turned to a memorial of salt looking at the lights of a forgotten city . . . in your affidavits, ancient Jews, you pour these like cups of coffee.

The woman who took men as snakes take rabbits, a rag and a bone and a hank of hair, she whose eyes called men to sea dreams and shark's teeth . . . in a poem you pour this like a cup of coffee, Kip.

Marching to the footlights in night robes with spots of blood, marching in white sheets muffling the faces, marching with heads in the air they come back and cough and cry and sneer: . . . in your poems, men, you pour these like cups of coffee.

Passports

SMOKE ROSE GOLD

THE dome of the capitol looks to the Potomac river.
Out of haze over the sunset,
Out of a smoke rose gold:
One star shines over the sunset.
Night takes the dome and the river, the sun and the smoke rose gold,
The haze changes from sunset to star.
The pour of a thin silver struggles against the dark.
A star might call: It's a long way across.

TANGIBLES

I HAVE seen this city in the day and the sun.
I have seen this city in the night and the moon.
And in the night and the moon I have seen a thing this city gave me
nothing of in the day and the sun.

The float of the dome in the day and the sun is one thing.
The float of the dome in the night and the moon is another thing.
In the night and the moon the float of the dome is a dream-whisper, a
croon of a hope: "Not today, child, not today, lover; maybe tomorrow,
child, maybe tomorrow, lover."

Can a dome of iron dream deeper than living men?
Can the float of a shape hovering among tree-tops—can this speak an
oratory sad, singing and red beyond the speech of the living men?

A mother of men, a sister, a lover, a woman past the dreams of the living—
Does she go sad, singing and red out of the float of this dome?

There is . . . something . . . here . . . men die for.

[WASHINGTON, *August, 1918*]

NIGHT MOVEMENT—NEW YORK

In the night, when the sea-winds take the city in their arms,
And cool the loud streets that kept their dust noon and afternoon;
In the night, when the sea-birds call to the lights of the city,
The lights that cut on the skyline their name of a city;
In the night, when the trains and wagons start from a long way off
For the city where the people ask bread and want letters;
In the night the city lives too—the day is not all.
In the night there are dancers dancing and singers singing,
And the sailors and soldiers look for numbers on doors.
In the night the sea-winds take the city in their arms.

NORTH ATLANTIC

When the sea is everywhere
from horizon to horizon . . .
  when the salt and blue
  fill a circle of horizons . . .
I swear again how I know
the sea is older than anything else
and the sea younger than anything else.

My first father was a landsman.
My tenth father was a sea-lover,
  a gypsy sea-boy, a singer of chanties.
  (Oh Blow the Man Down!)

The sea is always the same:
and yet the sea always changes.

    The sea gives all,
    and yet the sea keeps something back.

The sea takes without asking.
The sea is a worker, a thief and a loafer.
    Why does the sea let go so slow?
    Or never let go at all?

The sea always the same
day after day,
the sea always the same
night after night,
fog on fog and never a star,
wind on wind and running white sheets,
bird on bird always a sea-bird—
so the days get lost:
it is neither Saturday nor Monday,
it is any day or no day,
it is a year, ten years.

Fog on fog and never a star,
what is a man, a child, a woman,
to the green and grinding sea?
The ropes and boards squeak and groan.

On the land they know a child they have named Today.
On the sea they know three children they have named:
            Yesterday, Today, Tomorrow.

I made a song to a woman:—it ran:
      I have wanted you.
      I have called to you
      on a day I counted a thousand years.

In the deep of a sea-blue noon
many women run in a man's head,
phantom women leaping from a man's forehead
      . . . to the railings . . . into the sea . . . to the
      sea rim . . .
      . . . a man's mother . . . a man's wife . . . other
      women . . .
I asked a sure-footed sailor how and he said:
      I have known many women but there is only one sea.

I saw the North Star once
and our old friend, The Big Dipper,
      only the sea between us:

"Take away the sea
and I lift The Dipper,
swing the handle of it,
drink from the brim of it."

I saw the North Star one night
and five new stars for me in the rigging ropes,
and seven old stars in the cross of the wireless
        plunging by night,
        plowing by night—
Five new cool stars, seven old warm stars.

I have been let down in a thousand graves
        by my kinfolk.
I have been left alone with the sea and the sea's
        wife, the wind, for my last friends
And my kinfolk never knew anything about it at all.

Salt from an old work of eating our graveclothes is here.
    The sea-kin of my thousand graves,
    The sea and the sea's wife, the wind,
They are all here tonight
        between the circle of horizons,
        between the cross of the wireless
        and the seven old warm stars.
Out of a thousand sea-holes I came yesterday.
Out of a thousand sea-holes I come tomorrow.

I am kin of the changer.
        I am a son of the sea
        and the sea's wife, the wind.

FOG PORTRAIT

Rings of iron gray smoke; a woman's steel face . . . looking . . . looking.
Funnels of an ocean liner negotiating a fog night; pouring a taffy mass
    down the wind; layers of soot on the top deck; a taffrail . . . and a
    woman's steel face . . . looking . . . looking.

Cliffs challenge humped; sudden arcs form on a gull's wing in the storm's vortex; miles of white horses plow through a stony beach; stars, clear sky, and everywhere free climbers calling; and a woman's steel face . . . looking . . . looking . . .

FLYING FISH

I HAVE lived in many half-worlds myself . . . and so I know you.

I leaned at a deck rail watching a monotonous sea, the same circling birds and the same plunge of furrows carved by the plowing keel.

I leaned so . . . and you fluttered struggling between two waves in the air now . . . and then under the water and out again . . . a fish . . . a bird . . . a fin thing . . . a wing thing.

Child of water, child of air, fin thing and wing thing . . . I have lived in many half-worlds myself . . . and so I know you.

HOME THOUGHTS

THE sea rocks have a green moss.
The pine rocks have red berries.
I have memories of you.

. . . .

Speak to me of how you miss me.
Tell me the hours go long and slow.

Speak to me of the drag on your heart,
The iron drag of the long days.

I know hours empty as a beggar's tin cup on a rainy day, empty as a soldier's sleeve with an arm lost.

Speak to me . . .

IN THE SHADOW OF THE PALACE

LET us go out of the fog, John, out of the filmy persistent drizzle on the
streets of Stockholm, let us put down the collars of our raincoats, take
off our hats and sit in the newspaper office.

Let us sit among the telegrams—clickety-click—the kaiser's crown goes
into the gutter and the Hohenzollern throne of a thousand years falls
to pieces a one-hoss shay.

It is a fog night out and the umbrellas are up and the collars of the rain-
coats—and all the steamboats up and down the Baltic sea have their
lights out and the wheelsmen sober.

Here the telegrams come—one king goes and another—butter is costly:
there is no butter to buy for our bread in Stockholm—and a little
patty of butter costs more than all the crowns of Germany.

Let us go out in the fog, John, let us roll up our raincoat collars and go
on the streets where men are sneering at the kings.

TWO ITEMS

STRONG rocks hold up the riksdag bridge . . . always strong river waters
shoving their shoulders against them . . .
In the riksdag tonight three hundred men are talking to each other about
more potatoes and bread for the Swedish people to eat this winter.
In a boat among calm waters next to the running waters a fisherman sits
in the dark and I, leaning at a parapet, see him lift a net and let it
down . . . he waits . . . the waters run . . . the riksdag talks . . .
he lifts the net and lets it down . . .
Stars lost in the sky ten days of drizzle spread over the sky saying yes-yes.

. . . .

Every afternoon at four o'clock fifteen apple women who have sold their
apples in Christiania meet at a coffee house and gab.
Every morning at nine o'clock a girl wipes the windows of a hotel across
the street from the post office in Stockholm.

I have pledged them when I go to California next summer and see the
  orange groves splattered with yellow balls
I shall remember other people half way round the world.

STREETS TOO OLD

I WALKED among the streets of an old city and the streets were lean as the
  throats of hard seafish soaked in salt and kept in barrels many years.
How old, how old, how old, we are:—the walls went on saying, street walls
  leaning toward each other like old women of the people, like old mid-
  wives tired and only doing what must be done.
The greatest the city could offer me, a stranger, was statues of the kings,
  on all corners bronzes of kings—ancient bearded kings who wrote
  books and spoke of God's love for all people—and young kings who
  took forth armies out across the frontiers splitting the heads of their
  opponents and enlarging their kingdoms.
Strangest of all to me, a stranger in this old city, was the murmur always
  whistling on the winds twisting out of the armpits and fingertips of
  the kings in bronze:—Is there no loosening? Is this for always?
In an early snowflurry one cried:—Pull me down where the tired old mid-
  wives no longer look at me, throw the bronze of me to a fierce fire
  and make me into neckchains for dancing children.

SAVOIR FAIRE

CAST a bronze of my head and legs and put them on the king's street.
Set the cast of me here alongside Carl XII, making two Carls for the
  Swedish people and the utlanders to look at between the palace and
  the Grand Hotel.
The summer sun will shine on both the Carls, and November drizzles
  wrap the two, one in tall leather boots, one in wool leggings.
Also I place it in the record: the Swedish people may name boats after
  me or change the name of a long street and give it one of my nick-
  names.
The old men who beset the soil of Sweden and own the titles to the land
  —the old men who enjoy a silken shimmer to their chin whiskers
  when they promenade the streets named after old kings—if they for-

get me—the old men whose varicose veins stand more and more blue
on the calves of their legs when they take their morning baths at-
tended by old women born to the bath service of old men and young
—if these old men say another King Carl should have a bronze on the
king's street rather than a Fool Carl—

Then I would hurl them only another fool's laugh—

I would remember last Sunday when I stood on a jutland of fire-born red
granite watching the drop of the sun in the middle of the afternoon
and the full moon shining over Stockholm four o'clock in the after-
noon.

If the young men will read five lines of one of my poems I will let the
kings have all the bronze—I ask only that one page of my writings be
a knapsack keepsake of the young men who are the bloodkin of those
who laughed nine hundred years ago: We are afraid of nothing—
only—the sky may fall on us.

MOHAMMED BEK HADJETLACHE

This Mohammedan colonel from the Caucasus yells with his voice and
wigwags with his arms.

The interpreter translates, "I was a friend of Kornilov, he asks me what
to do and I tell him."

A stub of a man, this Mohammedan colonel . . . a projectile shape . . .
a bald head hammered . . .

"Does he fight or do they put him in a cannon and shoot him at the
enemy?"

This fly-by-night, this bull-roarer who knows everybody.

"I write forty books, history of Islam, history of Europe, true religion,
scientific farming, I am the Roosevelt of the Caucasus, I go to
America and ride horses in the moving pictures for $500,000, you
get $50,000 . . ."

"I have 30,000 acres in the Caucasus, I have a stove factory in Petrograd
the bolsheviks take from me, I am an old friend of the Czar, I am an
old family friend of Clemenceau . . ."

These hands strangled three fellow workers for the czarist restoration, took
their money, sent them in sacks to a river bottom . . . and scandal-
ized Stockholm with his gang of strangler women.

Mid-sea strangler hands rise before me illustrating a wish, "I ride horses

for the moving pictures in America, $500,000, and you get ten per
cent . . ."
This rider of fugitive dawns. . . .

HIGH CONSPIRATORIAL PERSONS

OUT of the testimony of such reluctant lips, out of the oaths and mouths
of such scrupulous liars, out of perjurers whose hands swore by God
to the white sun before all men,

Out of a rag saturated with smears and smuts gathered from the footbaths
of kings and the loin cloths of whores, from the scabs of Babylon and
Jerusalem to the scabs of London and New York,

From such a rag that has wiped the secret sores of kings and overlords
across the millenniums of human marches and babblings,

From such a rag perhaps I shall wring one reluctant desperate drop of
blood, one honest-to-God spot of red speaking a mother-heart.

[CHRISTIANIA, NORWAY, *December,* 1918]

BALTIC FOG NOTES

SEVEN days all fog, all mist, and the turbines pounding through high seas.
I was a plaything, a rat's neck in the teeth of a scuffling mastiff.
Fog and fog and no stars, sun, moon.
Then an afternoon in fjords, low-lying lands scrawled in granite languages
on a gray sky,
A night harbor, blue dusk mountain shoulders against a night sky,
And a circle of lights blinking: Ninety thousand people here.
Among the Wednesday night thousands in galoshes and coats
slickered for rain,
I learned how hungry I was for streets and people.

. . . .

I would rather be water than anything else.
I saw a drive of salt fog and mist in the North Atlantic and an iceberg
dusky as a cloud in the gray of morning.

And I saw the dream pools of fjords in Norway . . . and the scarf of
    dancing water on the rocks and over the edges of mountain shelves.
         . . . .

Bury me in a mountain graveyard in Norway.
Three tongues of water sing around it with snow from the mountains.

Bury me in the North Atlantic.
A fog there from Iceland will be a murmur in gray over me and a long
    deep wind sob always.

Bury me in an Illinois cornfield.
The blizzards loosen their pipe organ voluntaries in winter stubble and
    the spring rains and the fall rains bring letters from the sea.

                                    [BERGEN]

Circles of Doors

CIRCLES OF DOORS

I LOVE him, I love him, ran the patter of her lips
And she formed his name on her tongue and sang
And she sent him word she loved him so much,
So much, and death was nothing; work, art, home,
All was nothing if her love for him was not first
Of all; the patter of her lips ran, I love him,
I love him; and he knew the doors that opened
Into doors and more doors, no end of doors,
And full-length mirrors doubling and tripling
The apparitions of doors: circling corridors of
Looking-glasses and doors, some with knobs, some

With no knobs, some opening slow to a heavy push,
And some jumping open at a touch and a hello.
And he knew if he so wished he could follow her
Swift running through circles of doors, hearing
Sometimes her whisper, I love him, I love him,
And sometimes only a high chaser of laughter
Somewhere five or ten doors ahead or five or ten
Doors behind, or chittering *h-st, h-st*, among corners
Of the tall full-length dusty looking-glasses.
I love, I love, I love, she sang short and quick in
High thin beaten soprano and he knew the meanings,
The high chaser of laughter, the doors on doors
And the looking-glasses, the room to room hunt,
The ends opening into new ends always.

HATE

ONE man killed another. The saying between them had been "I'd give you
the shirt off my back."

The killer wept over the dead. The dead if he looks back knows the killer
was sorry. It was a shot in one second of hate out of ten years of love.

Why is the sun a red ball in the six o'clock mist?
Why is the moon a tumbling chimney? . . . tumbling . . . tumbling
. . . "I'd give you the shirt off my back" . . . And I'll kill you if my
head goes wrong.

TWO STRANGERS BREAKFAST

THE law says you and I belong to each other, George.
The law says you are mine and I am yours, George.
And there are a million miles of white snowstorms, a million furnaces of
hell,
Between the chair where you sit and the chair where I sit.
The law says two strangers shall eat breakfast together after nights on the
horn of an Arctic moon.

SNOW

Snow took us away from the smoke valleys into white mountains, we saw
    velvet blue cows eating a vermilion grass and they gave us a pink
    milk.

Snow changes our bones into fog streamers caught by the wind and spelled
    into many dances.

Six bits for a sniff of snow in the old days bought us bubbles beautiful to
    forget floating long-arm women across sunny autumn hills.

Our bones cry and cry, no let-up, cry their telegrams:
More, more—a yen is on, a long yen and God only knows when it will
    end.

In the old days six bits got us snow and stopped the yen—now the govern-
    ment says: No, no, when our bones cry their telegrams: More, more.

The blue cows are dying, no more pink milk, no more floating long-arm
    women, the hills are empty—us for the smoke valleys—sneeze and
    shiver and croak, you dopes—the government says: No, no.

DANCER

The lady in red, she in the chile con carne red,
Brilliant as the shine of a pepper crimson in the summer sun,
She behind a false-face, the much sought-after dancer, the most sought-
    after dancer of all in this masquerade,
The lady in red sox and red hat, ankles of willow, crimson arrow amidst
    the Spanish clashes of music,

> I sit in a corner
> watching her dance first with one man
> and then another.

PLASTER

"I KNEW a real man once," says Agatha in the splendor of a shagbark
hickory tree.

Did a man touch his lips to Agatha? Did a man hold her in his arms? Did
a man only look at her and pass by?

Agatha, far past forty in a splendor of remembrance, says, "I knew a real
man once."

CURSE OF A RICH POLISH PEASANT ON HIS SISTER WHO
RAN AWAY WITH A WILD MAN

FELIKSOWA has gone again from our house and this time for good, I hope.
She and her husband took with them the cow father gave them, and they
sold it.
She went like a swine, because she called neither on me, her brother, nor
on her father, before leaving for those forests.
That is where she ought to live, with bears, not with men.
She was something of an ape before and there, with her wild husband, she
became altogether an ape.
No honest person would have done as they did.
Whose fault is it? And how much they have cursed me and their father!
May God not punish them for it. They think only about money; they let
the church go if they can only live fat on their money.

WOMAN WITH A PAST

THERE was a woman tore off a red velvet gown
And slashed the white skin of her right shoulder
And a crimson zigzag wrote a finger nail hurry.

There was a woman spoke six short words
And quit a life that was old to her
For a life that was new.

There was a woman swore an oath
And gave hoarse whisper to a prayer
And it was all over.

She was a thief and a whore and a kept woman,
She was a thing to be used and played with.
She wore an ancient scarlet sash.

The story is thin and wavering,
White as a face in the first apple blossoms,
White as a birch in the snow of a winter moon.

The story is never told.
There are white lips whisper alone.
There are red lips whisper alone.

In the cool of the old walls,
In the white of the old walls,
The red song is over.

WHITE HANDS

For the second time in a year this lady with the white hands is brought
to the west room second floor of a famous sanatorium.
Her husband is a cornice manufacturer in an Iowa town and the lady has
often read papers on Victorian poets before the local literary club.
Yesterday she washed her hands forty-seven times during her waking
hours and in her sleep moaned restlessly attempting to clean imag-
inary soiled spots off her hands.
Now the head physician touches his chin with a crooked forefinger.

AN ELECTRIC SIGN GOES DARK

Poland, France, Judea ran in her veins,
Singing to Paris for bread, singing to Gotham in a fizz at the pop of a
bottle's cork.

"Won't you come and play wiz me" she sang . . . and "I just can't make
my eyes behave."
"Higgeldy-Piggeldy," "Papa's Wife," "Follow Me" were plays.

Did she wash her feet in a tub of milk? Was a strand of pearls sneaked
from her trunk? The newspapers asked.
Cigarettes, tulips, pacing horses, took her name.

Twenty years old . . . thirty . . . forty . . .
Forty-five and the doctors fathom nothing, the doctors quarrel, the doc-
tors use silver tubes feeding twenty-four quarts of blood into the veins,
the respects of a prize-fighter, a cab driver.
And a little mouth moans: It is easy to die when they are dying so many
grand deaths in France.

A voice, a shape, gone.
A baby bundle from Warsaw . . . legs, torso, head . . . on a hotel bed
at The Savoy.
The white chiselings of flesh that flung themselves in somersaults, strad-
dles, for packed houses:
A memory, a stage and footlights out, an electric sign on Broadway dark.

She belonged to somebody, nobody.
No one man owned her, no ten nor a thousand.
She belonged to many thousand men, lovers of the white chiseling of
arms and shoulders, the ivory of a laugh, the bells of song.

Railroad brakemen taking trains across Nebraska prairies, lumbermen
jaunting in pine and tamarack of the Northwest, stock ranchers in
the middle west, mayors of southern cities
Say to their pals and wives now: I see by the papers Anna Held is dead.

THEY BUY WITH AN EYE TO LOOKS

The fine cloth of your love might be a fabric of Egypt,
Something Sinbad, the sailor, took away from robbers,
Something a traveler with plenty of money might pick up
And bring home and stick on the walls and say:
"There's a little thing made a hit with me

When I was in Cairo—I think I must see Cairo again some day."
So there are cornice manufacturers, chewing-gum kings,
Young Napoleons who corner eggs or corner cheese,
Phenoms looking for more worlds to corner,
And still other phenoms who lard themselves in
And make a killing in steel, copper, permanganese,
And they say to random friends in for a call:
   "Have you had a look at my wife? Here she is.
   Haven't I got her dolled up for fair?"
O-ee! the fine cloth of your love might be a fabric of Egypt.

PROUD AND BEAUTIFUL

AFTER you have spent all the money modistes and manicures and man-
   nikins will take for fixing you over into a thing the people on the
   streets call proud and beautiful,
After the shops and fingers have worn out all they have and know and
   can hope to have and know for the sake of making you what the
   people on the streets call proud and beautiful,
After there is absolutely nothing more to be done for the sake of staging
   you as a great enigmatic bird of paradise and they must all declare
   you to be proud and beautiful,
After you have become the last word in good looks, in so far as good looks
   may be fixed and formulated, then, why then, there is nothing more
   to it then, it is then you listen and see how voices and eyes declare
   you to be proud and beautiful.

TELEGRAM

I SAW a telegram handed a two hundred pound man at a desk. And the
   little scrap of paper charged the air like a set of crystals in a chemist's
   tube to a whispering pinch of salt.
Cross my heart, the two hundred pound man had just cracked a joke
   about a new hat he got his wife, when the messenger boy slipped in
   and asked him to sign. He gave the boy a nickel, tore the envelope
   and read.
Then he yelled "Good God," jumped for his hat and raincoat, ran for the
   elevator and took a taxi to a railroad depot.

As I say, it was like a set of crystals in a chemist's tube and a whispering pinch of salt.

I wonder what Diogenes who lived in a tub in the sun would have commented on the affair.

I know a shoemaker who works in a cellar slamming half-soles onto shoes, and when I told him, he said: "I pay my bills, I love my wife, and I am not afraid of anybody."

GLIMMER

LET down your braids of hair, lady.
Cross your legs and sit before the looking-glass
And gaze long on lines under your eyes.
Life writes; men dance.
      And you know how men pay women.

WHITE ASH

THERE is a woman on Michigan Boulevard keeps a parrot and goldfish and two white mice.

She used to keep a houseful of girls in kimonos and three pushbuttons on the front door.

Now she is alone with a parrot and goldfish and two white mice . . . but these are some of her thoughts:

The love of a soldier on furlough or a sailor on shore leave burns with a bonfire red and saffron.

The love of an emigrant workman whose wife is a thousand miles away burns with a blue smoke.

The love of a young man whose sweetheart married an older man for money burns with a sputtering uncertain flame.

And there is a love . . . one in a thousand . . . burns clean and is gone leaving a white ash. . . .

And this is a thought she never explains to the parrot and goldfish and two white mice.

TESTIMONY REGARDING A GHOST

THE roses slanted crimson sobs
On the night-sky hair of the women,
And the long light-fingered men
Spoke to the dark-haired women,
"Nothing lovelier, nothing lovelier."
How could he sit there among us all
Guzzling blood into his guts,
Goblets, mugs, buckets—
Leaning, toppling, laughing
With a slobber on his mouth,
A smear of red on his strong raw lips,
How could he sit there
And only two or three of us see him?
   There was nothing to it.
He wasn't there at all, of course.

The roses leaned from the pots.
The sprays shot roses gold and red
And the roses slanted crimson sobs
   In the night-sky hair
And the voices chattered on the way
To the frappé, speaking of pictures,
Speaking of a strip of black velvet
Crossing a girlish woman's throat,
Speaking of the mystic music flash
Of pots and sprays of roses,
"Nothing lovelier, nothing lovelier."

PUT OFF THE WEDDING FIVE TIMES AND NOBODY COMES TO IT
(Handbook for Quarreling Lovers)

I THOUGHT of offering you apothegms.
I might have said, "Dogs bark and the wind carries it away."
I might have said, "He who would make a door of gold must knock a
   nail in every day."

So easy, so easy it would have been to inaugurate a high impetuous mo-
ment for you to look on before the final farewells were spoken.
You who assumed the farewells in the manner of people buying news-
papers and reading the headlines—and all peddlers of gossip who
buttonhole each other and wag their heads saying, "Yes, I heard all
about it last Wednesday."

I considered several apothegms.
"There is no love but service," of course, would only initiate a quarrel
over who has served and how and when.
"Love stands against fire and flood and much bitterness," would only
initiate a second misunderstanding, and bickerings with lapses of
silence.
What is there in the Bible to cover our case, or Shakespeare? What poetry
can help? Is there any left but Epictetus?

Since you have already chosen to interpret silence for language and
silence for despair and silence for contempt and silence for all things
but love,
Since you have already chosen to read ashes where God knows there was
something else than ashes,
Since silence and ashes are two identical findings for your eyes and there
are no apothegms worth handing out like a hung jury's verdict for
a record in our own hearts as well as the community at large,
I can only remember a Russian peasant who told me his grandfather
warned him: If you ride too good a horse you will not take the
straight road to town.

It will always come back to me in the blur of that hokku: The heart of
a woman of thirty is like the red ball of the sun seen through a mist.
Or I will remember the witchery in the eyes of a girl at a barn dance
one winter night in Illinois saying:
    Put off the wedding five times and nobody comes to it.

BABY VAMPS

Baby vamps, is it harder work than it used to be?
Are the new soda parlors worse than the old time saloons?
  Baby vamps, do you have jobs in the day time

or is this all you do?
do you come out only at night?
In the winter at the skating rinks, in the summer at the roller coaster
parks,
Wherever figure eights are carved, by skates in winter, by roller coasters
in summer,
Wherever the whirligigs are going and chicken spanish and hot dog are
sold,
There you come, giggling baby vamp, there you come with your blue
baby eyes, saying:
Take me along.

VAUDEVILLE DANCER

ELSIE FLIMMERWON, you got a job now with a jazz outfit in vaudeville.

The houses go wild when you finish the act shimmying a fast shimmy
to The Livery Stable Blues.

It is long ago, Elsie Flimmerwon, I saw your mother over a washtub in
a grape arbor when your father came with the locomotor ataxia shuffle.

It is long ago, Elsie, and now they spell your name with an electric sign.

Then you were a little thing in checked gingham and your mother wiped
your nose and said: You little fool, keep off the streets.

Now you are a big girl at last and streetfuls of people read your name
and a line of people shaped like a letter S stand at the box office hoping
to see you shimmy.

BALLOON FACES

THE balloons hang on wires in the Marigold Gardens.
They spot their yellow and gold, they juggle their blue and red, they
float their faces on the face of the sky.
Balloon-face eaters sit by hundreds reading the eat cards, asking, "What

shall we eat?"—and the waiters, "Have you ordered?" they are sixty
balloon faces sifting white over the tuxedoes.

Poets, lawyers, ad men, mason contractors, smart-alecks discussing "edu-
cated jackasses," here they put crabs into their balloon faces.

Here sit the heavy balloon-face women lifting crimson lobsters into their
crimson faces, lobsters out of Sargossa sea-bottoms.

Here sits a man cross-examining a woman, "Where were you last night?
What do you do with all your money? Who's buying your shoes now,
anyhow?"

So they sit eating whitefish, two balloon faces swept on God's night wind.

And all the time the balloon spots on the wires, a little mile of festoons,
they play their own silence play of film yellow and film gold, bubble
blue and bubble red.

The wind crosses the town, the wind from the west side comes to the
banks of marigolds boxed in the Marigold Gardens.

Night moths fly and fix their feet in the leaves and eat and are seen by
the eaters.

The jazz outfit sweats and the drums and the saxophones reach for the
ears of the eaters.

The chorus brought from Broadway works at the fun and the slouch of
their shoulders, the kick of their ankles, reach for the eyes of the
eaters.

These girls from Kokomo and Peoria, these hungry girls, since they are
paid-for, let us look on and listen, let us get their number.

Why do I go again to the balloons on the wires, something for nothing,
kin women of the half-moon, dream women?

And the half-moon swinging on the wind crossing the town—these two,
the half-moon and the wind—this will be about all, this will be
about all.

Eaters, go to it; your mazuma pays for it all; it's a knockout, a classy
knockout—and payday always comes.

The moths in the marigolds will do for me, the half-moon, the wishing
wind and the little mile of balloon spots on wires—this will be about
all, this will be about all.

Haze

HAZE

KEEP a red heart of memories
Under the great gray rain sheds of the sky,
Under the open sun and the yellow gloaming embers.
Remember all paydays of lilacs and songbirds;
All starlights of cool memories on storm paths.

Out of this prairie rise the faces of dead men.
They speak to me. I can not tell you what they say.

Other faces rise on the prairie.
⠀⠀⠀⠀⠀⠀⠀⠀⠀⠀⠀They are the unborn. The future.

Yesterday and tomorrow cross and mix on the skyline.
The two are lost in a purple haze. One forgets. One waits.

In the yellow dust of sunsets, in the meadows of vermilion eight o'clock
⠀⠀⠀June nights . . . the dead men and the unborn children speak to
⠀⠀⠀me . . . I can not tell you what they say . . . you listen and you
⠀⠀⠀know.

I don't care who you are, man:
I know a woman is looking for you
and her soul is a corn-tassel kissing a south-west wind.

(The farm-boy whose face is the color of brick-dust, is calling the cows;
⠀⠀⠀he will form the letter X with crossed streams of milk from the teats;
⠀⠀⠀he will beat a tattoo on the bottom of a tin pail with X's of milk.)

I don't care who you are, man:
I know sons and daughters looking for you

And they are gray dust working toward star paths
And you see them from a garret window when you laugh
At your luck and murmur, "I don't care."

I don't care who you are, woman:
I know a man is looking for you
And his soul is a south-west wind kissing a corn-tassel.

(The kitchen girl on the farm is throwing oats to the chickens and the
    buff of their feathers says hello to the sunset's late maroon.)

I don't care who you are, woman:
I know sons and daughters looking for you
And they are next year's wheat or the year after hidden in the dark and
    loam.

My love is a yellow hammer spinning circles in Ohio, Indiana. My love
    is a redbird shooting flights in straight lines in Kentucky and Ten-
    nessee. My love is an early robin flaming an ember of copper on her
    shoulders in March and April. My love is a graybird living in the
    eaves of a Michigan house all winter. Why is my love always a cry-
    ing thing of wings?

On the Indiana dunes, in the Mississippi marshes, I have asked: Is it only
    a fishbone on the beach?
Is it only a dog's jaw or a horse's skull whitening in the sun? Is the red
    heart of man only ashes? Is the flame of it all a white light switched
    off and the power-house wires cut?

Why do the prairie roses answer every summer? Why do the changing
    repeating rains come back out of the salt sea wind-blown? Why do
    the stars keep their tracks? Why do the cradles of the sky rock new
    babies?

CADENZA

THE knees
    of this proud woman
are bone.

The elbows
　of this proud woman
are bone.

The summer-white stars
　and the winter-white stars
never stop circling
　around this proud woman.

The bones
　of this proud woman
answer the vibrations
　of the stars.

　In summer
the stars speak deep thoughts
　In the winter
the stars repeat summer speeches.

The knees
　of this proud woman
know these thoughts
　and know these speeches
of the summer and winter stars.

MEMORANDA

THIS handful of grass, brown, says little. This quarter-mile field of it,
　waving seeds ripening in the sun, is a lake of luminous firefly
　lavender.

. . . .

Prairie roses, two of them, climb down the sides of a road ditch. In the
　clear pool they find their faces along stiff knives of grass, and cat-tails
　who speak and keep thoughts in beaver brown.

. . . .

These gardens empty; these fields only flower ghosts; these yards with
　faces gone; leaves speaking as feet and skirts in slow dances to slow
　winds; I turn my head and say good-by to no one who hears; I pro-
　nounce a useless good-by.

POTOMAC TOWN IN FEBRUARY

The bridge says: Come across, try me; see how good I am.
The big rock in the river says: Look at me; learn how to stand up.
The white water says: I go on; around, under, over, I go on.
A kneeling, scraggly pine says: I am here yet; they nearly got me last year.
A sliver of moon slides by on a high wind calling: I know why; I'll see
    you tomorrow; I'll tell you everything tomorrow.

BUFFALO DUSK

The buffaloes are gone.
And those who saw the buffaloes are gone.
Those who saw the buffaloes by thousands and how they pawed the
    prairie sod into dust with their hoofs, their great heads down pawing
    on in a great pageant of dusk,
Those who saw the buffaloes are gone.
And the buffaloes are gone.

CORN HUT TALK

Write your wishes
    on the door
    and come in.

Stand outside
    in the pools of the harvest moon.

Bring in
    the handshake of the pumpkins.

There's a wish
    for every hazel nut?
There's a hope
    for every corn shock?
There's a kiss
    for every clumsy climbing shadow?

Clover and the bumblebees once,
high winds and November rain now.

Buy shoes
for rough weather in November.
Buy shirts
to sleep outdoors when May comes.

Buy me
something useless to remember you by.
Send me
a sumach leaf from an Illinois hill.

In the faces marching in the firelog flickers,
In the fire music of wood singing to winter,
Make my face march through the purple and ashes.
Make me one of the fire singers to winter.

BRANCHES

THE dancing girls here . . . after a long night of it . . .
The long beautiful night of the wind and rain in April,
The long night hanging down from the drooping branches of the top of
    a birch tree,
Swinging, swaying, to the wind for a partner, to the rain for a partner.
What is the humming, swishing thing they sing in the morning now?
The rain, the wind, the swishing whispers of the long slim curve so little
    and so dark on the western morning sky . . . these dancing girls
    here on an April early morning . . .
They have had a long cool beautiful night of it with their partners learn-
    ing this year's song of April.

RUSTY CRIMSON
(*Christmas Day,* 1917)

THE five o'clock prairie sunset is a strong man going to sleep after a long
    day in a cornfield.

The red dust of a rusty crimson is fixed with two fingers of lavender.
    A hook of smoke, a woman's nose in charcoal and . . . nothing.

The timberline turns in a cover of purple. A grain elevator humps a
    shoulder. One steel star whisks out a pointed fire. Moonlight comes
    on the stubble.

. . . .

"Jesus in an Illinois barn early this morning, the baby Jesus . . . in
    flannels . . ."

LETTER S

THE river is gold under a sunset of Illinois.
It is a molten gold someone pours and changes.
A woman mixing a wedding cake of butter and eggs
Knows what the sunset is pouring on the river here.
The river twists in a letter S.
    A gold S now speaks to the Illinois sky.

WEEDS

FROM the time of the early radishes
To the time of the standing corn
Sleepy Henry Hackerman hoes.

There are laws in the village against weeds.
The law says a weed is wrong and shall be killed.
The weeds say life is a white and lovely thing
And the weeds come on and on in irrepressible regiments.
Sleepy Henry Hackerman hoes; and the village law uttering a ban on
    weeds is unchangeable law.

NEW FARM TRACTOR

SNUB nose, the guts of twenty mules are in your cylinders and transmission.

The rear axles hold the kick of twenty Missouri jackasses.

It is in the records of the patent office and the ads there is twenty horse-
    power pull here.

The farm boy says hello to you instead of twenty mules—he sings to you
    instead of ten span of mules.

A bucket of oil and a can of grease is your hay and oats.

Rain proof and fool proof they stable you anywhere in the fields with the
    stars for a roof.

I carve a team of long ear mules on the steering wheel—it's good-by now
    to leather reins and the songs of the old mule skinners.

PODS

Pea pods cling to stems.
Neponset, the village,
Clings to the Burlington railway main line.
Terrible midnight limiteds roar through
Hauling sleepers to the Rockies and Sierras.
The earth is slightly shaken
And Neponset trembles slightly in its sleep.

HARVEST SUNSET

Red gold of pools,
Sunset furrows six o'clock,
And the farmer done in the fields
And the cows in the barns with bulging udders.

Take the cows and the farmer,
Take the barns and bulging udders.
Leave the red gold of pools
And sunset furrows six o'clock.
The farmer's wife is singing.
The farmer's boy is whistling.
I wash my hands in red gold of pools.

NIGHT'S NOTHINGS AGAIN

WHO knows what I know
when I have asked the night questions
and the night has answered nothing
only the old answers?

Who picked a crimson cryptogram,
the tail light of a motor car turning a corner,
or the midnight sign of a chile con carne place,
or a man out of the ashes of false dawn muttering "hot-dog" to the night
      watchmen:
Is there a spieler who has spoken the word or taken the number of night's
      nothings? am I the spieler? or you?

Is there a tired head
the night has not fed and rested
and kept on its neck and shoulders?

Is there a wish
Of man to woman
and woman to man
the night has not written
and signed its name under?

Does the night forget
as a woman forgets?
and remember
as a woman remembers?

Who gave the night
this head of hair,
this gypsy head
calling: Come-on?

Who gave the night anything at all
and asked the night questions
and was laughed at?

Who asked the night
for a long soft kiss
and lost the half-way lips?
who picked a red lamp in a mist?

Who saw the night
fold its Mona Lisa hands
and sit half-smiling, half-sad,
nothing at all,
and everything,
all the world?

Who saw the night
let down its hair
and shake its bare shoulders
and blow out the candles of the moon,
whispering, snickering,
cutting off the snicker . . . and sobbing . . .
out of pillow-wet kisses and tears?

Is the night woven of anything else
than the secret wishes of women,
the stretched empty arms of women?
the hair of women with stars and roses?
I asked the night these questions.
I heard the night asking me these questions.

I saw the night
put these whispered nothings
across the city dust and stones,
across a single yellow sunflower,
one stalk strong as a woman's wrist;

And the play of a light rain,
the jig-time folly of a light rain,
the creepers of a drizzle on the sidewalks
for the policemen and the railroad men,
for the home-goers and the homeless,
silver fans and funnels on the asphalt,
the many feet of a fog mist that crept away;

I saw the night
put these nothings across
and the night wind came saying: Come-on:
and the curve of sky swept off white clouds
and swept on white stars over Battery to Bronx,
scooped a sea of stars over Albany, Dobbs Ferry, Cape Horn, Constanti-
     nople.

I saw the night's mouth and lips
strange as a face next to mine on a pillow
and now I know . . . as I knew always . . .
the night is a lover of mine . . .
I know the night is . . . everything.
I know the night is . . . all the world.

I have seen gold lamps in a lagoon
play sleep and murmur
with never an eyelash,
never a glint of an eyelid,
quivering in the water-shadows.

A taxi whizzes by, an owl car clutters, passengers yawn reading street signs,
     a bum on a park bench shifts, another bum keeps his majesty of stone
     stillness, the forty-foot split rocks of Central Park sleep the sleep of
     stone whalebacks, the cornices of the Metropolitan Art mutter their
     own nothings to the men with rolled-up collars on the top of a bus:
Breaths of the sea salt Atlantic, breaths of two rivers, and a heave of haw-
     sers and smokestacks, the swish of multiplied sloops and war dogs,
     the hesitant hoo-hoo of coal boats: among these I listen to Night
     calling:
I give you what money can never buy: all other lovers change: all others
     go away and come back and go away again:
          I am the one you slept with last night.
          I am the one you sleep with tonight and
               tomorrow night.
          I am the one whose passion kisses
               keep your head wondering
               and your lips aching
               to sing one song
               never sung before

at night's gypsy head
 calling: Come-on.

These hands that slid to my neck and held me,
these fingers that told a story,
this gypsy head of hair calling: Come-on:
can anyone else come along now
and put across night's nothings again?

I have wanted kisses my heart stuttered at asking,
I have pounded at useless doors and called my people fools.
I have staggered alone in a winter dark making mumble songs
to the sting of a blizzard that clutched and swore.

 It was the night in my blood:
  open dreaming night,
  night of tireless sheet-steel blue:
 The hands of God washing something,
  feet of God walking somewhere.

Panels

PANELS

THE west window is a panel of marching onions.
Five new lilacs nod to the wind and fence boards.
The rain dry fence boards, the stained knot holes,
 heliograph a peace.
(How long ago the knee drifts here and a blizzard
  howling at the knot holes,
  whistling winter war drums?)

DAN

EARLY May, after cold rain the sun baffling cold wind.
Irish setter pup finds a corner near the cellar door,
           all sun and no wind,
Cuddling there he crosses forepaws and lays his skull
Sideways on this pillow, dozing in a half-sleep,
Browns of hazel nut, mahogany, rosewood, played off
           against each other on his paws
           and head.

WHIFFLETREE

GIVE me your anathema.
Speak new damnations on my head.
The evening mist in the hills is soft.
The boulders on the road say communion.
The farm dogs look out of their eyes and keep thoughts from the corn
    cribs.
Dirt of the reeling earth holds horseshoes.
The rings in the whiffletree count their secrets.
Come on, you.

MASCOTS

I WILL keep you and bring hands to hold you against a great hunger.
I will run a spear in you for a great gladness to die with.
I will stab you between the ribs of the left side with a great love worth
    remembering.

THE SKYSCRAPER LOVES NIGHT

ONE by one lights of a skyscraper fling their checkering cross work on the
    velvet gown of night.

I believe the skyscraper loves night as a woman and brings her playthings
    she asks for, brings her a velvet gown,
And loves the white of her shoulders hidden under the dark feel of it all.

The masonry of steel looks to the night for somebody it loves,
He is a little dizzy and almost dances . . . waiting . . . dark . . .

NEVER BORN

THE time has gone by.
The child is dead.
The child was never even born.
Why go on? Why so much as begin?
How can we turn the clock back now
And not laugh at each other
As ashes laugh at ashes?

THIN STRIPS

IN a jeweler's shop I saw a man beating
out thin sheets of gold. I heard a woman
laugh many years ago.

Under a peach tree I saw petals scattered
. . . torn strips of a bride's dress. I heard
a woman laugh many years ago.

FIVE CENT BALLOONS

PIETRO has twenty red and blue balloons on a string.
They flutter and dance pulling Pietro's arm.
A nickel apiece is what they sell for.

Wishing children tag Pietro's heels.

He sells out and goes the streets alone.

MY PEOPLE

My people are gray,
    pigeon gray, dawn gray, storm gray.
I call them beautiful,
    and I wonder where they are going.

SWIRL

A swirl in the air where your head was once, here.
You walked under this tree, spoke to a moon for me
I might almost stand here and believe you alive.

WISTFUL

Wishes left on your lips
The mark of their wings.
Regrets fly kites in your eyes.

BASKET

Speak, sir, and be wise.
Speak choosing your words, sir,
    like an old woman over a bushel
    of apples.

FIRE PAGES

I will read ashes for you, if you ask me.
I will look in the fire and tell you from the gray lashes
And out of the red and black tongues and stripes,
I will tell how fire comes
And how fire runs far as the sea.

FINISH

DEATH comes once, let it be easy.
Ring one bell for me once, let it go at that.
Or ring no bell at all, better yet.

Sing one song if I die.
Sing John Brown's Body or Shout All Over God's Heaven.
Or sing nothing at all, better yet.

Death comes once, let it be easy.

FOR YOU

THE peace of great doors be for you.
Wait at the knobs, at the panel oblongs.
Wait for the great hinges.

The peace of great churches be for you,
Where the players of loft pipe organs
Practice old lovely fragments, alone.

The peace of great books be for you,
Stains of pressed clover leaves on pages,
Bleach of the light of years held in leather.

The peace of great prairies be for you.
Listen among windplayers in cornfields,
The wind learning over its oldest music.

The peace of great seas be for you.
Wait on a hook of land, a rock footing
For you, wait in the salt wash.

The peace of great mountains be for you,
The sleep and the eyesight of eagles,
Sheet mist shadows and the long look across.

The peace of great hearts be for you,
Valves of the blood of the sun,
Pumps of the strongest wants we cry.

The peace of great silhouettes be for you,
Shadow dancers alive in your blood now,
Alive and crying, "Let us out, let us out."

The peace of great changes be for you.
Whisper, Oh beginners in the hills.
Tumble, Oh cubs—tomorrow belongs to you.

The peace of great loves be for you.
Rain, soak these roots; wind, shatter the dry rot.
Bars of sunlight, grips of the earth, hug these.

The peace of great ghosts be for you,
Phantoms of night-gray eyes, ready to go
To the fog-star dumps, to the fire-white doors.

Yes, the peace of great phantoms be for you,
Phantom iron men, mothers of bronze,
Keepers of the lean clean breeds.

SLABS
OF THE SUNBURNT WEST

TO

HELGA

Slabs of the Sunburnt West

THE WINDY CITY

1

THE lean hands of wagon men
put out pointing fingers here,
picked this crossway, put it on a map,
set up their sawbucks, fixed their shotguns,
found a hitching place for the pony express,
made a hitching place for the iron horse,
the one-eyed horse with the fire-spit head,
found a homelike spot and said, "Make a home,"
saw this corner with a mesh of rails, shuttling
      people, shunting cars, shaping the junk of
      the earth to a new city.

The hands of men took hold and tugged
And the breaths of men went into the junk
And the junk stood up into skyscrapers and asked:
Who am I? Am I a city? And if I am what is my name?
And once while the time whistles blew and blew again
The men answered: Long ago we gave you a name,
Long ago we laughed and said: You? Your name is Chicago.

Early the red men gave a name to a river,
      the place of the skunk,
      the river of the wild onion smell,
      Shee-caw-go.

Out of the payday songs of steam shovels,
Out of the wages of structural iron rivets,
The living lighted skyscrapers tell it now as a name,

271

Tell it across miles of sea blue water, gray blue land:
I am Chicago, I am a name given out by the breaths of working men,
    laughing men, a child, a belonging.

So between the Great Lakes,
The Grand De Tour, and the Grand Prairie,
The living lighted skyscrapers stand,
Spotting the blue dusk with checkers of yellow,
    streamers of smoke and silver,
        parallelograms of night-gray watchmen,
Singing a soft moaning song: I am a child, a belonging.

2

How should the wind songs of a windy city go?
Singing in a high wind the dirty chatter gets blown
        away on the wind—the clean shovel,
                        the clean pickax,
                        lasts.

It is easy for a child to get breakfast and pack off
        to school with a pair of roller skates,
        buns for lunch, and a geography.
Riding through a tunnel under a river running backward,
        to school to listen . . . how the Pottawatomies . . .
        and the Blackhawks . . . ran on moccasins . . .
        between Kaskaskia, Peoria, Kankakee, and Chicago.

It is easy to sit listening to a boy babbling
        of the Pottawatomie moccasins in Illinois,
        how now the roofs and smokestacks cover miles
        where the deerfoot left its writing
        and the foxpaw put its initials
        in the snow . . . for the early moccasins . . . to read.

It is easy for the respectable taxpayers to sit in the
        streetcars and read the papers, faces of burglars,
        the prison escapes, the hunger strikes, the cost of
        living, the price of dying, the shop gate battles of
        strikers and strikebreakers, the strikers killing

scabs and the police killing strikers—the strongest,
the strongest, always the strongest.

It is easy to listen to the haberdasher customers hand each other their
    easy chatter—it is easy to die
    alive—to register a living thumbprint and be dead
    from the neck up.
And there are sidewalks polished with the footfalls of
    undertakers' stiffs, greased mannikins, wearing up-to-
    the-minute sox, lifting heels across doorsills,
    shoving their faces ahead of them—dead from the
    neck up—proud of their sox—their sox are the last
    word—dead from the neck up—it is easy.

3

Lash yourself to the bastion of a bridge
and listen while the black cataracts of people go by,
        baggage, bundles, balloons,
        listen while they jazz the classics:

      "Since when did you kiss yourself in
      And who do you think you are?
      Come across, kick in, loosen up.
      Where do you get that chatter?"

      "Beat up the short-change artists.
      They never did nothin' for you.
      How do you get that way?
      Tell me and I'll tell the world.
      I'll say so, I'll say it is."

      "You're trying to crab my act.
      You poor fish, you mackerel,
      You ain't got the sense God
      Gave an oyster—it's raining—
      What you want is an umbrella."

       "Hush baby—
      I don't know a thing.
      I don't know a thing.
       Hush baby."

"Hush baby,
It ain't how old you are,
It's how old you look.
It ain't what you got,
It's what you can get away with."

"Bring home the bacon.
Put it over, shoot it across.
    Send 'em to the cleaners.
What we want is results, re-sults
    And damn the consequences.
        Sh . . . sh. . . .
You can fix anything
If you got the right fixers."

"Kid each other, you cheap skates.
Tell each other you're all to the mustard—
You're the gravy."

"Tell 'em, honey.
Ain't it the truth, sweetheart?
    Watch your step.
    You said it.
    You said a mouthful.
We're all a lot of damn fourflushers."

"Hush baby!
    Shoot it,
    Shoot it all!
    Coo coo, coo coo"—
This is one song of Chicago.

4

It is easy to come here a stranger and show the whole works, write a
    book, fix it all up—it is easy to come and go away a muddle-headed
    pig, a bum and a bag of wind.

Go to it and remember this city fished from its
    depths a text: "independent as a hog on ice."

Venice is a dream of soft waters, Vienna and Bagdad recollections of dark
    spears and wild turbans; Paris is a thought in Monet gray on scab-
    bards, fabrics, façades; London is a fact in a fog filled with the moan-
    ing of transatlantic whistles; Berlin sits amid white scrubbed quad-
    rangles and torn arithmetics and testaments; Moscow brandishes a flag
    and repeats a dance figure of a man who walks like a bear.
Chicago fished from its depths a text: Independent
    as a hog on ice.

5

Forgive us if the monotonous houses go mile on mile
Along monotonous streets out to the prairies—
If the faces of the houses mumble hard words
At the streets—and the street voices only say:
"Dust and a bitter wind shall come."
Forgive us if the lumber porches and doorsteps
Snarl at each other—
And the brick chimneys cough in a close-up of
Each other's faces—
And the ramshackle stairways watch each other
As thieves watch—
And dooryard lilacs near a malleable iron works
Long ago languished
In a short whispering purple.

And if the alley ash cans
Tell the garbage-wagon drivers
The children play the alley is Heaven
And the streets of Heaven shine
With a grand dazzle of stones of gold
And there are no policemen in Heaven—
Let the rag-tags have it their way.

And if the geraniums
In the tin cans of the window sills
Ask questions not worth answering—
And if a boy and a girl hunt the sun
With a sieve for sifting smoke—
Let it pass—let the answer be—
"Dust and a bitter wind shall come."

Forgive us if the jazz timebeats
Of these clumsy mass shadows
Moan in saxophone undertones,
And the footsteps of the jungle,
The fang cry, the rip claw hiss,
The sneak-up and the still watch,
The slant of the slit eyes waiting—
If these bother respectable people
  with the right crimp in their napkins
  reading breakfast menu cards—
  forgive us—let it pass—let be.

If cripples sit on their stumps
And joke with the newsies bawling,
"Many lives lost! many lives lost!
Ter-ri-ble ac-ci-dent! many lives lost!"—
If again twelve men let a woman go,
"He done me wrong; I shot him"—
Or the blood of a child's head
Spatters on the hub of a motor truck—
Or a 44-gat cracks and lets the skylights
Into one more bank messenger—
Or if boys steal coal in a railroad yard
And run with humped gunnysacks
While a bull picks off one of the kids
And the kid wriggles with an ear in cinders
And a mother comes to carry home
A bundle, a limp bundle,
To have his face washed, for the last time,
Forgive us if it happens—and happens again—
And happens again.

  Forgive the jazz timebeat
  of clumsy mass shadows,
  footsteps of the jungle,
  the fang cry, the rip claw hiss,
  the slant of the slit eyes waiting.

Forgive us if we work so hard
And the muscles bunch clumsy on us

And we never know why we work so hard—
If the big houses with little families
And the little houses with big families
Sneer at each other's bars of misunderstanding;
Pity us when we shackle and kill each other
And believe at first we understand
And later say we wonder why.

Take home the monotonous patter
Of the elevated railroad guard in the rush hours:
"Watch your step. Watch your step. Watch your step."
Or write on a pocket pad what a pauper said
To a patch of purple asters at a whitewashed wall:
"Let every man be his own Jesus—that's enough."

6

The wheelbarrows grin, the shovels and the mortar
    hoist an exploit.
The stone shanks of the Monadnock, the Transportation,
    the People's Gas Building, stand up and scrape
    at the sky.
The wheelbarrows sing, the bevels and the blueprints
    whisper.
The library building named after Crerar, naked
    as a stock farm silo, light as a single eagle
    feather, stripped like an airplane propeller,
    takes a path up.
Two cool new rivets say, "Maybe it is morning,"
    "God knows."

Put the city up; tear the city down;
    put it up again; let us find a city.
Let us remember the little violet-eyed
    man who gave all, praying, "Dig and
    dream, dream and hammer, till your
    city comes."

Every day the people sleep and the city dies;
    every day the people shake loose, awake and
    build the city again.

The city is a tool chest opened every day,
    a time clock punched every morning,
    a shop door, bunkers and overalls
    counting every day.

The city is a balloon and a bubble plaything
    shot to the sky every evening, whistled in
    a ragtime jig down the sunset.

The city is made, forgotten, and made again,
    trucks hauling it away haul it back
    steered by drivers whistling ragtime
    against the sunsets.

Every day the people get up and carry the city,
    carry the bunkers and balloons of the city,
    lift it and put it down.

        "I will die as many times
        as you make me over again,
        says the city to the people,
I am the woman, the home, the family,
I get breakfast and pay the rent;
I telephone the doctor, the milkman, the undertaker;
    I fix the streets
    for your first and your last ride—
Come clean with me, come clean or dirty,
I am stone and steel of your sleeping numbers;
    I remember all you forget.
    I will die as many times
    as you make me over again."

Under the foundations,
Over the roofs,
The bevels and the blueprints talk it over.
The wind of the lake shore waits and wanders.
The heave of the shore wind hunches the sand piles.
The winkers of the morning stars count out cities
And forget the numbers.

7

At the white clock-tower
lighted in night purples
over the boulevard link bridge
only the blind get by without acknowledgments.

The passers-by, factory punch-clock numbers,
    hotel girls out for the air, teameoes,
    coal passers, taxi drivers, window washers,
    paperhangers, floorwalkers, bill collectors,
    burglar alarm salesmen, massage students,
    manicure girls, chiropodists, bath rubbers,
    booze runners, hat cleaners, armhole basters,
    delicatessen clerks, shovel stiffs, work plugs—
They all pass over the bridge, they all look up
    at the white clock-tower
    lighted in night purples
    over the boulevard link bridge—
    And sometimes one says, "Well, we hand it to 'em."

Mention proud things, catalogue them.
The jack-knife bridge opening, the ore boats,
    the wheat barges passing through.
Three overland trains arriving the same hour,
    one from Memphis and the cotton belt,
    one from Omaha and the corn belt,
    one from Duluth, the lumberjack and the iron range.
Mention a carload of shorthorns taken off the valleys of Wyoming last
    week, arriving yesterday, knocked in the head, stripped, quartered,
    hung in ice boxes today, mention the daily melodrama of this hum-
    drum, rhythms of heads, hides, heels, hoofs hung up.

8

It is wisdom to think the people are the city.
It is wisdom to think the city would fall to pieces
    and die and be dust in the wind.
If the people of the city all move away and leave no people at all to watch
    and keep the city.

It is wisdom to think no city stood here at all until the working men, the
     laughing men, came.
It is wisdom to think tomorrow new working men, new laughing men, may
     come and put up a new city—
Living lighted skyscrapers and a night lingo of lanterns testify tomorrow
     shall have its own say-so.

                              9

Night gathers itself into a ball of dark yarn.
Night loosens the ball and it spreads.
The lookouts from the shores of Lake Michigan
          find night follows day, and ping! ping! across
          sheet gray the boat lights put their signals.
Night lets the dark yarn unravel, Night speaks and the yarns change to
     fog and blue strands.

The lookouts turn to the city.
The canyons swarm with red sand lights
          of the sunset.
The atoms drop and sift, blues cross over,
          yellows plunge.
Mixed light shafts stack their bayonets,
          pledge with crossed handles.
So, when the canyons swarm, it is then the
          lookouts speak
Of the high spots over a street . . . mountain language
Of skyscrapers in dusk, the Railway Exchange,
The People's Gas, the Monadnock, the Transportation,
Gone to the gloaming.

The river turns in a half circle.
The Goose Island bridges curve
          over the river curve.
          Then the river panorama
          performs for the bridge,
          dots . . . lights . . . dots . . . lights,
          sixes and sevens of dots and lights,
          a lingo of lanterns and searchlights,
          circling sprays of gray and yellow.

10

A man came as a witness saying:
"I listened to the Great Lakes
And I listened to the Grand Prairie,
And they had little to say to each other,
A whisper or so in a thousand years.
'Some of the cities are big,' said one.
'And some not so big,' said another.
'And sometimes the cities are all gone,'
Said a black knob bluff to a light green sea."

Winds of the Windy City, come out of the prairie,
        all the way from Medicine Hat.
Come out of the inland sea blue water, come where
        they nickname a city for you.

Corn wind in the fall, come off the black lands,
        come off the whisper of the silk hangers,
        the lap of the flat spear leaves.

Blue water wind in summer, come off the blue miles
        of lake, carry your inland sea blue fingers,
        carry us cool, carry your blue to our homes.

White spring winds, come off the bag wool clouds,
        come off the running melted snow, come white
        as the arms of snow-born children.

Gray fighting winter winds, come along on the tear-
        ing blizzard tails, the snouts of the hungry
        hunting storms, come fighting gray in winter.

Winds of the Windy City,
Winds of corn and sea blue,
Spring wind white and fighting winter gray,
Come home here—they nickname a city for you.

The wind of the lake shore waits and wanders.
The heave of the shore wind hunches the sand piles.
The winkers of the morning stars count out cities
And forget the numbers.

WASHINGTON MONUMENT BY NIGHT

1

THE stone goes straight.
A lean swimmer dives into night sky,
Into half-moon mist.

2

Two trees are coal black.
This is a great white ghost between.
It is cool to look at.
Strong men, strong women, come here.

3

Eight years is a long time
To be fighting all the time.

4

The republic is a dream.
Nothing happens unless first a dream.

5

The wind bit hard at Valley Forge one Christmas.
Soldiers tied rags on their feet.
Red footprints wrote on the snow . . .
. . . and stone shoots into stars here
. . . into half-moon mist tonight.

6

Tongues wrangled dark at a man.
He buttoned his overcoat and stood alone.
In a snowstorm, red hollyberries, thoughts,
    he stood alone.

7

Women said: He is lonely
. . . fighting . . . fighting . . . eight years . . .

8

The name of an iron man goes over the world.
It takes a long time to forget an iron man.

9

. . . .
. . . .

AND SO TODAY

AND so today—they lay him away—
the boy nobody knows the name of—
the buck private—the unknown soldier—
the doughboy who dug under and died
when they told him to—that's him.

Down Pennsylvania Avenue today the riders go,
men and boys riding horses, roses in their teeth,
stems of roses, rose leaf stalks, rose dark leaves—
the line of the green ends in a red rose flash.

Skeleton men and boys riding skeleton horses,
the rib bones shine, the rib bones curve,
shine with savage, elegant curves—
a jawbone runs with a long white slant,
a skull dome runs with a long white arch,
bone triangles click and rattle,
elbows, ankles, white line slants—
shining in the sun, past the White House,
past the Treasury Building, Army and Navy Buildings,
on to the mystic white Capitol Dome—
so they go down Pennsylvania Avenue today,
skeleton men and boys riding skeleton horses,
stems of roses in their teeth,

rose dark leaves at their white jaw slants—
and a horse laugh question nickers and whinnies,
moans with a whistle out of horse head teeth:
why? who? where?

      ("The big fish—eat the little fish—
      the little fish—eat the shrimps—
      and the shrimps—eat mud"—
      said a cadaverous man—with a black umbrella—
      spotted with white polka dots—with a missing
      ear—with a missing foot and arms—
      with a missing sheath of muscles
      singing to the silver sashes of the sun.)

And so today—they lay him away—
the boy nobody knows the name of—
the buck private—the unknown soldier—
the doughboy who dug under and died
when they told him to—that's him.

If he picked himself and said, "I am ready to die,"
if he gave his name and said, "My country, take me,"
then the baskets of roses today are for the Boy,
the flowers, the songs, the steamboat whistles,
the proclamations of the honorable orators,
they are all for the Boy—that's him.

If the government of the Republic picked him saying,
"You are wanted, your country takes you"—
if the Republic put a stethoscope to his heart
and looked at his teeth and tested his eyes and said,
"You are a citizen of the Republic and a sound animal
in all parts and functions—the Republic takes you"—
then today the baskets of flowers are all for the Republic,
the roses, the songs, the steamboat whistles,
the proclamations of the honorable orators—
they are all for the Republic.

And so today—they lay him away—
and an understanding goes—his long sleep shall be

under arms and arches near the Capitol Dome—
there is an authorization—he shall have tomb companions—
the martyred presidents of the Republic—
the buck private—the unknown soldier—that's him.

The man who was war commander of the armies of the Republic
rides down Pennsylvania Avenue—
The man who is peace commander of the armies of the Republic
rides down Pennsylvania Avenue—
for the sake of the Boy, for the sake of the Republic.

    (And the hoofs of the skeleton horses
    all drum soft on the asphalt footing—
    so soft is the drumming, so soft the roll call
    of the grinning sergeants calling the roll call—
    so soft is it all—a camera man murmurs, "Moonshine.")

Look—who salutes the coffin—
lays a wreath of remembrance
on the box where a buck private
sleeps a clean dry sleep at last—
look—it is the highest ranking general
of the officers of the armies of the Republic.

    (Among pigeon corners of the Congressional Library—they file docu-
    ments quietly, casually, all in a day's work—this human document,
    the buck private nobody knows the name of—they file away in granite
    and steel—with music and roses, salutes, proclamations of the hon-
    orable orators.)

Across the country, between two ocean shore lines,
where cities cling to rail and water routes,
there people and horses stop in their foot tracks,
cars and wagons stop in their wheel tracks—
faces at street crossings shine with a silence
of eggs laid in a row on a pantry shelf—
among the ways and paths of the flow of the Republic
faces come to a standstill, sixty clockticks count—
in the name of the Boy, in the name of the Republic.

(A million faces a thousand miles from Pennsylvania Avenue stay frozen with a look, a clocktick, a moment—skeleton riders on skeleton horses—the nickering high horse laugh, the whinny and the howl up Pennsylvania Avenue: who? why? where?)

(So people far from the asphalt footing of Pennsylvania Avenue look, wonder, mumble—the riding white-jaw phantoms ride hi-eeee, hi-eeee, hi-yi, hi-yi, hi-eeee—the proclamations of the honorable orators mix with the top-sergeants whistling the roll call.)

If when the clockticks counted sixty,
when the heartbeats of the Republic
came to a stop for a minute,
if the Boy had happened to sit up,
happening to sit up as Lazarus sat up, in the story,
then the first shivering language to drip off his mouth
might have come as, "Thank God," or "Am I dreaming?"
or "What the hell" or "When do we eat?"
or "Kill 'em, kill 'em, the . . ."
or "Was that . . . a rat . . . ran over my face?"
or "For Christ's sake, gimme water, gimme water,"
or "Blub blub, bloo bloo. . . . . . ."
or any bubbles of shell-shock gibberish
from the gashes of No Man's Land.

Maybe some buddy knows,
some sister, mother, sweetheart,
maybe some girl who sat with him once
when a two-horn silver moon
slid on the peak of a house-roof gable,
and promises lived in the air of the night,
when the air was filled with promises,
when any little slip-shoe lovey
could pick a promise out of the air.

      "Feed it to 'em,
      they lap it up,
      bull . . . bull . . . bull,"
Said a movie newsreel camera man,
Said a Washington newspaper correspondent,

Said a baggage handler lugging a trunk,
Said a two-a-day vaudeville juggler,
Said a hanky-pank selling jumping-jacks.
"Hokum—they lap it up," said the bunch.

And a tall scar-face ball player,
Played out as a ball player,
Made a speech of his own for the hero boy,
Sent an earful of his own to the dead buck private:
    "It's all safe now, buddy,
    Safe when you say yes,
    Safe for the yes-men."

He was a tall scar-face battler
With his face in a newspaper
Reading want ads, reading jokes,
Reading love, murder, politics,
Jumping from jokes back to the want ads,
Reading the want ads first and last,
The letters of the word JOB, "J-O-B,"
Burnt like a shot of bootleg booze
In the bones of his head—
In the wish of his scar-face eyes.
The honorable orators,
Always the honorable orators,
Buttoning the buttons on their prinz alberts,
Pronouncing the syllables "sac-ri-fice,"
Juggling those bitter salt-soaked syllables—
Do they ever gag with hot ashes in their mouths?
Do their tongues ever shrivel with a pain of fire
Across those simple syllables "sac-ri-fice"?

(There was one orator people far off saw.
He had on a gunnysack shirt over his bones,
And he lifted an elbow socket over his head,
And he lifted a skinny signal finger.
And he had nothing to say, nothing easy—
He mentioned ten million men, mentioned them as having gone west,
    mentioned them as shoving up the daisies.

We could write it all on a postage stamp, what he said.
He said it and quit and faded away,
A gunnysack shirt on his bones.)

    Stars of the night sky,
    did you see that phantom fadeout,
    did you see those phantom riders,
    skeleton riders on skeleton horses,
    stems of roses in their teeth,
    rose leaves red on white-jaw slants,
    grinning along on Pennsylvania Avenue,
    the top-sergeants calling roll calls—
    did their horses nicker a horse laugh?
    did the ghosts of the boney battalions
    move out and on, up the Potomac, over on the Ohio,
    and out to the Mississippi, the Missouri, the Red River,
    and down to the Rio Grande, and on to the Yazoo,
    over to the Chattahoochee and up to the Rappahannock?
    did you see 'em, stars of the night sky?

    And so today—they lay him away—
    the boy nobody knows the name of—
    they lay him away in granite and steel—
    with music and roses—under a flag—
    under a sky of promises.

BLACK HORIZONS

    BLACK horizons, come up.
    Black horizons, kiss me.
    That is all; so many lies; killing so cheap;
    babies so cheap; blood, people, so cheap; and
    land high, land dear; a speck of the earth
    costs; a suck at the tit of Mother Dirt so
    clean and strong, it costs; fences, papers,
    sheriffs; fences, laws, guns; and so many
    stars and so few hours to dream; such a big
    song and so little a footing to stand and

sing; take a look; wars to come; red rivers
to cross.
Black horizons, come up.
Black horizons, kiss me.

SEA SLANT

On up the sea slant,
On up the horizon,
This ship limps.

The bone of her nose fog-gray,
The heart of her sea-strong,
She came a long way,
She goes a long way.

On up the horizon,
On up the sea-slant,
She limps sea-strong, fog-gray.

She is a green-lit night gray.
She comes and goes in sea fog.
Up the horizon slant she limps.

UPSTREAM

The strong men keep coming on.
They go down shot, hanged, sick,
    broken.
They live on fighting, singing,
    lucky as plungers.
The strong mothers pulling them
    on . . .
The strong mothers pulling them
    from a dark sea, a great prairie,
    a long mountain.
Call hallelujah, call amen, call
    deep thanks.
The strong men keep coming on.

FOUR STEICHEN PRINTS

THE earth, the rock and the oil of the earth, the slippery frozen places of the earth, these are for homes of rainbow bubbles, curves of the circles of a bubble, curves of the arcs of the rainbow prisms—between sun and rock they lift to the sun their foam feather and go.

. . .

Throw your neck back, throw it back till the neck muscles shine at the sun, till the falling hair at the scalp is a black cry, till limbs and knee bones form an altar, and a girl's torso over the fire-rock torso shouts hi yi, hi yee, hallelujah.

. . .

Goat girl caught in the brambles, deerfoot or fox-head, ankles and hair of feeders of the wind, let all the covering burn, let all stopping a naked plunger from plunging naked, let it all burn in this wind fire, let the fire have it in a fast crunch and a flash.

. . .

They threw you into a pot of thorns with a wreath in your hair and bunches of grapes over your head—your hard little buttocks in the thorns—then the black eyes, the white teeth, the nameless muscular flair of you, rippled and twisted in sliding rising scales of laughter; the earth never had a gladder friend; pigs, goats, deer, tawny tough-haired jaguars might understand you.

FINS

PLOW over bars of sea plowing,
the moon by moon work of the sea,
the plowing, sand and rock, must
be done.

Ride over, ride over bars of sea riding,
the sun and the blue riding of the sea—
sit in the saddles and say it, sea riders.

Slant up and go, silver breakers; mix
the high howls of your dancing; shoot
your laugh of rainbow foam tops.

Foam wings, fly; pick the comers, the fin pink,
the belly green, the blue rain sparks, the
white wave spit—fly, you foam wings.

The men of the sea are gone to work; the women
of the sea are off buying new hats, combs, clocks;
it is rust and gold on the roofs of the sea.

BEAT, OLD HEART

BEAT, old heart, these are the old bars
All strugglers have beat against.
Beat on these bars like the old sea
Beats on the rocks and beaches.
Beat here like the old winter winds
Beat on the prairies and timbers.
Old grizzlies, eagles, buffalo,
Their paws and beaks register this.
Their hides and heads say it with scars.

MOON RIDERS

1

WHAT have I saved out of a morning?
The earliest of the morning came with moon-mist
And the travel of a moon-spilt purple;
    Bars, horseshoes, Texas longhorns,
    Linked in night silver,
    Linked under leaves in moonlit silver,
    Linked in rags and patches
Out of the ice houses of the morning moon.
Yes, this was the earliest—
Before the cowpunchers on the eastern rims

Began riding into the sun,
Riding the roan mustangs of morning,
Roping the mavericks after the latest stars.
What have I saved out of a morning?
Was there a child face I saw once
Smiling up a stairway of the morning moon?

2

"It is time for work," said a man in the morning.
He opened the faces of the clocks, saw their works,
Saw the wheels oiled and fitted, running smooth.
"It is time to begin a day's work," he said again,
Watching a bull-finch hop on the rain-worn boards
Of a beaten fence counting its bitter winters.
The slinging feet of the bull-finch and the flash
Of its flying feathers as it flipped away
Took his eyes away from the clocks, his flying eyes.
He walked over, stood in front of the clocks again
And said, "I'm sorry; I apologize forty ways."

3

The morning paper lay bundled
Like a spear in a museum
Across the broken sleeping room
Of a moon-sheet spider.
The spinning work of the morning spider's feet
Left off where the morning paper's pages lay
In the shine of the web in the summer dew grass.
The man opened the morning paper, saw the first page,
The back page, the inside pages, the editorials,
Saw the world go by, eating, stealing, fighting,
Saw the headlines, date lines, funnies, ads,
The marching movies of the workmen going to work, the workmen striking,
The workmen asking jobs—five million pairs of eyes look for a boss and
    say, "Take me,"
People eating with too much to eat, people eating with nothing in sight
    to eat tomorrow, eating as though eating belongs where people belong.

"Hustle, you hustlers, while the hustling's good,"
Said the man, turning the morning paper's pages,

Turning among headlines, date lines, funnies, ads.
"Hustlers carrying the banner," said the man
Dropping the paper and beginning to hunt the city,
Hunting the alleys, boulevards, back-door by-ways,
Hunting till he found a blind horse dying alone,
Telling the horse, "Two legs or four legs—it's all the same with a work
    plug."

    A hayfield mist of evening saw him
    Watching moon riders lose the moon
    For new shooting stars—he asked,
"Christ, what have I saved out of a morning?"
He called up a stairway of the morning moon
And he remembered a child face smiling up that same stairway.

AT THE GATES OF TOMBS

    CIVILIZATIONS are set up and knocked down
    the same as pins in a bowling alley.

    Civilizations get into the garbage wagons
    and are hauled away the same as potato
    peelings or any pot scrapings.

    Civilizations, all the work of the artists,
    inventors, dreamers of work and genius,
    go to the dumps one by one.

    Be silent about it; since at the gates of tombs
    silence is a gift, be silent; since at the epitaphs
    written in the air, since at the swan songs hung in
    the air, silence is a gift, be silent; forget it.

    If any fool, babbler, gabby mouth, stand up and say:
    Let us make a civilization where the sacred and
    beautiful things of toil and genius shall last—

    If any such noisy gazook stands up and makes himself
    heard—put him out—tie a can on him—lock him up

in Leavenworth—shackle him in the Atlanta hoosegow
—let him eat from the tin dishes at Sing Sing—
slew him in as a lifer at San Quentin.

It is the law; as a civilization dies and goes down
to eat ashes along with all other dead civilizations
—it is the law all dirty wild dreamers die first—
gag 'em, lock 'em up, get 'em bumped off.

And since at the gates of tombs silence is a gift,
be silent about it, yes, be silent—forget it.

HAZARDOUS OCCUPATIONS

Jugglers keep six bottles in the air.
Club swingers toss up six and eight.
The knife throwers miss each other's
        ears by a hair and the steel quivers
        in the target wood.
The trapeze battlers do a back-and-forth
        high in the air with a girl's feet
        and ankles upside down.
So they earn a living—till they miss
        once, twice, even three times.
So they live on hate and love as gypsies
        live in satin skins and shiny eyes.
In their graves do the elbows jostle once
        in a blue moon—and wriggle to throw
        a kiss answering a dreamed-of applause?
Do the bones repeat: It's a good act—
        we got a good hand . . . ?

PROPS

1

Roll open this rug a minx is
in it; see her toe wiggling;
roll open the rug; she is a

runaway; or somebody is trying
to steal her; here she is;
here's your minx; how can we
have a play unless we have
this minx?

2

The child goes out in the storm
stage thunder; "erring daughter,
never darken this doorsill again";
the tender parents speak their curse;
the child puts a few knick-knacks in
a handkerchief; and the child goes;
the door closes and the child goes;
she is out now, in the storm on the
stage, out forever; snow, you son-of-a-gun,
snow, turn on the snow.

GYPSY MOTHER

IN a hole-in-a-wall on Halsted Street sits a gypsy woman,
In a garish gas-lit rendezvous, in a humpback higgling hole-in-a-wall.

The left hand is a tattler; stars and oaths and alphabets
Commit themselves and tell happenings gone, happenings to come, path-
ways of honest people, hypocrites.

"Long pointed fingers mean imagination; a star on the third finger says a
black shadow walks near."
Cross the gypsy's hand with fifty cents and she takes your left hand and
reads how you shall be happy in love, or not, and whether you die
rich, or not.
Signs outside the hole-in-a-wall say so, misspell the promises, scrawl the
superior gypsy mysteries.

A red shawl on her shoulders falls with a fringe hem to a green skirt;
Chains óf yellow beads sweep from her neck to her tawny hands.
Fifty springtimes must have kissed her mouth holding a calabash pipe.
She pulls slow contemplative puffs of smoke; she is a shape for ghosts of

contemplation to sit around and ask why something cheap as happiness is here and more besides, chapped lips, rough eyes, red shawl.
She is thinking about somebody and something the same as Whistler's mother sat and thought about somebody and something.

In a hole-in-a-wall on Halsted Street are stars, oaths, alphabets.

GOLD MUD
(For R. F.)

THE pot of gold at the rainbow end
    is a pot of mud, gold mud,
    slippery shining mud.

Pour it on your hair and you will
    have a golden hair.
Pour it on your cat and you will
    have a golden cat.
Pour it on your clock and you will
    have a golden clock.

Pour it on a dead man's thumb and
    you will have a golden thumb
    to bring you bad dreams.
Pour it on a dead woman's ear and
    you will have a golden ear
    to tell hard luck stories to.
Pour it on a horse chestnut and you
    will have a golden buckeye
    changing your luck.
Pour it in the shape of a holy cross,
    fasten it on my shirt for me to wear
    and I will have a keepsake.
I will touch it and say a prayer for you.

CROSSING THE PACES

The Sioux sat around their wigwam fires
in winter with some papooses hung up
and some laid down.
And the Sioux had a saying, "Love grows
like hair on a black bear's skin."

The Arabians spill this: The first gray
hair is a challenge of death.
A Polish blacksmith: A good black-
smith is not afraid of smoke.
And a Scandinavian warns: The world was born
in fire and he who is fire himself will be
at home anywhere on earth.
So a stranger told his children: You are
strangers—and warned them:

Bob your hair; or let it grow long;
Be a company, a party, a picnic;
Be alone, a nut, a potato, an orange blossom,
    a keg of nails; if you get lost try a
    want ad; if night comes try a long sleep.

COUPLES

Six miasmic women in green
danced an absinthe dance
hissing oaths of laughter
at six men they cheated.

Six miasmic men did the same
for six women they cheated.

It was a stand-off
in oaths of laughter hissed;

The dirt is hard where they danced.
The pads of their feet made a floor.

The weeds wear moon mist mourning veils.
The weeds come high as six little crosses,
   One little cross for each couple.

CALIGARI

MANNIKINS, we command you.
Stand up with your white beautiful skulls.
Stand up with your moaning sockets.
Dance your stiff limping dances.
We handle you with spic and span gloves.
We tell you when and how
And how much.

FEATHER LIGHTS

MACABRE and golden the moon opened a slant of light.

A triangle for an oriole to stand and sing, "Take me home."

A layer of thin white gold feathers for a child queen of gypsies.

So the moon opened a slant of light and let it go.

So the lonesome dogs, the fog moon, the pearl mist, came back.

PEARL HORIZONS

UNDER a prairie fog moon
in a circle of pearl mist horizons,
a few lonesome dogs scraping thongs,
midnight is lonely; the fog moon midnight
takes up again its even smooth November.

Memories: you can flick me and sting me.
Memories, you can hold me even and smooth.

A circle of pearl mist horizons
is not a woman to be walked up to and kissed,
nor a child to be taken and held for a good night,
nor any old coffee-drinking pal to be smiled at in the eyes and left with
    a grip and a handshake.

Pearl memories in the mist circling the horizon,
flick me, sting me, hold me even and smooth.

HOOF DUSK

THE dusk of this box wood
is leather gold, buckskin gold,
and the hoofs of a dusk goat
leave their heel marks on it.

The cover of this wooden box
is a last-of-the-sunset red,
a red with a sandman sand
fixed in evening siftings—
late evening sands are here.

The gold of old clocks,
forgotten in garrets,
hidden out between battles
of long wars and short wars,
the smoldering ember gold
of old clocks found again—
here is the small smoke fadeout
of their slow loitering.

Feel me with your fingers,
measure me in fire and wind:
maybe I am buckskin gold, old clock gold,
late evening sunset sand—
               Let go
               and loiter
               in the smoke fadeout.

HARSK, HARSK

1

Harsk, harsk, the wind blows tonight.
What a night for a baby to come into the world!
What a night for a melodrama baby to come
    And the father wondering
    And the mother wondering
What the years will bring on their stork feet
Till a year when this very baby might be saying
On some storm night when a melodrama baby is born:
    "What a night
    for a baby
    to come into the world!!"
Harsk, harsk, the wind blows tonight.

2

It is five months off.
Knit, stitch, and hemstitch.
Sheets, bags, towels, these are the offerings.
When he is older—or she is a big girl—
There may be flowers or ribbons or money
For birthday offerings. Now, however,
We must remember it is a naked stranger
Coming to us, and the sheath of the arrival
Is so soft we must be ready, and soft too.
Knit, stitch, hemstitch, it is only five months.

3

It would be easy to pick a lucky star for this baby
If a choice of two stars lay before our eyes,
One a pearl gold star and one pearl silver,
And the offer of a chance to pick a lucky star.

4

When the high hour comes
Let there be a light flurry of snow,
A little zigzag of white spots
    Against the gray roofs.
The snow-born all understand this as a luck-wish.

BRANCUSI

BRANCUSI is a galoot; he saves tickets to take him nowhere; a galoot with his baggage ready and no timetable; ah yes, Brancusi is a galoot; he understands birds and skulls so well, he knows the hang of the hair of the coils and plaits on a woman's head, he knows them so far back he knows where they came from and where they are going; he is fathoming down for the secrets of the first and the oldest makers of shapes.

Let us speak with loose mouths today not at all about Brancusi because he has hardly started nor is hardly able to say the name of the place he wants to go when he has time and is ready to start; O Brancusi, keeping hardwood planks around your doorsteps in the sun waiting for the hardwood to be harder for your hard hands to handle, you Brancusi with your chisels and hammers, birds going to cones, skulls going to eggs—how the hope hugs your heart you will find one cone, one egg, so hard when the earth turns mist there among the last to go will be a cone, an egg.

Brancusi, you will not put a want ad in the papers telling God it will be to his advantage to come around and see you; you will not grow gabby and spill God earfuls of prayers; you will not get fresh and familiar as if God is a next-door neighbor and you have counted His shirts on a clothes line; you will go stammering, stuttering and mumbling or you will be silent as a mouse in a church garret when the pipe organ is pouring ocean waves on the sunlit rocks of ocean shores; if God is saving a corner for any battling bag of bones, there will be one for you, there will be one for you, Brancusi.

AMBASSADORS OF GRIEF

THERE was a little fliv of a woman loved one man and lost out. And she took up with another and it was a blank again. And she cried to God the whole layout was a fake and a frame-up. And when she took up with Number Three she found the fires burnt out, the love power, gone. And she wrote a letter to God and dropped it in a mail-box. The letter said:

O God, ain't there some way you can fix it up so the little flivs of women, ready to throw themselves in front of railroad trains for men they love, can have a chance? I guessed the wrong keys, I battered on the wrong panels, I picked the wrong roads. O God, ain't there no way to guess again and start all over back where I had the keys in my hands, back where the roads all came together and I had my pick?

And the letter went to Washington, D. C., dumped into a dump where all letters go addressed to God—and no house number.

WITHOUT THE CANE AND THE DERBY
(For C. C.)

THE woman had done him wrong.
Either that . . . or the woman was clean as a white rose in the morning
gauze of dew.
It was either one or the other or it was the two things, right and wrong,
woven together like two braids of a woman's head of hair hanging
down woven together.

The room is dark. The door opens. It is Charlie playing for his friends
after dinner, "the marvelous urchin, the little genius of the screen,"
(chatter it like a monkey's running laughter cry.)
No . . . it is not Charlie . . . it is somebody else. It is a man, gray
shirt, bandana, dark face. A candle in his left hand throws a slant
of light on the dark face. The door closes slow. The right hand leaves
the door knob slow.

He looks at something. What is it? A white sheet on a table. He takes
two long soft steps. He runs the candle light around a hump in the
sheet. He lifts the sheet slow, sad like.
A woman's head of hair shows, a woman's white face. He takes the head
between his hands and looks long at it. His fingers trickle under the
sheet, snap loose something, bring out fingers full of a pearl neck-
lace.
He covers the face and the head of hair with the white sheet. He takes
a step toward the door. The necklace slips into his pocket off the
fingers of his right hand. His left hand lifts the candle for a good-by
look.

Knock, knock, knock. A knocking the same as the time of the human
heartbeat.

Knock, knock, knock, first louder, then lower. Knock, knock, knock, the
same as the time of the human heartbeat.

He sets the candle on the floor . . . leaps to the white sheet . . . rips it
back . . . has his fingers at the neck, his thumbs at the throat, and
does three slow fierce motions of strangling.

The knocking stops. All is quiet. He covers the face and the head of hair
with the white sheet, steps back, picks up the candle and listens.

Knock, knock, knock, a knocking the same as the time of the human
heartbeat.

Knock, knock, knock, first louder, then lower. Knock, knock, knock, the
same as the time of the human heartbeat.

Again the candle to the floor, the leap, the slow fierce motions of
strangling, the cover-up of the face and the head of hair, the step
back, the listening.

And again the knock, knock, knock . . . louder . . . lower . . . to the
time of the human heartbeat.

Once more the motions of strangling . . . then . . . nothing at all . . .
nothing at all . . . no more knocking . . . no knocking at all . . .
no knocking at all . . . in the time of the human heartbeat.

He stands at the door . . . peace, peace, peace everywhere only in the
man's face so dark and his eyes so lighted up with many lights, no
peace at all, no peace at all.

So he stands at the door, his right hand on the door knob, the candle
slants of light fall and flicker from his face to the straight white sheet
changing gray against shadows.

So there is peace everywhere . . . no more knocking . . . no knocking
at all to the time of the human heartbeat . . . so he stands at the
door and his right hand on the door knob.

And there is peace everywhere . . . only the man's face is a red gray
plaster of storm in the center of peace . . . so he stands with a
candle at the door . . . so he stands with a red gray face.

After he steps out the door closes; the door, the door knob, the table, the
white sheet, there is nothing at all; the owners are shadows; the
owners are gone; not even a knocking; not even a knock, knock,
knock . . . louder, lower, in the time of the human heartbeat.

The lights are snapped on. Charlie, "the marvelous urchin, the little
    genius of the screen" (chatter it with a running monkey's laughter
    cry) Charlie is laughing a laugh the whole world knows.
The room is full of cream yellow lights. Charlie is laughing . . . louder
    . . . lower . . .
And again the heartbeats laugh . . . the human heartbeats laugh. . . .

THE RAKEOFF AND THE GETAWAY

"SHALL we come back?" the gamblers asked.
"If you want to, if you feel that way," the answer.

And they must have wanted to,
they must have felt that way;
for they came back,
hats pulled down over their eyes
as though the rain or the policemen
or the shadows of a sneaking scar-face Nemesis
followed their tracks and hunted them down.

"What was the clean-up? Let's see the rakeoff,"
somebody asked them, looking into their eyes
far under the pulled-down hat rims;
and their eyes had only the laugh of the rain in them,
lights of escape from a sneaking scar-face Nemesis
hunting their tracks, hunting them down.

Anvils, pincers, mosquitoes, anguish, raspberries,
steaks and gravy, remorse, ragtime, slang,
a woman's looking-glass to be held in the hand
for looking at the face and the face make-up,
blackwing birds fitted onto slits
of the sunsets they were flying into,
bitter green waters, clear running waters,
standing pools ringing the changes
of all the triangles of the equinoxes of the sky,
    and a woman's slipper
    with a tarnished buckle,
    a tarnished Chinese silver buckle.

The gamblers snatched their hats off babbling,
"Some layout—take your pick, kid."

And their eyes had yet in them
the laugh of the rain
and the lights of their getaway
from a sneaking scar-face Nemesis.

TWO HUMPTIES

THEY tried to hand it to us on a platter,
Us hit in the eyes with marconigrams from moon dancers—
And the bubble busted, went flooey, on a thumb touch.

  So this time again, Humpty,
We cork our laughs behind solemn phizzogs,
Sweep the floor with the rim of our hats
And say good-a-by and good-a-by, just like that.

    Tomorrow maybe they will be hit
    in the eyes with marconigrams
    From moon dancers.
Good-a-by, our hats and all of us say good-a-by.

IMPROVED FARM LAND

TALL timber stood here once, here on a corn belt farm along the Monon.
Here the roots of a half mile of trees dug their runners deep in the loam
    for a grip and a hold against wind storms.
Then the axmen came and the chips flew to the zing of steel and handle—
    the lank railsplitters cut the big ones first, the beeches and the oaks,
    then the brush.
Dynamite, wagons and horses took the stumps—the plows sunk their
    teeth in—now it is first class corn land—improved property—and the
    hogs grunt over the fodder crops.
It would come hard now for this half mile of improved farm land along
    the Monon corn belt, on a piece of Grand Prairie, to remember once
    it had a great singing family of trees.

HELL ON THE WABASH

When country fiddlers held a convention in
Danville, the big money went to a barn dance
artist who played Turkey in the Straw, with
variations.
They asked him the name of the piece calling
it a humdinger and he answered, "I call it
'Hell On The Wabash.'"
The two next best were The Speckled Hen, and
Sweet Potatoes Grow in Sandy Land, with
variations.

THIS—FOR THE MOON—YES?

This is a good book? Yes?
Throw it at the moon.
Stand on the ball of your right foot
And come to the lunge of a center fielder
Straddling in a throw for the home plate,
Let her go—spang—this book for the moon
        —yes?
And then—other books, good books, even the
        best books—shoot 'em with a long twist
        at the moon—yes?

PRIMER LESSON

Look out how you use proud words.
When you let proud words go, it is
        not easy to call them back.
They wear long boots, hard boots; they
        walk off proud; they can't hear you
        calling—
Look out how you use proud words.

SLABS OF THE SUNBURNT WEST

1

Into the night, into the blanket of night,
Into the night rain gods, the night luck gods,
Overland goes the overland passenger train.

Stand up, sandstone slabs of red,
Tell the overland passengers who burnt you.

Tell 'em how the jacks and screws loosened you.
Tell 'em who shook you by the heels and stood you on your heads,
Who put the slow pink of sunset mist on your faces.

Panels of the cold gray open night,
Gates of the Great American Desert,
    Skies keeping the prayers of the wagon men,
    The riders with picks, shovels and guns,
On the old trail, the Santa Fé trail, the Raton pass
Panels, skies, gates, listen tonight while we send up our prayers on the
    Santa Fé trail.

    (A colossal bastard frog
    squats in stone.
    Once he squawked.
    Then he was frozen and
    shut up forever.)

Into the night the overland passenger train,
Slabs of sandstone red sink to the sunset red,
Blankets of night cover 'em up.
Night rain gods, night luck gods, are looking on.

March on, processions.
Tie your hat to the saddle and ride, O Rider.
Let your ponies drag their navels in the sand.
Go hungry; leave your bones in the desert sand.
When the desert takes you the wind is clean.
The winds say so on a noisy night.

The fingerbone of a man
lay next to the handle of a frying pan
and the footbone of a horse.
"Clean, we are clean," the winds whimper on a noisy night.

Into the night the overland passenger train,
And the engineer with an eye for signal lights,
And the porters making up berths for passengers,
And the boys in the diner locking the icebox—
And six men with cigars in the buffet car mention "civilization," "history," "God."

Into the blanket of night goes the overland train,
Into the black of the night the processions march,
      The ghost of a pony goes by,
      A hat tied to the saddle,
      The wagon tongue of a prairie schooner
      And the handle of a Forty-niner's pickax
      Do a shiver dance in the desert dust,
      In the coyote gray of the alkali dust.
And—six men with cigars in the buffet car mention "civilization," "history," "God."

Sleep, O wonderful hungry people.
Take a shut-eye, take a long old snooze,
      and be good to yourselves;
Into the night the overland passenger train
And the sleepers cleared for a morning sun
      and the Grand Canyon of Arizona.

2

      A bluejay blue
      and a gray mouse gray
      ran up the canyon walls.

A rider came to the rim
Of a slash and a gap of desert dirt—
A long-legged long-headed rider
On a blunt and a blurry jackass—
Riding and asking, "How come? How come?"

And the long-legged long-headed rider said:
"Between two ears of a blurry jackass
I see ten miles of auburn, gold and purple—
I see doors open over doorsills
And always another door and a doorsill.
Cheat my eyes, fill me with the float
Of your dream, you auburn, gold, and purple.
Cheat me, blow me off my pins onto footless floors.
Let me put footsteps in an airpath.
Cheat me with footprints on auburn, gold, purple
Out to the last violet shimmer of the float
Of the dream—and I will come straddling a jackass,
Singing a song and letting out hallelujahs
To the doorsill of the last footprint."

And the man took a stub lead pencil
And made a long memo in shorthand
On the two blurry jackass ears:—

"God sits with long whiskers in the sky."
I said it when I was a boy.
I said it because long-whiskered men
Put it in my head to say it.
        They lied . . . about you . . . God . . .
        They lied. . . .

The other side of the five doors
and doorsills put in my house—
how many hinges, panels, doorknobs,
how many locks and lintels,
put on the doors and doorsills
winding and wild between
the first and the last doorsill of all?

"Out of the footprints on ten miles
of auburn, gold and purple—an old song comes:
These bones shall rise again,
Yes, children, these bones shall rise.

"Yonder past my five doors
are fifty million doors, maybe,

stars with knobs and locks and lintels,
stars with riders of rockets,
stars with swimmers of fire.

"Cheat my eyes—and I come again—
straddling a jackass—singing a song—
letting out hallelujahs.

"If God is a proud and a cunning Bricklayer,
Or if God is a King in a white gold Heaven,
Or if God is a Boss and a Watchman always watching,
I come riding the old ride of the humiliation,
Straddling a jackass, singing a song,
Letting out hallelujahs.

"Before a ten mile float
of auburn, gold, and purple,
footprints on a sunset airpath haze,
     I ask:
How can I taste with my tongue a tongueless God?
How can I touch with my fingers a fingerless God?
How can I hear with my ears an earless God?
Or smell of a God gone noseless long ago?
Or look on a God who never needs eyes for looking?

"My head is under your foot, God.
My head is a pan of alkali dust
your foot kicked loose—your foot of air
with its steps on the sunset airpath haze.

          (A bluejay blue
          and a gray mouse gray
          ran up the canyon walls.)

"Sitting at the rim of the big gap
at the high lash of the frozen storm line,
I ask why I go on five crutches,
tongues, ears, nostrils—all cripples—
eyes and nose—both cripples—
I ask why these five cripples

limp and squint and gag with me,
why they say with the oldest frozen faces:
    Man is a poor stick and a sad squirt;
    if he is poor he can't dress up;
    if he dresses up he don't know any place to go.

"Away and away on some green moon
a blind blue horse eats white grass
    And the blind blue horse knows more than I do
    because he saw more than I have seen
    and remembered it after he went blind.

"And away and away on some other green moon
is a sea-kept child who lacks a nose I got
and fingers like mine and all I have.
And yet the sea-kept child knows more than
I do and sings secrets alien to me as light
to a nosing mole underground.
I understand this child as a yellow-belly
catfish in China understands peach pickers
at sunrise in September in a Michigan orchard.

    "The power and lift of the sea
    and the flame of the old earth fires under,
I sift their meanings of sand in my fingers.
I send out five sleepwalkers to find out who I am,
    my name and number, where I came from,
    and where I am going.
They go out, look, listen, wonder, and shoot a fire-white rocket across
    the night sky; the shot and the flare of the rocket dies to a whisper;
    and the night is the same as it always was.
They come back, my five sleepwalkers; they have an answer for me, they
    say; they tell me: *Wait*—the password all of them heard when the
    fire-white rocket shot across the sky and died to a whisper, the pass-
    word is: *Wait*.

"I sit with five binoculars, amplifiers, spectroscopes
I sit looking through five windows, listening, tasting, smelling, touching.
I sit counting five million smoke fogs.
Repeaters, repeaters, come back to my window-sills.

Some are pigeons coming to coo and coo and clean their tail feathers
    and look wise at me.
Some are pigeons coming with broken wings to die with pain in their
    eyes on my window-sills.

"I walk the high lash of the frozen storm line;
I sit down with my feet in a ten-mile gravel pit.
Here I ask why I am a bag of sea-water fastened
to a frame of bones put walking on land—here I
look at crawlers, crimson, spiders spotted with
purple spots on their heads, flinging silver nets,
two, four, six, against the sun.
Here I look two miles down to the ditch of the sea
and pick a winding ribbon, a river eater, a water
grinder; it is a runner sent to run by a stop-watch,
it is a wrecker on a rush job."

      (A bluejay blue
      and a gray mouse gray
      ran up the canyon walls.)

Battering rams, blind mules, mounted policemen,
trucks hauling caverns of granite, elephants
grappling gorillas in a death strangle, cathedrals,
arenas, platforms, somersaults of telescoped rail-
road train wrecks, exhausted egg heads, piles of
skulls, mountains of empty sockets, mummies of kings
and mobs, memories of work gangs and wrecking crews,
sobs of wind and water storms, all frozen and held
on paths leading on to spirals of new zigzags—

An arm-chair for a one-eyed giant;
two pine trees grow in the left arm of the chair;
a bluejay comes, sits, goes, comes again;
a bluejay shoots and twitters . . . out and across . . .
tumbled skyscrapers and wrecked battleships,
walls of crucifixions and wedding breakfasts;
ruin, ruin—a brute gnashed, dug, kept on—
kept on and quit: and this is It.

Falling away, the brute is working.
Sheets of white veils cross a woman's face.
An eye socket glooms and wonders.
The brute hangs his head and drags on to the job.
The mother of mist and light and air murmurs: Wait.

The weavers of light weave best in red,
    better in blue.
The weavers of shadows weave at sunset;
        the young black-eyed women run, run, run
        to the night star homes; the old women
        sit weaving for the night rain gods,
        the night luck gods.

Eighteen old giants throw a red gold shadow ball;
they pass it along; hands go up and stop it; they
bat up flies and practice; they begin the game, they
knock it for home runs and two-baggers; the pitcher
put it across in an out- and an in-shoot drop; the
Devil is the Umpire; God is the Umpire; the game
is called on account of darkness.

        A bluejay blue
        and a gray mouse gray
        ran up the canyon walls.

3

Good night; it is scribbled on the panels
of the cold gray open desert.
Good night; on the big sky blanket over the
Santa Fé trail it is woven in the oldest
Indian blanket songs.

Buffers of land, breakers of sea, say it and
say it, over and over, good night, good night.

        Tie your hat to the saddle
        and ride, ride, ride, O Rider.
        Lay your rails and wires
        and ride, ride, ride, O Rider.

The worn tired stars say
you shall die early and die dirty.
The clean cold stars say
you shall die late and die clean.

The runaway stars say
you shall never die at all,
never at all.

GOOD MORNING, AMERICA

TO

A. H.

TENTATIVE (FIRST MODEL)
DEFINITIONS OF POETRY

1 *Poetry is a projection across silence of cadences arranged to break that silence with definite intentions of echoes, syllables, wave lengths.*

2 *Poetry is an art practised with the terribly plastic material of human language.*

3 *Poetry is the report of a nuance between two moments, when people say, 'Listen!' and 'Did you see it?' 'Did you hear it? What was it?'*

4 *Poetry is the tracing of the trajectories of a finite sound to the infinite points of its echoes.*

5 *Poetry is a sequence of dots and dashes, spelling depths, crypts, cross-lights, and moon wisps.*

6 *Poetry is a puppet-show, where riders of skyrockets and divers of sea fathoms gossip about the sixth sense and the fourth dimension.*

7 *Poetry is a plan for a slit in the face of a bronze fountain goat and the path of fresh drinking water.*

8 *Poetry is a slipknot tightened around a time-beat of one thought, two thoughts, and a last interweaving thought there is not yet a number for.*

9 *Poetry is an echo asking a shadow dancer to be a partner.*

10 *Poetry is the journal of a sea animal living on land, wanting to fly the air.*

11 *Poetry is a series of explanations of life, fading off into horizons too swift for explanations.*

12 *Poetry is a fossil rock-print of a fin and a wing, with an illegible oath between.*

13 *Poetry is an exhibit of one pendulum connecting with other and unseen pendulums inside and outside the one seen.*

14 *Poetry is a sky dark with a wild-duck migration.*

15 *Poetry is a search for syllables to shoot at the barriers of the unknown and the unknowable.*

16 *Poetry is any page from a sketchbook of outlines of a doorknob with thumb-prints of dust, blood, dreams.*

17 *Poetry is a type-font design for an alphabet of fun, hate, love, death.*

18 *Poetry is the cipher key to the five mystic wishes packed in a hollow silver bullet fed to a flying fish.*

19 *Poetry is a theorem of a yellow-silk handkerchief knotted with riddles, sealed in a balloon tied to the tail of a kite flying in a white wind against a blue sky in spring.*

20 *Poetry is a dance music measuring buck-and-wing follies along with the gravest and stateliest dead-marches.*

21 *Poetry is a sliver of the moon lost in the belly of a golden frog.*

22 *Poetry is a mock of a cry at finding a million dollars and a mock of a laugh at losing it.*

23 *Poetry is the silence and speech between a wet struggling root of a flower and a sunlit blossom of that flower.*

24 *Poetry is the harnessing of the paradox of earth cradling life and then entombing it.*

25 *Poetry is the opening and closing of a door, leaving those who look through to guess about what is seen during a moment.*

26 *Poetry is a fresh morning spider-web telling a story of moonlit hours of weaving and waiting during a night.*

27 *Poetry is a statement of a series of equations, with numbers and symbols changing like the changes of mirrors, pools, skies, the only never-changing sign being the sign of infinity.*

28 *Poetry is a packsack of invisible keepsakes.*

29 *Poetry is a section of river-fog and moving boat-lights, delivered be-
tween bridges and whistles, so one says, 'Oh!' and another,
'How?'*

30 *Poetry is a kinetic arrangement of static syllables.*

31 *Poetry is the arithmetic of the easiest way and the primrose path,
matched up with foam-flanked horses, bloody knuckles, and
bones, on the hard ways to the stars.*

32 *Poetry is a shuffling of boxes of illusions buckled with a strap of facts.*

33 *Poetry is an enumeration of birds, bees, babies, butterflies, bugs, bam-
binos, babayagas, and bipeds, beating their way up bewildering
bastions.*

34 *Poetry is a phantom script telling how rainbows are made and why
they go away.*

35 *Poetry is the establishment of a metaphorical link between white
butterfly-wings and the scraps of torn-up love-letters.*

36 *Poetry is the achievement of the synthesis of hyacinths and biscuits.*

37 *Poetry is a mystic, sensuous mathematics of fire, smoke-stacks, waffles,
pansies, people, and purple sunsets.*

38 *Poetry is the capture of a picture, a song, or a flair, in a deliberate
prism of words.*

GOOD MORNING, AMERICA

1

In the evening there is a sunset sonata comes to the cities.

There is a march of little armies to the dwindling of drums.

The skyscrapers throw their tall lengths of walls into black bastions on the red west.

The skyscrapers fasten their perpendicular alphabets far across the changing silver triangles of stars and streets.

And who made 'em? Who made the skyscrapers?

Man made 'em, the little two-legged joker, Man.

Out of his head, out of his dreaming, scheming skypiece,

Out of proud little diagrams that danced softly in his head—Man made the skyscrapers.

With his two hands, with shovels, hammers, wheelbarrows, with engines, conveyors, signal whistles, with girders, molds, steel, concrete—

Climbing on scaffolds and falsework with blueprints, riding the beams and dangling in mid-air to call, Come on, boys—

Man made the skyscrapers.

When one tall skyscraper is torn down

To make room for a taller one to go up,

Who takes down and puts up those two skyscrapers?

Man . . . the little two-legged joker . . . Man.

2

"There's gold in them hills,"

Said old timers on their wagon seats.

And on the wagons was a scribble:

Pike's Peak or Bust.

The Rocky Mountains are stacked tall on the skyline.
Sunrise and dawns wash on the skyline every morning.
Sunset feathers of foam float red and fade pink.

   And so,
    Quite so,
Facts are facts, nailed down, fastened to stay.
And facts are feathers, foam, flying phantoms.
Niagara is a fact or a little bluebird cheeping in a flight over the Falls—
Chirping to itself: What have we here?
                And how come?

The stone humps of old mountains
Sag and lift in a line to the sky.
The sunsets come with long shadowprints.
The six-cylinder go-getters ask:
    What time is it?
    Who were the Aztecs and the
        Zunis anyhow?
    What do I care about Cahokia?
    Where do we go from here?
    What are the facts?

3

Facts stay fastened; facts are phantom.
An old one-horse plow is a fact.
A new farm tractor is a fact.
Facts stay fastened; facts fly with bird wings.
Blood and sweat are facts, and
The commands of imagination, the looks back and ahead,
The spirals, pivots, landing places, fadeaways,
The signal lights and dark stars of civilizations.

Now the head of a man, his eyes, are facts.
He sees in his head, as in looking-glasses,
A cathedral, ship, bridge, railroad—a skyscraper—
And the plans are drawn, the blueprints fixed,
The design and the line, the shape written clear.
So fact moves from fact to fact, weaves, intersects.
Then come more, then come blood and sweat.

Then come pain and death, lifting and groaning,
And a crying out loud, between paydays.
Then the last ghost on the job walks.
The job stands up, the joined stresses of facts,
The cathedral, ship, bridge, railroad—the skyscraper—
Speaks a living hello to the open sky,
Stretches forth as an acknowledgement:
    "The big job is done.
      By God, we made it."
Facts stay fastened; facts fly with phantom bird wings.

4

I have looked over the earth and seen the swarming of different people
    to a different God—
White men with prayers to a white God, black men with prayers to a
    black God, yellow-faces before altars to a yellow-face God—
Amid burning fires they have pictured God with a naked skin; amid
    frozen rocks they have pictured God clothed and shaggy as a polar
    bear—
I have met stubs of men broken in the pain and mutilation of war say-
    ing God is forgetful and too far off, too far away—
I have met people saying they talk with God face to face; they tell God,
    hello God and how are you God; they get familiar with God and
    hold intimate conversations—
Yet I have met other people saying they are afraid to see God face to
    face for they would ask questions even as God might ask them
    questions.
I have seen these facts of God and man and anxious earthworms hunt-
    ing for a home.

I have seen the facts of humblebees and scarlet butterflies, orioles and
    flickers, goldwing moths and pink lady-bugs—
I have seen the spotted sunset sky filled with flights and wings—and I
    have heard high in the twilight blue the propellers of man and the
    evening air mail droning from Omaha to Chicago, droning across
    Iowa and Illinois—
I have said: The prints of many new wings, many fresh flights, many
    clean propellers, shall be on the sky before we understand God and
    the work of wings and air.

5

I have seen the figures of heroes set up as memorials, testimonies of fact—

Leif Ericson in a hard, deep-purple bronze, stands as a frozen shadow, lean, with searching eyes, on a hill in Wisconsin overlooking Lake Michigan—

Columbus in bronze is the center of a turmoil of traffic from world ends gathered on Manhattan Island—

Washington stands in marble shaped from life, in the old Romanesque temple on Capitol Hill, in Richmond, Virginia, with an arrogant laughter heard from circling skyscrapers—

Andrew Jackson in bronze on a bronze horse, a rocking horse on its hind legs with forepaws in the air, the tail brandishing, as the General lifts a cockade from his head in salutation to the citizens and soldiers of the Republic—

Ulysses S. Grant, somber and sober, is on a pony high in bronze listening to the endless white horses of Lake Michigan talking to Illinois—

Robert E. Lee, recumbent in white stone, sleeps a bivouac sleep in peace among loved ones of the southern Shenandoah Valley—

Lincoln's memory is kept in a living, arterial highway moving across state lines from coast to coast to the murmur, Be good to each other, sisters; don't fight, brothers.

6

And may we ask—is a flower a fact?
Shall a thin perishable blossom
Mount out of homeland soil
And give the breath of its leaves
For a memorial printed a few days,
For a symbol kept by the bees and the wind?
Shall each state pick its favorite flower

And say, This is Me, Us, this comes from the dirt of the earth, the loam, the mulch, this is a home greeting to our eyes, these leaves touch our footloose feet, our children and our children's children.

The blue cornflower along the railroad tracks in Illinois—
The pink moccasin hiding in the big woods of Minnesota—
The wild prairie rose scrambling along Iowa roads—
Golden poppy of California, giant cactus of Arizona—
Apple blossom of Michigan, Kentucky's trumpet vine—
The rhododendrons of Washington and West Virginia—

The Indian paintbrush of Wyoming, Montana's bitter root—
Vital and endless goldenrod crossing Nebraska—
Mariposa lily of Utah, pasque flower of South Dakota—
Ox-eyed daisy of North Carolina, Florida's orange blossom—
The magnolia of Louisiana, the Delaware peach blossom—
The silent laughing salutations of the Kansas sunflower—
The old buffalo clover, the marching Texas bluebonnet—
The pine cone and tassel of the lonesome State of Maine—
    Shall these be among our phantom facts?

7

Facts are phantom; facts begin
With a bud, a seed, an egg.

A hero, a hoodlum, a little of both,
A toiling two-faced driven destiny,
Sleeps in the secret traceries of eggs.
If one egg could speak and answer the question,
    Egg, who are you, what are you, where did you
        come from and where are you going?
If one egg could break through the barriers, pass
    all interference and tell that much, then we
    could tell how the earth came—
            how we came with hair, lungs, noses
            to sit on the earth and eat our breakfasts,
            to sleep with our mates
            and to salute the moon between sleeps,
            to meditate on worms in the dust
            and how they fail to divulge the designs
            of the dark autocracies of their fates.
Let one egg tell and we would understand a billion eggs.
The newborn child, dried behind the ears,
Swaddled in soft cloths and groping for nipples,
Comes from a payday of love so old,
So involved, so traced with circles of the moon,
So cunning with secrets of the salts of blood,
It must be older than the moon, older than the salt sea.
And do nations go back to the secret traceries of eggs?
To beginnings that fail to divulge the designs?
Can we say to the unborn, Egg, who are you? Egg, divulge your design.

Nations begin young the same as babies.
They suckle and struggle; they grow up;
They toil, fight, laugh, suffer, die.
They obey the traced circles of the moon.
They follow the ordained times of night, morning, afternoon, evening,
and night again.
They stand up and have their day on the pavilion of the Four Winds.
The night sky of stars watches them begin, wear out, and fade away be-
fore newcomers, before silence, before empty pavilions.
They leave flags, slogans, alphabets, numbers, tools, tales of flaming per-
formances; they leave moths, manuscripts, memories.

And so, to the pavilion of the four winds
Came the little one they called America,
One that suckled, struggled, toiled, laughed, grew.
America began young the same as a baby.
The little new republic had its swaddling cloths,
Its child shirt, its tussle to knit long bone joints.
    And who can read the circle of its moons now?
    And who shall tell beforehand the secrets of its
        salts and blood?

8

Turn back and look at those men riding horses, sitting in saddles, smell-
ing of leather, going to Boston, to Richmond, in velvet knicker-
bockers, in silk stockings, in slippers with silver buckles, white-
powdered wigs on their heads, speaking of "the honor of a gentle-
man," singing "God rest ye, merry gentlemen," meeting carpenters
who built staircases and gables with their hands, the work-day was
sunup till sundown; they drove handwrought nails; the smoothing of
their own hands was on their woodwork.

Look back; they are pinching their fingers in silver and gold snuff boxes,
lifting tankards of ale, discussing titles to many miles of land, coun-
ties and townships of land; a gentleman rides all day to round his
boundaries; and the jail doors cling to their brass locks holding the
dregs, the convicts of debt.

    Look back,
    And that was long ago.

America was new born.
The republic was a baby, a child,
Fresh wiped behind the ears,
Blinking, tussling to knit the long
     new bone joints.

Look back; there is an interlude; men in covered wagons, in buckskin,
    with plows, rifles, six-shooters, sweep west; the Havana cigar, the
    long pantaloons, the Mississippi steamboat, the talking wires, the
    iron horse.

Yes, there was an interlude.
Something happened, always something happens.
History is a living horse laughing at a wooden horse.
History is a wind blowing where it listeth.
History is no sure thing to bet on.
History is a box of tricks with a lost key.
History is a labyrinth of doors with sliding panels, a book of ciphers with
    the code in a cave of the Sargossa sea.
History says, if it pleases, Excuse me, I beg your pardon, it will never
    happen again if I can help it.

Yes, there was an interlude,
And phantoms washed their white shirts
Over and over again in buckets of blood—
And the saddest phantom of all stood up at Gettysburg
And tried to tell right from wrong and left the most
    of it unsaid, in the air.

The years go by with their numbers, names,
    So many born, so many gone.
Again the Four Horsemen take their laughter.
Men walk on air and tumble from the sky.
Men grapple undersea and soak their bones along rust-brown, rust-flaked
    turbines on the sea bottom.
Men bite the dust from bullets, bombs, bayonets, gas,
Till ten million go west without time for a good-by,
Till double ten million are cripples for life,

Blind, shocked, broken storm children.
Boys singing Hinky Dinky Parley Voo
Come back from the oversea vortex,
From the barrages of No Man's Land,
Saying with gleams deep in their eyes,
"There is nothing to say, ask me no questions."

9

Steel, coal, oil, the test tube arise as facts, dominions,
Standing establishments with world ambassadors.
Between two seashores comes a swift interweaving of blood and bones,
    nerves and arteries, rail and motor paths, airways and airports, tun-
    nels, wires, broadcasts on high and low frequencies to the receiving
    sets.
The train callers call All Aboard for transcontinental flyers; it is seaboard
    to seaboard; and the tincan tourists buy gas and follow the bird
    migrations.

The concrete highways crack under the incessant tires of two-ton, ten-ton
    trucks—and the concrete mixers come with laughing bellies filled with
    gravel for the repair jobs.
The talk runs—of the boll-weevil in the cotton, the doodle bug in the oil
    fields, the corn borer—of the lame duck in Congress, the farm bloc,
    the Ku Klux, a new sucker born every minute, sales canvass and sell-
    ing spiels—
The talk runs—of crime waves, boy murderers, two women and a man,
    two men and a woman, bootleggers, the beer racket and the high-
    jackers, gang fights, cloud-bursts, tornadoes, floods, the Lakes-to-Gulf
    waterway, Boulder Dam—
The latest songs go from Broadway west across the country—the latest
    movies go from Hollywood east across the country—in a million
    homes they set their dials and listen to jazz numbers, the classics, the
    speech of the President in Washington, the heavyweight champion-
    ship fight, the symphonies of the music masters.

10

Voices—telling mankind to look itself in the face—who are you? what
    are you? we'll tell you—here is the latest—this is what Man has done
    today on the pavilion of the four winds, on the arcs of the globe—

As the dusty red sun settles in the dayend the sport sheets blaze forth
telling the box scores, the touchdowns, the scandals—pictures of
dying champions, of new claimants, fresh aspirants calling challenges
—of over-sea flyers, winners and losers—of new and old darlings of
destiny—

Fate's crapshooters fading each other, big Dick or snake eyes, midnights
and deuces, chicken one day and feathers the next, the true story of
how an ash can became a verandah and vice versa.

11

A code arrives; language; lingo; slang;
behold the proverbs of a people, a nation:
Give 'em the works. Fix it, there's always
a way. Be hard boiled. The good die young.

Be a square shooter. Be good; if you can't
be good be careful. When they put you in
that six foot bungalow, that wooden kimono,
you're through and that's that.

Sell 'em, sell 'em. Make 'em eat it. What
if we gyp 'em? It'll be good for 'em. Get their
names on the dotted line and give 'em the haha.

The higher they go the farther they drop.
The fewer the sooner. Tell 'em. Tell 'em.
Make 'em listen. They got to listen when
they know who you are. Don't let 'em know
what you got on your hip. Hit 'em where
they ain't. It's good for whatever ails
you and if nothing ails you it's good for
that. Where was you raised—in a barn?

They're a lot of muckers, tin horns; show
those slobs where they get off at. Tell 'em
you're going to open a keg of nails. Beat 'em
to a fare-thee-well. Hand 'em the razz-berries.
Clean 'em and then give 'em carfare home.

Maybe all you'll get from 'em you can put in
your ear, anyhow.

They got a fat nerve to try to tie a can
on you. Send 'em to the cleaners. Put the
kibosh on 'em so they'll never come back.
You don't seem to know four out of five
have pyorrhea in Peoria.

Your head ain't screwed on wrong, I trust.
Use your noodle, your nut, your think tank,
your skypiece. God meant for you to use it.
If they offer to let you in on the ground
floor take the elevator.

Put up a sign: Don't worry; it won't last;
nothing does. Put up a sign: In God we
trust, all others pay cash. Put up a sign:
Be brief, we have our living to make. Put
up a sign: Keep off the grass.

Aye, behold the proverbs of a people:
The big word is Service.
Service—first, last and always.
Business is business.
What you don't know won't hurt you.
Courtesy pays.
Fair enough.
The voice with a smile.
Say it with flowers.
Let one hand wash the other.
The customer is always right.
Who's your boy friend?
Who's your girl friend?
O very well.
God reigns and the government at Washington lives.
Let it go at that.
There are lies, dam lies and statistics.
Figures don't lie but liars can figure.
There's more truth than poetry in that.
You don't know the half of it, dearie.

It's the roving bee that gathers the honey.[1]
A big man is a big man whether he's a president or a prizefighter.[2]
Name your poison.
Take a little interest.
Look the part.
It pays to look well.
Be yourself.
Speak softly and carry a big stick.[3]
War is hell.
Honesty is the best policy.
It's all in the way you look at it.
Get the money—honestly if you can.
It's hell to be poor.
Well, money isn't everything.
Well, life is what you make it.
Speed and curves—what more do you want?
I'd rather fly than eat.[4]
There must be pioneers and some of them get killed.[4]
The grass is longer in the backyard.[5]
Give me enough Swedes and snuff and I'll build a railroad to hell.[6]
How much did he leave? All of it.[7]
Can you unscramble eggs? [8]
Early to bed and early to rise and you never meet any prominent people.[9]
Let's go. Watch our smoke. Excuse our dust.
Keep your shirt on.

12

First come the pioneers, lean, hungry, fierce, dirty.
They wrangle and battle with the elements.

[1] On hearing from his father "A rolling stone gathers no moss," John L. Sullivan won one of his important early fights and telegraphed this reply.

[2] John L. Sullivan's greeting spoken to President Theodore Roosevelt in the White House.

[3] A Spanish proverb first Americanized by Theodore Roosevelt.

[4] Charles A. Lindbergh.

[5] Based on a Republican campaign story in 1892 alleging that a man on all fours eating grass on the White House lawn told President Grover Cleveland, "I'm hungry," and was advised, "The grass is longer in the backyard."

[6] A saying that took rise from James J. (Jim) Hill.

[7] A folk tale in Chicago chronicles two ditch diggers on the morning after Marshall Field I died, leaving an estate of $150,000,000, as having this dialogue.

[8] J. Pierpont Morgan's query as to court decrees dissolving an inevitable industrial combination.

[9] George Ade.

They gamble on crops, chills, ague, rheumatism.
They fight wars and put a nation on the map.
They battle with blizzards, lice, wolves.
They go on a fighting trail
To break sod for unnumbered millions to come.

Then the fat years arrive when the fat drips.
Then come the rich men baffled by their riches,
Bewildered by the silence of their tall possessions.
Then come the criers of the ancient desperate taunt:
    Stuff your guts
    and strut your stuff,
    strut it high and handsome;
    when you die you're dead
    and there's no comeback
    and not even the winds
    will say your name—
    feed, oh pigs, feed, oh swine.

Old timer, dust of the earth so kindly,
Old timer, dirt of our feet and days.
Old time gravel and gumbo of the earth,
Take them back kindly,
These pigs, these swine.
The bones of them and their brothers blanch to the same yellow of the
    years.

13

Since we sell the earth with a fence around it,
Since one man sells the ocean to another and guarantees a new roof and
    all modern conveniences,
Since we sell everything but the blue sky and only the Blue Sky Laws
    stop us selling that,
Since we sell justice, since we sell pardons for crimes,
Since we sell land titles, oil claims, ninety-nine year options, all-day
    suckers and two-minute eggs—
Since we have coined a slogan, Never give the sucker an even break and
    the Old Army Game goes—
Since the selling game is the big game and unless you know how to sell
    you're a bum and that ain't all—

Since the city hicks and the hicks from the sticks go to the latest Broad-
way hit hoping to fix their glims on a birdie with her last feather off
in a bathtub of booze—
Let the dance go on—let the stalking stuffed cadavers of old men run the
earth and call up the Four Horsemen. . . .

14

Now it's Uncle Sam sitting on top of the world.
Not so long ago it was John Bull and, earlier yet, Napoleon and the
eagles of France told the world where to get off at.
Spain, Rome, Greece, Persia, their blunderbuss guns, their spears, cata-
pults, ships, took their turn at leading the civilizations of the earth—
One by one they were bumped off, moved over, left behind, taken for
a ride; they died or they lost the wallop they used to pack, not so
good, not so good.
One by one they no longer sat on top of the world—now the Young
Stranger is Uncle Sam, is America and the song goes, "The stars and
stripes forever!" even though "forever" is a long time.
Even though the oldest kings had their singers and clowns calling, "Oh
king, you shall live forever."

15

In God we trust; it is so written.
The writing goes onto every silver dollar.
The fact: God is the great One who made us all.
We is you and me and all of us in the United States of America.
And trusting God means we give ourselves, all of ourselves, the whole
United States of America, to God, the great One.
Yes . . . perhaps . . . is that so?

16

The silent litany of the workmen goes on—
Speed, speed, we are the makers of speed.
We make the flying, crying motors,
Clutches, brakes, and axles,
Gears, ignitions, accelerators,
Spokes and springs and shock absorbers.
The silent litany of the workmen goes on—
Speed, speed, we are the makers of speed;
Axles, clutches, levers, shovels,

We make the signals and lay the way—
   Speed, speed.
The trees come down to our tools.
We carve the wood to the wanted shape.
The whining propeller's song in the sky,
The steady drone of the overland truck,
Comes from our hands; us; the makers of speed.

Speed; the turbines crossing the Big Pond,
Every nut and bolt, every bar and screw,
Every fitted and whirling shaft,
They came from us, the makers,
Us, who know how,
Us, the high designers and the automatic feeders,
Us, with heads,
Us, with hands,
Us, on the long haul, the short flight,
We are the makers; lay the blame on us—
The makers of speed.

17

   There is a Sleepwalker
   goes walking and talking—
I promise you nothing, there are too many promises.
I bring you a package so little, so thin, you can hide it anywhere, in your
   shoes, in your ear, in a corner of your heart.
I bring you a handkerchief, so filmy a gauze of silk, so foamy a fabric,
   you pick it up and put it away as you put away a bubble, a morning
   cobweb in the sun, a patch of moon dropped from two lilacs.
I bring you gold, beaten so thin with so many little hammers it is thinner
   than the morning laughter of hummingbirds flitting among diamond
   dewdrops yet hard as an anvil wearing out the strongest hammers.

There is a Sleepwalker
goes walking and talking—

Go alone and away from all books, go with your own heart into the
   storm of human hearts and see if somewhere in that storm there are
   bleeding hearts, sacred hearts taking a bitter wages of doom, red-
   soaked and crimson-plunged hearts of the Redeemer of Man.

Walk by yourself and find the silence where a whisper of your lips is the same as a pounding and a shouting at the knobs and panels of great doors.

Walk again where the mass human shadows foregather, where the silhouettes and pantomimes of the great human procession wind with a crying out loud, and rotten laughters mix with raging tumults—

And between the being born and the being dead of the generations they march, march, march, to the drums, drums, drums, of the three facts of arriving, living, departing—

Go where the shadows string from winding pilgrim cohorts, where the line of the march twists and reels, and a hundred years is nothing much and a thousand or a million years nothing much, as they march, march, march, to the drums, drums, drums, of the three facts.

Go there and let your heart be soft, fading as rainbows on slants of rain in the sun: let your heart be full of riddles as white steel and its blue shadows.

There is a sleepwalker
goes walking and talking—

We are afraid. What are we afraid of?
We are afraid of what we are afraid of.
We are afraid of this, that, these, those, them.

We are afraid the earth will blow up and bomb the human family out of its sleep, its slumber, its sleepwalking, its pass and repass of shadows.

We are afraid the sky will come apart and fall on us and in a rain of stars we will wash out into the Great Alone, the Deep Dark, saying, "Good-by old Mother Earth, we always were afraid of you."

We are afraid; what are we afraid of? We are afraid of nothing much, nothing at all, nothing in the shape of god, man or beast, we can eat any ashes offered us, we can step out before the fact of the Fact of Death and look it in the eye and laugh, "You are the beginning or the end of something, I'll gamble with you, I'll take a chance."

18

And we, us, the people,
We who of course are no sleepwalkers,
Perhaps we may murmur—

Perhaps as the airmen slip into their leather coats,
Gambling for the timetables as against the skull and crossbones,
Riding with mail sacks across orange blossoms, the desert cactus, the
    Rockies, the Great Plains, the Mississippi, the corn belt, the Appa-
    lachians,
Riding with mail sacks, with a clutch on the steering wheels in storms
    and stars, with a passing cry, "Good luck and God bless you,"
Perhaps while they ride and gamble on the new transcontinental sky
    paths, perhaps we may ask and murmur—
            Good morning, America.
            Good morning, Mr. Who, Which, What.
            Good morning, let's all of us tell our
                real names.
            Good morning, Mr. Somebody, Nobody, Any-
                body-who-is-Anybody-at-all.
            Good morning, Worms in the Dust, Eagles
                in the Air, Climbers to the Top of
                the Sky.

                        19

You have kissed good-by to one century, one little priceless album.
You will yet kiss good-by to ten, twenty centuries. Ah! you shall have
    such albums!
Your mothers, America, have labored and carried harvests of generations—
Across the spillways come further harvests, new tumultuous populations,
    young strangers, crying, "We are here! We belong! look at us!"
Good morning, America!
Morning goes as morning-glories go!
High noon goes, afternoon goes!
Twilight, sundown, gloaming—
The hour of writing: Good night, America!
Good night, sleep, peace, and sweet dreams!

                        20

The prints of many new ships shall be on the sky.
The Four Horsemen shall ride again in a bitter dust,
The granaries of great nations shall be the food of fat rats,
And the shooting stars shall write new alphabets on the sky
        Before we come home,
        Before we understand.

Off in our western sky,
Off in a burning maroon,
Shall come in a wintrish haze,
Shall come in points and crystals—
A shovel of stars.

Let us wigwag the moon.
Let us make new propellers,
Go past old spent stars
And find blue moons on a new star path.

Let us make pioneer prayers.
Let working clothes be sacred.
Let us look on
And listen in
On God's great workshop
Of stars . . . and eggs . . .

There shall be—
Many many girls in a wild windy moonlight,
Many many mothers carrying babies.

21

Sea sunsets, give us keepsakes.
Prairie gloamings, pay us for prayers.
Mountain clouds on bronze skies—
    Give us great memories.
Let us have summer roses.
Let us have tawny harvest haze in pumpkin time.
Let us have springtime faces to toil for and play for.
Let us have the fun of booming winds on long waters.
Give us dreamy blue twilights—of winter evenings—to wrap us in a coat
    of dreaminess.
Moonlight, come down—shine down, moonlight—meet every bird cry
    and every song calling to a hard old earth, a sweet young earth.

Spring Grass

SPRING GRASS

Spring grass, there is a dance to be danced
 for you.
Come up, spring grass, if only for young feet.
Come up, spring grass, young feet ask you.

Smell of the young spring grass,
You're a mascot riding on the wind horses.
You came to my nose and spiffed me. This is
 your lucky year.

Young spring grass just after the winter,
Shoots of the big green whisper of the year,
Come up, if only for young feet.
Come up, young feet ask you.

MOIST MOON PEOPLE

The moon is able to command the valley tonight.
The green mist shall go a-roaming, the white river shall
 go a-roaming.
Yet the moon shall be commanding, the moon shall take a
 high stand on the sky.
When the cats crept up the gullies,
And the goats fed at the rim a-laughing,
When the spiders swept their rooms in the burr oaks,
And the katydids first searched for this year's accordions,
And the crickets began a-looking for last year's concer-
 tinas—

I was there, I saw that hour, I know God had grand
    intentions about it.
If not, why did the moon command the valley, the green
    mist and white river go a-roaming, and the moon by
    itself take so high a stand on the sky?
If God and I alone saw it, the show was worth putting on,
Yet I remember others were there, Amos and Priscilla,
    Axel and Hulda, Hank and Jo, Big Charley and
    Little Morningstar,
They were all there; the clock ticks spoke with castanet
    clicks.

SPRING CRIES

1

CALL us back, call us with your sliding silver,
Frogs of the early spring, frogs of the later days
When spring crosses over, when spring spills over
And spills the last of its sliding silvers
Into the running wind, the running water, of summer.
Call us back then, call over, call under—only call—
Frogs of the early spring, frogs of the later days.

2

Birds we have seen and known and counted,
Birds we have never learned the names of,
Call us back, you too, call us back.
Out of the forks and angles of branches,
High out of the blacksmith arms of oak and ash,
Sweet out of the Lombardy poplar's arrow head,
Soft out of the swinging, swaying,
The bending and almost broken branch
Of the bush of the home of the wild gooseberry—
Yellow feather, white throat, gray neck, red wing,
Scarlet head, blue shoulder, copper silver body line—
All you birds—call us back—call us under, over—
Birds we know, birds we never can know,
Birds spilling your one-two-three
Of a slur and a cry and a trill—
Call us back, you too call us.

3

Warble us easy and old ones.
Open your gates up the sunset in the evening.
Lift up your windows of song in the morning lights.
Wind on your spiral and zigzag ways.
Birds, we have heard baskets of you, bushes of you.
In a tree of a hundred windows ten of you sat
On the song sills of every window.
Warble us easy and old ones now.
Call us back, spill your one-two-three
Of a slur and a cry and a trill.

FROG SONGS

THE silver burbles of the frogs wind and swirl.
The lines of their prongs swing up in a spray.
They cut the air with bird line curves.
The eye sees nothing, the ear is filled, the head remembers
The beat of the swirl of frog throat silver prongs
In the early springtime when eggs open, when feet learn,
When the crying of the water begins a new year.

LUMBER YARD POOLS AT SUNSET

THE rain pools in the old lumber yard
change as the sky changes.

No sooner do lightfoot sunset maroons
cross the west than they cross the rain
pools too.

So now every blue has a brother
and every singing silver a sister.

SPRING CARRIES SURPRISES

BE gay now.
Shadows go fast these days
Unlocking the locks of blossoms.

The lilacs never know how,
The oleanders along the old walls,
The peach trees over the hills—
Out of the lock-ups they go,
Out and crying with leaves.
They never know how.
Be gay—this is the time.

The little keys of the climbing runners,
The opening of the doors again,
The letting loose of the shut-ins—
Here is the time—be gay now.

Ask spring why.
Ask in your heart why.
Go around gay and foolish asking why.
God be easy on your fool heart
If you don't go around asking spring
In your heart, "Why, why, why,"
        Three times like that, or else
        One long, "Why?"

Be gay now.

MORE COUNTRY PEOPLE

THE six pigs at the breast of their mother
Equal six spots of young brown against a big spot of old brown.
The bleating of the sheep was an arithmetic
Of the long wool coats thick after winter.

The collar of white hair hung on the neck of the black hog,
The roosters of the Buff Cochin people strutted.

Cherry branches stuck their blossoms against the sky.
Elbows joined elbows of white blossoms.
Zigzags blent into a mass.
"Look once at us—today is the day we call today."

SPRING WIND

Be flip with us if you want to, spring wind.
Be gay and make us sniff at your slow secrets.
 Be easy with us, spring wind.
Be lovely and yet be lovely not too fast with us.

If a child came crying out of a snowstorm
And sat down with secrets of new playthings,
Crying because lovelier things than ever came that year—

If a child came crying out of sheet ice,
A white carving of a lithe running torso,
Holding in its hands new baffling playthings—

If a child came crying so,
Wet and smiling, smelling of promises
Of yellow roses blowing in the river backwashes,
Potato blossoms across the prairie flat lands,
And even so much as one new honest song to sing—

If a child came so,
We would say, 'Come and sit on our back porch;
Listen with us and tell us more, tell us all you know;
Tell us the secrets of the spring wind;
Tell us if this is a lucky year;
Be lovely and yet be lovely not too fast with us.'

CRISSCROSS

Spring crosses over into summer.
This is as it always was.

Buds on the redhaw, beetles in the loam,
And the interference of the green leaves
At the blue roofs of the spring sky
Crossing over into summer—
These are ways, this is out and on.
This always was.

The tumble out and the push up,
The breaking of the little doors,
The look again at the mother sun,
The feel of the blue roofs over—
This is summer? This always was?

The whispering sprigs of buds stay put.
The spiders are after the beetles.
The farmer is driving a tractor turning furrows.
The hired man drives a manure spreader.
The oven bird hops in dry leaves.
The woodpecker beats his tattoo.
Is this it? Is spring crossing over?
Is it summer? And this always was?
The whispering pinks, the buds on the redhaw,
The blue roofs of the sky . . . stay put.

BABY SONG OF THE FOUR WINDS

LET me be your baby, south wind.
Rock me, let me rock, rock me now.
Rock me low, rock me warm.
Let me be your baby.

Comb my hair, west wind.
Comb me with a cowlick.
Or let me go with a pompadour.
Come on, west wind, make me your baby.

North wind, shake me where I'm foolish.
Shake me loose and change my ways.
Cool my ears with a blue sea wind.
I'm your baby, make me behave.

And you, east wind, what can I ask?
A fog comfort? A fog to tuck me in?
Fix me so and let me sleep.
I'm your baby—and I always was.

BLOSSOM THEMES

1

LATE in the winter came one day
When there was a whiff on the wind,
a suspicion, a cry not to be heard
    of perhaps blossoms, perhaps green
    grass and clean hills lifting roll-
    ing shoulders.
Does the nose get the cry of spring
    first of all? is the nose thankful
    and thrilled first of all?

2

If the blossoms come down
so they must fall on snow
because spring comes this year
before winter is gone,
then both snow and blossoms look sad;
peaches, cherries, the red summer apples,
all say it is a hard year.
The wind has its own way of picking off
the smell of peach blossoms and then
carrying that smell miles and miles.
    Women washing dishes in lonely farmhouses
    stand at the door and say, "Something is
    happening."
A little foam of the summer sea
    of blossoms,
    a foam finger of white leaves,
    shut these away—
    high into the summer wind runners.
Let the wind be white too.

SMALL HOMES

THE green bug sleeps in the white lily ear.
The red bug sleeps in the white magnolia.
Shiny wings, you are choosers of color.
You have taken your summer bungalows wisely.

Corn Belt

SHE OPENS THE BARN DOOR EVERY MORNING

OPEN the barn door, farm woman,
It is time for the cows to be milked.
Their udders are full from the sleep night.
Open the door with your right hand shuttling a cleat,
Your left hand pulling a handle.
The smell of the barn is let out to the pastures.
Dawn lets itself in at the open door.
A cow left out in the barnyard all the night
Looks on as though you do this every morning.
Open the barn door, farm woman, you do it
As you have done it five hundred times.
As a sleep woman heavy with the earth,
Clean as a milk pail washed in the sun,
You open the barn door a half mile away
And a cow almost turns its head and looks on.

MILK-WHITE MOON, PUT THE COWS TO SLEEP

MILK-WHITE moon, put the cows to sleep.
Since five o'clock in the morning,
Since they stood up out of the grass,
Where they slept on their knees and hocks,
They have eaten grass and given their milk
And eaten grass again and given milk,
And kept their heads and teeth at the earth's face.
 Now they are looking at you, milk-white moon.
 Carelessly as they look at the level landscapes,
 Carelessly as they look at a pail of new white milk,
 They are looking at you, wondering not at all, at all,
 If the moon is the skim face top of a pail of milk,
 Wondering not at all, carelessly looking.
 Put the cows to sleep, milk-white moon,
 Put the cows to sleep.

SLOW PROGRAM

THE iron rails run into the sun.
The setting of the sun chooses an hour.
The red rail ribbons run into the red ball sun.
The ribbons and the ball change like red water lights.
The picture floats with a slow program of red haze lights.

FIELD PEOPLE

IN the morning eyes of the brown-eyed Susans,
in the toadflax sheaves smiling butter-and-eggs,
in the white mushrooms sprung from air into air
since yesterday morning, since yesterday evening,
in the corn row corridor walls of cornstalks—
the same southwest wind comes again, knowing—

How the field people go away,
the corn row people, the toadflax, mushroom,
 thistlebloom people,

how they rise, sing songs they learn, and then go away,
leaving in the air no last will and testament at all,
leaving no last whisper at all on how this sister,
that brother, this friend, such and such a sweetheart
is remembered with a gold leaf, a cup rainbow home,
a cricket's hut for counting its summer heartbeats,
a caught shimmer of one haunted moonray to be passed on—
the running southwest wind knows them all.

SUNSETS

THERE are sunsets who whisper a good-by.
It is a short dusk and a way for stars.
Prairie and sea rim they go level and even
And the sleep is easy.

There are sunsets who dance good-by.
They fling scarves half to the arc,
To the arc then and over the arc.
Ribbons at the ears, sashes at the hips,
Dancing, dancing good-by. And here sleep
Tosses a little with dreams.

GRASSROOTS

GRASS clutches at the dark dirt with finger holds.
Let it be blue grass, barley, rye or wheat,
Let it be button weed or butter-and-eggs,
Let it be Johnny-jump-ups springing clean blue streaks.
Grassroots down under put fingers into dark dirt.

CANADIANS AND POTTAWATOMIES

I HAVE seen a loneliness sit
in the dark and nothing lit up.
I have seen a loneliness sit

in the dark lit up like a Christ-
mas tree, a Hallowe'en pumpkin.

If two Canadians understand snow
they are then both Canadians.
If one Canadian understands snow
and another doesn't understand
snow at all, then one is a Canadian
and the other is no Canadian at all.

The Pottawatomie Indians sang something
like this in their early winter songs.
They sang it digging holes in the ice to
let down fish-hooks, they chattered it in
the wigwams when blizzards shook the wigwams.

CORN AND BEANS

HAVING looked long at two gardens rows
And seen how the rain and dirt have used them
I have decided the corn and beans shall have names.

And one is to be known as the Thwarted Corn of a Short Year
While the other shall be called the Triumphant Beans of Plenty Rain.

If I change these names next Sunday I shall let you know about it.

MOCKERS GO TO KANSAS IN SPRING

RIDING from Topeka, Kansas, to Manhattan, Kansas,
Marco saw and heard three mockingbirds.
He mentioned it to the Kansas Authors' Club.
Two mockers were heard that night in Manhattan.
A man from Chicago sleeping in the Gillett House
Heard one of the mockers before breakfast the morning after.
This is evidence, testimony, offered in behalf of those who do not under-
    stand how mockers roam north from Texas and Arkansas, sometimes
    as far north as Manhattan, Kansas.

BIRD TALK

AND now when the branches were beginning to be heavy,
It was the time when they once had said, "This is the
    beginning of summer."
The shrilling of the frogs was not so shrill as in the
    first weeks after the broken winter;
The birds took their hops and zigzags a little more
    anxious; a home is a home; worms are worms.
The yellow spreads of the dandelions and buttercups
    reached across the green pastures.
Tee whee and tee whee came on the breezes, and the grackles
    chuzzled their syllables.
And it was the leaves with a strong soft wind over them
    that talked most of all and said more than any others
    though speaking the fewest words.
It was the green leaves trickling out the gaunt nowhere
    of winter, out on the gray hungry branches—
It was the leaves on the branches, beginning to be heavy,
    who said as they said one time before, "This is the be-
    ginning of summer."

We shall never blame the birds who come
    where the river and the road make the Grand Crossing
    and talk there, sitting in circles talking bird talk.
If they ask in their circles as to who is here
    and as to who is not here and who used to be here,
Or if instead of counting up last year as against
    this year, they count up this year as against next
    year, and have their bird chatter about who is here
    this year who won't be here next year,
We shall never blame the birds.

If I have put your face among leaf faces, child,
Or if I have put your voice among bird voices,
Blame me no more than the bluejays.

KANSAS LESSONS

OFTEN the mockingbird is only a mocker
singing the songs of other birds,
pouring their trills over the bushes.
    And sometimes the mocker is all alone
    the child playing all-aloney all—aloney.
And sometimes the mocker calls, calls, calls,
the fables, texts and cries of all heartbreaks,
all the wild nights a blood-gold moon can buy.

CRICKET MARCH

As the corn becomes higher
The one shrill of a summer cricket
Becomes two and ten
With a shrilling surer than last month.

As the banners of the corn
Come to their highest flying in the wind,
The summer crickets come to a marching army.

SUMMER GRASS

SUMMER grass aches and whispers.

It wants something; it calls and sings; it pours
    out wishes to the overhead stars.

The rain hears; the rain answers; the rain is slow
    coming; the rain wets the face of the grass.

NOCTURN CABBAGE

CABBAGES catch at the moon.
It is late summer, no rain, the pack of the soil
    cracks open, it is a hard summer.

In the night the cabbages catch at the moon, the
        leaves drip silver, the rows of cabbages are
        series of little silver waterfalls in the moon.

CRABAPPLES

SWEETEN these bitter wild crabapples, Illinois
October sun. The roots here came from the
wilderness, came before man came here. They
are bitter as the wild is bitter.

Give these crabapples your softening gold,
October sun, go through to the white wet
seeds inside and soften them black. Make
these bitter apples sweet. They want you, sun.

The drop and the fall, the drop and the fall,
the apples leaving the branches for the black
earth under, they know you from last year,
the year before last year, October sun.

POPLAR AND ELM

SILVER leaves of the last of summer,
Poplar and elm silver leaves,
Leaves not least of all of the Lombardy poplar,
Standing before the autumn moon and the autumn wind
        as a woman waits in a doorway for some one who
        must be coming,
All you silver leaf people, you I have seen and heard
        in a hundred summer winds,
It is October, it is a week, two weeks, till the rain and frost
        break on us and the leaves are washed off, washed
        down.
In January when the trees fork gray against a clear winter
        blue in the spare sun silver of winter or the lengthened
        frost silver of the long nights—
I shall remember then the loans of the sun to you in June,
        I shall remember the hundred winds who kissed you.

BROWN GOLD

THE time of the brown gold comes softly.
Oat shocks are alive in brown gold belts,
 the short and the shambling oat shocks
 sit on the stubble and straw.
The timothy hay, the fodder corn, the cabbage
 and the potatoes, across their leaves are
 footsteps.
There is a bold green up over the cracks in
 the corn rows where the crickets go criss-
 cross errands, where the bugs carry pack-
 ages.
Flutter and whirr, you birdies, you newcomers
 in lines and sashes, tellers of harvest
 weather on the way, belts of brown gold
 coming softly.
It is very well the old time streamers take
 up the old time gold haze against the west-
 ern timber line.
It is the old time again when months and birds
 tell each other, "Oh, very well," and repeat it
 where the fields and the timber lines meet
 in belts of brown gold hazes, "Oh, very
 well, Oh, very well."

RIPE CORN

THE wind blows. The corn leans. The corn leaves go rustling. The march
time and the windbeat is on October drums. The stalks of fodder bend
all one way, the way the last windstorm passed.

"Put on my winter clothes; get me an ulster; a yellow ulster to lay down
in January and shut my eyes and cover my ears in snow drifts."

The wind blows. The corn leans. The fodder is russet. October says to the
leaves, "Rustle now to the last lap, to the last leg of the year."

AUBURN

AUBURN autumn leaves, will you come back?
Auburn autumn oaks, foxprints burning soft,
    burning the oaken autumn coats, burning
    the auburn autumn fire—
How can you burn so, how can you go on with
    all this burning, and bring back more to
    burn next year?
Ask and let go, lift this burning of this year
    so much like last year's burning; let next
    year's burning come; ask; let go.
The burnings of the auburn autumn leaves, the
    slow burnt foxprints of the oaken auburns,
    house of leaves and branches, house of leaves
    to burn and branches to be here in the
    white howling, the white quiet of winter—
Going so, going so, auburn house-roof of eaves and
    leaves, the child and the old man, the child and
    the old woman shoot a good-by to you.

The tall old man with clean bones, clean-shape toes
    counting ten against the bed footboard—
This is the tall old man telling a son with clean
    bones a passover auburn and oaken secret—
There are fall leaves, foxprint burnings, this year,
    last year, next year, in all houses, and
Most of all in the house of the tall old man with
    clean bones, clean-shape toes counting ten against
    the bed footboard.
In all houses are leaves burnt and burning, in all hous-
    es branches to be here in the white howling, the patched
    black quiet of winter.

REDHAW RAIN

    THE red rain spatter under the redhaw
    tree, the hut roof branches of the red-
    haw tree, the floor level loam under the

redhaw tree, the meeting place of the
fall red rain and the loam of the first
fall frost—the Pottawatomies took this
into their understanding of why October
so seldom fails, why October so often
brings the red rain spatter under the red-
haw tree.

The slow rain soaks. The farmers fix
wagon axles, patch the barn roof shin-
gles, peek in the thatch of the empty
swallow homes. The farm wives keep to
the kitchens cleaning pans. The slow
rain soaks.

The head at the end of a horse's neck
holds its bone and meat, teeth and eye-
balls, tongue and ears, to the west, to
the east, to the browse of the last of
the sweetgrass range this year. Snow
comes soon, out of the north, to the south
and south. The tongue of the head in
the sweetgrass knows.

The gray west opens for a spear of blue
longer than fifty, a hundred and fifty,
prairie miles.

The gray west opens a triangle silver,
an arch of bar clouds over the prairie.

And the sun washes the spear, the arch,
the triangle, over and over.

WITHOUT NOTICE BEFOREHAND

THE frozen rain of the first November days
came down without notice beforehand
the same as the wind and the frost
loosening the leaves of the buckeye tree,
dropping a yellow rain of flat swirling leaves,
all without notice beforehand, came down,

the same as the far hiding out of lady bugs,
woggle bugs spotted black polka dots
on box car red, on banana yellow,
the same as this going away of the bug families
all went on without notice beforehand.

Under the hedgethorn tree the bugs got together,
families from many directions; they dappled
the dark soil and made a red weather
of the Indian summer afternoon among thorns;
if a man should live a day for every bug
with a paint of box car red, a lamp shade red
on his back, a man would live many years
counting a day for a bug under the Indian summer
hedgethorn afternoon; the farmers husked their
corn in old fashioned Studebaker wagons;
the cream and gold corn ears sent a shine
between the green wagon boards, over the tops
of the green wagon boards; so the bug families
held a pow wow, making a red weather
among thorns in sun patches of Indian summer;
it seemed to be all in a bug family lifetime
coming as it did with no warnings ahead,
no shadow line to tell how soon or late
the frozen rain of the first November days,
coming without notice beforehand.

The buckeye built itself a house of gold and black,
the green leaf roof, the green leaf walls of summer
belted their eaves with bucklers of gold,
changed their arches and let the rich glooms
of the black inside rafters play out;
the shine was loam crossing its heart with gold,
the running out of russet and cream yellow
on the loam black of the forks of the branches
was a sign of summer people leaving
the house the buckeye built itself; and this too
came with no warnings ahead, no shadow line
of the frozen rain of the first November days
coming without notice beforehand.

CORN PRATTLINGS

THE wind came across the corn laughing.
It was late in summer, the limit of summer,
The deadline of early fall time,
And the wind in the laughing corn,
The wind came across.

The wind ran on the tops of the corntassels,
And the pointed long leaves hung over,
Hands obedient to the wind.
And the wind ran once and again for each leaf,
Each pointed long leaf, the wind sang running
Across the corntassels and leaves of corn.

There is a floor the corn grows on,
The roots of the corn go under and twist and hold.
The trunk of the corn stands over the floor,
The leaf and the corntassel signal our winds
And take notice of the path of the sun.

The ears laugh in the husks now.
The big job of the year is done.
It's all over again till next year.
Out of maroon silk and fading greens,
Up over the wandering pumpkin stems,
The yellow and gold kernels laugh.
The big job is over and the laugh of the yellow ears
And the laugh of the running wind go together.
They come across together now late, late, in summer
Early in the fall time of the corntassels.

HAZE GOLD

SUN, you may send your haze gold
Filling the fall afternoon
With a flimmer of many gold feathers.
Leaves, you may linger in the fall sunset

Like late lingering butterflies before frost.
Treetops, you may sift the sunset cross-lights
Spreading a loose checkerwork of gold and shadow.
Winter comes soon—shall we save this, lay it by,
Keep all we can of these haze gold yellows?

WINTER GOLD

THE same gold of summer was on the winter hills,
the oat straw gold, the gold of slow sun change.

The stubble was chilly and lonesome,
the stub feet clomb up the hills and stood.

The flat cry of one wheeling crow faded and came,
ran on the stub gold flats and faded and came.

Fade-me, find-me, slow lights rang their changes
on the flats of oat straw gold on winter hills.

MAROON WITH SILVER FROST

WHISPERS of maroon came on the little river.
The slashed hill took up the sunset,
Took up the evening star.
The brambles crackled in a fire call
To the beginnings of frost.
"It is almost night," the maroon whispered
        in widening blood rings on the little river.
"It is night," the sunset, the evening star
        said later over the hump of the slashed hill.
"What if it is?" the brambles crackled across
        the sure silver beginnings of frost.

CORNFIELD RIDGE AND STREAM

THE top of the ridge is a cornfield.
It rests all winter under snow.
It feeds the broken snowdrifts in spring

To a clear stream cutting down hill to the river.
Late in summer the stream dries; rabbits run and
    birds hop along the dry mud bottom.
Fall time comes and it fills with leaves; oaks and
    shagbark hickories drop their summer hats,
    ribbons, handkerchiefs.
"This is how I keep warm all winter," the stream
    murmurs, waiting till the snowdrifts melt and
    the ice loosens and the clear singing babble
    of spring comes back.

ON A RAILROAD RIGHT OF WAY

STREAM, go hide yourself.
In the tall grass, in the cat-tails,
In the browns of autumn, the last purple
    asters, the yellow whispers.
On the moss rock levels leave the marks
    of your wave-lengths.
Sing in your gravel, in your clean gully.
Let the moaning railroad trains go by.
Till they stop you, go on with your song.

The minnies spin in the water gravel,
In the spears of the early autumn sun.
There must be winter fish.
Babies, you will be jumping fish
In the first snow month.

SO TO SPEAK

DREAMS, graves, pools, growing
flowers, cornfields—these are
silent, so to speak.

Northwest blizzards, sea rocks
apounding in high wind, southeast
sleet after a thaw—these are heard,
so to speak.

Valley Mist

SILVER POINT

THE silver point of an evening star
dropping toward the hammock of new moon
over Lake Okoboji, over prairie waters in Iowa,—
it was framed in the lights just after twilight.

MIST MARCHES ACROSS THE VALLEY

MIST marches across the valley.
Down a long slope the mist marches
And then up a long slope the mist marches
And kingdoms, armies, guns, magic of bookmen, axmen,
The mist marches through them all, gathers them all
And goes to the next valley, goes to the next night,
Goes to the next lookers-on, gathers them all,
Gathers valleys, nights, lookers-on.

Come on down the valley: come on, oh mist.
Whiten us with some of your white.
Show us your gift, your great gift, your white gift
Of gathering all, gathering kingdoms, armies, guns,
Magic of bookmen, axmen, gathering valleys, nights, lookers-on.
Whiten us, oh mist, whiten us with some of this strong soft white of
       yours.

METHUSALEH SAW MANY REPEATERS

METHUSALEH was a witness to many cabbages and kings,
Many widows of the sod and many grass widows,
Many a mother-in-law, many a triangle of one woman and two men or
    one man and two women,

Many who died hungry and crying for their babies, many who died
hungry and no babies at all to cry for.

Methusaleh must have lived eight hundred years or a thousand or two
hundred years.
Methusaleh was an old man when he died and you if you see what
Methusaleh saw,
You will be an old man or an old woman when you die.

Repeat it: Methusaleh saw many cabbages and kings, he was a witness,
a looker-on like me, like you.
Repeat it: Methusaleh was an old man, he saw much before he was
through, and you or I, if we see what Methusaleh saw, if we see it
all before we are through,
You and I will be old, old as Methusaleh, old with our looking on at
cabbages and kings, widows of the sod and the grass, triangles, and
people with babies to cry for and no babies at all to cry for.
Repeat it: Methusaleh was a witness of repeating figures, sea patterns in
the sea sand, land patterns of the land wind, Methusaleh was a wit-
ness, a looker-on like me, like you.

SKETCH OF A POET

HE wastes time walking and telling the air, "I am superior even to the
wind."

On several proud days he has addressed the wide circumambient atmos-
phere, "I am the wind myself."

He has poet's license 4-11-44; he got it even before writing of those "silver
bugs that come on the sky without warning every evening."

He stops for the buzzing of bumblebees on bright Tuesdays in any
summer month; he performs with a pencil all alone among dun cat-
tails, amid climbing juniper bushes, notations rivaling the foot tracks of
anxious spiders; he finds mice homes under beach logs in the sand and
pursues inquiries on how the mice have one room for bed-room, dining-
room, sitting-room and how they have no front porch where they sit pub-
licly and watch passers-by.

He asks himself, "Who else is the emperor of such elegant english? Who else has slipped so often on perilous banana peels and yet lived to put praise of banana peels on sonorous pages?"

One minute he accuses God of having started the world on a shoestring; the next minute he executes a simple twist of the wrist and a slight motion of the hand and insinuates these bones shall rise again.

Yet he wastes time walking and telling the air, "I am superior to the wind," or on proud days, "I am the wind myself."

WHIFFS OF THE OHIO RIVER AT CINCINNATI

1

A YOUNG thing in spring green slippers, stockings,
    silk vivid as lilac-time grass,
And a red line of a flaunt of fresh silk again up under
    her chin—
She slipped along the street at half-past six in the evening,
    came out of the stairway where her street address is,
    where she has a telephone number—
Just a couple of blocks from the street next to the
    Ohio river, where men sit in chairs tipped back,
    watching the evening lights on the water of the
    Ohio river—
She started out for the evening, dark brown calf eyes,
    roaming and hunted eyes,
And her young wild ways were not so young any more,
    nor so wild.

Another evening primrose stood in a stairway, with a
    white knit sweater fitting her shoulders and ribs close.
She asked a young ballplayer passing for a few kind words
    and a pleasant look—and he slouched up to her like an
    umpire calling a runner out at the home plate—he
    gave her a few words and passed on.
She had bells on, she was jingling, and yet—her young
    wild ways were not so young any more, nor so wild.

2

When I asked for fish in the restaurant facing the Ohio river, with fish
  signs and fish pictures all over the wooden, crooked frame of the fish
  shack, the young man said, "Come around next Friday—the fish is
  all gone today."

So, I took eggs, fried, straight up, one side, and he murmured, humming,
  looking out at the shining breast of the Ohio river, "And the next
  is something else; and the next is something else."

The customer next was a hoarse roustabout, handling nail kegs on a
  steamboat all day, asking for three eggs, sunny side up, three, noth-
  ing less, shake us a mean pan of eggs.

And while we sat eating eggs, looking at the shining breast of the Ohio
  river in the evening lights, he had his thoughts and I had mine
  thinking how the French who found the Ohio river named it La
  Belle Riviere meaning a woman easy to look at.

SUBURBAN SICILIAN SKETCHES

1

THE cockleburs came on the burdocks,
a little of thistle, a little of flower,
a light red purple tip on raw green bur.

The burdocks came like hoodlums come;
they came with neither permits nor requests;
they took what they wanted. "If anybody
asks you, this is us, and we are here because
we decided to come to the party—we invited
ourselves and we are welcome."

Listen in the summer when the roots dig in,
the hoodlum roots of the burdock gangs;
what each one sings is much like—
"I'm gonna live anyhow until I die."

In the time of the turning leaves
the light red purple tip and the raw green bur
pass and turn to a brown, to a drab and dirty brown.

2

In Mel-a-rose among the sons of Sicily
I saw a sheep, a dirty undersized sheep,
In the front yard cabbage patch of a son of Sicily,
And the wool of the sheep had never been combed,
The wool of the sheep was snarled and knotted.
And the burdock gang was there,
Burs in the wool with a drab and hoodlum mutter,
'This is us, we invited ourselves and we're welcome.'

3

The sober-faced goat crops grass next to the sidewalk.
A clinking chain connects the collar of the goat with a steel pin driven
    in the ground.
Next to the sidewalk the goat crops November grass,
Pauses seldom, halts not at all, incessantly goes after grass.

4

The playhouse of the Sicilian children
thatched with maple branches their father
threw over for a roof in summer,
the playhouse roof is dry;
It sags and crackles in the west wind.

5

The Sicilian father is tying cornstalks
for a winter vest at the roots of the young apple tree.
This, and the red peppers drying on the cellar door,
this is one of the signs of November.

FLAT WATERS OF THE WEST IN KANSAS

AFTER the sunset in the mountains
there are shadows and shoulders
standing to the stars.
After the sunset on the prairie
there are only the stars,
the stars standing alone.

The flat waters of the west in Kansas
take up the sunset lights
one by one and all—
the bars, the barriers, the slow-down,
the loose lasso handy on the saddle,
the big hats, the slip-knot handkerchiefs,
the cattle horns, the hocks and haunches
ready for the kneel-down, the sleep
of the humps and heads in the grass,
the pony with a rump to the wind
or curving a neck to a front foot—
if a baby moon comes after the sunset
it is a witness of many homes,
many home-makers under the night sky-shed—
and the flat waters of the west in Kansas
take up the baby moon, the witness,
take it and let it ride,
take it and let it have a home.

The great plains
gave the buffalo grass.

The great plains
gave the buffalo grass.

THREE SLANTS AT NEW YORK

New York is a city of many cats.
Some say New York is Babylon.
There is a rose and gold mist New York.

New York is a city of many cats; they eat the swill of the poor and the
swell swill; they rub their backs against fire escapes and weep to each
other from alley barrels; they are born to the cat life of New York.

Some say New York is Babylon; here are Babylonian dancers stripped to
the flash of the navel, while the waiters murmur, "Yes," in undertones
to regular customers calling for the same whiskey as last time; and having
seen a thing of much preparation, toil and genius, having spoken to each

other of how marvelous it is, they eat and drink till it is forgotten; and the topics are easy topics, such as which bootleggers take the biggest risks, and what light risks superior bootleggers travel under.

There is a rose and gold New York of evening lights and sunsets; there is a mist New York seen from steamboats, a massed and spotted hovering ghost, a shape the fists of men have lifted out of dirt and work and daylight and early morning oaths after sleep nights.

> New York is a city of many cats.
> Some say New York is Babylon.
> There is a rose and gold mist New York.

LANDSCAPE INCLUDING THREE STATES OF THE UNION

THE mountains stand up around the main street in Harper's Ferry.
Shadows stand around the town, and mist creeps up the flanks of tall rocks.
A terrible push of waters sometime made a cloven way for their flood here.
On the main street the houses huddle; the walls crouch for cover.
And yet—up at Hilltop House, or up on Jefferson's Rock, there are lookouts;
There are the long curves of the meeting of the Potomac and the Shenandoah;
There is the running water home of living fish and silver of the sun.
The lazy flat rocks spread out browns for green and blue silver to run over.
Mascots of silver circles move around Harper's Ferry.
No wonder John Brown came here to fight and be hanged.
No wonder Thomas Jefferson came here to sit with his proud red head writing notes on the great State of Virginia.
Borders hem the town, borders of Virginia, West Virginia, Maryland;
Be absent minded a minute or two and you guess at what state you are in.
Harper's Ferry is a meeting place of winds and waters, rocks and ranges.

CROSSING OHIO WHEN POPPIES BLOOM IN ASHTABULA

1

Go away. Leave the high winds of May
blowing over the fields of grape vines
near the northwest corner of Pennsylvania.
    Leave the doorstep peonies
    pushing high bosoms at passers-by
    in northern Ohio towns in May.

Leave the boys flying light blue kites
on a deep blue sky; and the yellow, the
yellow spilling over the drinking rims
of the buttercups, piling their yellows
into foam blown sea rims of yellow;
    Go away; go to New York,
    Broadway, Fifth Avenue, glass
    lights and leaves, glass faces,
    fingers; go . . .

2

    Pick me poppies in Ohio,
    mother.
    Pick me poppies in a back yard
    in Ashtabula.
May going, poppies coming, summer humming:
make it a poppy summer, mother; the leaves
sing in the silk, the leaves sing a tawny
red gold; seven sunsets saved themselves
to be here now.

Pick me poppies, mother; go, May; wash me,
summer; shoot up this back yard in Ashta-
bula, shoot it up, give us a daylight fire-
works in Ohio, burn it up with tawny red
gold.

MARCH OF THE HUNGRY MOUNTAINS

ACROSS Nevada and Utah
Look for the march of the hungry mountains.

They are cold and white,
They are taking a rest,
They washed their faces in awful fires,
They lifted their heads for heavy snows.

White, O white, are the vapors,
And the wind in the early morning,
White are the hungry mountains.

The tireless gray desert,
The tireless salt sea,
The tireless mountains,
They are thinking over something.
They are wondering, "What next?"
They are thankful, thinking it over,
Waiting, sleeping, drying their faces from awful fires,
Lifting their heads into higher snow,
White in the early morning wind.

"Come and listen to us,"
Said the marching, hungry mountains.
"You will hear nothing at all,
And you will learn only a little,
And, yet listening, your ears may grow longer and softer;
You may yet have long, clear, listening ears.
Come and listen," said the mocking, hungry mountains.

DIALOGUE

LAKE MICHIGAN: We have been here quite a while.

ILLINOIS PRAIRIE: Maybe.

LAKE: We have seen ten cities.

PRAIRIE: Eleven.

LAKE: Eleven with Chicago.

SMOKE BLUE

THE mountains stood on their bottom ends;
the smoky mountains stood around in blue;
the blue mountains stood around in smoke;

The higher the line of the burnt timber climbed,
the lower the line of the green timber crept;
the creep of the burnt and the green
was a couple of shadows moving through each other.

The farms and the fences came,
And the farmers fixing fences.
The snake rail fences measured the farms;
Hog tight, horse high, they held for the owners
The hogs for hams and the horses for hauls.

The farms came to the valley,
And the mountains stood on their bottom ends;
The mountains stood in a smoke and a blue.

The cities came, the lumber wagons,
The lumber carpenters, the lathers, the plasterers;
The bricklayers came in their overalls,
And the hod-carriers up and down the ladders with mortar
And the bricklayers calling down to the hod-carriers,
         "Mort!"
And the concrete mixers came with their endless bellies
For sand and crushed stone and gravel and cement;
The cities came, stood up, and swore, "This is us, by God."
The cities, the families, the tall two-fisted men, swearing,
    "This is us, by God, this is God's country."

   The boomers boomed the boosters,
   The boosters boosted the boomers.

And the mountains stood on their bottom ends.
The mountains stood in a smoke and a blue.

AGAIN?

OLD MAN WOOLWORTH put up a building.
There it was; his dream; all true;
The biggest building in the world.
Babel, the Nineveh Hanging Gardens,
Karnak, all old, outclassed.
And now, here at last, what of it?
What about it? Well, every morning
We'll walk around it and look up.
And every morning we'll ask what
It means and where it's going.
It's a dream; all true; going somewhere,
That's a cinch; women buying mousetraps,
Wire cloth dishrags, ten cent sheet music,
They paid for it; the electric tower
Might yell an electric sign to the inbound
Ocean liners, 'Look what the washerwomen
Of America can do with their nickels,' or
'See what a nickel and a dime can do,'
And that wouldn't clear Old Man Woolworth's
Head; it was a mystery, a dream, the biggest
Building in the world; Babel, the Nineveh
Hanging Gardens, Karnak, all old,
Outclassed. So the old man cashes in,
The will of the old man is dug out,
And the widow gets thirty million dollars,
Enough to put up another building,
Another bigger than any in the world,
Bigger than Babel, the Nineveh Hanging Gardens,
Karnak, another mystery, another dream
To stand and look up at
And ask what it means.

EVEN NUMBERS

1

A HOUSE like a man all lean and coughing,
a man with his two hands in the air at a cry,
"Hands up."

A house like a woman shrunken and stoop-shouldered,
shrunken and done with dishes and dances.

These two houses I saw going uphill in Cincinnati.

2

Two houses leaning against each other like drunken
brothers at a funeral,

Two houses facing each other like two blind wrestlers
hunting a hold on each other,

These four scrawny houses I saw on a dead level
cinder patch in Scranton, Pennsylvania.

3

And by the light of a white moon in Waukesha, Wisconsin,
I saw a lattice work in lilac time . . . white-mist lavender
. . . a sweet moonlit lavender . . .

CHILLICOTHE

THERE was a man walked out
Of a house in Chillicothe, Ohio,—
Or the house was in Chillicothe, Illinois,
Or again in Chillicothe, Missouri,—

And the man said to himself,
Speaking as men speak their thoughts
To themselves after a funeral or a wedding,
After seeing a baby born with raw, red toes

And the toe-nails pink as the leaves of fresh flowers,
Or after seeing a kinsman try to hold on
To the fading door-frames of life
And then languish, let go, and sleep,—

Speaking his own thoughts,
Or what he believed in so far as he knew
To be thoughts peculiar to himself alone,
At that hour of time, under the clocks and suns,
He said, and to himself:

"I have never seen myself live a day.
I have told myself I get up in the morning,
I wash my face, I reach for a towel, I find a razor,
I shave off a day- or a two-day growth of whiskers.
I look in the looking-glass and say,
'Birdie, whither away today?' or I say,
'You old hound dog, are you on to yourself?' or
'What's in the wind for this evening?' or,
'Who put the fish in efficiency?' or,
'What packages will be handed us this morning?'

"Yes, I stand in front of the looking-glass,
And while I am shaving I sometimes ask questions
Exactly as though the house I am shaving in
Is a wagon crossing Oklahoma looking for a home,
Or a steamboat on the tossing salt, two days from Sandy
        Hook,
Or a Pullman sleeper crossing the divide in Colorado—
This must be why I say to the looking-glass,
'You are the same when I am shaving, always,
Whether we are in Oklahoma, off Sandy Hook,
Or hitting the high spot of the Colorado divide;
Your business as a looking-glass is to say 'Me, too,'
'Here it is,' 'Here you are,' 'I don't want to tell you no lie.
If I tell a lie, I lose out as a looking-glass.'

"There are hinged elbows of arms, sockets in shoulder-
        bones.
And out beyond the elbows are finger-bones, finger-ends.

And after a while the command runs out to the finger-ends
To wipe off the lather, throw a hot towel, witch hazel,
Then dry smooth the face, talcum, and call it a once over.
This action finished, I can testify all day, 'I shaved this
          morning'
Or if there is a murder or a robbery, and I am called as a
          witness
In the matter of an identity or an alibi or *corpus delicti,*
I can solemnly swear at this hour I shaved my face, at this
          hour
I commanded the members and parts of my body in these
          performances.
I shaved this morning.

"Yet all this is only a whiff, a little comic beginning.
Ever since I have owned more than one shirt
I have had to decide which shirt to wear today.
There was a year when I had only one shirt,
And even then I had to decide whether I would wear that
          one shirt
Or whether I would get along with no shirt at all.
Now, having six shirts, I must pick one and let five others
          go.
If there are buttons off the shirt, I decide
How many new buttons go on.

"Decisions—see? It is early in the day, it is not a half-hour
Since I was in the sheets of unremembering slumber.
Yet the day's decisions have mounted steadily as the climb
          of the sun
Up and on across the elements of the sky.

"Yes? Quite so. And sure, Mike.
These things count for nothing much.
There is no special destiny about them.
They are different from falling in love
Or calling up a doctor to tie an artery
Or writing a lawyer about a bastardy case,
Or telling a panhandler you are broke yourself,
And do your shopping by looking in the show-windows.

"Yes, they are all different.
Yet they all connect up with civilization
Or tombs and ramparts earlier than civilization.
So God help your soul when you get tired of them and say:
'I want something new. I want two and two to be five. I want a miracle
    to happen, miracles now and henceforth. I want the light that never
    was on land or sea.' "

And all the time it is the same man speaking,
The same man who walked out of his house
In Chillicothe, Ohio, Chillicothe, Illinois, or Chillicothe,
        Missouri;
It is the same man speaking his own thoughts,
As if thoughts come to him and belong to him alone,
And as though it is useless to pass them on—
It is the same man speaking.

"I have never seen myself live a day.
I have pulled up a chair to the breakfast table
And watched children tuck napkins under their chin,
Spill the yellow of eggs down their bibs,
Clean their plates, lick their spoons, call for more to eat,
While they banged their spoons and bowls on the table
And went on yammering for more to eat.
I have seen them use their tongues as cats and dogs
Employ their tongues, as utensils, conveniences,
With laughters shining in their eyes.
And when they began talking, they lied to each other,
They lied with an importance of falsifying large.
They broke out with impossible propositions.
They acted as though they live in a republic of separate
        laws,
Under a government whose laws go deeper than the speech
Of people expert and renowned for their ways of speech.
Their laughter ran as the water of waterfalls runs.

"They were so proud, so sure, in all their ways, I said:
'What goes? What drops off? What is the sheath they lose
When they grow up and get big and leave behind them
Their republic of separate laws,

Their government of laws deeper than speech,
Their civilization of impossible propositions?
Why shall they seem no longer so proud, so sure,
With laughter running as the water of waterfalls runs?'

"I ask myself just that question.
I asked it far inside of myself.
And it was such a far-off question, if I had whispered it
They would have known it was not to be answered."

And this was only one morning
Among the many mornings of that man
Speaking to himself what he considered his own thoughts
Going out of the door of his house in Chillicothe.

And these are only a few of the thoughts of that one morning.
For, when he reached the gate and stepped to the sidewalk,
He said again to himself:

"I have never seen myself live a day."

SPLINTER

THE voice of the last cricket
across the first frost
is one kind of good-by.
It is so thin a splinter of singing.

SANTA FE SKETCHES

1

THE valley was swept with a blue broom to the west.

And to the west, on the fringes of a mesa sunset,
there are blue broom leavings, hangover blue wisps—
bluer than the blue floor the broom touched
before and after it caught the blue sweepings.

The valley was swept with a blue broom to the west.

2

When a city picks a valley—and a valley picks a city—
it is a marriage—and there are children.

Since the bluebirds come by twenties
and the blackbirds come by forties
in March, when the snow skirls in a sunshine wind;
since they come up the valley to the city, heading north,
it is taken as a testimony of witnesses.

When the bluebird barriers drop,
when the redwing bars go down,
the flurries of sun flash now on the tail feathers—
it is up the valley—up and on—
by twenties and forties—
and the tail feathers flashing.

In the cuts of the red dirt arroyos,
at the change of the mist of the mountain waterfalls,
in cedars and piñons, at the scars and gashes,
at the patches where new corn will be planted,
at the Little Canyon of the Beans,
they stop and count how far they have come,
the twenties and forties stop and count.

> Whoever expected them to remember,
> to carry little pencils between their toes,
> notebooks under their wings?
> By twenties, by forties—it is enough;
> "When wings come, and sun, and a new wind
> out of the Southwest whispering—
> and especially wings—we forget—
> we forget."

They saw Navajos ride with spears and arrows,
Spaniards ride with blunderbusses,
cowboys ride with Colts and Winchesters—
they saw the changing shooting irons—
and now the touring-car and flivver
creep up the red dirt valley, among the rabbit bushes,

passing the clean-piled clean-cut woodpiles
on the backs of mountain-born burros.

3

The valley sits with its thoughts.

"Have I not had my thoughts by myself
four hundred years?" she asks.

"Have I not seen the guns of Spain, Mexico
and America go up and down the valley?

"Is not holy faith and the name of a saint
in my name?

"Was I not called La Villa de Sante Fé de
San Francisco de Assisi?

"Do they not name a railroad from Chicago
to Los Angeles after me?

"Did they not give a two-thousand-mile wagon
trail of the first gold diggers, the forty-niners,
my name, the short pet name, Santa Fé?

"Do you wonder I sit here, like an easy woman,
not young, not old—
Do you wonder I sit here, shrewd, faded, asking:
What next? who next?
And answering my own questions: I don't care—
let the years worry."

4

By twenties and forties,
the bluebirds and the redwings,
out of the bars, the barriers,
in a flash of tail feathers
on and up the valley—
"When wings come
and the Southwest whispering,
we forget."

5

The valley city sits among its brooding facts,
"Six years ago—only ponies, bridles, saddles circled
around the public square, the plaza, the place of the
Summer band concerts—
And now—the varnished motor-cars stand with funeral
faces filling the old pony hitching places.

"I have seen candles keep the night watch till the coal
oil came and then the live wires—
Thirty miles away the mountain villages see two strings
of lights hung like Summer flies—the penitentiary night
lights of Santa Fé.

"The fast travelers with extra tires come in a hurry
and solve me and pass on to say all their lives,
'Santa Fé? oh yes, Santa Fé, I have seen Santa Fé.'
'Hurry up,' is their first and last word on my zigzag
streets, my lazy 'dobe corners.
'Hurry up, we must see the Old Church, the Old Bell, the
Oldest House in the United States, touch the doors,
and then go on—hurry up!'

"They are afraid grass will grow under their feet—they
say so as a proverb—
And I am afraid they will knock loose some cool green
whisper of moss in a chink of a wall."

6

In April the little farmers go out in the foothills,
up the mountain patches.
They go to gamble against the weather, the rain.

"If the rain comes like last year, we shall have a fat
winter,
If the rain comes like year before last, it is a lean
Christmas for us."

They put in their beans, the magic frijole, the chile,
they stretch open hands to the sky,
and tell the rain to come,
to come, come, come.

With a willing rain the gamblers win.
If the rain says, "Not this year," they lose.

So the little farmers go out in the foothills,
up the mountain patches in April,
telling every bean in the sack
to send up a wish to God
for water to come . . . out of the sky.

7

A loose and changeable sky
looks on a loose and changeable land.

The rain rips the wagon road ruts
    too deep for wheels—the wagons make a new road,
    the rain makes a new little arroyo.
Pack burros tussling under bundled woodpiles go by
    with eyes murmuring, "Everything is the same as it
    always was."
The tough little tussling foot of a burro, the wag of
    a left ear to a right ear, are they joking, "Every-
    thing is the same as it always was?"

8

Proud and lazy Spaniards with your pearl swords
    of conquest, your blunderbuss guns of flags and
    victory—
Who did you conquer and fasten down as your vassals?

The blood is dry and mixed in a mixing-bowl.
The passion kiss and the sunlit blaze of the Indian woman's eye—the
    faces and the hair of Spain and the Aztecs, Moors and the Navajos—
    are mixed in a mixing-bowl—and a passer-by writes:

"In Mexico nobody knows how to sing
 and everybody sings."

Come back and pick up your pearl-handled swords,
your blunderbuss guns.
Sniff with the tourists in the Santa Fé Museum—

See them look at their stop-watches—
"A little gas now—and we're on our way—come on
kid—on your way."

9

The valley was swept with a blue broom to the west,
there are blue broom leavings on the sky,
hangover blue wisps.
The valley city sits with its thoughts.
"Have I not had my thoughts by myself
four hundred years?" she asks.
"Do you wonder I sit here, shrewd, faded,
asking: What next? who next?
And answering: I don't care—let the
years worry."

10

By twenties and forties,
the bluebirds and the redwings,
out of the bars, the barriers,
in a flash of tail feathers
on and up the valley—
"When wings come
and the Southwest whispering,
we forget."

Little Album

NEW HAMPSHIRE AGAIN

I REMEMBER black winter waters,
I remember thin white birches,
I remember sleepy twilight hills,

I remember riding across New
Hampshire lengthways.
I remember a station named
"Halcyon," a brakeman call-
ing to passengers "Halcyon!!
Halcyon!!"
I remember having heard the
gold diggers dig out only
enough for wedding rings.
I remember a stately child tell-
ing me her father gets letters
addressed "Robert Frost, New
Hampshire."
I remember an old Irish saying,
"His face is like a fiddle and
every one who sees him must
love him."
I have one remember, two re-
members, ten remembers; I
have a little handkerchief
bundle of remembers.

One early evening star just over
a cradle moon,
One dark river with a spatter of
later stars caught,
One funnel of a motorcar head-
light up a hill,
One team of horses hauling a
bobsled load of wood,
One boy on skis picking himself
up after a tumble—
I remember one and a one and a
one riding across New Hamp-
shire lengthways: I have a lit-
tle handkerchief bundle of re-
members.

A COUPLE

HE was in Cincinnati, she in Burlington.
He was in a gang of Postal Telegraph linemen.
She was a pot rassler in a boarding house.
"The crying is lonely," she wrote him.
"The same here," he answered.
The winter went by and he came back and they married
And he went away again where rainstorms knocked down telegraph
    poles and wires dropped with frozen sleet.
And again she wrote him, "The crying is lonely."
And again he answered, "The same here."
Their five children are in the public schools.
He votes the Republican ticket and is a taxpayer.
They are known among those who know them
As honest American citizens living honest lives.
Many things that bother other people never bother them.
They have their five children and they are a couple,
A pair of birds that call to each other and satisfy.
As sure as he goes away she writes him, "The crying is
          lonely"
And he flashes back the old answer, "The same here."
It is a long time since he was a gang lineman at Cincinnati
And she was a pot rassler in a Burlington boarding house;
Yet they never get tired of each other; they are a couple.

CHICAGO BOY BABY

THE baby picked from an ash barrel by the night police
came to the hospital of the Franciscan brothers
in a diaper and a white sheet.

It was a windy night in October, leaves and geese scurrying
across the north sky, and the curb pigeons more ravenous
than ever for city corn in the cracks of the street stones.

The two policemen who picked the baby from the ash barrel
are grayheads; they talk about going on the pension list

soon; they talk about whether the baby, surely a big man
now, votes this year for Smith or Hoover.

JOKE GOLD

It arose with him as a joke,
His saying so often with a mystical gesture
Known to all as a joke,
"There's gold in them hills, Jack."
All of us laughed and he laughed most
At the comic illusion of gold hunters
Picking hills to gamble in, with
Hopes and shovels, burros and frying pans,
The yellow shine of the high lure
Overlying life's high points.
It was all there in his sudden interjection,
"There's gold in them hills, Jack."
His wife, his other women, his new jobs
One after the other, his swaggering neckties,
Sport shirts, and allusions to men with fat
Checkbooks he lunched with chummily,
It all tied in with his always saying
Gold lay in hills beyond, joke gold
In joke hills to be made into real gold
In real hills for wishing, for only enough
Wishing—it was all in his voice when he
Went away and was never heard from again,
Stepping on the outbound train west
Saying, "Gold in them hills, Jack."

THE OLD FLAGMAN

The old flagman has great-grandchildren.
Ruddy as a hard nut, hair in his ears, clear sea lights in his eyes,
He goes out of his shanty and lifts a sign: Stop.

"Y'see where the sign is dented?
I hit a fellah over the head with it,

The only way to stop him gettin' run over.
They want to get killed; I have to stop 'em.
That's my job."

He was twenty years a policeman in Chicago.
"I carry a bullet in my guts an I got an abscess in my gall bladder—
     I picked this shanty for a rest.
I go slow and careful; I got a leak in the heart; if
I laugh too hard my heart stops—and I fall down;
I have to watch myself."

A third rail car hoots up the line.
He goes out with a warning in his hand: Stop.
"These damn fools, they want to get under the wheels.
I have to stop 'em."

Ruddy as a hard nut, hair in his ears, clear sea lights in his eyes.

IGLITS AND HIS WIFE

IGLITS' wife spoke of her own novel, of a Norwegian's novel and came finally to speak of Whimsley and Whimsley's wife and egg spots on the wallpaper and fly specks on the new white kalsomining of the sleeping room of Whimsley and Whimsley's wife.
> Iglits' wife went on patching a picture together in clean polite language, hearsay and circumstance.

The cool abstraction of the scientist, the mocking sleight-of-hand passes of the artist, the galloping babble of the gossip who mixes names and dates for the sake of the story and only asks a laugh or a giggle before going on to another laugh—
> These were lost in the list of witnesses ready to testify to the egg spots on the wallpaper, the fly specks on the new white kalso-mining of the sleeping room of Whimsley and Whimsley's wife.

Iglits mentions the weather to the housemaid serving washed apricots for breakfast, mentions letters and filing devices to the stenographer in the downtown office.
> Iglits buys whiskey from two booze runners; a bottle is in his desk always; Iglits says he wants to be lit up a little every day.

MEDLEY

IGNORANCE came in stones of gold;
The ignorant slept while the hangmen
Hanged the keepers of the lights
Of sweet stars: such were the apothegms,
Offhand offerings of mule-drivers
Eating sandwiches of rye bread,
Salami and onions.

"Too Many Books," we always called him;
A landscape of masterpieces and old favorites
Fished with their titles for his eyes
In the upstairs and downstairs rooms
Of his house. Whenever he passed
The old-time bar-room where Pete Morehouse
Shot the chief of police, where
The sponge squads shot two bootleggers,
He always remembered the verse story,
The Face on the Bar-room Floor—
The tramp on a winter night,
Saddened and warmed with whiskey,
Telling of a woman he wanted
And a woman who wanted him,
How whiskey wrecked it all;
Taking a piece of chalk,
Picturing her face on the bar-room floor,
Fixing the lines of her face
While he told the story,
Then gasping and falling with finished heartbeats,
Dead.

And whenever he passed over the bridge at night
And took the look up the river to smaller bridges,
Barge lights, and looming shores,
He always thought of Edgar Allan Poe,
With a load of hootch in him,
Going to a party of respectable people
Who called for a speech,

Who listened to Poe recite the Lord's Prayer,
Correctly, word for word, yet with lush, unmistakable
Intonations, so haunting the dinner-party people
All excused themselves to each other.

Whenever Too Many Books
Passed over the town bridge in the gloaming,
He thought of Poe breaking up that party
Of respectable people. Such was Too Many Books—
We called him that.

IMPLICATIONS

WHEN the charge of election bribery was brought against an Illinois senator, he replied, "I read the Bible and believe it from cover to cover."

When his accusers specified five hundred dollars of corruption money was paid in a St. Louis hotel bathroom, his friends answered, "He is faithful to his wife and always kind to his children."

When he was ousted from the national senate and the doors of his bank were closed by government receivers and a grand jury indicted him, he took the vows of an old established church.

When a jury acquitted him of guilt as a bank wrecker, following the testimony of prominent citizens that he was an honest man, he issued a statement to the public for the newspapers, proclaiming he knew beforehand no jury would darken the future of an honest man with an unjust verdict.

TO THE GHOST OF JOHN MILTON

IF I should pamphleteer twenty years against royalists,
With rewards offered for my capture dead or alive,
And jails and scaffolds always near,

And then my wife should die and three ignorant daughters
Should talk about their father as a joke, and steal the
Earnings of books, and the poorhouse always reaching for
    me,

If I then lost my eyes and the world was all dark and I
Sat with only memories and talk—

I would write "Paradise Lost," I would marry a second wife
And on her dying I would marry a third pair of eyes to
Serve my blind eyes, I would write "Paradise Regained," I
Would write wild, foggy, smoky, wordy books—

I would sit by the fire and dream of hell and heaven,
Idiots and kings, women my eyes could never look on again,
And God Himself and the rebels God threw into hell.

HEAVY AND LIGHT

And you, old woman, are carrying scrub buckets tonight.
Just like last year, just like the year before,
Every Saturday night you come gripping the handles,
Throwing the suds, cleaning this room's floor.
They call you "Mrs. Swanson," your hair is thin and gray,
It is a lean little wiry frame you move in.
In your eyes you are ready for whatever comes next.
Your sons have scrubbed ship decks, an uncle somewhere
Stood at a wheel in a Baltic storm—why must there be
Some rag of romance, some slant of a scarlet star
Over and around your scrub buckets?

         · · ·

Fritters used to say, "There is poetry in neckties."
He picked neckties with a theory of color and design.
He knew haberdashers the way book bugs know where second-hand book-
    stores are.
For a picnic he wore pink, for a fall fog day a gray blue,
And a four-in-hand, a bow, a bat-eye, each in its separate individual silk,
    plain or striped or spotted,
Each had its message, its poem, its reminders, for Fritters.
"I know how to pick 'em," he used to say, "I know the right scarf for
    either a wedding or a funeral or a poker party, there is poetry in
    neckties."

EARLY HOURS
(*To A. W. F.*)

SINCE you packed your rubber bottom boots
And took the night train for northern Wisconsin
To hunt deer in the ten days allowed by law,
I have remembered your saying the hunters
Get up out of bed and dress for shooting,
For reading snow tracks, circling, waiting, firing,
At the hour of half past four in the morning;
Now this has been in my mind sometimes
When after a long day's work and more than half a night
I opened the east window before going to bed
At half past three o'clock in the morning
And there were deer feet and horns of stars on the sky.
I listened to the chiming of a watch and said,
"A couple of hours and Jim'll kill a deer, maybe."
There are different kinds of early hours.

HUNGRY AND LAUGHING MEN

LOVE to keep? There is no love to keep.
There is memory to keep of running water,
        running horses, running weather, running days.

When I see the rain-glad eaves filling and the
        beat of the running spills on the ferns,
Or if I come to a pony heel mark, a half loop on
        a smooth Kentucky blue grass,
Or stand in a Dutch landscape of running threats
        in changing lights of interchangeable running
        sun and rain-cloud—
I shall take old note-books of Hokusai and Hiroshige,
        memoirs of the wonderful hungry laughing men, and in
        an off corner, write my code:
            Love to keep? There is no love to keep.
            There is memory of runners, foot-glad flingers,
            heel marks in the blue grass, running
            threats of interchangeable sun and rain-cloud.

FATE

FATE comes with pennies or dollars.
An Indian head or the Goddess of Liberty:
    it is all the same to Fate.
One day copper, one day silver, and these
    are samples:
        The cry held back
        the kiss kept under
        the song choked down
        the wish never spoken.
They are pennies and dollars these.
The girl at the sink washing dishes knows them.
The girl who has breakfast in bed knows them.

CHEAP BLUE

HILL blue among the leaves in summer,
Hill blue among the branches in winter—
Light sea blue at the sand beaches in winter,
Deep sea blue in the deep deep waters—
Prairie blue, mountain blue—
    Who can pick a pocketful of these blues,
        a handkerchief of these blues,
    And go walking, talking, walking as though
    God gave them a lot of loose change
    For spending money, to throw at the birds,
    To flip into the tin cups of blind men?

LAVENDER LILIES

THE lavender lilies in Garfield Park lay lazy in the morning sun.
A cool summer wind flicked at our eyebrows and the pansies fixed their
    yellow drops and circles for a day's show.
The statue of Lincoln, an ax in his hand, a bronze ax, was a chum of five
    bluejays crazy and calling, "Another lovely morning, another lovely
    morning."

And the headline of my newspaper said, "Thirty dead in race riots."
And Lincoln with the ax, and all the lavender lilies and the cool summer
wind and the pansies, the living lips of bronze and leaves, the living
tongues of bluejays, all they could say was,
"Another lovely morning, another lovely morning."

HALF WAY

AT the half-way house the pony died.
The road stretched ahead, the sunny hills,
    people in the fields, running waters,
    towns with new names, windmills pointing
    circles in the air at holy crossroads.
It was here we stopped at the half-way house,
    here where the pony died.
Here the keeper of the house said, "It is strange
    how many ponies die here."

BETWEEN WORLDS

AND he said to himself
in a sunken morning moon
between two pines,
between lost gold and lingering green:

I believe I will count up my worlds.
There seem to me to be three.
There is a world I came from which is Number One.
There is a world I am in now, which is Number Two.
There is a world I go to next, which is Number Three.

There was the seed pouch, the place I lay dark in, nursed and shaped in
    a warm, red, wet cuddling place; if I tugged at a latchstring or
    doubled a dimpled fist or twitched a leg or a foot, only the Mother
    knew.

There is the place I am in now, where I look back and
    look ahead, and dream and wonder.

There is the next place—

And he took a look out of a window
at a sunken morning moon
between two pines,
between lost gold and lingering green.

M'LISS AND LOUIE

When M'Liss went away from the old home
with its purple lilacs in front and white
fence pickets and green grass—

Where the slow black covers of evening and
night came dropping softly before the gold
moon came on the yellow roses—

Louie, the lonesome, spoke his thoughts to himself,
sitting in that same moonlight coming on the lilacs,
the roses:—

> Let her win her own thoughts; let her be
> M'Liss always; let her sit alone after
> whatever happens and see some of the outs
> and ins of it;
>
> Let her know the feel of the bones of
> one of her hands resting on the other;
>
> Let her lose love, gold,
> names, promises, savings;
>
> Let her know hot lips, crazy love letters,
> cool heels, good wings, birds crossing big
> windows of blue skies, time, oh God, time to
> think things over; let her be M'Liss;
>
> Let her be easy with all meanings of quiet
> new sunsets, quiet fresh mornings, and long
> sleeps in the old still moonlight;
>
> Let her be M'Liss always.

Well . . . well . . . it was growing late in the evening of that day
when M'Liss went away, late, late into the night, as Louie, the lone-

some, sat sleepy in the gold of that same moon coming on the fence pickets and the green grass, the purple lilacs, the yellow roses.

He was sleepy. Yet he could not sleep.

Bitter Summer Thoughts

PHIZZOG

THIS face you got,
This here phizzog you carry around,
You never picked it out for yourself,
    at all, at all—did you?
This here phizzog—somebody handed it
    to you—am I right?
Somebody said, "Here's yours, now go see
    what you can do with it."
Somebody slipped it to you and it was like
    a package marked:
"No goods exchanged after being taken away"—
This face you got.

BITTER SUMMER THOUGHTS

THE riders of the wind
Weave their shadows,
Trample their time-beats,
Take their time-bars,
Shake out scrolls,
And run over the oats, the barley,
Over the summer wheat-fields.

The farmer and the horse,
The steel and the wagon
Come and clean the fields
And leave us stubble.
The time-bars of the wind are gone;
The shadows, time-beats, scrolls,
They are woven away, put past,
Into the hands of threshers,
Into chaff, into dust,
Into rust and buff of straw stacks,
Into sliding, shoveling oats and wheat.
Over the wheat-fields,
Over the oats,
Summer weaves, is woven away, put past,
Into dust, into rust and buff.

Indian runners ran along this river road.
They cleaned the wind they clutched in ribs and lungs,
Up over the clean ankles, the clean elbows.
The Frenchmen came with lessons and prayers.
The Scotchmen came with horses and rifles.
Cities, war, railroads came.

In the rain storms, in the blizzards,
This river road is clean.

BITTER SUMMER THOUGHTS—NO. 3

FIRECRACKERS came from China.
Watermelons came from Egypt.
The horses of the sun hoist their heads and nicker at the fence where the
first old evening stars fish for faces.
And the light of the eyes of a child at a morning window calling to an
early morning snow, this too is a stranger among strangers.

The splendors of old books may be counted.
The spears of brass lights, shining in the dawn of the tug-boats and ware-
houses, throw other splendors.
Yet a corn wind is in my ears, a rushing of corn leaves swept by summer,
it is in my ears, the corn wind.

BITTER SUMMER THOUGHTS—NO. XXII

QUICKER AND EASIER

THE billboards and the street car signs told the people,
"Say it with flowers" and those who could buy flowers
And who knew no other way of saying found themselves
In the habit of saying it with flowers.
Men whose personal fragrance had no special whiff
Of fresh air, clean dirt, and growing things,
Found it easier to telephone the florist
And say it with flowers—quicker and easier.

YES, SAY IT WITH FLOWERS!

Women rather wear flowers than no flowers.
Gift flowers never tell where they came from.
A woman's flowers ought to whisper she has
        secrets worth hearing told.
If a woman tells a man, "Send me no flowers,"
        that is the end.
All women try to guess who would send an armful
        of roses for the coffin if one dies, if one has
        a funeral, if all one's friends know there is a
        funeral.
Each woman knows what one flower she would wear if
        called on to wear a flower at a wedding tomorrow.

BARS

BEAT at the bars.
Cry out your cry of want.
Let yourself out if you can.
Find the sea, find the moon,
        if you can.
Shut the windows, open the doors.
There are no windows, are no doors?
There is no sea, is no moon?
Cry your cry, let yourself out if you can.

THEY ASK: IS GOD, TOO, LONELY?

WHEN God scooped up a handful of dust,
And spit on it, and molded the shape of man,
And blew a breath into it and told it to walk—
That was a great day.

And did God do this because He was lonely?
Did God say to Himself he must have company
And therefore He would make man to walk the earth
And set apart churches for speech and song with God?

These are questions.
They are scrawled in old caves.
They are painted in tall cathedrals.
There are men and women so lonely they believe
    God, too, is lonely.

TWO NOCTURNS

1

THE sea speaks a language polite people never repeat.
It is a colossal scavenger slang and has no respect.
Is it a terrible thing to be lonely?

2

The prairie tells nothing unless the rain is willing.
It is a woman with thoughts of her own.
Is it a terrible thing to love much?

USELESS WORDS

So long as we speak the same language and never understand each other,
So long as the spirals of our words snarl and interlock
And clutch each other with the irreckonable gutturals,
Well . . .

WANTING THE IMPOSSIBLE

SUPPOSE he wishes balloon routes
            to five new moons, one woman,
            and a two-acre bean farm with
            bean poles and waltzing scare-
            crows wearing clown hats:
Ah-hah, ah-hah, this to God,
            this to me, this is something.

MONEY, POLITICS, LOVE AND GLORY

WHO put up that cage?
Who hung it up with bars, doors?
Why do those on the inside want to get out?
Why do those outside want to get in?
What is this crying inside and out all the time?
What is this endless, useless beating of baffled
      wings at these bars, doors, this cage?

THE WAY OF THE WORLD
(After Gustave Fröding in the Swedish)

THE sea roars, the storm whistles,
Waves roll ashen gray;
"Man overboard, captain!"
      Is that so?

"You can save his life yet, captain!"
The sea roars, the storm whistles.
"Throw a rope to him, you can reach him."
      Is that so?

Waves roll ashen gray.
"He's gone down, you can't see him
      any more, captain!"
      Is that so?
The sea roars, the storm whistles.

EARLY LYNCHING

Two Christs were at Golgotha.
One took the vinegar, another looked on.
One was on the cross, another in the mob.
One had the nails in his hands, another the stiff
    fingers holding a hammer driving nails.
There were many more Christs at Golgotha, many more
    thief pals, many many more in the mob howling the
    Judean equivalent of, "Kill Him! Kill Him!"
The Christ they killed, the Christ they didn't kill,
    those were the two at Golgotha.

Pity, pity, the bones of these broken ankles.
Pity, pity, the slimp of these broken wrists.
The mother's arms are strong to the last.
She holds him and counts the heart drips.

The smell of the slums was on him.
Wrongs of the slums lit his eyes.
Songs of the slums wove in his voice
The haters of the slums hated his slum heart.

The leaves of a mountain tree,
Leaves with a spinning star shook in them,
Rocks with a song of water, water, over them,
Hawks with an eye for death any time, any time,
The smell and the sway of these were on his sleeves,
    were in his nostrils, his words.

The slum man they killed, the mountain man lives on.

PLUNGER

EMPTY the last drop.
Pour out the final clinging heartbeat.
Great losers look on and smile.
Great winners look on and smile.

Plunger:
Take a long breath and let yourself go.

Rain Winds

RAIN WINDS BLOW DOORS OPEN

Dreaming of grips at her heart
She asked in a sleep and between sleeps,
"What is mercy and why am I asking mercy?"

The doors in her dreams opened
And a rain wind blew in the doorway
And treetops moaned under footsteps over.

Dreaming of a road running off
Into the roads gone crossways on the sky,
She shook in a dream and cried between sleeps,
"How many miles, how many days, how many years?"

The strips of the sun
Spelled a name on the floor in the morning.
She tried to spell out the name, the letters.
"A rain wind blows in the doorway," she said,
"And a road goes crossways on the sky," she said,
"And the night lets nobody know how many miles,
     how many days, how many years."

WIND HORSES

Roots, go deep: wrap your coils; fasten your knots:
Fix a loop far under, a four-in-hand far under:
The wind drives wild horses, gnashers, plungers:
     Go deep, roots.
Hold your four-in-hand knots against all wild horses.

RIVER MOON

THE moon in the river, mother, is a red, red moon tonight.
I am going away on the wild, wild moon, the moon so red on the river
    tonight, mother.

A man with a wild dream on his tongue, a flying wild dream in his
    head and his heart,
A man is here with a runaway drum in his ribs, and shots of the sun in
    the runners of his blood.

I am going away on the red, wild runaway moon.
The moon on the river, mother, is red tonight.

The mist on the river is white and the moon on the mist is white.
I remember, mother, I remember he came when the moon was red, with
    a runaway drum in his ribs.
I remember, mother, the shots of the sun in the runners of his blood,
    the flying wild dream on his tongue.
Tonight I remember, tonight with the mist on the river white and the
    moon on the mist white.

Something is gone—is it him that's gone or is it the red, wild runaway
    moon that's gone?

THEY MET YOUNG

1

"I COULD cry for roses, thinking of you,
Thinking of your lips, so like roses,
Thinking of the meetings of lips
And the crying of eyes meeting."

"I could love you in shadows, drinking
Of you, drinking till a morning sun.
I could touch the young heart of you
And learn all your red songs."

"I could answer the metronomes of blood,
The time-beats of your sweet kisses.
I could sing a star song or a sun song
In the crying of eyes meeting."

2

"Give me your lips.
Let Egypt come or Egypt go.
Open a window of stars.
Let a bag of shooting stars fall.
Wind us with a winding silk.
Pick us a slouching, foolish moon.
Take us to a silver blue morning.
It is too much—let your lips go.
The hammers call, the laws of the
        hammers knock on gongs, beat and
        beat on gongs.
It is too much—give me your lips
        —let your lips go."

YELLOW EVENING STAR

THE flush pink runner of the sun
Ran out with a ribbon leap
In the line of a yellow evening star.

Was there a murmur?
"Whither thou goest thither will I go?"
Was there a run and a jump—
Then old sea cliffs, clean high bastions?

FACE

I WOULD beat out your face in brass.
The side of your head I would beat out in brass.
The nose, the mouth, the hang of the hair thick over
        your head, the cool straight-looking forehead,

I would take a hammer and a sheet of brass and beat
    them out till your face would be set against rain,
    frost, storm, sea-water and sea-salt, against hoofs,
    wheels, nails, against tidewater, rust, verdigris.
I would set your face at a blue crossways of sea beaches,
    a dream of blue and brass.

HEAD

HERE is a head with a blur of horizons.
She sits where a sweep of leaves is on.
When the wind swept in the spring leaves,
When the wind swept out the autumn leaves,
She sat here with her head a blur of horizons.
She sat here and a worker in brass asked her.
And no answer came and the winds swept on
And the leaves swept on and her head took form
Against the blur of horizons.

EXPLANATIONS OF LOVE

THERE is a place where love begins and a place
where love ends.

There is a touch of two hands that foils all
dictionaries.

There is a look of eyes fierce as a big Bethlehem open hearth
furnace or a little green-fire acetylene torch.

There are single careless bywords portentous as a
big bend in the Mississippi River.

Hands, eyes, bywords—out of these love makes
battlegrounds and workshops.

There is a pair of shoes love wears and the coming
is a mystery.

There is a warning love sends and the cost of it
is never written till long afterward.

There are explanations of love in all languages
and not one found wiser than this:

There is a place where love begins and a place
where love ends—and love asks nothing.

SEVEN ELEVEN

Among the grackles in a half circle on the grass
Two walked side by side on two legs apiece.

Treetops bent in the wind and bird nests shuddered.
This was why and only why the grackles sat in a half circle.

Seven grackles came at first and sat in the half circle.
Then there were eleven came with two legs apiece and sat in.

They might have been crapshooters full of hope and hot
        breaths.
They might have been believers in luck, come seven, come
        eleven.

SPRAY

I wonder what they called
Across the beaten spray,
Across the night's forehead.

"The long kiss lasts," he told her.
"I'm crazy about you," she answered.

So they called
    to the beaten spray,
    to the night's forehead.

BROKEN HEARTED SOPRANO

WHEN the soprano sang,
"Ask the stars, O beloved,"
There was a wind piling a cover,
Over the sky a cover of black.

And the soprano was feeling
With a left hand over her heart
Trying to feel the deep hurt places,
Trying to measure the tired depths.

There is a wind piles covers.
The sky knows that wind out of old times.
The stars know that wind out of old times.

. . .

Have you pointed a finger
And beckoned a loose hand
Up at one star and found no answer?

EPISTLE

JESUS loved the sunsets on Galilee.
Jesus loved the fishing boats forming silhouettes
    against the sunsets on Galilee.
Jesus loved the fishermen on the fishing boats forming
    silhouettes against the sunsets on Galilee.
When Jesus said: Good-by, good-by, I will come again:
    Jesus meant that good-by for the sunsets, the fishing boats, the fish-
    ermen, the silhouettes all and any against the sunsets on Galilee:
    the good-by and the promise meant all or nothing.

MONKEY OF STARS

THERE was a tree of stars sprang up on a vertical panel of the south.
And a monkey of stars climbed up and down in this tree of stars.
And a monkey picked stars and put them in his mouth, tall up in a tree
    of stars shining in a south sky panel.

I saw this and I saw what it meant and what it means was five, six,
  seven, that's all, five, six, seven.
Oh hoh, yah yah, loo loo, the meaning was five, six, seven, five, six, seven.

Panels of changing stars, sashes of vapor, silver tails of meteor streams,
  washes and rockets of fire—
It was only a dream, oh hoh, yah yah, loo loo, only a dream, five, six,
  seven, five, six, seven.

Great Rooms

SEA CHEST

THERE was a woman loved a man
as the man loved the sea.
Her thoughts of him were the same
as his thoughts of the sea.
They made an old sea chest for their belongings
together.

WE HAVE GONE THROUGH GREAT ROOMS TOGETHER

AND when on the dark steel came the roads
Of a milky mist, and a spray of stars,
Bunches and squares and a spatter of stars,
We counted stars, one by one, a million and a million.
And we remembered those stars as fishermen remember fish,
As bees remember blossoms, as crops remember rains.
And these were rooms too; we can so reckon.
We can always say we have gone through great rooms together.

LOVE IN LABRADOR

ONE arch of the sky
Took on a spray of jewels.

The crystals gleamed on the windows
Weaving their wintrish alphabets
Of spears and ovals fixed in frost
Fastened to a glass design
With a word: This must be.

There are shooters of the moon far north.
There are dying eyes holding diadems.
There are deaths sweet as laughing waters.
There are gold heelprints on the fading
      staircases of the stars.

SLEEP IMPRESSION

THE dark blue wind of early autumn
ran on the early autumn sky
in the fields of yellow moon harvest.
      I slept, I almost slept,
      I said listening:
Trees you have leaves rustling like rain
When there is no rain.

MAYBE

MAYBE he believes me, maybe not.
Maybe I can marry him, maybe not.
Maybe the wind on the prairie,
The wind on the sea, maybe,
Somebody somewhere, maybe, can tell.
I will lay my head on his shoulder
And when he asks me I will say yes,
Maybe.

BUG SPOTS

THIS bug carries spots on his back.
Last summer he carried these spots.
Now it is spring and he is back here again
With a domino design over his wings.
All winter he has been in a bedroom,
In a hole, in a hammock, hung up, stuck away,
Stashed while the snow blew over
The wind and the dripping icicles,
The tunnels of the frost.
Now he has errands again in a rotten stump.

UNDERSTANDINGS IN BLUE

THE bird sat on a red handle
Counting five star flowers,
Five clover leafs.

The bird was a pigeon
Wearing a quiet understanding
Of how to wear blue.

There is pigeon blue
Picked out of baskets of big sky
When the springtime is blue.

This was the blue fadeout fire
Resting on the pigeon wings
In a quiet understanding.

The red handle, the star flowers,
The green clover leafs,
Wove into the weaves of blue.

The big sky stood back of it all
With a basket of springtime blue
And an understanding all alone.

LET THEM ASK YOUR PARDON

CHILD, what can those old men bring you?
If they can bring you a new handful
Absolutely warm and soft as summer rain,
Let them ask your pardon and do it soon.
Otherwise, why are they old?
Otherwise, why should they look at you
And carry assumptions in their old eyes
And speak such words as "ig-no-rance"
And "wisdom"—let them ask your pardon
Showing you how summer rain is an old pal
Of the wriggle of the angleworm,
The flip of the muskalonge,
And the step of the walking rain
Across the prairie. If the old men, child,
Tell you no stories about rockets,
Shooting stars, horses of high ranges,
Let them ask your pardon, excuse themselves,
And go away.

STRIPED CATS, OLD MEN AND PROUD STOCKINGS

1

RIDE a black horse with tan feet.
Let him have splashes of white,
Peninsulas of milk white.
Tell him, "Giddap, paint horse."
Ride him then with a bridle in your left hand
     and a hawk sitting on your right wrist.
Wear a yellow dress and an orange bandana
     tied over your forehead.
So should a proud woman ride a proud horse.
So should a woman ride to a horse show, a bird show,
To a public procession, to a secret wedding,
To a crying menagerie of proud striped cats.

2

The old men who sit cross-legged in Hindustan
Naming the wedding days, the hungry days, the work days,
Handling their whiskers softly where the cascades
Come down numbering the years and the facts—
The old men look better close to the earth, cross-legged,
Pegged near the dirt, the home of the roots,
The home of years, facts.

3

They have chosen stockings to cover their legs
By a feeling for choices fine as air.
The appeal of stripes came to this one,
And spots, diamonds, clocks, anchors, to others,
The feeling for these choices was airy, fine,
Born of the deliberation of childbirths,
Thrust out with decision on the ends of their tongues.
If a black horse wishes white sox
Or a white horse calls for tan footwear
Or an ankle covering of pigeon blue gray—
It is a balance born of deliberations, childbirths.

MOON HAMMOCK

When the moon was a hammock of gold,
And the gold of the moon hammock kept changing
Till there was a blood hammock of a moon—
And the slow slipping down of it in the west,
The idle easy slipping down of it
Left a bridge of stars
And marchers among the stars—
That was an evening, a calendar date,
A curve of lines in an almanac.
People said it was an hour in September or April.
The astronomers stood at the mirror angles
Putting down another movement of the moon
The same as so many other movements of the moon
Put down in the big books of the regular watchers

Of the moon. This is the way things go by.
The gold hammock of a moon changes to blood,
Slips down, leaves a bridge of stars, marchers, almanacs.

THIMBLE ISLANDS

THE sky and the sea put on a show.
Every day they put on a show.
There are dawn dress rehearsals.
There are sweet monotonous evening monologues.
The acrobatic lights of sunsets dwindle and darken.
The stars step out one by one with a bimbo, bimbo.

The red ball of the sun hung a balloon in the west,
And there was half a balloon, then no balloon at all,
And ten stars marched out and ten thousand more,
And the fathoms of the sky far over met the fathoms of the sea far
    under, among the thimble islands.

In the clear green water of dawn came a float of silver filaments, feelers
    circling a pink polyp's mouth;
The feelers ran out, opened and closed, opened and closed, hungry and
    searching, soft and incessant, floating the salt sea inlets sucking the
    green sea water as land roses suck the land air.

Frozen rock humps, smooth fire-rock humps—
Thimbles on the thumbs of the wives of prostrate sunken
        giants—
God only knows how many sleep in the slack of the
        seven seas.

There in those places
under the sun balloons,
and fathoms, filaments, feelers—

The wind and the rain
sew the years
stitching one year into another.

Heavy hammers and high blowouts
take their pay, fill their contracts—
And there are dawn dress rehearsals, sweet
    monotonous evening monologues.

CLEFS

THE little moon rode up a high corner.
The woman in a little room sat alone.
A violin the woman had sang for her.
The gut strings and the bow bent
A series of clefs climbing for memories.
"For remembering," she said, "A little moon
Up a high corner and climbing violin clefs."

THE GREAT PROUD WAGON WHEELS GO ON

THE great proud wagon wheels
go on. Out of night and night's
nothings a steel shaft, a white
fire, a new star.

The great proud wagon wheels
go on. Out of night and night's
nothings a proud head, a skull
shape, a thing looking, a face
and eyes.

The great proud wagon wheels
go on. Night again and night's
nothings again and the star and
the skull and face gone.

I wait. I know. Look! The great
proud wagon wheels go on. Now
what? Now who? . . . coming . . .
out of night and night's nothings
. . . coming . . . you? . . . and you? . . .

TALL TIMBER

NIGHT calls many witnesses
to supply evidence, to report honestly,
the meaning of dying, loving, being born.

Night has no better witnesses
than tall timber, rich in a moon, roaming in mist,
swearing a corroboration of relevant circumstances.

Call others to the courthouses of earth;
let them have counsel and all benefits of doubt;
let them report all they have seen and heard.

Then let Night come into court.
The tall timber testifies, the moon, the mist, testify.
Let us hear the oaths of these unimpeachable witnesses.

PROUD TORSOS

JUST before the high time of autumn
Comes with the crush of its touch,
And the leaves fall, the leaves one by one,
The leaves by a full darkening sky fall,
The trees look proud, the horse chestnut
Stands with a gathered pride, the ivies
Are gathered around the stumps,
The ivies are woven thick with a green coat
Covering the stumps. Yes, the trees
Look proud now, it is the big time.
Have they not all had summer?
Didn't they all flimmer with faint
Lines of green in the spring,
A thin green mist as if it might
Be air or it might be new green leaves?
So, the first weeks of September are on
And each tree stands with a murmur,

"I stand here with a count of one more year,
One more number, one more ring in my torso."
Two weeks, five, six weeks, and the trees
Will be standing . . . stripped . . . gaunt . . .
The leaves gone . . . the coat of green gone . . .
And they will be proud but no longer
With the gathered pride of the days
In the high time.

TO KNOW SILENCE PERFECTLY

THERE is a music for lonely hearts nearly always.
If the music dies down there is a silence
Almost the same as the movement of music.
To know silence perfectly is to know music.

Sky Pieces

SKY PIECES

PROUDLY the fedoras march on the heads of the somewhat
    careless men.
Proudly the slouches march on the heads of the still more
    careless men.
Proudly the panamas perch on the noggins of dapper
    debonair men.
Comically somber the derbies gloom on the earnest solemn
    noodles.
And the sombrero, most proud, most careless, most dapper and debonair

of all, somberly the sombrero marches on the heads of important
men who know what they want.
Hats are skypieces; hats have a destiny; wish your hat
 slowly; your hat is you.

LOVABLE BABBLERS

WHAT did that old philosopher say?
"The deadest deaths are the best."
For he was the same who said to a friend:
When you cry I cry, when you shake hands with
  me and ease my luck telling me it's too
  bad and the world's all wrong, it melts
  something inside of me and I break down.
So there are babblers we love for what they are.

OOMBA

OOMBA went along years
Lugging a head
On a pikestaff of human neck.
"It is mine," said Oomba,
"If it is not mine who does it
Belong to?" he asked,
Oomba putting a straight quiz
To Oomba himself.

"Here it is," he muttered,
"Here on my neck, here on
My pikestaff of human neck;
And what is it for and how did I get it
And why do I say it is mine
And because it is mine it belongs to me?"
So Oomba went on talking to Oomba
Asking the simplest, oldest questions
Of himself.

SEVENTEEN MONTHS

THIS girl child speaks five words.
No for no and no for yes, "no" for either
    no or yes.
"Teewee" for wheat or oats or corn or barley
    or any food taken with a spoon.
"Go way" as an edict to keep your distance
    and let her determinations operate.

"Spoon" for spoon or cup or anything to be handled,
    all instruments, tools, paraphernalia of utility
    and convenience are SPOONS.
Mama is her only epithet and synonym for God and the
    Government and the one force of majesty and in-
    telligence obeying the call of pity, hunger, pain,
    cold, dark—MAMA, MAMA, MAMA.

SARAH'S LETTER TO PETER

WHEN Sarah wrote Peter how she slept
among silver leaf poplars, waking to see
a light wind moving the under-side of the leaves—

She told him how to the north and east
there came a bath of light, a slow flush,
and the larks shot out into the air,
curved up and sang to meet the rose-red dawn.

But it wasn't dawn.
Four dark hours crept on till dawn arrived.
And the larks crept back to their nests
And later met the dawn that came and stayed,
Met it only with silence, with sore, dumb hearts.

Does every love have a false dawn?

She wrote her lover:
Others are but the showers of April, whilst
    thou art the seven seas.
Making a rendezvous and then not keeping it is wrong.
Do not be a false dawn; I want thee forever.

And this was one of the chapters.

DESTROYERS

GRANDFATHER and grandfather's uncle stand looking at the harbor. "Look there," says grandfather, "and you see a torpedo boat. Next to it is a torpedo boat destroyer. And next to the torpedo boat destroyer is a destroyer of torpedo boat destroyers."

And grandfather's uncle says, "I heard my grandfather's uncle say every echo has a destroyer and for every echo destroyer there is a destroyer of echo destroyers."

And grandfather's uncle says, "I remember hearing my grandfather's uncle say every destroyer carries a pocket of eggs and the eggs wait and when they are ready they go blooey and the works of the destroyer blows up."

So they stand looking at the harbor, grandfather a grand old gray-whiskered monochromic sea-dog and grandfather's uncle a grand old gray-whiskered monochromic landlubber.

"Columbus," says grandfather, "Columbus was only a little dago, a ginny, a wop, and he changed the shape of the earth; before Columbus came the shape of the earth in the heads of men was square and flat and he made it round and round in the heads of men."

"Yes," said grandfather's uncle, "he was bugs, he was loony, he saw things in a pig's eye, he had rats in his garret, bats in his belfry, there was a screw loose somewhere in him, he had a kink and he was a crank, he was nuts and belonged in a booby hatch."

And the two grand old gray-whiskered monochromic men, one a sea-dog, the other a landlubber, laughed, laughed, laughed in each other's sea-green, land-gray eyes.

TWO WOMEN AND THEIR FATHERS

1

HER father was a policeman who went fishing summer Sundays and caught a carp once with an old Spanish coin in its belly. As for her she picks up a good living high in the air in pink tights on a trapeze working for Ringling's circus.

2

Her father wore hip rubber boots and stood in yellow clay digging a tunnel for street cars to dip under the Chicago river. As for her she goes by a Hawaiian name and is known for a dance wherein she takes off one garment after another till there is a semblance of no garments at all.

VERY VERY IMPORTANT

I HAVE no doubt that it is very important and so are you.
Put in two more of the word 'very' as a prefix to the
　　word 'important' if you like.
Make it read: I have no doubt it is very very very im-
　　portant and so are you.
Thus there are three of the word 'very' standing in a row
　　as prefixes to 'important.'
If you wish more of the word 'very' go to the same place
　　these came from.

FOOLISH ABOUT WINDOWS

I WAS foolish about windows.
The house was an old one and the windows
　　were small.
I asked a carpenter to come and open the
　　walls and put in bigger windows.
"The bigger the window the more it costs,"
　　he said.
"The bigger the cheaper," I said.
So he tore off siding and plaster and laths
And put in a big window and bigger windows.
I was hungry for windows.

One neighbor said, "If you keep on you'll be
    able to see everything there is."
I answered, "That'll be all right, that'll be
    classy enough for me."
Another neighbor said, "Pretty soon your house
    will be all windows."
And I said, "Who would the joke be on then?"
And still another, "Those who live in glass
    houses gather no moss."
And I said, "Birds of a feather should not throw
    stones and a soft answer turneth away rats."

LOVE LETTER TO HANS CHRISTIAN ANDERSEN

THE kitchen chair speaks to the bread knife,
"Why have you no legs?"
The bread knife answers, "And you no teeth?"
It was a quarrel on a summer day.
It ran on till winter
And on to another winter and another.
In the cellar ultimately
The kitchen chair said,
"Your teeth are gone,"
And the bread knife,
"I see you have no legs."
It was quiet in the cellar, they found,
No yammering of people, no soup nor nuts,
A pile of coal, old mops, and broken tools,
These they could talk with . . . and mostly
None of them talked at all.

MYSTERIOUS BIOGRAPHY

CHRISTOFO COLOMBO was a hungry man,
hunted himself half way round the world;
he began poor, panhandled, ended in jail,
Christofo so hungry, Christofo so poor,
Christofo in the chilly, steel bracelets,
honorable distinguished Christofo Colombo.

RAT RIDDLES

THERE was a gray rat looked at me
with green eyes out of a rathole.

"Hello, rat," I said,
"Is there any chance for me
to get on to the language of the rats?"

And the green eyes blinked at me,
blinked from a gray rat's rathole.

"Come again," I said,
"Slip me a couple of riddles;
there must be riddles among the rats."

And the green eyes blinked at me
and a whisper came from the gray rathole:
"Who do you think you are and why is a rat?
  Where did you sleep last night and why do
      you sneeze on Tuesdays? And why is the
      grave of a rat no deeper than the grave
      of a man?"

And the tail of a green-eyed rat
Whipped and was gone at a gray rathole.

WINTER WEATHER

IT is cold.
The bitter of the winter
whines a story.
It is the colder weather when the truck
drivers sing it would freeze the whiskers
off a brass monkey.
It is the bitterest whining of the winter
now.

Well, we might sit down now, have a cup of coffee
apiece, and talk about the weather.
We might look back on things that happened long
ago, times when the weather was different.
Or we might talk about things ahead of us, funny
things in the days, days, days to come, days when
the weather will be different again.

Yes, a cup of coffee apiece.
Even if this winter weather is bitter,
The truck drivers are laughing:
It would freeze the whiskers off a brass monkey.

THE DINOSAUR BONES

The dinosaur bones are dusted every day.
The cards tell how old we guess the dinosaur
    bones are.
Here a head was seven feet long, horns with a
    hell of a ram,
Humping the humps of the Montana mountains.
          The respectable school children
Chatter at the heels of their teacher who ex-
    plains.
The tourists and wonder hunters come with
    their parasols
And catalogues and arrangements to do the
    museum
In an hour or two hours.
          The dinosaur bones
            are dusted
            every day.

UNINTENTIONAL PAINT

The flat gray banana store front
is visited by a union painter with no intentions
and a bucket of high maroon paint
and a pot of high yellow.

The high maroon banana store front
sings its contralto with two stripes
of yellow soprano on the door.

The union painter meant nothing
and we can not attribute intentions
to a bucket of maroon nor a pot of yellow.

The door and the lintels sing.
Two banjos strum on the threshold.
Two people hum a snatch of song
They know well from singing together often.
        I must come this way often
        and not only for bananas.

PEOPLE OF THE EAVES, I WISH YOU GOOD MORNING

THE wrens have troubles like us. The house of a wren will not run itself any more than the house of a man.

They chatter the same as two people in a flat where the laundry came back with the shirts of another man and the shimmy of another woman.

The shirt of a man wren and the shimmy of a woman wren are a trouble in the wren house. It is this or something else back of this chatter a spring morning.

Trouble goes so quick in the wren house. Now they are hopping wren jigs beaten off in a high wren staccato time.

People of the eaves, I wish you good morning, I wish you a thousand thanks.

WEDDING POSTPONED

THE arrangements are changed.
We were going to marry at six o'clock.
Now we shall not marry at all.

The bridegroom was all ready.
And the best man of the bridegroom was ready.

The bride fixed out in orchids and a long veil,
The bride and six bridesmaids were all ready.

Then the arrangements changed.
The date was changed not from six o'clock till later.
The date was changed to no time at all, to never.

Why the arrangements were changed is a long story.
Tell half of it and it is better than nothing at all.
Tell it with a hint and a whisper and it is told wrong.

We know why it was put off,
Why the arrangements shifted,
Why the organist was told to go,
Why the minister ready for the ring ceremony
Was told to drive away and be quick about it, please.
We know this in all its results and circumstances.

The disappointment of the best man,
The sorry look on the faces of the bridesmaids,
We, who chose them out of many, we could understand.

And we told them only what is told here:
The arrangements are changed, there will be no wedding,
We shall not marry at all, not today, not tomorrow, no
       time.

TWO WOMEN

THEY told me in an old book
about the wine-dark sea.

I saw the sea foam-lit and
green, sunset-red and changing.

I saw the sea wine-dark only
when I thought of you and your eyes.
    . . .

The fabrics shift in her eyes.
Persian cat fur is soft,

A Navajo blanket beautifully woven,
And is there anything more restful
        than a Japanese sea-mist silk?
The fabrics shift in her voice.

SNATCH OF SLIPHORN JAZZ

ARE you happy? It's the only
way to be, kid.
Yes, be happy, it's a good nice
way to be.
But not happy-happy, kid, don't
be too doubled-up doggone happy.
It's the doubled-up doggone happy-
happy people . . . bust hard . . . they
do bust hard . . . when they bust.
Be happy, kid, go to it, but not too
doggone happy.

LANDSCAPE

ON a mountain-side the real estate agents
Put up signs marking the city lots to be sold there.
A man whose father and mother were Irish
Ran a goat farm half-way down the mountain;
He drove a covered wagon years ago,
Understood how to handle a rifle,
Shot grouse, buffalo, Indians, in a single year,
And now was raising goats around a shanty.
Down at the foot of the mountain
Two Japanese families had flower farms.
A man and woman were in rows of sweet peas
Picking the pink and white flowers
To put in baskets and take to the Los Angeles market.
They were clean as what they handled
There in morning sun, the big people and baby-faces.
Across the road high on another mountain
Stood a house saying, "I am it," a commanding house.
There was the home of a motion picture director

Famous for lavish doll house interiors,
Clothes ransacked from the latest designs for women
In the combats of "male against female."
The mountain, the scenery, the layout of the landscape,
And the peace of the morning sun as it happened,
The miles of houses pocketed in the valley beyond—
It was all worth looking at, worth wondering about,
How long it might last, how young it might be.

[HOLLYWOOD, 1923]

DIFFERENT KINDS OF GOOD-BY

GOOD-BY is a loose word, a yellow ribbon
    fluttering in the wind.
Good-by is a stiff word, a steel slide rule—
    a fixed automatic phone number.
A thousand people? And you must say good-by
    to all? One at a time?—yes, I guess you
    need a thousand different good-bys.
There is a good-by for the Johnsons and another
    for the Smiths and another for the Poindexters
    and the Van Rensselaers.
And there is the big grand good-by to the thousand
    all at once, the whole works.

THREE HILLS LOOK DIFFERENT IN THE MOONSHINE

THE hill of the white skull in the summer moon
shines; the hill of the red heart is a neighbor
in the summer moonshine; the hill of the climbing
clumsy shadows is another.

PROUD OF THEIR RAGS

THEY come down from the mountains, proud of their rags.
"What do you know about loons, panthers, hawks?
Wings, winds, slides—what do you know?

Hunger and hope, and how do you know who tore my rags?"
They come down from the mountains, proud of their rags,
    five or six out of sixty; they come down with proud
    heads.

BROKEN SKY

THE sky of gray is eaten in six places,
    Rag holes stand out.
    It is an army blanket and the sleeper
        slept too near the fire.

HELLS AND HEAVENS

EACH man pictures his hell or heaven different.
Some have snug home-like heavens, suburban, well-kept.
Some have a wild, storm-swept heaven; their happiness has
    been in storms, heaven must have storms mixed with
    fair weather.
And hell for some is a jail, for others a factory, for others
    a kitchen, for others a place of many polite liars full
    of blah, all gah gah.

THREE FRAGMENTS FOR FISHERS OF DESTINY

METHUSALEH was a witness to many cabbages and kings.
They marched in procession for him like the marching
    harvests of onions lift their green spears in Maytime
    and go down the wind in thistledown fluff with the
    leaves of October.

The same wind blew its crescendo and diminuendo in the
    long beards of clear-eyed prophets and again in the
    whiskers of the muddleheads who only called them-
    selves prophets.

Methusaleh saw the old muddleheads sniff at the sun
And proclaim their wisdom as beyond the sun.

Timber Moon

TIMBER MOON

THERE is a way the moon looks into the timber at night
And tells the walnut trees secrets of silver sand—
There is a way the moon makes a lattice work
Under the leaves of the hazel bushes—
There is a way the moon understands the hoot owl
Sitting on an arm of a sugar maple throwing its
One long lonesome cry up the ladders of the moon—
There is a way the moon finds company early in the fall-
        time.

FLOWERS TELL MONTHS

GOLD buttons in the garden today—
Among the brown-eyed susans the golden spiders are
    gambling
The blue sisters of the white asters speak to each other.

        After the travel of the snows—
        Buttercups come in a yellow rain,
        Johnny-jump-ups in a blue mist—
        Wild azaleas with a low spring cry.

LANDSCAPE

SEE the trees lean to the wind's way of learning.
See the dirt of the hills shape to the water's
    way of learning.
See the lift of it all go the way the biggest
    wind and the strongest water want it.

COUNTING

SWEET lips, there are songs about kisses now.
Looking backward are kisses of remembrance
Looking ahead are kisses to be wished-for.
So time is counted, so far back, so far ahead, in
    measurements of sweet kisses.

OAK ARMS

THE broken arm of the black oak
blisters in the list of numbers:
    "The sky hissed; I stand and remember."

And the gold of the gloaming flushes, floods by,
And the haze gold is cut across with the cricket's
    wisp of silver.

MOON PATH

CREEP up, moon, on the south sky.
Mark the moon path of this evening.
The day must be counted.
The new moon is a law.
The little say-so of the moon must be listened to.

THERE ARE DIFFERENT GARDENS

FLOWERS can be cousins of the stars.
The closing and speaking lips of the lily
And the warning of the fire and the dust—
They are in the gardens and the sky of stars.
Beyond the shots of the light of this sun
Are the little sprinkles, the little twinklers
Of suns to whose lips this lily never sent
A whisper from its closing and speaking lips.

WINDFLOWER LEAF

THIS flower is repeated
out of old winds, out of
old times.

The wind repeats these, it
must have these, over and
over again.

New windflowers so fresh,
oh beautiful leaves, here
now again.

　　The domes over
　　fall to pieces.
　　The stones under
　　fall to pieces.
　　Rain and ice
　　wreck the works.
The wind keeps, the windflowers
　　keep, the leaves last,
The wind young and strong lets
　　these last longer than stones.

LITTLE SKETCH

THERE are forked branches of trees
Where the leaves shudder obediently,
Where the hangover leaves
Flow in a curve downward;
And between the forks and leaves,
In patches and angles, in square handfuls,
The orange lights of the done sunset
Come and filter and pour.

BUTTER COLORS

THE light of the yellow flowers
leaps to the light of the pool.

Butter under the chin of this slip
slides to the level water mirror.

Fan yellow films of light play fast
slipping all day on, on, to the water home.

Home, come home, water calls to light.
Fan yellow films leap and slide.

WEBS

EVERY man spins a web of light circles
And hangs this web in the sky
Or finds it hanging, already hung for him,
Written as a path for him to travel.
The white spiders know how this geography goes.
Their feet tell them when to spin,
How to weave in a criss-cross
Among elms and maples, among radishes and button weeds,
Among cellar timbers and old shanty doors.
Not only the white spiders, also the yellow and blue,
Also the black and purple spiders
Listen when their feet tell them to spin one.
And while every spider spins a web of light circles
Or finds one already hung for him,
So does every man born under the sky.

PEACE, NIGHT, SLEEP

"You shall have peace with night and sleep.
It was written in the creep of the mist,
In the open doors of night horizons.

Peace, night, sleep, all go together.
In the forgetting of the frogs and the sun,
In the losing of the grackle's off cry
And the call of the bird whose name is gone—
You shall have peace; the mist creeps, the doors open.
Let night, let sleep, have their way."

BUNDLES

I HAVE thought of beaches, fields,
Tears, laughter.

I have thought of homes put up—
And blown away.

I have thought of meetings and for
Every meeting a good-by.

I have thought of stars going alone,
Orioles in pairs, sunsets in blundering
Wistful deaths.

I have wanted to let go and cross over
To a next star, a last star.

I have asked to be left a few tears
And some laughter.

MAN AND DOG ON AN EARLY WINTER MORNING

THERE was a tall slough grass
Too tough for the farmers to feed the cattle,
And the wind was sifting through, shaking the grass;
Each spear of grass interfered a little with the wind
And the interference sent up a soft hiss,
A mysterious little fiddler's and whistler's hiss;
And it happened all the spears together
Made a soft music in the slough grass

Too tough for the farmers to cut for fodder.
"This is a proud place to come to
    On a winter morning, early in winter,"
    Said a hungry man, speaking to his dog,
Speaking to himself and the passing wind,
"This is a proud place to come to."

PRECIOUS MOMENTS

BRIGHT vocabularies are transient as rainbows.
Speech requires blood and air to make it.
Before the word comes off the end of the tongue,
While the diaphragms of flesh negotiate the word,
In the moment of doom when the word forms
It is born, alive, registering an imprint—
Afterward it is a mummy, a dry fact, done and gone.
The warning holds yet: Speak now or forever hold
    your peace.
Ecce homo had meanings: Behold the Man! Look at
    him! Dying he lives and speaks!

OCTOBER PAINT

FLAME blue wisps in the west,
Wrap yourselves in these leaves
And speak to winter about us.
Tell winter the whole story.

Red leaves up the oaken slabs,
You came, little and green spats
Four months ago; your climbers
Put scroll after scroll around
The oaken slabs. "Red, come red,"
Some one with an October paint
Pot said. And here you are,
Fifty red arrowheads of leaf paint
Or fifty mystic fox footprints
Or fifty pointed thumbprints.

Hold on, the winds are to come
Blowing, blowing, the gray slabs
Will lose you, the winds will
Flick you away in a whiff
One by one, two by two . . . Yet
I have heard a rumor whispered;
Tattlers tell it to each other
Like a secret everybody knows . . .
Next year you will come again.
Up the oaken slabs you will put
Your pointed fox footprints
Green in the early summer
And you will be red arrowheads
In the falltime . . . Tattlers
Slip this into each other's ears
Like a secret everybody knows.
. . . If I see some one with an
October paint pot I shall be
Full of respect and say,
"I saw your thumbprints everywhere;
How do you do it?"

MANY HATS

1

WHEN the scrapers of the
deep winds were done, and
the haulers of the tall
waters had finished, this
was the accomplishment.

The drums of the sun never
get tired, and first off
every morning, the drums of
the sun perform an intro-
duction of the dawn here.

The moon goes down here
as a dark bellringer doing

once more what he has done
over and over already in
his young life.

Up on a long blue platform
comes a line of starprints.

If the wind has a song, it
is moaning; Good Lawd, I
done done what you told me
to do.

2

Whose three-ring circus is this? Who stipulated in a contract for this to
be drunken, death-defying, colossal, mammoth, cyclopean, mystic as the
light that never was on land or sea, bland, composed, and imperturbable
as a cool phalanx of sphinxes? Why did one woman cry, The silence is
terrible? Why did another smile, There is a sweet gravity here? Why do
they come and go here and look as in a looking-glass?

The Grand Canyon of Arizona, said one, this is it, hacked out by the
broadax of a big left-handed God and left forgotten, fixed over and embel-
lished by a remembering right-handed God who always comes back.

If you ask me, said an old railroader, I'll never tell you who took the exca-
vation contract for this blowout—it took a lot of shovels and a lot of dyna-
mite—several large kegs, I would guess—and maybe they had a case or two
of T N T.

Yes, he went on, the Grand Canyon, the daddy of 'em all—the undisputed
champeen—that range rider sure was righto—the elements had a hell of
a rassle here.

The Grand Canyon—a long ride from where Brigham Young stands in
bronze gazing on the city he bade rise out of salt and alkali—a weary walk
from Santa Fé and the Mountains of the Blood of Christ—a bitter hike
from where the Sonora dove at Tucson mourns, No hope, no hope—a
sweet distance from where Balboa stripped for his first swim in the Pacific—
a mean cross-country journey to where Roy Bean told the muchacho, By
the white light of a moon on the walls of an arroyo last Tuesday you killed

a woman and next Tuesday we're going to hang you—a traveler's route of many days and sleeps to reach the place of the declaration, God reigns and the government at Washington lives.

Shovel into this cut of earth all past and present possessions, creations, belongings of man; shovel furioso, appassionata, pizzicato; shovel cities, wagons, ships, tools, jewels; the bottom isn't covered; the wild burros and the trail mules go haw-hee, haw-hee, haw-hee.

Turn it into a Hall of Fame, said a rambler, let it be a series of memorials to the Four Horsemen, to Napoleon, Carl the Twelfth, Caesar, Alexander the Great, Hannibal and Hasdrubal, and all who have rode in blood up to the bridles of the horses, calling, Hurrah for the next who goes—let each have his name on a truncated cyclops of rock—let passers-by say, He was pretty good but he didn't last long.

Now I wonder, I wonder, said another, can they all find room here? Elijah fed by the ravens, Jonah in the belly of the whale, Daniel in the lion's den, Lot's wife transmogrified into salt, Elijah riding up into the sky in a chariot of fire—can they all find room? Are the broken pieces of the Tower of Babel and the Walls of Jericho here? Should I look for the ram's horn Joshua blew?

3

A phantom runner runs on the rim. "I saw a moon man throw hats in, hats of kings, emperors, senators, presidents, plumed hats of knights, red hats of cardinals, five-gallon hats of cowboys, tasselled hats of Bavarian yodelers, mandarin hats, derbies, fedoras, chapeaus, straws, lady picture hats out of Gainsborough portraits—

"Hats many proud people handed over, dying and saying, Take this one too—hats furioso, appassionata, pizzicato—hats for remembrance, good-by, three strikes and out, fade me, there's no place to go but home—hats for man alone, God alone, the sky alone."

4

Think of the little birds, said another, the wee birdies—before God took a hunk of mud and made Man they were here, the birds, the robins, juncoes, nuthatches, bats, eagles, cedar birds, chickadees, bluejays, I saw a blackbird gleaming in satin, floating in the scrolls of his glamorous wings, stopping on an airpath and standing still with nothing under his feet, looking at the gray Mojave desert level interrupted by the Grand Canyon—the birds belong, don't they?

5

Comes along a hombre saying, Let it be dedicated to Time; this is what is left of the Big Procession when Time gets through with it; the sun loves its stubs; we will give a name to any torso broken and tumbled by Time; we will leave the vanished torsos with no names.

Comes along a hombre accidentally remarking, Let it be dedicated to Law and Order—the law of the Strong fighting the Strong, the Cunning out-witting the Less Cunning—and the Weak Ones ordered to their places by the Strong and Cunning—aye—and ai-ee—Law and Order.

Comes along another hombre giving his slant at it, Now this sure was the Gyarden of Eden, smooth, rich, nice, watered, fixed, no work till tomorrow, Adam and Eve satisfied and sitting pretty till the day of the Snake Dance and the First Sin; and God was disgusted and wrecked the works; he or-dered club-foot angels with broken wings to shoot the job; now look at it.

Comes another hombre all wised up, This was the Devil's Brickyard; here were the kilns to make the Kitchens of Hell; after bricks enough were made to last Hell a million years, the Devil said, "Shut 'er down"; they had a big payday night and left it busted from hell to breakfast; the Hopis looked it over and decided to live eighty miles away where there was water; then came Powell, Hance, the Santa Fé, the boys shooting the rapids, and Fred Harvey with El Tovar.

6

Now Hance had his points; they asked him how he come to find the Canyon and he told 'em, I was ridin' old Whitey and the Mojaves after me when we comes to this gap miles across; I told Whitey, It's you now for the longest jump you ever took; Whitey jumped and was half way across when I pulled on the bridle, turned him around, and we come back to the same place on the Canyon rim we started from.

Yes, Hance told 'em, if they asked, how he come to dig the Canyon. "But where did you put all the dirt?" "Took it away in wheelbarrows and made San Francisco Peaks."

Hance sleeping near a big rock, woke up and saw seven rattlesnakes circle seven times around the rock, each with the tail of the snake ahead in his mouth, and all of them swallowing, till after a while there wasn't a snake left. Hance's wife got her leg caught between two rocks; couldn't get her loose, said Hance, so I had to shoot her to save her from starving to death; look down there between those two rocks and you can see her bones, said Hance.

This is where we find the original knuckle snake; he breaks to pieces if you try to pick him up; and when you go away he knuckles himself together again; yes, and down here, is the original echo canyon; we holler, "Has Smith been here?" and the echo promulgates back, "Which Smith?"

7

Down at the darkest depths, miles down, the Colorado River grinds, toils, driving the channel deeper—is it free or convict?—tell me—will it end like a great writer crying, I die with my best books unwritten?

Smooth as glass run the streaming waters—then a break into rapids, into tumblers, into spray, into voices, roars, growls, into commanding mono-tones that hunt far corners and jumping-off places.

And how should a beautiful, ignorant stream of water know it heads for an early release—out across the desert, running toward the Gulf, below sea level, to murmur its lullaby, and see the Imperial Valley rise out of burn-ing sand with cotton blossoms, wheat, watermelons, roses, how should it know?

8

The hombres keep coming; here comes another; he says, says he, I met four people this morning, the poker face, the baby stare, the icy mitt, and the peace that passeth understanding—let this place be dedicated to X, the unknown factor, to the Missing Link, to Jo Jo the dog-faced boy, to the Sargossa Sea, to Humpty Dumpty, to Little Red Riding Hood crying for her mother, to those who never believe in Santa Klaus, to the man who turned himself inside out because he was so sleepy.

9

Steps on steps lift on into the sky; the lengths count up into stairways; let me go up for the Redeemer is up there; He died for me; so a Spanish Indian was speaking—and he asked, When the first French Jesuit looked from Yavapai four hundred years ago, did he murmur of a tall altar to go on a mile-long rock shelf down there on a mesa? did he whisper of an unspeakably tall altar there for the raising of the ostensorium and the swinging of censers and the calling up of the presence of the Heart of the Living Christ? And he went on, Where the Son of God is made known surely is a place for the removal of shoes and the renewal of feet for the journey—surely this is so.

10

Came a lean, hungry-looking hombre with Kansas, Nebraska, the Dakotas on his wind-bitten face, and he was saying, Sure my boy, sure my girl, and you're free to have any sweet bluebird fancies you please, any wild broncho thoughts you choose to have, when you stand before this grand scrap-pile of hats, hammers, haciendas, and hidalgos. He went on, Yes, let this be dedicated to Time and Ice; a memorial of the Human Family which came, was, and went; let it stand as a witness of the short miserable pilgrimage of mankind, of flame faiths, of blood and fire, and of Ice which was here first and will be here again—Faces once frozen you shall all be frozen again—the little clocks of Man shall all be frozen and nobody will be too late or too early ever again.

11

On the rim a quizzical gray-glinting hombre was telling himself how it looked to him—the sun and the air are endless with silver tricks—the light of the sun has crimson stratagems—the changes go on in stop-watch split seconds—the blues slide down a box of yellow and mix with reds that melt into gray and come back saffron clay and granite pink—a weaving gamble of color twists on and it is anybody's guess what is next.

A long sand-brown shawl shortens to a glimmering turquoise scarf—as the parapets and chimneys wash over and out in the baths of the sunset and the floats of the gloaming, one man says, There goes God with an army of banners, and another man, Who is God and why? who am I and why?

> He told himself, This may be
> something else than what I
> see when I look—how do I
> know? For each man sees him-
> self in the Grand Canyon—
> each one makes his own Canyon
> before he comes, each one brings
> and carries away his own Canyon—
> who knows? and how do I know?

12

If the wind has a song, it
is moaning: Good Lawd, I
done done what you told me
to do.

When the scrapers of the
deep winds were done, and
the haulers of the tall
waters had finished, this
was the accomplishment.

The moon goes down here
as a dark bellringer doing
once more what he has done
over and over already in
his young life.

Up on a long blue platform
comes a line of starprints.

The drums of the sun never
get tired, and first off
every morning, the drums of
the sun perform an intro-
duction of the dawn here.

THE PEOPLE, YES

*Being several stories and psalms nobody would
want to laugh at*

*interspersed with memoranda variations worth a
second look*

*along with sayings and yarns traveling on grief and
laughter*

*running sometimes as a fugitive air in the classic
manner*

*breaking into jig time and tap dancing nohow
classical*

*and further broken by plain and irregular sounds
and echoes from*

*the roar and whirl of street crowds, work gangs,
sidewalk clamor,*

*with interludes of midnight cool blue and inviolable
stars*

over the phantom frames of skyscrapers.

DEDICATED
TO CONTRIBUTORS
DEAD AND LIVING

The People, Yes

1

FROM the four corners of the earth,
from corners lashed in wind
and bitten with rain and fire,
from places where the winds begin
and fogs are born with mist children,
tall men from tall rocky slopes came
and sleepy men from sleepy valleys,
their women tall, their women sleepy,
with bundles and belongings,
with little ones babbling, "Where to now?
    what next?"

The people of the earth, the family of man,
wanted to put up something proud to look at,
a tower from the flat land of earth
on up through the ceiling into the top of the sky.

 And the big job got going,
 the caissons and pilings sunk,
 floors, walls and winding staircases
 aimed at the stars high over,
 aimed to go beyond the ladders of the moon.

 And God Almighty could have struck them dead
 or smitten them deaf and dumb.

 And God was a whimsical fixer.
 God was an understanding Boss
 with another plan in mind,

And suddenly shuffled all the languages,
    changed the tongues of men
    so they all talked different
And the masons couldn't get what the hodcarriers said,
The helpers handed the carpenters the wrong tools,
Five hundred ways to say, "W h o a r e y o u?"
Changed ways of asking, "Where do we go from here?"
Or of saying, "Being born is only the beginning,"
Or, "Would you just as soon sing as make that noise?"
Or, "What you don't know won't hurt you."
And the material-and-supply men started disputes
With the hauling gangs and the building trades
And the architects tore their hair over the blueprints
And the brickmakers and the mule skinners talked back
To the straw bosses who talked back to the superintendents
And the signals got mixed; the men who shovelled the bucket
Hooted the hoisting men—and the job was wrecked.

Some called it the Tower of Babel job
And the people gave it many other names.
The wreck of it stood as a skull and a ghost,
a memorandum hardly begun,
swaying and sagging in tall hostile winds,
held up by slow friendly winds.

2

From Illinois and Indiana came a later myth
Of all the people in the world at Howdeehow
For the first time standing together:
From six continents, seven seas, and several archipelagoes,
From points of land moved by wind and water
Out of where they used to be to where they are,
The people of the earth marched and travelled
To gather on a great plain.

At a given signal they would join in a shout,
    So it was planned,
One grand hosannah, something worth listening to.
    And they all listened.
    The signal was given.

And they all listened.
And the silence was beyond words.
They had come to listen, not to make a noise.
They wanted to hear.
So they all stood still and listened,
Everybody except a little old woman from Kalamazoo
Who gave out a long slow wail over what she was missing
        because she was stone deaf.

This is the tale of the Howdeehow powpow,
One of a thousand drolls the people tell of themselves,
Of tall corn, of wide rivers, of big snakes,
Of giants and dwarfs, heroes and clowns,
Grown in the soil of the mass of the people.

3

In the long flat panhandle of Texas
far off on the grassland of the cattle country
near noon they sight a rider coming toward them
and the sky may be a cold neverchanging gray
or the sky may be changing its numbers
back and forth all day even and odd numbers
and the afternoon slides away somewhere
and they see their rider is alive yet
their rider is coming nearer yet
and they expect what happens and it happens again
he and his horse ride in late for supper
yet not too late
and night is on and the stars are out
and night too slides away somewhere
night too has even and odd numbers.

The wind brings "a norther"
to the long flat panhandle
and in the shivering cold they say:
        "Between Amarilla and the North Pole
        is only a barbwire fence,"
which they give a twist:
        "Out here the only windbreak
        is the North Star."

4

THE people know what the land knows
the numbers odd and even of the land
the slow hot wind of summer and its withering
or again the crimp of the driving white blizzard
and neither of them to be stopped
neither saying anything else than:
   "I'm not arguing. I'm telling you."

The old timer on the desert was gray
and grizzled with ever seeing the sun:
   "For myself I don't care whether it rains.
   I've seen it rain.
   But I'd like to have it rain
   pretty soon sometime.
   Then my son could see it.
   He's never seen it rain."

"Out here on the desert,"
  said the first woman who said it,
   "the first year you don't believe
   what others tell you
   and the second year you don't
   believe what you tell yourself."
  "I weave thee, I weave thee,"
  sang the weaving Sonora woman.
  "I weave thee,
   thou art for a Sonora fool."

And the fool spoke of her,
over wine mentioned her:
"She can teach a pair of stilts to dance."

"What is the east? Have you been in the east?"
the New Jersey woman asked the little girl
the wee child growing up in Arizona who said:
"Yes, I've been in the east,
the east is where trees come
between you and the sky."

Another baby in Cleveland, Ohio,
in Cuyahoga County, Ohio—
why did she ask:
>"Papa,
>what is the moon
>supposed to advertise?"

And the boy in Winnetka, Illinois who wanted to know:
"Is there a train so long you can't count the cars?
Is there a blackboard so long it will hold all the numbers?"

What of the Athenian last year on whose bosom
a committee hung a medal to say to the world
here is a champion heavyweight poet?
He stood on a two-masted schooner
and flung his medal far out on the sea bosom.
>"And why not?
>Has anybody ever given the ocean a medal?
>Who of the poets equals the music of the sea?
>And where is a symbol of the people
>>unless it is the sea?"
"Is it far to the next town?"
asked the Arkansas traveller
who was given the comfort:
>"It seems farther than it is
>but you'll find it ain't."

Six feet six was Davy Tipton
and he had the proportions
as kingpin Mississippi River pilot
nearly filling the pilothouse
as he took the wheel with a laugh:
"Big rivers ought to have big men."

On the homestretch of a racetrack
in the heart of the bluegrass country
in Lexington, Kentucky
they strewed the ashes of a man
who had so ordered in his will.

He loved horses
and wanted his dust
in the flying hoofs of the homestretch.

5

FOR sixty years the pine lumber barn
had held cows, horses, hay, harness, tools, junk,
amid the prairie winds of Knox County, Illinois
and the corn crops came and went, plows and wagons,
and hands milked, hands husked and harnessed
and held the leather reins of horse teams
in dust and dog days, in late fall sleet
till the work was done that fall.
And the barn was a witness, stood and saw it all.
    "That old barn on your place, Charlie,
    was nearly falling last time I saw it,
    how is it now?"
    "I got some poles to hold it on the east side
    and the wind holds it up on the west."

6

AND you take hold of a handle
    by one hand or the other
    by the better or worse hand
    and you never know
    maybe till long afterward
    which was the better hand.

    And you give an anecdote
out of profound and moving forms of life
and one says you're an odd bird to tell it
and it was whimsical entertaining thank you
while another takes it as a valentine
    and a fable not solved offhand
    a text for two hours talk and
        several cigars smoked—
You might say there never was a man who cut
    off his nose to spite his face.

Yet the cartoon stands for several nations
 and more than one ruler of a realm.
Likewise the man who burned his barn to get
 rid of the rats
Or the woman who said her "No" meant "Perhaps"
 and her "Perhaps" meant "Yes"
Or Monte Cristo yes he was a case.

Monte Cristo had a list, a little roll call.
And one by one he took them each for a ride
Saying One and Two and Three and so on
Till the names were all crossed off
And he had cleansed the world of a given number
Of betrayers who had personally wronged him.
He was judge, jury, and executioner,
On a par with Frankie who shot Johnnie,
Only far colder than Frankie.
 "He created a solitude
  and called it peace."
He was cold, sure, and what they call elevated,
Meaning it was justice and not personal malice
Handing out stiff death with regards, compliments,
Calling each number like Nemesis in knickerbockers.
 The show he put on was a little too good.
 He was a lone wolf all on his own.
 And Jesse James beat his record.
And John Brown was a far more profound sketch,
John Brown who was locked up and didn't stay locked,
John Brown who was buried deep and didn't stay so.

 In a Colorado graveyard
 two men lie in one grave.
They shot it out in a jam over who owned
One corner lot: over a piece of real estate
They shot it out: it was a perfect duel.
Each cleansed the world of the other.
Each horizontal in an identical grave
Had his bones cleaned by the same maggots.
They sleep now as two accommodating neighbors.
They had speed and no control.
They wanted to go and didn't know where.

"Revenge takes time and is a lot of bother,"
   said a released convict who by the code
   of Monte Cristo should have shot twelve
   jurymen and hanged one judge and cruci-
   fied one prosecuting attorney and hung by
   thumbs two police officers and four prom-
   inent citizens.
"In my case," he added, "it pays to have a
   good forgettery."

7

NEITHER wife nor child had Mr. Eastman and the manner of his death
   was peculiar.

Around a fireplace in his home one night he entertained eight old friends,
   saying to one woman at the door at eleven o'clock, "I'm leaving
   you," she rejoining, "No, I'm leaving you."

But Mr. Eastman, the kodak king of exactly how many millions he
   wasn't sure, knew better as to whether he was leaving her or she him.

After a good night of sleep and breakfast he met two lawyers and a sec-
   retary, rearranging codicils in his will

And when they lingered and delayed about going, he said, "You must
   be going, I have some writing to do,"

And they had a feeling, "Well, this is one of Mr. Eastman's jokes, he
   has always had his odd pleasantries."

And again Mr. Eastman knew better than they that there was a little
   writing to be done and nobody else could do it for him.

They went—and Mr. Eastman stepped into a bathroom, took his reliable
   fountain pen and scribbled on a sheet of paper:
                   "My work is finished. Why wait?"

He had counted the years one by one up to seventy-seven, had come
   through one paralytic stroke, had seen one lifelong friend reduced
   by a series of strokes to childish play at papercutting four years in
   bed and the integrity of the mind gone.

He had a guess deep in his heart that if he lived he might change his
   will; he could name cases; as the will now stood it was a keen dis-
   persal for science, music, research, and with a changing mind he
   might change his will.

Cool he was about what he was doing for he had thought about it along
   the slopes of the Genesee Valley of New York and along the coasts
   of Africa and amid babbling apes of the jungle.

He inspects in the bathroom an automatic revolver, a weapon tested
and trusted, loaded, oiled, operating.

He takes a towel and wets it, placing it over the heart, the idea being that
in case he shoots himself there will be no soot nor splatter and a
clean piece of workmanship.

His preparations are considered and thorough and he knows the credit
for the deed can never possibly go to anyone but himself.

Then he steps out, the hammer falls, he crosses over, takes the last barrier.

He knows thereafter no console organist will call of a morning to play
Bach or Handel while he eats breakfast.

His last testament stands secure against the childishness of second child-
hood.

8

MILDRED KLINGHOFER whirled through youth in bloom.

One baby came and was taken away, another came and was taken away.

From her windows she saw the cornrows young and green

And later the final stand of the corn and the huddled shocks

And the blue mist of a winter thaw deepening at evening.

In her middle forties her first husband died.

In her middle sixties her second husband died.

In her middle seventies her third husband died.

And she died at mid-eighty with her fourth husband at the bedside.

Thus she had known an editor, a lawyer, a grocer, a retired farmer.

To the first of them she had borne two children she had hungered for.

And deep in her had stayed a child hunger.

In the last hours when her mind wandered, she cried imperiously, "My
baby! give me my baby!"

And her cries for this child, born of her mind, in her final moments of
life, went on and on.

When they answered, "Your baby isn't here" or "Your baby is coming
soon if you will wait," she kept on with her cry, "My baby! let me
hold my baby!"

    And they made a rag doll

    And laid it in her arms

And she clutched it as a mother would.

And she was satisfied and her second childhood ended like her first,
with a doll in her arms.

There are dreams stronger than death.

Men and women die holding these dreams.

Yes, "stronger than death": let the hammers beat on this slogan.
Let the sea wash its salt against it and the blizzards drive wind and winter
 at it.
Let the undersea sharks try to break this bronze murmur.
Let the gentle bush dig its root deep and spread upward to split one boul-
 der.
Blame the frustrate? Some of them have lived stronger than death.
Blame only the smug and scrupulous beyond reproach.
Who made the guess Shakespeare died saying his best plays didn't get
 written?
Who swindles himself more deeply than the one saying, "I am holier than
 thou"?

> "I love you,"
> said a great mother.
> "I love you for what you are
> knowing so well what you are.
> And I love you more yet, child,
> deeper yet than ever, child,
> for what you are going to be,
> knowing so well you are going far,
> knowing your great works are ahead,
> ahead and beyond,
> yonder and far over yet."

9

A FATHER sees a son nearing manhood.
What shall he tell that son?
"Life is hard; be steel; be a rock."
And this might stand him for the storms
and serve him for humdrum and monotony
and guide him amid sudden betrayals
and tighten him for slack moments.
"Life is a soft loam; be gentle; go easy."
And this too might serve him.
Brutes have been gentled where lashes failed.
The growth of a frail flower in a path up
has sometimes shattered and split a rock.
A tough will counts. So does desire.

So does a rich soft wanting.
Without rich wanting nothing arrives.
Tell him too much money has killed men
and left them dead years before burial:
the quest of lucre beyond a few easy needs
has twisted good enough men
sometimes into dry thwarted worms.
Tell him time as a stuff can be wasted.
Tell him to be a fool every so often
and to have no shame over having been a fool
yet learning something out of every folly
hoping to repeat none of the cheap follies
thus arriving at intimate understanding
of a world numbering many fools.
Tell him to be alone often and get at himself
and above all tell himself no lies about himself
whatever the white lies and protective fronts
he may use amongst other people.
Tell him solitude is creative if he is strong
and the final decisions are made in silent rooms.
Tell him to be different from other people
if it comes natural and easy being different.
Let him have lazy days seeking his deeper motives.
Let him seek deep for where he is a born natural.
    Then he may understand Shakespeare
    and the Wright brothers, Pasteur, Pavlov,
    Michael Faraday and free imaginations
bringing changes into a world resenting change.
    He will be lonely enough
    to have time for the work
    he knows as his own.

1 0

THE Australian mounted infantryman now teaches
    in a western state college.
Once he studied at the University of Heidelberg
    and took a doctor's degree.
Once he slept on newspapers, pink sheets, three
    weeks in Grant Park, Chicago

Keeping a tight hold on his certificate awarded
    by the University of Heidelberg.
Once he lived six weeks in a tent looking in the
    face the Great Sphinx of Egypt.
Once of a morning shaving he happened to ask the
    battered and worndown Sphinx,
"What would you say if I should ask you to tell
    me something worth telling?"
And the Sphinx broke its long silence:
              "Don't expect too much."

1 1

AN Englishman in the old days
presented the Empress of Russia
with a life-sized flea made of gold
and it could hop.

She asked the court:
"What can we Russians do
to equal this marvel?"

A Minister took it away
and brought it back soon after.
He had seen to it
and had the monogram of the Empress
engraved on each foot of the flea
though it would no longer hop.

This is a case in point
as told by Salzman
who came from the Caucasus
and had it from a man who was there.

In Tiflis, his home town,
Salzman knew a merchant
who stood in the front door
and spoke to passers-by,
to possible customers:
    "Come inside.

We've got everything—
even bird's milk."

And this merchant weighed his hand
along with what he sold his patrons
and each evening after business hours
he threw holy water on his hand
saying, "Cleanse thyself, cleanse thyself."

Among the peasants Salzman heard:
"He should be the owner of the land
who rubs it between his hands every spring."

Wood rangers in the forest of the czar
came in and talked all night.
They spoke of forest sounds:
"The cry of a virgin tree at its first cut
    of the ax stays in the air.
"The sound of the blow that kills a snake
    is in the air till sundown.
"The cry of the child wrongfully punished
    stays in the air."

And this was in the old days
and they are a fine smoke
a thin smoke.

The people move
in a fine thin smoke,
the people, yes.

1 2

THE scaffolding holds the arch in place
till the keystone is put in to stay.
Then the scaffolding comes out.
Then the arch stands strong as all the
massed pressing parts of the arch
and loose as any sag or spread
failing of the builders' intention, hope.

"The arch never sleeps."
Living in union it holds.
So long as each piece does its work
the arch is alive, singing, a restless choral.

1 3

THE outstraw green turns gold turns ashen and
    prepares for snow.
The earth and the grass hold grand international
    confabulations with the sun.
Along the Arkansas or the Po grass testifies to
    loam of earth alive yet.
The rivers of the earth run into the sea, return
    in fog and rain alive yet.
The shuttlings go on between field and sky and
    keep corn potatoes beans alive yet.
The Illinois corn leaves spoken to in high winds
    run in sea waves of sun silver.
Alive yet the spillover of last night's moonrise
    brought returns of peculiar cash
    a cash of thin air alive yet.

On the shores of Lake Michigan
high on a wooden pole, in a box,
two purple martins had a home
and taken away down to Martinique
and let loose, they flew home,
thousands of miles to be home again.
    And this has lights of wonder
    echo and pace and echo again.
The birds let out began flying
north north-by-west north
till they were back home.
How their instruments told them
of ceiling, temperature, air pressure,
how their control-boards gave them
reports of fuel, ignition, speeds,
is out of the record, out.
    Across spaces of sun and cloud,
    in rain and fog, through air pockets,

wind with them, wind against them,
stopping for subsistence rations,
whirling in gust and spiral,
these people of the air,
these children of the wind,
had a sense of where to go and how,
how to go north north-by-west north,
till they came to one wooden pole,
till they were home again.
 And this has lights of wonder
 echo and pace and echo again
for other children, other people, yes.

The red ball of the sun in an evening mist
Or the slow fall of rain on planted fields
Or the pink sheath of a newborn child
Or the path of a child's mouth to a nipple
Or the snuggle of a bearcub in mother paws
Or the structural weave of the universe
Witnessed in a moving frame of winter stars—
 These hold affidavits of struggle.

1 4

THE people is Everyman, everybody.
Everybody is you and me and all others.
What everybody says is what we all say.
 And what is it we all say?

Where did we get these languages?
Why is your baby-talk deep in your blood?
What is the cling of the tongue
To what it heard with its mother-milk?

They cross on the ether now.
They travel on high frequencies
Over the border-lines and barriers
Of mountain ranges and oceans.
When shall we all speak the same language?
And do we want to have all the same language?
Are we learning a few great signs and passwords?

Why should Everyman be lost for words?
The questions are put every day in every tongue:
          "Where you from, Stranger?
          Where were you born?
          Got any money?
          What do you work at?
          Where's your passport?
          Who are your people?"

Over the ether crash the languages.
          And the people listen.
As on the plain of Howdeehow they listen.
          They want to hear.
They will be told when the next war is ready.
The long wars and the short wars will come on the air,
How many got killed and how the war ended
And who got what and the price paid
And how there were tombs for the Unknown Soldier,
     The boy nobody knows the name of,
The boy whose great fame is that of the masses,
The millions of names too many to write on a tomb,
The heroes, the cannonfodder, the living targets,
The mutilated and sacred dead,
The people, yes.

Two countries with two flags
are nevertheless one land, one blood, one people—
     can this be so?
And the earth belongs to the family of man?
     can this be so?

The first world war came and its cost was laid on the people.
The second world war—the third—what will be the cost?
And will it repay the people for what they pay?

15

FROM the people the countries get their armies.
By the people the armies are fed, clothed, armed.
Out of the smoke and ashes of the war

The people build again their two countries with two flags
Even though sometimes it is one land, one blood, one people.

Hate is a vapor fixed and mixed.
Hate is a vapor blown and thrown.
And the war lasts till the hate dies down
And the crazy Four Horsemen have handed the people
Hunger and filth and a stink too heavy to stand.
Then the earth sends forth bright new grass
And the land begins to breathe easy again
Though the hate of the people dies slow and hard.
        Hate is a lingering heavy swamp mist.

And the bloated horse carcass points four feet to the sky
And the tanks and caterpillar tractors are buried deep in shell holes
And rust flakes the big guns and time rots the gas masks on skeleton faces:
Deep in the dirt the dynamite threw them with an impersonal detonation:
        war is "Oh!" and "Ah!": war is "Ugh!"

                And after the strife of war
                begins the strife of peace.

16

Hope is a tattered flag and a dream out of time.
Hope is a heartspun word, the rainbow, the shadblow in white,
The evening star inviolable over the coal mines,
The shimmer of northern lights across a bitter winter night,
The blue hills beyond the smoke of the steel works,
The birds who go on singing to their mates in peace, war, peace,
The ten-cent crocus bulb blooming in a used-car salesroom,
The horseshoe over the door, the luckpiece in the pocket,
The kiss and the comforting laugh and resolve—
Hope is an echo, hope ties itself yonder, yonder.

The spring grass showing itself where least expected,
The rolling fluff of white clouds on a changeable sky,
The broadcast of strings from Japan, bells from Moscow,
Of the voice of the prime minister of Sweden carried
Across the sea in behalf of a world family of nations

And children singing chorals of the Christ child
And Bach being broadcast from Bethlehem, Pennsylvania
And tall skyscrapers practically empty of tenants
And the hands of strong men groping for handholds
And the Salvation Army singing God loves us. . . .

17

"The people is a myth, an abstraction."
And what myth would you put in place
        of the people?
And what abstraction would you exchange
        for this one?
And when has creative man not toiled
        deep in myth?
And who fights for a bellyful only and
        where is any name worth remembering
        for anything else than the human ab-
        straction woven through it with in-
        visible thongs?
"Precisely who and what is the people?"
Is this far off from asking what is grass?
        what is salt? what is the sea? what is
        loam?
What are seeds? what is a crop? why must
        mammals have milk soon as born or they
        perish?
And how did that alfalfaland governor
        mean it: "The common people is a mule
        that will do anything you say except
        stay hitched"?

18

Let the nickels and dimes explain.
They are made for the people.
Millions every day study the buffalo on the nickel,
Study the torch of liberty on the dime
And the words "In God We Trust,"
Study before spending the nickel, the dime,

For a handkerchief, a mousetrap, a bowl of soup.
    These with their nickels and dimes
    Bring the street its roar and whirl,
    These in their wants and spending,
These are the bottom pedestals of steel-ribbed skyscrapers.
These are the buyers and payers whose mass flood of nickels
    and dimes is a life stream of a system.

And how come the hey-you-
    -listen-to-this billboard, the you-can't-
    -get-away-from-this electric sign, the
    show window robots and dummies, the loud-
    speaker clamor, the bargains brandished
    with slambang hoots and yells, nods and
    winks, gee-whizz sales?
The liar in print who first lies to you
    about your health and then lies about
    what will fix it, the scare liar who hopes
    his lies will scare you into buying what
    he is lying about,
The better-than-all-others liar, the easy-pay-
    ments liar, the greatest-on-earth liar, the
    get-rich-quick liar
Befouling words and mutilating language and
    feeding rubbish and filth to the human mind
    for the sake of sales, selling whatever can
    be sold for a profit—
Out of this seething whirl, this merciless fight
    of the selling game, what happens to buyers
    and sellers? why does the question rise:
        "How can you compete with a skunk?"

The endless lines of women buying steel-wool dishrags are among the
    people, the customers, the mass buyers who pay
For the barons and counts the American girl goes shopping for, trying
    one and another.
"What is doing in dukes today and how much for a marquis a markee?"
    asks the chain store princess, the daughter of the railroad reorgani-
    zation looter,
While the shoppers and commuters who constitute their meal tickets

pick the aisles amid frying pans, flannelette apparel, leatherette
notions, genuine toys and imitation jewelry.

Out of the needs of life and the wants of the people rises a jungle of
tall possessions bewildering to its owners and their sons and daugh-
ters who step in when the will is read and say, "Now it's ours."
From then on the bank and its branches appurtenant thereto, the mills
and mines, the patents, the oil wells and pipe lines, the monopoly
rights, the coast-to-coast chain of stores, belong to the new gen-
eration,
To a daughter sometimes nothing special, just another cutie; to a son who
knows neckties and chorines and wisecracks at parting, "Abyssinia."
Out of this rigamarole come czars of definite domains, owners of control
saying, "We don't have to own it. What's ownership anyhow if we
hold control and the affiliates and subsidiaries of the main holding
company are fixed our way?"

19

THE people, yes, the people,
Everyone who got a letter today
And those the mail-carrier missed,
The women at the cookstoves preparing meals,
    in a sewing corner mending, in a basement
    laundering, woman the homemaker,
The women at the factory tending a stitching
    machine, some of them the mainstay of the
    jobless man at home cooking, laundering,
Streetwalking jobhunters, walkers alive and keen,
    sleepwalkers drifting along, the stupefied and
    hopeless down-and-outs, the game fighters
    who will die fighting,
Walkers reading signs and stopping to study
    windows, the signs and windows aimed
    straight at their eyes, their wants,
Women in and out of doors to look and feel, to
    try on, to buy and take away, to order and
    have it charged and delivered, to pass by on
    account of price and conditions,
The shopping crowds, the newspaper circulation,

the bystanders who witness parades, who
  meet the boat, the train, who throng in
  wavelines to a fire, an explosion, an accident—
  The people, yes—
Their shoe soles wearing holes in stone steps, their
  hands and gloves wearing soft niches in ban-
  isters of granite, two worn foot-tracks at the
  general-delivery window,
Driving their cars, stop and go, red light, green
  light, and the law of the traffic cop's fingers,
  on their way, loans and mortgages, margins to
  cover,
Payments on the car, the bungalow, the radio, the
  electric icebox, accumulated interest on loans
  for past payments, the writhing point of
  where the money will come from,
Crime thrown in their eyes from every angle,
  crimes against property and person, crime in
  the prints and films, crime as a lurking
  shadow ready to spring into reality, crime as
  a method and a technic,
Comedy as an offset to crime, the laughmakers,
  the odd numbers in the news and the movies,
  original clowns and imitators, and in the best
  you never know what's coming next even
  when it's hokum,
And sports, how a muff in the seventh lost yes-
  terday's game and now they are learning to
  hit Dazzy's fadeaway ball and did you hear
  how Foozly plowed through that line for a
  touchdown this afternoon?
And daily the death toll of the speed wagons; a
  cripple a minute in fenders, wheels, steel and
  glass splinters; a stammering witness before a
  coroner's jury, "It happened so sudden I
  don't know what happened."
And in the air a decree: life is a gamble; take a
  chance; you pick a number and see what you
  get: anything can happen in this sweepstakes:
  around the corner may be prosperity or the

worst depression yet: who knows? nobody:
you pick a number, you draw a card, you
shoot the bones.

In the poolrooms the young hear, "Ashes to
ashes, dust to dust, If the women don't get
you then the whiskey must," and in the
churches, "We walk by faith and not by sight,"

Often among themselves in their sessions of can-
dor the young saying, "Everything's a racket,
only the gyp artists get by."

And over and beyond the latest crime or comedy
always that relentless meal ticket saying
dont-lose-me, hold your job, glue your mind
on that job or when your last nickel is gone
you live on your folks or sign for relief,

And the terror of these unknowns is a circle of
black ghosts holding men and women in toil
and danger, and sometimes shame, beyond
the dreams of their blossom days, the days
before they set out on their own.

What is this "occupational disease" we hear
about? It's a sickness that breaks your health
on account of the work you're in. That's all.
Another kind of work and you'd have been
as good as any of them. You'd have been
your old self.

And what is this "hazardous occupation"? Why
that's where you're liable to break your neck
or get smashed on the job so you're no good
on that job any more and that's why you
can't get any regular life insurance so long as
you're on that job.

These are heroes then—among the plain people—
Heroes, did you say? And why not? They
give all they've got and ask no questions and
take what comes and what more do you
want?

On the street you can see them any time, some
with jobs, some nothing doing, here a down-
and-out, there a game fighter who will die
fighting.

20

Who shall speak for the people?
Who knows the works from A to Z
    so he can say, "I know what the
    people want"? Who is this phenom?
    where did he come from?
When have the people been half as rotten
    as what the panderers to the people
    dangle before crowds?
When has the fiber of the people been as
    shoddy as what is sold to the people
    by cheaters?
What is it the panderers and cheaters of
    the people play with and trade on?
The credulity of believers and hopers—and
    when is a heart less of a heart because
    of belief and hope?
What is the tremulous line between credu-
    lity on the one side and on the other
    the hypotheses and illusions of inven-
    tors, discoverers, navigators who chart
    their course by what they hope and
    believe is beyond the horizon?
What is a stratosphere fourteen miles from
    the earth or a sunken glass house on
    the sea-bottom amid fish and feather-
    stars unless a bet that man can shove
    on beyond yesterday's record of man
    the hoper, the believer?
How like a sublime sanctuary of human
    credulity is that room where amid
    tubes, globes and retorts they shoot
    with heavy hearts of hydrogen and
    batter with fire-streams of power hop-
    ing to smash the atom:
Who are these bipeds trying to take apart
    the atom and isolate its electrons and
    make it tell why it is what it is? Be-
    lievers and hopers.

Let the work of their fathers and elder
     brothers be cancelled this instant and
     what would happen?
Nothing—only every tool, bus, car, light,
     torch, bulb, print, film, instrument or
     communication depending for its life
     on electrodynamic power would stop
     and stand dumb and silent.

2 1

Who knows the people, the migratory harvest hands and berry pickers,
     the loan shark victims, the installment house wolves,
The jugglers in sand and wood who smooth their hands along the mold
     that casts the frame of your motorcar engine,
The metal polishers, solderers, and paint-spray hands who put the final
     finish on the car,
The riveters and bolt-catchers, the cowboys of the air in the big city, the
     cowhands of the Great Plains, the ex-convicts, the bellhops, redcaps,
     lavatory men—
The union organizer with his list of those ready to join and those hesi-
     tating, the secret paid informers who report every move toward or-
     ganizing,
The house-to-house canvassers, the doorbell ringers, the good-morning-
     have-you-heard boys, the strike pickets, the strikebreakers, the hired
     sluggers, the ambulance crew, the ambulance chasers, the picture
     chasers, the meter readers, the oysterboat crews, the harborlight
     tenders—
          who knows the people?

Who knows this from pit to peak? The people, yes.

2 2

The people is a lighted believer and
     hoper—and this is to be held against
     them?
The panderers and cheaters are to have
     their way in trading on these lights
     of the people?

Not always, no, not always, for the people
    is a knower too.
With Johannson steel blocks the people
    can measure itself as a knower
Knowing what it knows today with a deeper
    knowing than ever
Knowing in millionths and billionths of
    an inch
Knowing in the mystery of one automatic
    machine expertly shaping for your eyes
    another automatic machine
Knowing in traction, power-shafts, transmis-
    sion, twist drills, grinding, gears—
Knowing in the night air mail, the news-
    reel flicker, the broadcasts from Tokyo,
    Shanghai, Bombay and Somaliland—
The people a knower whose knowing
    grows by what it feeds on
The people wanting to know more, wanting.
The birds of the air and the fish of the sea
    leave off where man begins.

23

"THE kindest and gentlest here are the
    murderers," said the penitentiary warden.
"I killed the man because I loved him,"
    said the woman the police took yesterday.
"I had such a good time," said the woman leaving a movie theater with
    tears in her eyes. "It was a swell picture."
"A divorced man goes and marries the same kind of a woman he is just
    rid of," said the lawyer.
"Life is a gigantic fake," read the farewell note of the high school boy
    who killed himself.
"I pick jurors with nonconvicting faces,"
    said the lawyer who usually cleared his man.
"We earn and we earn and all that we earn goes into the grave," said the
    basement-dwelling mother who had lost six of her eight children from
    the white plague.
"Don't mourn for me but organize," said the Utah I.W.W. before a firing

squad executed sentence of death on him, his last words running:
"Let her go!"
"Look out or you'll be ready for one of these one-man bungalows with
silver handles," laughed the traffic cop.
"Tie your hat to the saddle and let's ride,"
yelled one in a five-gallon hat in Albuquerque.
"If I never see you again don't think the time long," smiled an old timer
in Wyoming moonlight.
On tiptoe and whispering so no one else could hear, a little girl at Browns-
ville spoke into the ear of the chief executive of the great State of
Texas: "How does it feel to be Governor?"
Why when the stock crash came did the man in black silk pajamas let
himself headfirst off a fire escape down ten floors to a stone sidewalk?
His sixty million dollars had shrunk to ten million and he didn't see
how he could get along.
"If she was a wicked witch she wouldn't say so, she would be so wicked
she wouldn't know it," said little Anne.
"God will forgive me, it's his line of business,"
said the dying German-Jewish poet in his garret.

The little girl saw her first troop parade and asked,
          "What are those?"
"Soldiers."
"What are soldiers?"
"They are for war. They fight and each tries to kill
as many of the other side as he can."
The girl held still and studied.
"Do you know . . . I know something?"
"Yes, what is it you know?"
"Sometime they'll give a war and nobody will come."

One of the early Chicago poets,
One of the slouching underslung Chicago poets,
Having only the savvy God gave him,
Lacking a gat, lacking brass knucks,
Having one lead pencil to spare, wrote:
          "I am credulous about the destiny of man,
          and I believe more than I can ever prove
          of the future of the human race
          and the importance of illusions,

the value of great expectations.
I would like to be in the same moment
an earthworm (which I am) and
a rider to the moon (which I am)."

2 4

WHO shall speak for the people?
who has the answers?
where is the sure interpreter?
who knows what to say?
Who can write the music jazz-classical
smokestacks-geraniums hyacinths-biscuits
now whispering easy
now boom doom crashing angular
now tough monotonous tom tom
Who has enough split-seconds and slow sea-tides?

The ships of the sea and the mists of
night and the sheen of old battle-
fields and the moon on the city
rubbish dumps belong to the people.
The crops this year, last and next year,
and the winds and frosts in many
orchards and tomato gardens, are
listed in the people's acquaintance.
Horses and wagons, trucks and tractors,
from the shouting cities to the sleep-
ing prairies, from worn pavements
to mountain mule paths, the people
have strange possessions.
The plow and the hammer, the knife and
the shovel, the planting hoe and the
reaping sickle, everywhere these are
the people's possessions by right of
use.
Their handles are smoothed to the grain
of the wood by the enclosing
thumbs and fingers of familiar
hands,

Maintenance-of-way men in a Tennessee
    gang singing, "If I die a railroad
    man put a pick and shovel at my
    head and my feet and a nine-pound
    hammer in my hand,"
Larry, the Kansas section boss, on his
    dying bed asking for one last look at
    the old hand-car,
His men saying in the coffin on his chest
    he should by rights have the spike
    maul, the gauge and the old claw-bar.

The early morning in the fields, the
    brown thrush warbling and the imi-
    tations of the catbird, the neverend-
    ing combat with pest and destroyer,
    the chores of feeding and watching,
    seedtime and harvest,
The clocking of the months toward a
    birthing day, the newly dropped
    calves and the finished steers loaded
    in stock-cars for market, the gamble
    on what we'll get tomorrow for
    what we put in today—
These are belongings of the people, dusty
    with the dust of earth, merciless as
    sudden hog cholera, hopeful as a
    rainwashed hill of moonlit pines.

2 5

"You do what you must—this world and then the next—one world at a
    time."
The grain gamblers and the price manipulators and the stock-market
    players put their own twist on the text: In the sweat of thy brow shalt
    thou eat thy bread.
The day's work in the factory, mill, mine—the whistle, the bell, the alarm
    clock, the timekeeper and the paycheck, your number on the assembly
    line, what the night shift says when the day shift comes—the blood

of years paid out for finished products proclaimed on billboards yell-
ing at highway travellers in green valleys—
These are daily program items, values of blood and mind in the everyday
rituals of the people.

2 6

You can drum on immense drums
the monotonous daily motions of the people
taking from earth and air
their morsels of bread and love,
a carryover from yesterday into tomorrow.

You can blow on great brass horns
the awful clamors of war and revolution
when swarming anonymous shadowshapes
obliterate old names Big Names
and cross out what was
and offer what is on a fresh blank page.

2 7

In the folded and quiet yesterdays
Put down in the book of the past
Is a scrawl of scrawny thumbs
And a smudge of clutching fingers
And the breath of hanged men,
Of thieves and vagabonds,
Of killers saying welcome as an ax fell,
Of traitors cut in four pieces
And their bowels thrust over their faces
According to the ancient Anglo-Saxon
Formula for the crime of treason,
Of persons covered with human filth
In due exaction of a penalty,
Of ears clipped, noses slit, fingers chopped
For the identification of vagrants,
Of loiterers and wanderers seared
"with a hot iron in the breast the mark V,"
Of violence as a motive lying deep
As the weather changes of the sea,

Of gang wars, tong wars, civil tumults,
Industrial strife, international mass murders,
Of agitators outlawed to live on thistles,
Of thongs for holding plainspoken men,
Of thought and speech being held a crime,
And a woman burned for saying,
"I listen to my Voices and obey them,"
And a thinker locked into stone and iron
              For saying, "The earth moves,"
              And the pity of men learning by shocks,
              By pain and practice,
              By plunges and struggles in a bitter pool.

        In the folded and quiet yesterdays
        how many times has it happened?
The leaders of the people estimated as to price
And bought with bribes signed and delivered
Or waylaid and shot or meshed by perjurers
Or hunted and sent into hiding
Or taken and paraded in garments of dung,
Fire applied to their footsoles:
        "Now will you talk?"
Their mouths basted with rubber hose:
        "Now will you talk?"
Thrown into solitary, fed on slops, hung by thumbs,
Till the mention of that uprising is casual, so-so,
As though the next revolt breeds somewhere
In the bowels of that mystic behemoth, the people.
"And when it comes again," say watchers, "we are ready."
        How many times
        in the folded and quiet yesterdays
        has it happened?

              "You may burn my flesh and bones
              and throw the ashes to the four winds,"
              smiled one of them,   •
              "Yet my voice shall linger on
              and in the years yet to come
              the young shall ask what was the idea
              for which you gave me death

and what was I saying
that I must die for what I said?"

2 8

In the days of the cockade and the brass pistol
Fear of the people brought the debtors' jail.
The creditor said, "Pay me or go to prison,"
And men lacking property lacked ballots and citizenship.
Into the Constitution of the United States they wrote a fear
In the form of "checks and balances," "proper restraints"
On the people so whimsical and changeable,
So variable in mood and weather.

Lights of tallow candles fell on lawbooks by night.
The woolspun clothes came from sheep near by.
Men of "solid substance" wore velvet knickerbockers
And shared snuff with one another in greetings.
One of these made a name for himself with saying
You could never tell what was coming next from the people:
"Your people, sir, your people is a great beast,"
Speaking for those afraid of the people,
Afraid of sudden massed action of the people,
The people being irresponsible with torch, gun and rope,
The people being a child with fire and loose hardware,
The people listening to leather-lunged stump orators
Crying the rich get richer, the poor poorer, and why?
The people undependable as prairie rivers in floodtime,
The people uncertain as lights on the face of the sea
Wherefore high and first of all he would write
God, the Constitution, Property Rights, the Army and the Police,
After these the rights of the people.

    The meaning was:
The people having nothing to lose take chances.
The people having nothing to take care of are careless.
The people lacking property are slack about property.
Having no taxes to pay how can they consider taxes?
"And the poor have they not themselves to blame for their poverty?"

Those who have must take care of those who have not
Even though in the providence of events some of
Those who now have *not* once *had* and what they had *then*
Was taken away from them by those who *now have.*

>   Naughts are naughts into riffraff.
>   Nothing plus nothing equals nothing.
>   Scum is scum and dregs are dregs.
>   "This flotsam and jetsam."
There is the House of Have and the House of Have-Not.
God named the Haves as caretakers of the Have-Nots.
This shepherding is a divine decree laid on the betters.
"And surely you know when you are among your betters?"

>   This and a lot else was in the meaning:
>   "Your people, sir, is a great beast."
The testament came with deliberation
Cold as ice, warm as blood,
Hard as a steel hand steel-gloved,
A steel foot steel-shod
for contact with another testament:
"All men are born free and equal."
The cow content to give milk and calves,
The plug work-horse plowing from dawn till dark,
The mule lashed with a blacksnake when balking—
Fed and sheltered—or maybe not—all depending—
A pet monkey leaping for nuts thrown to it,
A parrot ready to prattle your words
And repeat after you your favorite oaths—
Or a nameless monster to be guarded and tended
Against temper and flashes of retaliation—
These were the background symbols:
>   "Your people, sir, is a great beast."

29

>   THE people, yes—
Born with bones and heart fused in deep and violent secrets
Mixed from a bowl of sky blue dreams and sea slime facts—
A seething of saints and sinners, toilers, loafers, oxen, apes

In a womb of superstition, faith, genius, crime, sacrifice—
The one and only source of armies, navies, work gangs,
The living flowing breath of the history of nations,
Of the little Family of Man hugging the little ball of Earth,
And a long hall of mirrors, straight, convex and concave,
Moving and endless with scrolls of the living,
Shimmering with phantoms flung from the past,
Shot over with lights of babies to come, not yet here.

    The honorable orators, the gazettes of thunder,
    The tycoons, big shots and dictators,
    Flicker in the mirrors a few moments
    And fade through the glass of death
    For discussion in an autocracy of worms
While the rootholds of the earth nourish the majestic people
And the new generations with names never heard of
Plow deep in broken drums and shoot craps for old crowns,
Shouting unimagined shibboleths and slogans,
Tracing their heels in moth-eaten insignia of bawdy leaders—
Piling revolt on revolt across night valleys,
Letting loose insurrections, uprisings, strikes,
Marches, mass-meetings, banners, declared resolves,
Plodding in a somnambulism of fog and rain
Till a given moment exploded by long-prepared events—
    Then again the overthrow of an old order
    And the trials of another new authority
    And death and taxes, crops and droughts,
    Chinch bugs, grasshoppers, corn borers, boll weevils,
    Top soil farms blown away in a dust and wind,
    Inexorable rains carrying off rich loam,
    And mortgages, house rent, groceries,
    Jobs, pay cuts, layoffs, relief
    And passion and poverty and crime
    And the paradoxes not yet resolved
    Of the shrewd and elusive proverbs,
    The have-you-heard yarns,
    The listen-to-this anecdote
    Made by the people out of the roots of the earth,
    Out of dirt, barns, workshops, timetables,
    Out of lumberjack payday jamborees,

Out of joybells and headaches the day after,
Out of births, weddings, accidents,
Out of wars, laws, promises, betrayals,
Out of mists of the lost and anonymous,
Out of plain living, early rising and spare belongings:

3 0

WE'LL see what we'll see.
Time is a great teacher.
Today me and tomorrow maybe you.
This old anvil laughs at many broken hammers.
What is bitter to stand against today may be sweet to remember tomorrow.
Fine words butter no parsnips. Moonlight dries no mittens.
Whether the stone bumps the jug or the jug bumps the stone it is bad
    for the jug.
One hand washes the other and both wash the face.
Better leave the child's nose dirty than wring it off.
We all belong to the same big family and have the same smell.
Handling honey, tar or dung some of it sticks to the fingers.
    The liar comes to believe his own lies.
He who burns himself must sit on the blisters.
    God alone understands fools.
The dumb mother understands the dumb child.
To work hard, to live hard, to die hard, and then to go to hell after all
    would be too damned hard.
You can fool all the people part of the time and part of the people all the
    time but you can't fool all of the people all of the time.
    It takes all kinds of people to make a world.

What is bred in the bone will tell.
Between the inbreds and the cross-breeds the argu-
    ment goes on.
You can breed them up as easy as you can breed
    them down.
"I don't know who my ancestors were," said a
    mongrel, "but we've been descending for a
    long time."
"My ancestors," said the Cherokee-blooded Okla-
    homan, "didn't come over in the *Mayflower*
    but we was there to meet the boat."

> "Why," said the Denver Irish policeman as he
> arrested a Pawnee Indian I.W.W. soapboxer,
> "why don't you go back where you came from?"

An expert is only a damned fool a long ways from home.
You're either a thoroughbred, a scrub, or an in-between.
Speed is born with the foal—sometimes.
Always some dark horse never heard of before is coming under the wire
    a winner.
A thoroughbred always wins against a scrub, though you never know for
    sure: even thoroughbreds have their off days: new blood tells: the
    wornout thoroughbreds lose to the fast young scrubs.

> There is a luck of faces and bloods
> Comes to a child and touches it.
> It comes like a bird never seen.
> It goes like a bird never handled.
> There are little mothers hear the bird,
> Feel the flitting of wings never seen,
> And the touch of the givers of luck,
> The bringers of faces and bloods.

31

> "Your low birth puts you beneath me,"
> said Harmodius, Iphicrates replying,
> "The difference between us is this.
>   My family begins with me.
>   Yours ends with you."

"A long, tall man won't always make a good fireman," said the Santa Fé
    engineer to a couple of other rails deadheading back. "Out of a dozen
    wants to be firemen you can pick 'em. Take one of these weakly
    fellers he'll do his best but he's all gone time you get nine miles.
    Take a short, stout feller, low down so he can get at his coal, and he'll
    beat one of those tall fellers has to stoop. But if a tall feller's got long
    arms he can do wonders. I knowed one engineer used to say he had
    a fireman he never saw him throw a shovel of coal on the fire—his
    arms was so long he just reached and laid the coal on!"

He can turn around on a dime.
He has an automobile thirst and a wheelbarrow income.

I don't know where I'm going but I'm on my way.

I'll knock you so high in the air you'll starve coming down.

A bonanza is a hole in the ground owned by a champion liar.

All you get from him you can put in your eye.

He tried to get a bird in the hand and two in the bush but what he got was a horse of another color.

If the government tried to pay me for what I don't know there wouldn't be enough money in all the mints to pay me.

You can't tell him anything because he thinks he knows more now than he gets paid for.

It's a slow burg—I spent a couple of weeks there one day.

He bit off more than he could chew.

Don't take a mouthful bigger than your mouth.

Let's take it apart to see how it ticks.

If we had a little ham we could have some ham and eggs if we had some eggs.

He always takes off his hat when he mentions his own name.

What's the matter with him? The big I, always the big I.

"Why didn't you zigzag your car and miss him?" "He was zigzagging himself and outguessed me."

"Are you guilty or not guilty?" "'What else have you?"

"Are you guilty or not guilty?" "I stands mute."

3 2

WHAT the people learn out of lifting and hauling and waiting and losing and laughing

Goes into a scroll, an almanac, a record folding and unfolding, and the music goes down and around:

The story goes on and on, happens, forgets to happen, goes out and meets itself coming in, puts on disguises and drops them.

"Yes yes, go on, go on, I'm listening." You hear that in one doorway.

And in the next, "Aw shut up, close your trap, button your tongue, you talk too much."

      The people, yes, the people,

To the museum, the aquarium, the planetarium, the zoo, they go by thousands, coming away to talk about mummies, camels, fish and stars,

The police and constables holding every one of them either a lawbreaker or lawabiding.

The fingerprint expert swears no two of them ever has finger lines and
    circlings the same.
The handwriting expert swears no one of them ever writes his name twice
    the same way.
To the grocer and the banker they are customers, depositors, investors.
The politician counts them as voters, the newspaper editor as readers, the
    gambler as suckers.
The priest holds each one an immortal soul in the care of Almighty God.
        bright accidents from the chromosome
        spill   from the color bowl of the
        chromosomes some go under in early
        bubbles some learn from desert blos-
        soms how to lay up and use thin
        hoardings of night mist

    In an old French town
    the mayor ordered the people
    to hang lanterns in front of their houses
    which the people did
    but the lanterns gave no light
    so the mayor ordered they must
    put candles in the lanterns
    which the people did
    but the candles in the lanterns gave no light
    whereupon the mayor ordered
    they must light the candles in the lanterns
    which the people did
    and thereupon there was light.

The cauliflower is a cabbage with a college education.
All she needs for housekeeping is a can opener.
    They'll fly high if you give them wings.
Put all your eggs in one basket and watch that basket.
Everybody talks about the weather and nobody does anything about it.
The auk flies backward so as to see where it's been.
    Handle with care women and glass.
    Women and linen look best by candlelight.
One hair of a woman draws more than a team of horses.
Blessed are they who expect nothing for they shall not be disappointed
You can send a boy to college but you can't make him think.

The time to sell is when you have a customer.
Sell the buffalo hide after you have killed the buffalo.
The more you fill a barrel the more it weighs unless you fill it with holes.
A pound of iron or a pound of feathers weighs the same.
Those in fear they may cast pearls before swine are often lacking in pearls.
May you live to eat the hen that scratches over your grave.
He seems to think he's the frog's tonsils but he looks to me like a plugged
　　nickel.
If you don't like the coat bring back the vest and I'll give you a pair of
　　pants.
The coat and the pants do the work but the vest gets the gravy.
"You are singing an invitation to summer," said the teacher, "you are not
　　defying it to come."

　　　"Sargeant, if a private calls you
　　　a dam fool, what of it?"
　　　"I'd throw him in the guard house."
　　　"And if he just thinks you're a dam
　　　fool and don't say it, then what?"
　　　"Nothing."
　　　"Well, let it go at that."

　　　　　The white man drew a small circle in the sand
　　　　　and told the red man, "This is what the Indian
　　　　　knows," and drawing a big circle around the
　　　　　small one, "This is what the white man knows."
　　　　　The Indian took the stick and swept an immense
　　　　　ring around both circles: "This is where the
　　　　　white man and the red man know nothing."

　　　　On the long dirt road from Nagadoches to Austin
　　　　The pioneer driving a yoke of oxen and a cart
　　　　met a heavy man in a buggy driving a team
　　　　of glossy black horses.
　　　　　　"I am Sam Houston, Governor of the State of Texas,
　　　　　　and I order you to turn out of the road for me."
　　　　　　"I am an American citizen and a taxpayer of Texas
　　　　　　and I have as much right to the road as you."
　　　　　　"That is an intelligent answer and I salute you
　　　　　　and I will turn out of the road for you."

What did they mean with that Iowa epitaph:
    "She averaged well for this vicinity"?
And why should the old Des Moines editor
    say they could write on his gravestone:
    "He et what was sot before him"?

"I never borrowed your umbrella," said a
    borrower, "and if I did I brought it back."
He was quiet as a wooden-legged man on a tin
    roof and busy as a one-armed paper-hanger
    with the hives.
When a couple of fried eggs were offered the
    new hired man he said, "I don't dirty my
    plate for less than six."

Why did the top sergeant tell the rookie, "Put
    on your hat, here comes a woodpecker"?
"Whiskey," taunted the Irish orator, "whiskey
    it is that makes you shoot at the landlords
    —and miss 'em!"
"Unless you learn," said the father to the son,
    "how to tell a horse chestnut from a chest-
    nut horse you may have to live on soup made
    from the shadow of a starved pigeon."
Said Oscar neither laughing nor crying: "We fed
    the rats to the cats and the cats to the rats
    and was just getting into the big money when
    the whole thing went blooey on account of the
    overproduction of rats and cats."

    Where you been so long?
    What good wind blew you in?
Snow again, kid, I didn't get your drift.
Everything now is either swell or lousy.
"It won't be long now," was answered,
    "The worst is yet to come."
Of the dead merchant prince whose holdings
    were colossal the ditch-digger queried,
    "How much did he leave? All of it."

"What do you want to be?"
T. R. asked.
Bruere answered, "Just an
earthworm turning over a
little of the soil near me."
"Great men never feel great,"
say the Chinese.
"Small men never feel small."

3 3

REMEMBER the chameleon. He was a well-behaved chameleon and noth-
ing could be brought against his record. As a chameleon he had done
the things that should have been done and left undone the things
that should have been left undone. He was a first-class unimpeach-
able chameleon and nobody had anything on him. But he came to a
Scotch plaid and tried to cross it. In order to cross he had to imitate
six different yarn colors, first one and then another and back to the first
or second. He was a brave chameleon and died at the crossroads true
to his chameleon instincts.

What kind of a liar are you?
People lie because they don't remember clear what they saw.
People lie because they can't help making a story better than it was the
way it happened.
People tell "white lies" so as to be decent to others.
People lie in a pinch, hating to do it, but lying on because it might be
worse.
And people lie just to be liars for a crooked personal gain.
What sort of a liar are you?
Which of these liars are you?

3 4

IF you can imagine love letters written back and forth between Mary
Magdalene and Judas Iscariot, if you can see Napoleon dying and
saying he was only a sawdust emperor and an imitation of the real
thing, if you can see judges step down from the bench and take death
sentences from murderers sitting in black robes, if you can see big
thieves protected by law acknowledging to petty thieves handcuffed
and convicted that they are both enemies of society, if you can vision

an opposite for every reality, then you can shake hands with yourself
and murmur, "Pardon my glove, what were we saying when inter-
rupted?"

3 5

THE sea moves always, the wind moves always.
They want and want and there is no end to their wanting.
What they sing is the song of the people.
Man will never arrive, man will be always on the way.
It is written he shall rest but never for long.
The sea and the wind tell him he shall be lonely, meet love, be shaken
    with struggle, and go on wanting.

"When I was born in the Chicago Lying-in Hospital," said the pioneer's
    grandson, "there was a surgeon with multiple instruments, two
    nurses in starched uniforms with silk, gauze, antiseptics, and the
    obliterating cone of the grateful anesthesia. When my grandfather
    was born in the naked cornlands of Nebraska there was only a granny
    woman with a few clean rags and a pail of warm water."

You can go now yes go now. Go east or west, go north or south, you can
    go now. Or you can go up or go down now. And after these there
    is no place to go. If you say no to all of them then you stay here.
    You don't go. You are fixed and put. And from here if you choose
    you send up rockets, you let down buckets. Here then for you is the
    center of things.

3 6

"I AM zero, naught, one cipher,"
meditated the symbol preceding the numbers.
"Think of nothing. I am the sign of it.
I am bitter weather, zero.
In heavy fog the sky ceiling is zero.
Think of nowhere to go. I am it.
Those doomed to nothing for today
and the same nothing for tomorrow,
those without hits, runs, errors,
I am their sign and epitaph,
the goose egg : 0 :
even the least of these—that is me."

When they told those who had no money
"Save your money"
Those who had no money flashed back
"Would you ask those with nothing to eat
to eat less?"

"The stairway of time ever echoes
with the wooden shoe going up
the polished boot coming down."

    Ghost and rich man:
"What do you see out of the window?"
"The people."
"And what do you see in the mirror?"
"Myself."
"Yet the glass in the mirror is the
same only it is silvered."

"If I am a queen and you are a queen,
who fetches the water?" inquire the
Hindus, the Turks asking: "If you are
a gentleman and I am a gentleman, who
will milk the cow?" and the Irish:
"If you're a lady and I'm a lady,
who'll put the sow out of the house?"

"The man put green spectacles on his cow and fed her sawdust.
Maybe she would believe it was grass.
But she didn't. She died on him."

When the horses gagged at going farther up the steep hill, the driver
    shouted:
        "First class passengers, keep your seats.
        Second class passengers, get out and walk.
        Third class passengers, get out and shove."

Said the scorpion of hate: "The poor hate the rich. The rich hate the
    poor. The south hates the north. The west hates the east. The
    workers hate their bosses. The bosses hate their workers. The coun-
    try hates the towns. The towns hate the country. We are a house

divided against itself. We are millions of hands raised against each
other. We are united in but one aim—getting the dollar. And when
we get the dollar we employ it to get more dollars."

37

"So you want to divide all the money there is
and give every man his share?"
"That's it. Put it all in one big pile and split
it even for everybody."
"And the land, the gold, silver, oil, copper, you want
that divided up?"
"Sure—an even whack for all of us."
"Do you mean that to go for horses and cows?"
"Sure—why not?"
"And how about pigs?"
"Oh to hell with you—you know I got a couple of
pigs."

In the night and the mist these voices:
What is mine is mine and I am going to keep it.
What is yours is yours and you are welcome to keep it.
You will have to fight me to take from me what is mine.
Part of what is mine is yours and you are welcome to it.
What is yours is mine and I am going to take it from you.
          In the night and the mist
          the voices meet
          as the clash of steel on steel
Over the rights of possession and control and the points:
          what is mine? what is yours?
          and who says so?

The poor were divided into
the deserving and the undeserving
and a pioneer San Franciscan lacked words:
"It's hard enough to be poor
but to be poor and undeserving . . ."
He saw the slumborn illborn wearyborn
from fathers and mothers the same
out of rooms dank with rot

and scabs, rags, festerings, tubercles, chancres,
the very doorways quavering,
   "What's the use?"

"I came to a country,"
said a wind-bitten vagabond,
"where I saw shoemakers barefoot
saying they had made too many shoes.
I met carpenters living outdoors
saying they had built too many houses.
Clothing workers I talked with,
bushelmen and armhole-basters,
said their coats were on a ragged edge
because they had made too many coats.
And I talked with farmers, yeomanry,
the backbone of the country,
so they were told,
saying they were in debt and near starvation
because they had gone ahead like always
and raised too much wheat and corn
too many hogs, sheep, cattle.
When I said, 'You live in a strange country,'
they answered slow, like men
who wouldn't waste anything, not even language:
'You ain't far wrong there, young feller.
We're going to do something, we don't know what.'"

   The drowning man in the river
   answered the man on the bridge:
   "I don't want to die,
   I'll lose my job in the molding room of
   the Malleable Iron and Castings Works."
   And the living man on the bridge
   hotfooted to the molding room foreman
   of the Malleable Iron and Castings Works
   and got a short answer:
   "You're ten minutes late. The man who
   pushed that fellow off the bridge
   is already on the job."

"What do you want?" a passing stranger asked
a County Kerry farmer.
"What is it I'm wantin'? Me byes and girruls
is gone. The rain has rotted the prathies.
The landlord has taken me pig for the rint.
All I'm wantin' is the Judgment Day."

"The poor of the earth hide themselves together," wrote Job meaning in
   those days too they had a shantytown.
"As wild asses in the wilderness they must go forth, to seek food as their
   task," wrote Job meaning then too they carried the banner and
   hoped to connect with board and clothes somehow.
"In a field not theirs they harvest," wrote Job as though in Judea then
   the frontier was gone, as now in America instead of free homesteads
   the signs say: No Trespassing.
"The weaklings groan and the souls of the wounded cry for help," wrote
   Job taking special notice of those "forced to garner the vineyard of
   the wicked one," mentioning footless wanderers of Bible times as
   though the devices of men then too had an edge against the prop-
   ertyless.

In the Sunflower State 1928 Anno Domini
a Jayhawker sunburnt and gaunt
drove to a loading platform
and took what he got for his hogs
and spoke before two other hog raisers:
        "Everything's lopsided.
"I raise hogs and the railroads and the banks take them away from me
   and I get hit in the hind end.
"The more hogs I raise the worse my mortgages look.
"I try to sleep and I hear those mortgages gnawing in the night like rats
   in a corn crib.
"I want to shoot somebody but I don't know who.
"We'll do something. You wait and see.
"We don't have to stand for this skin game if we're free Americans."

                "Get off this estate."
                "What for?"
                "Because it's mine."
                "Where did you get it?"

"From my father."
"Where did he get it?"
"From his father."
"And where did he get it?"
"He fought for it."
"Well, I'll fight you for it."

3 8

Have you seen men handed refusals
        till they began to laugh
        at the notion of ever landing a job again—
Muttering with the laugh,
        "It's driving me nuts and the family too,"
Mumbling of hoodoos and jinx,
        fear of defeat creeping in their vitals—
Have you never seen this?
        or do you kid yourself
        with the fond soothing syrup of four words
        "Some folks won't work"??
Of course some folks won't work—
        they are sick or wornout or lazy
        or misled with the big idea
the idle poor should imitate the idle rich.

Have you seen women and kids
        step out and hustle for the family
        some in night life on the streets
        some fighting other women and kids
        for the leavings of fruit and vegetable markets
        or searching alleys and garbage dumps for scraps?

Have you seen them with savings gone
        furniture and keepsakes pawned
        and the pawntickets blown away in cold winds?
        by one letdown and another ending
        in what you might call slums—
To be named perhaps in case reports
        and tabulated and classified
        among those who have crossed over
        from the employables into the unemployables?

What is the saga of the employables?
      what are the breaks they get?
What are the dramas of personal fate
      spilled over from industrial transitions?
      what punishments handed bottom people
      who have wronged no man's house
      or things or person?

      Stocks are property, yes.
      Bonds are property, yes.
Machines, land, buildings, are property, yes.
      A job is property,
      no, nix, nah nah.

The rights of property are guarded
      by ten thousand laws and fortresses.
The right of a man to live by his work—
            what is this right?
            and why does it clamor?
            and who can hush it
            so it will stay hushed?
            and why does it speak
            and though put down speak again
            with strengths out of the earth?

39

THERE have been thousands of Andy Adams
only Andy was one of the few who had the words.
"Our men were plainsmen and were at home
as long as they could see the North Star."
They got his drift when he laughed:
"Blankets? Never use them. Sleep on your belly and
      cover it with your back and get up with the
      birds in the morning.
"Saddles? Every good cowman takes his saddle
      wherever he goes though he may not have
      clothes enough to dust a fiddle."
They could ride long hours in rain and sleet dozing
      and taking short sleeps in their saddles, resting
      to linger over their morning coffee.

This breed of men gone to a last roundup?
They will be heard from.
They tell us now any Texas girl is worth marrying.
"No matter what happens, she has seen worse."

     In oak and walnut
Those old New England carpenters hoisted and
     wrought.
Sunup till sundown they hoisted and wrought in
     oak and walnut.
Wood had a meaning and wood spoke to the feel of
     the fingers.
The hammer handles and the handwrought nails
     somehow had blessings.

And they are gone now? their blood is no longer
     alive and speaking?
They no longer come through telling of the hands
     of man having craft?
Let their beds and staircases, chairs and gables now
     lingering testify:
The strong workman whose blood goes into his
     work no more dies than the people die.

         "I'm holding my own,"
         said more than one pioneer.
         "I didn't have anything
         when I landed here
         and I ain't got anything now
         but I got some hope left.
         I ain't lost hope yet.
         I'm a wanter and a hoper."

4 0

     "WE live only once."
Of course the people buy great big hump-backed
     double-jointed fresh-roasted peanuts at ten
     a sack folks ten a sack—
Of course the people go to see the greatest

aggregation of concatenated curiosities and
monstrosities ever assembled beneath one
canvas—
Of course they enjoy the oily slant-eyed spieler
with his slick bazoo selling tickets and gab-
bing One at a time please One at a time,
and inside the tent Tom Thumb and Jumbo,
the hippodrome charioteers, the clowns and
tumblers, the lighted pink moment when a
lithe woman is flung into empty air from
one flying trapeze to another.
     "We live only once."

Of course the greatest showman on earth who
excused himself with saying, "The people
love to be humbugged," was himself hum-
bugged and lost the first of his fortunes to
the fate that humbugged him out of it.

     Do this, buy now, go here,
     stand up, come down, watch
     me and you will see I have
     nothing up my sleeve and I
     merely execute a twist of
     the wrist and a slight mo-
     tion of the hand. Do this,
     buy now, go here, plans,
     programs, inventions, promises,
     games, commands, suggestions,
     hints, insinuations, pour
     from professional schemers
     into the ears of the people.

41

"WHY did the children
put beans in their ears
when the one thing we told the children
they must not do
was put beans in their ears?"

"Why did the children
pour molasses on the cat
when the one thing we told the children
they must not do
was pour molasses on the cat?"

4 2

WHY repeat? I heard you the first time.
You can lead a horse to water, if you've
    got the horse.
The rooster and the horse agreed not to
    step on each other's feet.
The caterpillar is a worm in a raccoon
    coat going for a college education.
The cockroach is always wrong when it
    argues with the chicken.
If I hadn't done it Monday somebody
    else would have done it Tuesday.
Money is like manure—good only when
    spread around.
You're such a first-class liar I'll take a
    chance with you.
A short horse is soon curried.
A still pig drinks the swill.
Small potatoes and few in a hill.
A fat man on a bony horse: "I feed my-
    self—others feed the horse."
No peace on earth with the women, no
    life anywhere without them.
Some men dress quick, others take as
    much time as a woman.
"You're a liar." "Surely not if you say
    so."
He tried to walk on both sides of the
    street at once.
He tried to tear the middle of the street
    in two.
"When is a man intoxicated?" "When he
    tries to kiss the bartender good night."

"He says he'll kick me the next time we
    meet. What'll I do?" "Sit down."
He's as handy as that bird they call the
    elephant.
Now that's settled and out of the way
    what are you going to do next?
"From here on," said the driver at an
      imaginary line near the foothills of
      the Ozarks, "the hills don't get any
      higher but the hollers get deeper
      and deeper."
So slick he was his feet slipped out from
    under him.
The ground flew up and hit him in the
    face.
Trade it for a dog, drown the dog, and
    you'll be rid of both of them.
There'll be many a dry eye at his funeral.
"Which way to the post office, boy?"
      "I don't know." "You don't know
      much, do you?" "No, but I ain't
      lost."

43

WHEN we say fresh eggs we mean fresh.
Buying or selling strictly fresh eggs we mean
    strictly.
If eggs are guaranteed extra special what more
    could be asked?
A rotten egg can't be spoiled and a shrewd
    buyer knows an asking price from a sell-
    ing price.
Why do they say of some fellows, "He knows
    all about the Constitution and the price
    of eggs"?
Eggs offered as plain and ordinary means as
    eggs they are not bad.
The egg market punster noted of one buyer,
    "He dozen't eggsspect eggs speckled."

Eggs spotted or dirty of course are priced
　　accordingly.
Broken eggs can never be mended: they go
　　in a barrel by themselves.
What sort of an egg are you ??
Just today or yesterday someone was saying
　　you are a good egg or a bad egg or not-
　　so-bad or hard to classify.
Under a microscope Agassiz studied one egg:
　　chaos, flux, constellations, rainbows:
　　"It is a universe in miniature."

44

WHY should any man try to find the distance to the moon by guessing
　　half way and then multiplying by two?
To never see a fool you lock yourself in your room and smash the looking-
　　glass.
The new two dollar a day street-sprinkler driver took his job so serious he
　　went right on driving while the rain poured down.
"What! you saw a man drowning and didn't help him?" "Well, he didn't
　　ask me to."
"Help! help! I'm drowning." "Tuesday is the day I help the drowning
　　and I'll be here Tuesday."
"The peacock has a beautiful tail," said the other birds. "But look at
　　those legs! and what a voice!"
The farther up the street you go the tougher they get and I live in the
　　last house.
There's only two in the country and I'm both of 'em.
I can live without you in the daytime but oh when that evening sun goes
　　down it's nighttime that's killing me.
When the hotel waitress saw the traveling man eat fourteen ears of corn-
　　on-the-cob one summer noon in the horse-and-buggy days, she asked,
　　"Don't you think it would be cheaper for you to board at a livery-
　　stable?"
The fresh young hotel clerk pulled a fast one on the internationally famous
　　scientist who asked if they had an Encyclopaedia Britannica in the
　　house: "No, we haven't, but what is it you'd like to know?"
The degree B.B.D.P.B.B.B. means Big Bass Drum Player Boston Brass
　　Band.

The letter of recommendation read, "This man worked for me one week and I am satisfied."

If he had a little more sense he'd be a half-wit.

He opened his mouth and put his foot in it.

"Do you think it will rain?" "Be a long dry spell if it don't."

"Got enough, sonny?" "No, but I've got down to where it don't taste good any more."

>Yesterday's hits win no runs today.
>
>Nothing is so dead as yesterday's newspaper.
>
>Do right by any man and don't write any woman.
>
>The best throw of the dice is to throw 'em away.

"Give me something to eat," grinned a hobo. "I'm so thirsty I don't know where I'm going to sleep tonight."

"When he whittles toward him he's in good humor, but let him alone when he cuts the other way," they said of a Union Stockyards pioneer.

"And now," said the justice of the peace, "by the authority of the State of Wisconsin in me vested I do hereby pronounce you man and woman."

"Don't analyze me—please," the stenographer pleaded. "Sometimes when I think about you I'm afraid my heart will strip a gear."

45

THEY have yarns

Of a skyscraper so tall they had to put hinges

On the two top stories so to let the moon go by,

Of one corn crop in Missouri when the roots

Went so deep and drew off so much water

The Mississippi riverbed that year was dry,

Of pancakes so thin they had only one side,

Of "a fog so thick we shingled the barn and six feet out on the fog,"

Of Pecos Pete straddling a cyclone in Texas and riding it to the west coast where "it rained out under him,"

Of the man who drove a swarm of bees across the Rocky Mountains and the Desert "and didn't lose a bee,"

Of a mountain railroad curve where the engineer in his cab can touch the caboose and spit in the conductor's eye,

Of the boy who climbed a cornstalk growing so fast he would have starved to death if they hadn't shot biscuits up to him,

Of the old man's whiskers: "When the wind was with him his whiskers arrived a day before he did,"

Of the hen laying a square egg and cackling, "Ouch!" and of hens laying eggs with the dates printed on them,

Of the ship captain's shadow: it froze to the deck one cold winter night,

Of mutineers on that same ship put to chipping rust with rubber hammers,

Of the sheep counter who was fast and accurate: "I just count their feet and divide by four,"

Of the man so tall he must climb a ladder to shave himself,

Of the runt so teeny-weeny it takes two men and a boy to see him,

Of mosquitoes: one can kill a dog, two of them a man,

Of a cyclone that sucked cookstoves out of the kitchen, up the chimney flue, and on to the next town,

Of the same cyclone picking up wagon-tracks in Nebraska and dropping them over in the Dakotas,

Of the hook-and-eye snake unlocking itself into forty pieces, each piece two inches long, then in nine seconds flat snapping itself together again,

Of the watch swallowed by the cow—when they butchered her a year later the watch was running and had the correct time,

Of horned snakes, hoop snakes that roll themselves where they want to go, and rattlesnakes carrying bells instead of rattles on their tails,

Of the herd of cattle in California getting lost in a giant redwood tree that had hollowed out,

Of the man who killed a snake by putting its tail in its mouth so it swallowed itself,

Of railroad trains whizzing along so fast they reach the station before the whistle,

Of pigs so thin the farmer had to tie knots in their tails to keep them from crawling through the cracks in their pens,

Of Paul Bunyan's big blue ox, Babe, measuring between the eyes forty-two ax-handles and a plug of Star tobacco exactly,

Of John Henry's hammer and the curve of its swing and his singing of it as "a rainbow round my shoulder."

> "Do tell!"
> "I want to know!"
> "You don't say so!"
> "For the land's sake!"

"Gosh all fish-hooks!"
"Tell me some more.
I don't believe a word you say
but I love to listen
to your sweet harmonica
to your chin-music.
Your fish stories hang together
when they're just a pack of lies:
you ought to have a leather medal:
you ought to have a statue
carved of butter: you deserve
a large bouquet of turnips."

"Yessir," the traveler drawled,
"Away out there in the petrified forest
everything goes on the same as usual.
The petrified birds sit in their petrified nests
and hatch their petrified young from petrified eggs."

A high pressure salesman jumped off the Brooklyn Bridge and was saved
by a policeman. But it didn't take him long to sell the idea to the
policeman. So together they jumped off the bridge.

One of the oil men in heaven started a rumor of a gusher down in hell.
All the other oil men left in a hurry for hell. As he gets to thinking
about the rumor he had started he says to himself there might be
something in it after all. So he leaves for hell in a hurry.

"The number 42 will win this raffle, that's my number." And when he
won they asked him whether he guessed the number or had a
system. He said he had a system, "I took up the old family album
and there on page 7 was my grandfather and grandmother both on
page 7. I said to myself this is easy for 7 times 7 is the number that
will win and 7 times 7 is 42."

Once a shipwrecked sailor caught hold of a stateroom door and floated
for hours till friendly hands from out of the darkness threw him a
rope. And he called across the night, "What country is this?" and
hearing voices answer, "New Jersey," he took a fresh hold on the
floating stateroom door and called back half-wearily, "I guess I'll float
a little farther."

An Ohio man bundled up the tin roof of a summer kitchen and sent it
    to a motorcar maker with a complaint of his car not giving service.
    In three weeks a new car arrived for him and a letter: "We regret
    delay in shipment but your car was received in a very bad order."
A Dakota cousin of this Ohio man sent six years of tin can accumula-
    tions to the same works, asking them to overhaul his car. Two weeks
    later came a rebuilt car, five old tin cans, and a letter: "We are also
    forwarding you five parts not necessary in our new model."
Thus fantasies heard at filling stations in the midwest. Another relates
    to a Missouri mule who took aim with his heels at an automobile
    rattling by. The car turned a somersault, lit next a fence, ran right
    along through a cornfield till it came to a gate, moved onto the road
    and went on its way as though nothing had happened. The mule
    heehawed with desolation, "What's the use?"
Another tells of a farmer and his family stalled on a railroad crossing,
    how they jumped out in time to see a limited express knock it into
    flinders, the farmer calling, "Well, I always did say that car was no
    shucks in a real pinch."

When the Masonic Temple in Chicago was the tallest building in the
    United States west of New York, two men who would cheat the
    eyes out of you if you gave 'em a chance, took an Iowa farmer to the
    top of the building and asked him, "How is this for high?" They
    told him that for $25 they would go down in the basement and turn
    the building around on its turn-table for him while he stood on the
    roof and saw how this seventh wonder of the world worked. He
    handed them $25. They went. He waited. They never came back.
This is told in Chicago as a folk tale, the same as the legend of Mrs.
    O'Leary's cow kicking over the barn lamp that started the Chicago
    fire, when the Georgia visitor, Robert Toombs, telegraphed an
    Atlanta crony, "Chicago is on fire, the whole city burning down,
    God be praised!"

Nor is the prize sleeper Rip Van Winkle and his scolding wife forgotten,
    nor the headless horseman scooting through Sleepy Hollow
Nor the sunken treasure-ships in coves and harbors, the hideouts of gold
    and silver sought by Coronado, nor the Flying Dutchman rounding
    the Cape doomed to nevermore pound his ear nor ever again take
    a snooze for himself
Nor the sailor's caretaker Mother Carey seeing to it that every seafaring

man in the afterworld has a seabird to bring him news of ships and
women, an albatross for the admiral, a gull for the deckhand

Nor the sailor with a sweetheart in every port of the world, nor the ships
that set out with flying colors and all the promises you could ask,
the ships never heard of again,

Nor Jim Liverpool, the riverman who could jump across any river and
back without touching land he was that quick on his feet,

Nor Mike Fink along the Ohio and the Mississippi, half wild horse and
half cock-eyed alligator, the rest of him snags and snapping turtle.
"I can out-run, out-jump, out-shoot, out-brag, out-drink, and out-fight,
rough and tumble, no holts barred, any man on both sides of the river
from Pittsburgh to New Orleans and back again to St. Louis. My
trigger finger itches and I want to go redhot. War, famine and blood-
shed puts flesh on my bones, and hardship's my daily bread."

Nor the man so lean he threw no shadow: six rattlesnakes struck at him
at one time and every one missed him.

4 6

THE gang in its working clothes
the picnic bunch in its best bib and tucker
hicks from the sticks and big town hicks
they sing whatever they want to
and it may be The Old Rugged Cross
or The Old Gray Mare or a late hit.
        They are hit by the hit songs.
It's a hit only when it hits them.
They soon drop it like a hot potato
or they hold on to it for keeps.
And whenever they keep changing a song
with tunes twisted forty ways
and new verses you never heard of—
        at last then it's a folk song.

"Everybody is cleverer than anybody,"
    said a smooth old fox
    who once ran France with his left hand.

Of the woman born deaf, blind and dumb, the vaudeville audience
asked questions:

"Have you ever thought of getting married? Why has
a cow two stomachs? How much is too many? Do you
believe in ghosts? Do you think it is a blessing to
be poor? Do you dream? Do you think business is looking up? Am I
going on a trip?"
And the woman enjoyed answering these questions from people born
with sight and hearing:
"I liked it. I liked to feel the warm tide of human
life pulsing round and round me."
Her face lighted when a burst of handclapping and light laughter swept
the audience.
"How do you know when we applaud you?" they asked.
And she answered the vibrations in the boards of the
stage floor under her feet told her of every shading
of applause.

In the farm house passing another crock of apples,
On the streetcar riding to the roller coasters,
At picnics, clambakes, or the factory workbench
They have riddles, good and bad conundrums:
    Which goes through the plank first, the bullet or the hole?
    Where does the music go when the fiddle is put in the box?
    Where does your lap go when you stand up? The same place your
        fist goes when you open your hand.
    What are the two smallest things mentioned in the Bible? The
        widow's mite and the wicked flee.
    Who are the shortest people mentioned in the Bible? Bildad the
        Shuhite, Knee-high-miah, and the man who had nothing but
        from whom even that which he had was taken away.
    What was the last thing Paul Revere said to his horse on the famous
        ride? "Whoa!"
    "Did you hear about the empty barrel of flour?" "No." "Nothing
        in it."
    What is there more of in the world than anything else? Ends.

    They have Irish bulls timeworn and mossgrown:
You are to be hanged and I hope it will prove a warning to you.
I took so much medicine I was sick a long time after I got well.
I can never get these boots on till I have worn them for a while.

One of us must kill the other—let it be me. We were boys together—at
    least I was.
If all the world were blind what a melancholy sight it would be.
This will last forever and afterward be sold for old iron.
They would cut us into mince-meat and throw our bleeding heads on the
    table to stare us in the face.
On the dim and faroff shore of the future we can see the footprint of an
    unseen hand.
We pursue the shadow, the bubble bursts, and leaves in our hands only
    ashes.

> "Ah there tootsie wootsie," has its day
> till the good old summertime has gone
> with the kit and caboodle of its day
> into the second-hand bins, the rummage sales,
> and another whim emerges in, "Okay toots!"

The people, yes, the customers,
In short-order lunch rooms they read signs:
    If the ice-box gets on fire ring the towel.
    Don't tip the waiters—it upsets them.
    Eat here—why go somewhere else to be cheated?
    Your face is good but it won't go in the cash register.
"There ain't no strong coffee, there's only weak people," said one heavy
    on the java.

The people is a child at school writing howlers,
writing answers half wrong and half right:
    The government of England is a limited mockery.
    Gravitation is that which if there were none we would all fly away.
    There were no Christians among the early Gauls; they were mostly
        lawyers.

47

WHO made Paul Bunyan, who gave him birth as a myth, who joked him
    into life as the Master Lumberjack, who fashioned him forth as an
    apparition easing the hours of men amid axes and trees, saws and
    lumber? The people, the bookless people, they made Paul and had
    him alive long before he got into the books for those who read. He
    grew up in shanties, around the hot stoves of winter, among socks

and mittens drying, in the smell of tobacco smoke and the roar of laughter mocking the outside weather. And some of Paul came over-seas in wooden bunks below decks in sailing vessels. And some of Paul is old as the hills, young as the alphabet.

The Pacific Ocean froze over in the winter of the Blue Snow and Paul Bunyan had long teams of oxen hauling regular white snow over from China. This was the winter Paul gave a party to the Seven Axmen. Paul fixed a granite floor sunk two hundred feet deep for them to dance on. Still, it tipped and tilted as the dance went on. And because the Seven Axmen refused to take off their hob-nailed boots, the sparks from the nails of their dancing feet lit up the place so that Paul didn't light the kerosene lamps. No women being on the Big Onion river at that time the Seven Axmen had to dance with each other, the one left over in each set taking Paul as a partner. The commotion of the dancing that night brought on an earthquake and the Big Onion river moved over three counties to the east.

One year when it rained from St. Patrick's Day till the Fourth of July, Paul Bunyan got disgusted because his celebration on the Fourth was spoiled. He dived into Lake Superior and swam to where a solid pillar of water was coming down. He dived under this pillar, swam up into it and climbed with powerful swimming strokes, was gone about an hour, came splashing down, and as the rain stopped, he explained, "I turned the dam thing off." This is told in the Big North Woods and on the Great Lakes, with many particulars.

Two mosquitoes lighted on one of Paul Bunyan's oxen, killed it, ate it, cleaned the bones, and sat on a grub shanty picking their teeth as Paul came along. Paul sent to Australia for two special bumblebees to kill these mosquitoes. But the bees and the mosquitoes inter-married; their children had stingers on both ends. And things kept getting worse till Paul brought a big boatload of sorghum up from Louisiana and while all the bee-mosquitoes were eating at the sweet sorghum he floated them down to the Gulf of Mexico. They got so fat that it was easy to drown them all between New Orleans and Galveston.

Paul logged on the Little Gimlet in Oregon one winter. The cook stove at that camp covered an acre of ground. They fastened the side of

a hog on each snowshoe and four men used to skate on the griddle
while the cook flipped the pancakes. The eating table was three miles
long; elevators carried the cakes to the ends of the table where boys
on bicycles rode back and forth on a path down the center of the
table dropping the cakes where called for.

Benny, the Little Blue Ox of Paul Bunyan, grew two feet every time Paul
looked at him, when a youngster. The barn was gone one morning
and they found it on Benny's back; he grew out of it in a night. One
night he kept pawing and bellowing for more pancakes, till there were
two hundred men at the cook shanty stove trying to keep him fed.
About breakfast time Benny broke loose, tore down the cook shanty,
ate all the pancakes piled up for the loggers' breakfast. And after that
Benny made his mistake; he ate the red hot stove; and that finished
him. This is only one of the hot stove stories told in the North Woods.

4 8

ONE of the Cherokees in Oklahoma, having a million or so from oil
rights, went to a motorcar dealer, looked over the different new
makes, and in a corner of the salesroom noticed a brand-new white
hearse, embellished, shining, emblazoned. "This one for me," he
said, and he rode away, his chauffeur driving and himself seated in-
side the glittering white funeral car. They tell this in Oklahoma as
a folk tale. It is.

In Honolulu they have cockroach races and bet on the winner.
In Japan they have grasshopper stables, each grasshopper in a little stall
by himself.
In Mexico they sit around a table each man having a cube of sugar and
the first to have a fly sit on his sugar wins the money.

> Didn't he belong to the people, that Gallic eater
> and drinker whose will was short and read: "I have
> nothing, I owe much, I leave the remainder to the
> poor"?

> And why shouldn't they say of one windbag in
> Washington, D. C., "An empty taxicab drew up to
> the curb and Senator So-and-So stepped out"?

"The hungry hog follows his nose to the warm
    swill," said an old farmer.
"He could live on the smell of an oil rag," they
    said of an old sailor on a tramp steamer.
"When the wind favors you can smell a slave-ship
    seven miles," they said in days now gone.

"Baby, baby, you will get new shoes at the gate of
    heaven," sing the Mexican mothers to the mu-
    chacho.

"How are crops this year?"
"Not so good for a good year
but not so bad for a bad year."

"Didn't you hear me holler for help?"
"Yes but you're such a liar
I didn't think you meant it."

What about that railroad engineer
running on the Pennsy
twenty-two years out of Chicago
leaving his mother $12,000
directing in his will
they should burn his body
as a piece of rolling-stock
beyond rehabilitation or repair
and take the ashes to his pet locomotive
and when they had run her
to the Beverly curve at 87th Street
where the open prairie view was special
and his eyes had so often
met a changing sky of red and gold—
there from the old cab of locomotive No. 8152
they could empty his firebox
they could throw his ashes
strew the last cinders and clinkers
of an engineer, an old hogger

    thankful he had lived—
    Always when he had rounded that curve

his run was over and he could go home—
What did he have?
They obliged him. Why shouldn't they?
They were glad to. "But he was peculiar, wasn't he?"

"Haven't you had a little too much?" the White House guard asked the
    Sioux warrior who shifted a blanket: "A little too much is just
    enough."
When Chicago has a debate whether there is a hell someone always says,
    "Down in hell they debate whether there is a Chicago."
"Too bad you have to work in this kind of a soup parlor," the customer
    sympathized, the waiter refusing the sympathy: "I work here but I
    don't eat here."
A short-order lunch room in Waterloo hangs up a sign for visiting
    Hawkeyes: "We eat our own hash—think it over."
A college boarding house in Ann Arbor instructs the scissorbill: "God
    hates a glutton—learn to say No."
The slim little wiry Texas Ranger answering a riot call heard from the
    town committee that they certainly expected at least a company of
    troopers, which brought his query, "There's only one riot—isn't
    there?"
"Are you happy?" the evangelist asked the new half-convert. "Well,
    parson, I'm not damn happy, just *happy*, that's all."

49

HE was a king or a shah, an ahkoond or rajah,
the head man of the country,
and he commanded the learned men of the books
they must put all their books in one,
which they did,
and this one book into a single page,
which they did.
"Suppose next," said the head man, who was
either a king or shah, an ahkoond or rajah,
"Suppose now you give my people
the history of the world and its peoples
in three words—come, go to work!"
And the learned men sat long into the night
and confabulated over their ponderings

and brought back three words:
   "Born,
    troubled,
     died."
This was their history of Everyman.
"Give me next for my people," spoke the head man,
"in one word the inside kernel of all you know,
the knowledge of your ten thousand books
with a forecast of what will happen next—
this for my people in one word."
And again they sat into the peep of dawn
and the arguments raged
and the glass prisms of the chandeliers shook
and at last they came to a unanimous verdict
     and brought the head man one word:
      "Maybe."

     And in that country and in other countries
     over mountain ranges where white clouds rested
     and beyond the blue sea and its endless tumblers
     the people by sunlight, by candlelight, by lanterns
     by the new white bulbs spoken to with buttons,
     the people had sayings touching the phrase
      "Born, troubled, died,"
carrying farther the one word: "maybe,"
spacing values between serenity and anguish,
from daily humdrum and the kitchen stove
to the inevitable rainbow or evening star,
sayings:

What should I say when it is better to say nothing?
What is said is said and no sponge can wipe it out.
   Ask the young people—they know everything.
   They say—what say they? Let them say.
Have you noticed painted flowers give no smell?
A woman and a melon are not to be known by their outsides.
The handsomest woman can give only what she has.
The miser and the pig are no use till dead.
An old man in love is a flower in winter.
   Bean by bean we fill the sack.
   Step by step one goes far.

No matter how important you are, you may get the measles.
    Wash a dog, comb a dog, still a dog.
    Fresh milk is not to be had from a statue.
    Apes may put on finery but they are still apes.
Every man must eat his peck of dirt before he dies.
    God knows well who are the best pilgrims.
    The ache for glory sends free people into slavery.
He who is made of honey will be eaten to death by flies.
No matter how cheap you make shoes geese will go barefoot.
He drives the wind from his house with his hat.

      Wedlock is a padlock.
    Take a good look at the mother before
    getting tied up with the daughter.
    Let a mother be ever so bad she wishes
    her daughter to be good.
    The man hardly ever marries the woman
    he jokes about: she often marries the
    man she laughs at.
    Keep your eyes open before marriage,
    half-shut afterward.

In heaven an angel is nobody in particular.
Even if your stomach be strong, eat as few
    cockroaches as possible.
The curse of the Spanish gypsy: May you be
    a mail carrier and have sore feet.
Well lathered is half shaved.
A wife is not a guitar you hang on the wall after playing it.
The liar forgets.
A redheaded man in the orchestra is a sure sign
    of trouble.
The shabby genteel would better be in rags.
As sure as God made little apples he was busy
    as a cranberry merchant.
It will last about as long as a snowball in hell.
I wouldn't take a million dollars for this baby and
    I wouldn't give ten cents for another.

      Blue eyes say love me or I die.
      Black eyes say love me or I kill you.

The sun rises and sets in her eyes.
  Wishes won't wash dishes.
May all your children be acrobats.
  Leave something to wish for.
  Lips however rosy must be fed.
  Some kill with a feather.
  By night all cats are gray.
Life goes before we know what it is.
  One fool is enough in a house.
Even God gets tired of too much hallelujah.
Take it easy and live long as brothers.
  The baby's smile pays the bill.

Yesterday is gone, tomorrow may never come,
  today is here.
The sins of omission are those we should have
  committed and didn't.
May you live to pick flowers off your enemies' graves.
Some of them are so lazy they get up early in the morning
  so as to have more time to lay around and do nothing.
Some of them are dirty as a slut that's too lazy to lick herself.
Let the guts be full for they carry the legs.
The hypocrite talks like a saint and hides his cat claws.
The half-wit was asked how he found the lost horse no others could
  locate and explained, "I thought to myself where I would go if I
  was a horse and I went there and he had."
He who has one foot in a brothel has another in a hospital.
When the boy is growing he has a wolf in his belly.
Handsome women generally fall into the hands of men not worth a
  second look.
When someone hits you with a rock hit him with a piece of cotton.
Love your neighbor as yourself but don't take down your fence.
A fence should be horse-high, pig-tight, bull-strong.
  Except in fairy stories the bashful get less.
  A beggar's hand has no bottom.
  Polite words open iron gates.
  Be polite but not too polite.

50

FROM what graveyards and sepulchers have they come,
these given the public eye and ear
who chatter idly of their personal success
as though they flowered by themselves alone
saying "I," "I," "I,"
crediting themselves with advances and gains,
"I did this, I did that,"
and hither and thither, "It was me, Me,"
the people, yes, the people, being omitted
or being mentioned as incidental
or failing completely of honorable mention,
as though what each did was by him alone
and there is a realm of personal achievement
wherein he was the boss, the big boy,
and it wasn't luck nor the breaks
nor a convenient public
but it was him, "I," "Me,"
and the idea and the inference is
the pay and the praise should be his—
from what graveyards have they strolled
and do they realize their sepulchral manners
and what are the farther backgrounds?

Desecrate the landscape with your billboards, gentlemen,
Let no green valleys meet the beholder's eye without
Your announcements of gas, oil, beans, soup, whiskey, beer,
Your proclamations of shaving cream, tooth-paste, pills, tonics.
On the rocks and rugged hills, along clear streams and pastures
Set up your billboard brag and swagger, your raucous yells.
Desecrate the landscape, gentlemen, go to it, hit 'em in the eye.
Sell 'em. Make 'em eat it. Sell 'em the name, the idea, the habit.
If a rock stands proud and grand anywhere sling your signs up on it.

The machine yes the machine
never wastes anybody's time
never watches the foreman
never talks back

never talks what is right or wrong
never listens to others talking or if
    it does listen it doesn't hear
never says we've been thinking, or, our
    feeling is like this
the machine yes the machine cuts your production cost
a man is a man and what can you do with him?
but a machine now you take a machine
no kids   no woman   never hungry   never thirsty
all a machine needs is a little regular attention and plenty of grease.

        We raise more corn
        to feed more hogs
        to buy more land
        to raise more corn
        to feed more hogs
        to. . . .

Once there was a frontier. Year by year it moved west. At last it moved
into the Pacific Ocean. Word passed, "The frontier is gone, there is
no frontier any more." From then on no more frontiersmen, from
then on only jokers advising, "Go west, young man." This was long
after the old timers started west in covered wagons emblazoned "Ho
for California" "Oregon or Death" or "The Eleventh Command-
ment: Mind Your Own Business." One with a sign reading "Pikes
Peak or Bust" came back with another: "Busted by Gosh!" And you
can go now yes go now though the old frontiers are gone and the free
homesteads are few. Now you can stay where you are and send up
rockets, let down buckets. Now with less land you will have less
children.

    What happened in that buried city they
        found in Africa?
    Once it had streets and people and business
        and politics.
    Once it saw the weddings of young men and
        women
    And the children cried "mama" as the first
        word
    And they had news from day to day of food,
        love, work, people.

Now it is covered over with a level of snails,
    hills of snails.
The streets, houses, city hall, department of
    public works,
Houses of money lenders, huts of the poor,
    tabernacles,
Filled up and smoothed over by long proces-
    sions of snails,
Legions of plodding thoughtless misbegotten
    snails.

"Isn't that an iceberg on the horizon, Captain?"
"Yes, Madam."
"What if we get in a collision with it?"
"The iceberg, Madam, will move right along
    as though nothing had happened."

You can't come back to a home unless it was a
    home you went away from.
Between hay and grass neither one nor the other.
Can't you be useful as well as ornamental?
Why don't you go roll a peanut around the corner?
    When did they let you out?
The mules went to ask horns and came back without ears.
When you get hold of a good thing freeze onto it.
    Nothing to do and all day to do it in.
So dumb he spent his last dollar buying a pocketbook to put it in.
    A little more sandpaper and this will be smooth.
Write on one side of the paper and both sides of the subject.
Swear to it on a stack of Bibles and they wouldn't believe you.
    Be not a baker if your head be of butter.
Yesterday? It's a nickel thrown on a Salvation Army drum.
How could I let go when it was all I could do to hold on?
Thousands drink themselves to death before one dies of thirst.
    He didn't have much till he married a hunk of tin.
    There's always a nut on every family tree.
    The mosquitoes organized and drove me out of bed.
We'll fight till hell freezes over and then write on the ice, "Come on
    you bastards."
The yes-man spent his vacation yelling, "No! no! I tell you No!"

A man having nothing to feed his cow sang to her of the fresh green grass to come: this is the tune the old cow died on.

The man feeding a hatful of doughnuts to a horse explained to the curious, "I want to see how many he'll eat before he asks for a cup of coffee."

"I fired the man," said the new section boss, "not because I had anything agin him but because I had the authority."

"Don't I argue? Don't I sputify?" the backwoods preacher inquired of the complaining committee whose chairman responded, "Yes, you do argue and you do sputify but you don't tell wherein!"

The late riser is asked, "Are you up for all day?"

Shut the door—do you want to heat all outdoors?

He won't go to a wedding unless he's the bride nor a funeral unless he's the corpse.

"May you have the sevenyear itch," was answered, "I hope your wife eats crackers in bed."

He was always a hell of a big fellow in Washington when he was in Rhode Island and a hell of a big fellow in Rhode Island when he was in Washington.

You say you are going to Warsaw (or Boston) because you want me to think you are going to Lemberg (or Buffalo) but I know you are going to Warsaw (or Boston).

He got on a horse and rode off in all directions at once.

Did they let you out or did you let yourself out?

"Why!" said a Republican Governor of Illinois, "Why the Democrats can't run the government! It's all us Republicans can do."

This will last a thousand years and after that to the end of the world.

When a member died the newspaper men of the Whitechapel Club of Chicago gave the toast:

"Hurrah for the next who goes!"

In Vermont a shut-mouthed husband finally broke forth to his wife, "When I think of how much you have meant to me all these years, it is almost more than I can do sometimes to keep from telling you so."

5 1

THE blood of all men of all nations being red
the Communist International named red its banner color.
Pope Innocent IV gave cardinals their first red hats

saying a cardinal's blood belonged to the holy mother church.
The bloodcolor red is a symbol.

A Scotsman keeps the Sabbath and anything else he can lay his hands on,
say the English.
A fighting Frenchman runs away from even a she-goat, say the Germans.
A Russian, say the Poles, can be cheated only by a gypsy, a gypsy by a Jew,
a Jew by a Greek, and a Greek by the devil.
"If I owned Texas and hell I would rent Texas and move to hell," said
a famous general.
"That's right," wrote a Texas editor. "Every man for his own country."
The Peloponnesians pulled these long ago, so did the Russians, the Chi-
nese, even the Fijis with rings in their noses. Likewise:
An American is an Anglo-Saxon when an Englishman wants something
from him: or:
When a Frenchman has drunk too much he wants to dance, a German to
sing, a Spaniard to gamble, an Italian to brag, an Irishman to fight,
an American to make a speech: or:
"What is dumber than a dumb Irishman?" "A smart Swede."
These are in all tongues and regions of men. Often they bring laughter and
sometimes blood.
The propagandas of hate and war always monkey with the buzz-saw of race
and nationality, breed and kin, seldom saying, "When in doubt hold
your tongue."
In breathing spells of bloody combat between Christian nations the order
goes out: "Don't let the men in the front-line trenches fraternize!"

The sea has fish for every man.
Every blade of grass has its share of dew.
The longest day must have its end.
Man's life? A candle in the wind, hoar-frost
on stone.
Nothing more certain than death and nothing
more uncertain than the hour.
Men live like birds together in a wood; when
the time comes each takes his flight.
As wave follows wave, so new men take old
men's places.

The copperfaces, the red men, handed us tobacco,
the weed for the pipe of friendship,

also the bah-tah-to, the potato, the spud.
Sunflowers came from Peruvians in ponchos.
Early Italians taught us of chestnuts,
walnuts and peaches being Persian mementoes,
Siberians finding for us what rye might do,
Hindus coming through with the cucumber,
Egyptians giving us the onion, the pea,
Arabians handing advice with one gift:
"Some like it, some say it's just spinach."
    To the Chinese we have given
     kerosene, bullets, bibles
and they have given us radishes, soy beans, silk,
poems, paintings, proverbs, porcelain, egg foo yong,
gunpowder, Fourth of July firecrackers, fireworks,
and labor gangs for the first Pacific railways.
    Now we may thank these people
    or reserve our thanks
    and speak of them as outsiders
    and imply the request,
"Would you just as soon get off the earth?"
holding ourselves aloof in pride of distinction
saying to ourselves this costs us nothing
as though hate has no cost
as though hate ever grew anything worth growing.
Yes we may say this trash is beneath our notice
or we may hold them in respect and affection
as fellow creepers on a commodious planet
saying, "Yes you too you too are people."

"When God finished making the world
He had a few stinking scraps of mud left over
and used it to make a yellow dog"
    (and when they hate any race or nation
    they name that race or nation
    in place of the yellow dog).
They say and they say and the juice of prejudice drips from it.
They say and they say and in the strut of fool pride spit in the wind.
And the first of the seven rottening sins is this one: pride.
They set up a razzle-dazzle and get caught in their own revolving mirrors.
"We are the greatest city, the greatest people. Nothing like us ever was."

They set out for empire not knowing men and nations can die of empire.
And the earth is strewn with the burst bladders of the puffed-up.

> The best preacher is the heart,
> say the Jews of faith.
> The best teacher is time.
> The best book is the world.
> The best friend is God.

> The three worst waters,
> say the Irish:
> brown rain at the fall of the leaf,
> black rain at the springing of roots,
> the gray rain of May.

Love, a cough, an itch, or a fat paunch cannot be hid.
Love, a cough, smoke, money or poverty, are hard to hide.

Three things you can't nurse: an old woman, a hen, and a sheep.
Three who have their own way: a mule, a pig, and a miser.
Three to stay away from: a snake, a man with an oily tongue, and a loose
woman.
Three things dear to have: fresh eggs, hickory smoked ham, and old
women's praise.
Three things always pleasing: a cat's kittens, a goat's kid, and a young
woman.
The three prettiest dead: a little child, a salmon, a black cock.
Three of the coldest things: a man's knee, a cow's horn, and a dog's nose.
Three who come unbidden: love, jealousy, fear.
Three soon passing away: the beauty of a woman, the rainbow, the echo
of the woods.
Three worth wishing: knowledge, grain, and friendship.

Men are made of clay but women are made of men.
An old friend is better than two new ones.
He gets up early who pleases everybody.
Two fools in a house are a couple too many.
"I have forgotten your name" is better than "I don't
remember you."

Some can eat nails, others break their teeth on apple-
    sauce.
"Run home, your house is on fire." "No, that can't be.
    I locked the house when I left home."
"So now he's dead." "Yes." "What did he die of?"
    "The want of breath."
There are two good men, say the Chinese, one dead,
    the other not born yet.
The seller can get along with one eye, the buyer
    needs a hundred.

        The ragged colt may prove a good horse.
        The hasty bitch brings forth blind whelps.

He's eaten off many a dish and never washed a dish.
He's the sort that would haul rock with a race-horse.
It would be like him to drown in a spoonful of water.
If he had learned the hatter's trade, men would have
    been born without heads.
Ugly? Sleep stays away from him till he
    covers his face.
Poor? He can't raise money enough to buy
    lumber for a backhouse.
Big feet? Buying shoes he don't ask for a
    number, he says, "Lemme see the biggest
    you got."

        "Slave, I have bought you."
        "God knows you have."
        "Now you belong to me."
        "God knows I do."
        "And you'll not run away?"
        "God knows."

In the days of the faroff Pharaohs
in the days of Nebuchadnezzar
the king who ate grass
and reconsidered many former decisions—
one of the masters straddling a slave:
        "I think about you often
        and I would be willing

to do many kind things
almost anything for you."
And the man under:
"Almost anything except get off my back."

5 2

WHO was that early sodbuster in Kansas? He leaned at the gatepost and
studied the horizon and figured what corn might do next year and
tried to calculate why God ever made the grasshopper and why two
days of hot winds smother the life out of a stand of wheat and why
there was such a spread between what he got for grain and the price
quoted in Chicago and New York. Drove up a newcomer in a covered
wagon: "What kind of folks live around here?" "Well, stranger, what
kind of folks was there in the country you come from?" "Well, they
was mostly a lowdown, lying, thieving, gossiping, backbiting lot of
people." "Well, I guess, stranger, that's about the kind of folks you'll
find around here." And the dusty gray stranger had just about blended
into the dusty gray cottonwoods in a clump on the horizon when
another newcomer drove up: "What kind of folks live around here?"
"Well, stranger, what kind of folks was there in the country you come
from?" "Well, they was mostly a decent, hardworking, lawabiding,
friendly lot of people." "Well, I guess, stranger, that's about the kind
of folks you'll find around here." And the second wagon moved off
and blended with the dusty gray cottonwoods on the horizon while
the early sodbuster leaned at his gatepost and tried to figure why two
days of hot winds smother the life out of a nice stand of wheat.

> In the dry farming country they said:
> "Here you look farther and see less,
> and there are more creeks and less water,
> and more cows and less milk,
> and more horses and less grass,
> than anywhere else in the world."

White man: "I have no time to do anything."
Indian: "Why you have all the time there
is, haven't you?"

They said to the cows, "When you die we will
wrap you in fine linen sheets."

The cows: "We shall be satisfied if we keep
our hides."

Of one piece of Pennsylvania a Quaker poet wrote:
"God might have made a more beautiful region than Chester County—
but He never did."
An Oklahoma newspaper woman rewrote it: "God might have made a
more beautiful country than Oklahoma—but He never did."

All flesh is grass. From the sod the grazers derive their food and pass it
on to man. Out of the grasslands man takes his meat and milk and
lives. Wherever is a rich banquet it goes back to the grass. Howso-
ever men break bread together or eat alone it is grass giving them life
and they could pray: "Give us this day our daily grass."
And many, many are the grass families. From oats and corn to blue grass
and timothy hay, from rye and rice to clover and alfalfa, the grass
families are many and humble and hard to kill unless misused and
overdriven. The populations of the grass are lush and green with care
in the sun and rain and recurring seasons. The grass carries benedic-
tions and fables of service, toil and misuse. To whom does the grass
belong if not to the people?

5 3

COME on, superstition, and get my goat.
I got mascots.
The stars of my birthday favor me.
The numbers from one to ten are with me.
I was born under a lucky star and nothing can stop me.
The moon was a waxing moon and not a waning moon when I was born.
Every card in the deck and both of the seven-eleven bones are with me.
So you hear them tell it and they mean if it works it's good and if it don't
it costs nothing.
How to win love, how to win games, the spells and conjurations are named
for fever, burns, convulsions, snakebite, milksick, balking horses, rheu-
matism, warts.
"Tie the heart of a bat with a red silk string to your right arm and you
will win every game at which you play."
If your right foot itches you will soon start on a journey, if it's your left
foot you will go where you are not wanted.

If you sing before breakfast you will cry before night, if you sneeze before
   breakfast you will see your true love before Saturday night.
Lightning in the north means rain, lightning in the south means dry
   weather.
Frost three months after the first katydid is heard. Three white frosts and
   then a rain.

For toothache the faith doctor wrote the words "galla gaffa gassa" on the
   wall. With a nail he pointed at each letter of the words, asking if the
   toothache was better. At the letter where the tooth was feeling easier
   he drove the nail in and the tooth stopped aching. Galla gaffa gassa.
   Gassa galla gaffa.

> Goofer dust comes from the goofer tree.
> Sprinkle it in the shoes of the woman you love and
>   she can never get away from you.
>   Galla gaffa gassa.

> Even a lousy cur has his lucky days.
> Sweep dirt out of the door after night and
>   you sweep yourself out of a home.
> Shake the tablecloth out of doors after sunset
>   and you will never marry.
> The first to drive a hearse is the next to die.
> Kill cats, dogs or frogs and you die in rags.
> Point at a shooting star or even speak of it and
>   you lose your next wish.

> Better born lucky than rich.
> Marry in May, repent always.
> May is the month to marry bad wives.

> The son of the white hen brings luck.
> So does a horse with four white feet.

> He planted gravel and up came potatoes.
> When a bitch litters pigs that is luck.
> The lucky fellow gets eggs from his rooster
>   and his hen eggs have two yolks.
> Luck for the few, death for the many.

Ladders of luck, let us
climb your yellow rungs.
Ropes of the up-and-up
send us silver sky-hooks.
Black horses, let us saddle
you with silk belly-bands.
Black cats with orange spots
bring us big ships loaded
with wild Spanish women.
Galloping cubes of fate
hand us sevens elevens
hand us the pretty numbers.
Black moonlight, let a little
of that old gold drop down.
      Black roses? Yes
there must be cool black roses.
Out of the deep night came to us all
    the kiss of the black rose.

5 4

TYLOR believed it important; he put it down; he asks us to read it, to look
    at it and see what happens.
"In the islands of the Indian Archipelago whose tropical forests swarm
    both with high apes and low savages, the confusion between the two
    in the minds of the half-civilized inhabitants becomes almost inex-
    tricable.
Tylor dwelt on the tales of men with tails, homo caudatus or satyr, how
    you hear about them if you go hither and yon over the earth.
"To people who at once believe monkeys a kind of savages, and savages a
    kind of monkeys, men with tails are creatures coming under both defi-
    nitions."
The longer you look at it the more the confusions shift in the shaded
    areas denoting who belongs where.

5 5

ON Lang Syne Plantation they had a prayer:
"When we rise in the morning
to see the sun plowing his furrow across the elements,

we are thankful.
For the rising of the east moon we have seen tonight
and for the setting of the west moon we shall see,
we are thankful.
And O Lord—
When my room is like a public hall,
when my face is like a looking-glass,
when my teeth shut against a silence,
mother do me no good then,
father do me no good then,
sister, brother, friend, do me no good then.
Help us to know—
when our hands rest from the plow handle and lie still—
when we are like hills gone down in darkness—
when our nostrils are empty of breath—
then let us know when we trust in Thee—
        Thou art a crutch to the lame,
        a mother to the motherless,
        a father to the fatherless,
        a strong arm to the widow,
        a shade from the heat,
        a bridge over deep water."

The little lake with the long name in Massachusetts is called: Chaugh
    Jog a Gog Maugh Chaugh a Gog Chaugh Buna Guncha Maugh
    wherein the red men intended: We own to the middle of the lake on
    this side, you own to the middle of the lake on the other side, and
    both of us own the middle.

            Oh angel, oh angel,
     I don't want to be buried in the storm.
        Who's going to close these dying eyes?
        Dig my grave with a golden spade.
        Lower me down with a silver chain.
        The coffin lid will screw me down.
     I don't want to be buried in the storm.
        Who's going to close these dying eyes?
          Oh angel, oh angel.

5 6

THE sacred legion of the justborn—
how many thousands born this minute?
how many fallen for soon burial?
what are these deaths and replacements?
what is this endless shuttling of shadowlands
where the spent and done go marching into one
and from another arrive those crying Mama Mama?

In the people is the eternal child,
the wandering gypsy, the pioneer homeseeker,
the singer of home sweet home.

The people say and unsay,
put up and tear down
and put together again—
a builder, wrecker, and builder again—
this is the people.

The shrouding of obedience to immediate necessity,
The mask of "What do I care?" to cover "What else can I do?"
One half-real face put on to hide a more real face under,
The waiting of the hope of the inner face while the outer face
Holds to its look and says yes to immediate necessity,
Says yes to whatever is for the immediate moment—
This is the pokerface of the populace never read till long afterward.

The people in several longdrawn chapters seems a monster turtle.
Heavy years go by, heavy hundreds of years, till a shroud and mask drop,
Till the faces of events command the new faces of people,
And new chapters begin with new faces.

Protective coloration is only for birds and moths who take on the look
    of the leaves and bark they live in?
Out of long usage the ruled-over acquire devices by the ways of animals
  ˙ who blend with the landscape.
They can drop into long deep sleeps, they can hide out and hibernate till
    a time of release develops.

In the long night streets of snakeline lights
when there is bitter crying for leadership
and no leadership steps forth
is it because the masses and the intelligentsia
both are a wornout soil so thin and acrid
they cannot fling up leaders?
When the creative breath blows not over the waters
and elders are filled with hypocritical effluvia,
when the silent workers in pure science
are considered inferior to public utility manipulators
is this the time for the young to begin movements,
to question the ways of hypocritical elders
in the long night streets of snakeline lights?

> aw nuts aw go peddle yer papers
> where did ja cop dat monkeyface
>> jeez ja see dat skirt
>> did ja glom dat moll
> who was tellin you we wuz brudders
> how come ya get on dis side deh street
> go home and tell yer mudder she wants yuh
> chase yer shadder aroun deh corner
> yuh come to me wid a lot uh arkymalarky
>> a bing in de bean fer you yeah
> how come ya get on dis side deh street
> go home and get yer umbreller washed
>> den get yer face lifted
> dis corner is mine—see—dis corner is mine
> gwan ja tink ya gonna get dis f'm me fer nuttin
>> nobody gets nuttin fer nuttin
>> gwan monkeyface peddle yer papers
> ya can't kiss yerself in here dis is all fixed

> Those without a leader perish,
> says the Sanskrit,
> those without a youthful leader perish,
> those without a female leader perish,
> those without many leaders perish.

The people pause for breath, for wounds and bruises to heal,
For food again after famine, for regaining stamina,

For preparations and migration to greener pastures, to canaan, to america,
    to the argentine, australia, new zealand, alaska,
To farflung commonwealths lacking precedent or tradition.
They guess and toil and rest and try to make out and get along
And some would rather not talk about what they had to go through
In the first years of finding out what the soil might do for them,
In the first winter of snow too deep for travel, or
The first summer when the few clouds showing went away without rain, or
The day the grasshoppers came and tore a black path where the crops had
    stood.

    The people is a monolith,
    a mover, a dirt farmer,
    a desperate hoper.
The prize liar comes saying, "I know how, listen to me and I'll bring you
    through."
The guesser comes saying, "The way is long and hard and maybe what I
    offer will work out."
The people choose and the people's choice more often than not is one
    more washout.
Yet the strong man, the priceless one who wants nothing for himself and
    has his roots among his people,
Comes often enough for the people to know him and to win through into
    gains beyond later losing,
Comes often enough so the people can look back and say, "We have come
    far and will go farther yet."
        The people is a trunk of patience, a monolith.

    "And the king wanted an inscription
    good for a thousand years and after
    that to the end of the world?"
    "Yes, precisely so."
    "Something so true and awful that no
    matter what happened it would stand?"
    "Yes, exactly that."
    "Something no matter who spit on it or
    laughed at it there it would stand
    and nothing would change it?"
    "Yes, that was what the king ordered
    his wise men to write."

"And what did they write?"
"Five words: THIS TOO SHALL PASS AWAY."

5 7

LINCOLN?
He was a mystery in smoke and flags
saying yes to the smoke, yes to the flags,
yes to the paradoxes of democracy,
yes to the hopes of government
of the people by the people for the people,
no to debauchery of the public mind,
no to personal malice nursed and fed,
yes to the Constitution when a help,
no to the Constitution when a hindrance,
yes to man as a struggler amid illusions,
each man fated to answer for himself:
Which of the faiths and illusions of mankind
must I choose for my own sustaining light
to bring me beyond the present wilderness?

Lincoln? was he a poet?
and did he write verses?
"I have not willingly planted a thorn
in any man's bosom."
"I shall do nothing through malice; what
I deal with is too vast for malice."

Death was in the air.
So was birth.
What was dying few could say.
What was being born none could know.

He took the wheel in a lashing roaring
hurricane.
And by what compass did he steer the course
of the ship?
"My policy is to have no policy," he said in
the early months,
And three years later, "I have been controlled
by events."

He could play with the wayward human mind, saying at Charleston, Illinois, September 18, 1858, it was no answer to an argument to call a man a liar.

"I assert that you [pointing a finger in the face of a man in the crowd] are here today, and you undertake to prove me a liar by showing that you were in Mattoon yesterday.

"I say that you took your hat off your head and you prove me a liar by putting it on your head."

He saw personal liberty across wide horizons.

"Our progress in degeneracy appears to me to be pretty rapid," he wrote Joshua F. Speed, August 24, 1855. "As a nation we began by declaring that 'all men are created equal, except negroes.' When the Know-Nothings get control, it will read 'all men are created equal except negroes and foreigners and Catholics.' When it comes to this, I shall prefer emigrating to some country where they make no pretense of loving liberty."

    Did he look deep into a crazy pool
    and see the strife and wrangling
    with a clear eye, writing the military
    head of a stormswept area:
    "If both factions, or neither, shall abuse
    you, you will probably be about right. Beware of being assailed by one and praised
    by the other"?

    Lincoln? was he a historian?
    did he know mass chaos?
    did he have an answer for those
    who asked him to organize chaos?

"Actual war coming, blood grows hot, and blood is spilled. Thought is forced from old channels into confusion. Deception breeds and thrives. Confidence dies and universal suspicion reigns.

"Each man feels an impulse to kill his neighbor, lest he be first killed by him. Revenge and retaliation follow. And all this, as before said, may be among honest men only; but this is not all.

"Every foul bird comes abroad and every dirty reptile rises up. These add crime to confusion.

"Strong measures, deemed indispensable, but harsh at best, such men
   make worse by maladministration. Murders for old grudges, and mur-
   ders for pelf, proceed under any cloak that will best cover for the
   occasion. These causes amply account for what has happened in Mis-
   souri."

Early in '64 the Committee of the New York Workingman's Democratic
   Republican Association called on him with assurances and he medi-
   tated aloud for them, recalling race and draft riots:
"The most notable feature of a disturbance in your city last summer
   was the hanging of some working people by other working people.
   It should never be so.
"The strongest bond of human sympathy, outside of the family rela-
   tion, should be one uniting all working people, of all nations
   and tongues and kindreds.
"Let not him who is houseless pull down the house of another, but let
   him labor diligently and build one for himself, thus by example
   assuring that his own shall be safe from violence when built."

          Lincoln? did he gather
          the feel of the American dream
          and see its kindred over the earth?

      "As labor is the common burden of our race,
      so the effort of some to shift
      their share of the burden
      onto the shoulders of others
      is the great durable curse of the race."

          "I hold,
      if the Almighty had ever made a set of men
      that should do all of the eating
      and none of the work,
      he would have made them
      with mouths only, and no hands;
      and if he had ever made another class,
      that he had intended should do all the work
      and none of the eating,
      he would have made them
      without mouths and all hands."

"—the same spirit that says, 'You toil and work and earn bread, and I'll eat it.' No matter in what shape it comes, whether from the mouth of a king who seeks to bestride the people of his own nation and live by the fruit of their labor, or from one race of men as an apology for enslaving another race, it is the same tyrannical principle."

"As I would not be a *slave*, so I would not be a *master*. This expresses my idea of democracy. Whatever differs from this, to the extent of the difference, is no democracy."

"I never knew a man who wished to be himself a slave. Consider if you know any *good* thing that no man desires for himself."

"The sheep and the wolf
      are not agreed upon a definition
      of the word liberty."

"The whole people of this nation
         will ever do well
            if well done by."

"The plainest print cannot be read
   through a gold eagle."

"How does it feel to be President?" an Illinois friend asked.

"Well, I'm like the man they rode out of town on a rail. He said if it wasn't for the honor of it he would just as soon walk."

Lincoln? he was a dreamer.
He saw ships at sea,
he saw himself living and dead
in dreams that came.

Into a secretary's diary December 23, 1863
went an entry: "The President tonight
had a dream. He was in a party of plain
people, and, as it became known who
he was, they began to comment on his
appearance. One of them said: 'He is a
very common-looking man.' The Presi-
dent replied: 'The Lord prefers com-
mon-looking people. That is the reason
he makes so many of them.'"

He spoke one verse for then and now:
"If we could first know where we are,
and whither we are tending,
we could better judge
what to do, and how to do it."

5 8

THE people, yes,
Out of what is their change
from chaos to order
and chaos again?

"Yours till the hangman doth us part,"
Don Magregor ended his letters.

"It annoys me to die,"
said a philosopher.
"I should like to see what follows."

To those who had ordered them to death,
one of them said:
"We die because the people are asleep
and you will die because the people will awaken."

Greek met Greek when Phocion and Democritus spoke.
"You will drive the Athenians mad some day and they will kill you."
"Yes, me when they go mad, and as sure as they get sane again, you."

59

THE transient tar-paper shack
comes from the hands of the people.
So does the floodlighted
steel-and-concrete skyscraper.
  The rough-lumber two-room houseboat
  is from the hands of the people.
  So is the turbine-driven steamboat
  with ballroom, orchestra, swimming-pool,
  the fat of the land,
  moving in the mid-atlantic ocean.

Every day the people of the city haul it away,
  take it apart, and put it together again.
Every day around the globe and its atmos-
  pheric fringe the people of the earth live
  the unwritten saga of one day.
Today the fishing boats go out and little men
  shade their eyes and study the treacher-
  ous, rolling, free-handed sea.
Today the steel-and-aluminum streamlined
  passenger train cuts through a blizzard,
  the transcontinental planes are hung up,
  and a liner at sea sends a distress wireless.
Today strikes break out where strikes were
  never heard of before, the lumber trade
  stands in fear of steel-fabricated houses,
  and farming in Somaliland is a hazard.
Every hour thousands of six-decker novels
  lived, every minute millions of long and
  short stories.
Today homes are lost, farms won, cars traded
  in, old furniture lacquered, pigs littered,
  an albatross shot, pearls lost in Vienna
  found in a fishcan in Omaha.

Today jobs landed and lost, contracts signed
    and broken, families scattered and joined,
    girls after long waiting saying Yes to men
    No to men.
The books of man have begun only a short
    stammering memorandum of the toil,
    resources and stamina of man,
Of the required errands, the dramatic impulses,
    the irresistible songs of this given moment,
    this eyeblink now.
Every day the people of the city haul it away,
    take it apart, and put it together again.
The how and the why of the people so doing
    is the saga not yet written.

Is the story true or a make-believe?
In an ancient clan the elders found one of the
    younger, a man of dreaminess, writing a
    scroll and record.
Where he had picked up letters and the for-
    bidden art of putting down one word
    after another so as to make sense, they
    didn't know and he refused to tell.
On sheets to be read long after by other
    generations he was doing an eye-witness
    tale of their good and evil doings.
And he swore to them: "I will be the word of
    the people! Mine is the bleeding mouth
    from which the gag is snatched!"
So they took and killed him and set his bloody
    head on a pike for public gaze. Who had
    asked him to be the word of the people?
    When they wanted a history written they
    would elect someone to write it as they
    would have it written.

"You will see me surrender,"
said one old Viking,
"when hair grows in the palm of my hand."

"What are you fellows scared of? nothing?"
this too they asked the old Viking who said,
"Yes, one thing we are scared of, we are scared
the sky might come tumbling down on us."

6 0

THE grass lives, goes to sleep, lives again,
and has no name for it.
The oaks and poplars know seasons while standing
to take what comes.
The grinding of the earth on its gnarled axis
touches many dumb brothers.
Time toils on translations of fire and rain into
air, into thin air.

In the casual drift of routine
in the day by day run of mine
in the play of careless circumstance
the anecdotes emerge
alive with people in words, errands,
motives and silhouettes
taller than the immediate moment:

> "You have fourteen sons in the war?"
> "Yes."
> "And you have more children at home?"
> "Five."
> "And they all came one by one?"
> "No, they was four pair twins, two sets triplets."

"I remember," said the fond Irish mother to the white-
headed boy, "I remember when you was nothing but a
beautiful gleam in your father's eye."

"Breath is made out of air," wrote the schoolboy.
"We breathe with our lungs. If it wasn't for our breath we
would die when we slept. Our breath keeps the life go-
ing through the nose when we sleep."

Back and forth strode the campaign orator,
back and forth till an Irishman shouted:
"If you're talkin' stop walkin'!
If you're walkin' stop talkin'!"

The classical orator from Massachusetts had pronounced the words "Vox
Populi" five times in an Indianapolis speech when one Hoosier Con-
gressman bet another he didn't know what Vox Populi meant. The
money was put up and the winner of the bet freely translated Vox
Populi to mean "My God, my God, why hast Thou forsaken me?"

"There on the same track I saw the westbound passenger train coming
fifty miles an hour and the eastbound freight forty miles an hour."
"And what did you think?"
"I thought what a hell of a way to run a railroad!"

"Is you married?" the elder negro asked his son.
"I ain't sayin' I is and I ain't sayin' I ain't."
"I ain't askin' you is you ain't. Ise askin' you ain't you is."

They were ninety years old and of their seventeen children had just buried
the firstborn son who died seventy-two years of age.
"I told you," said the old man as he and his hillborn wife sat on the cabin
steps in the evening sunset, "I told you long ago we would never raise
that boy."

"I am John Jones."
"Take a chair."
"Yes, and I am the son of John
Throckmorton Jones."
"Is that possible? Take two chairs."

"What's the matter up there?"
"Playing soldier."
"But soldiers don't make that kind of noise."
"We're playing the kind of soldier that
makes that kind of noise."

"No, captain, I never stole nothing to eat out
of that chest. Why, captain, when I

looked in that chest to see if there was
anything to eat in it I met a cockroach
coming out of it with tears in his eyes."

"How do you do, my farmer friend?"
"Howdy."
"Nice looking country you have here."
"Fer them that likes it."
"Live here all your life?"
"Not yit."

61

THE nickels click off fares in the slot machines of the subway, the elevated.
"Fare, please," say the bus conductors to millions every day of the week.
Riders they are, riders to work, to home, to fun, to grief, each nickel and
     dime audited and accounted for as current income payable for taxes,
     overhead, upkeep, rehabilitation, surplus, dividends, flimflam.
To the whang and purr of steel and motors, streets and stations, the fares,
     the riders, with nickels and dimes, go and return, return and go.
One in a thousand says, "Whither goest thou?" but mostly "Where you
     going?"
Mostly they are in accord with the Minnesota Swede:
"Maybe I don't know so much but what I do know I know to beat hell."
Like tools tested for grinding and cutting and durability, they have gath-
     ered them clews of wisdom and they talk things over in the bus, the
     elevated, the subway:
     "The penitentiary is to learn to behave better, to think things over,
          it is lonesome."
     "A comedian acts funny and gets paid to make people laugh if he
          can."
     "Shakespeare is the greatest writer of them all, a dead Englishman
          and you have to read him in high school or you don't pass."
     "The police pass examinations and then get a club and a star to
          show who they are. They keep order and arrest you unless you
          got a pull."
     "Handkerchief is to carry in the pocket and blow your nose with and
          tie nickels in the corner of for carfare and church."
     "Economy is when you save without being stingy."
     "Banks keep money when you have some left over. They let nobody
          else get it. And they let you take money out if you pay for it and
          do what is regular."

"The Constitution tells how the government runs. It is a paper in Washington for the lawyers."

"War is when two nations go to it killing as many as you can for the government."

"The army is men in uniforms, they go away and fight till they come back or you hear from them."

"The president is the same as a king four years signing bills in the White House and meeting people. He can do whatever he wants to unless he is stopped."

"Oath is what you swear to in court that you will tell everything God help you and hold nothing back no matter what."

"Poverty is when you work hard, live cheap and can't pay up, you figure and you can't tell where you're coming out at."

"Liberty is when you are free to do what you want to do and the police never arrest you if they know who you are and you got the right ticket."

"The past is long ago and you can't touch it. Tomorrow today will be yesterday and belong in the past, like that, see?"

The ingenuity of the human mind and what passes the time of day for the millions who keep their serenity amid the relentless processes of wresting their provender from the clutch of tongs organized against them—this is always interesting and sometimes marvelous.

Daily is death and despair stood off by those who in hard trials know how and when to laugh.

The fox counts hens in his dreams. The eagle has an empire in the air. Man under his hat has several possessions of comedy.

The name of a stub line under the Lone Star banner is The Houston Eastern and Western Texas railroad.

On the passenger and freight cars is the monogram, the initials H. E. W. T.

And nearly everybody in the territory traversed and the adjacent right of way calls it "Hell Either Way you Take It."

The Never Did and Couldn't railway is the N.D. & C. Newburgh, Duchess and Connecticut.

The Delay Linger and Wait is the D. L. & W., the Delaware, Lackawanna and Western.

Come Boys and Quit Railroading ran the slogan of the 1888 engineers'
strike on the C. B. & Q. RR., the Chicago Burlington & Quincy
Rail Road.

The floors of the new horse stables were translucent tile, the drink-
ing fountains of marble, the mangers of mahogany, the feed-
boxes furbished with silver trimmings and inlays.
"Well, gentlemen," said the proprietor to his inspecting friends, "is
there anything you can think of that is lacking?"
"I can think of nothing," said an irreverent one, "unless you want
to put in a sofa for each horse."

62

WITHOUT the daily chores of the people
the milk trucks would have no milk
the markets neither meat nor potatoes
the railroad and bus timetables
would be on the fritz
and the shippers saying, "Phooey!"
And daily the chores are done
with heavy toil here, light laughter there,
the chores of the people, yes.

In a drought year when one dust storm came
    chasing another across a western town
Out of a Santa Fé day coach a passenger stuck
    his head and queried a citizen
"What's the name of this mean measly dirty
    dreary dried-up low-down burg?"
The citizen responding, "That's near enough,
    stranger, let it go at that."

When the railway stockholder reminded the
    brakeman of orders to call stations in a
    clear tenor voice, the brakeman inquired:
    "What kind of a tenor voice do you ex-
    pect for forty dollars a month?"

The meat wholesaler took in hand one of his
    salesmen: "You've got a bright head and

your ideas run away with you. Don't be
so bright when you tackle a customer. Be
dumb. Look dumb. They will appreciate
you better that way."

On a Baton Rouge headstone they carved:
His last words were:
"I die as I lived—
a Christian and a Democrat."

An Arkansas huckleberry cavalry commander
got his men into action with:
"Prepare to git on your creeters—git!"

"How many of yez down in the pit?"
"Five."
"The half of yez come up and be quick."

"Men, will yez fight or will yez run?"
"We will."
"Yez will what?"
"We will not."
"I t'ought yez would."

The restaurant cashier glanced at the check
he handed her and told him: "I am very sorry
but we have an arrangement with the banks
that they don't sell soup and we don't take
checks."

Phone girl: "I'm sorry I gave you the wrong number."
Man: "I'm sorry too, I know it was a perfectly good
number you gave me but I just couldn't use it."

"I'd hate to be up there in that," murmured one studying
an airplane in a tailspin, another murmuring, "I'd hate
to be up there and *not* be in that."

Man going up elevator:
"We eat, work, sleep, then we die—eh?"
Elevator boy: "Yeah."

The people laugh.
From a light easy humming
to the raucous guffaw and the brutal jeer
   the people laugh.
   The decisions of the people
   as to how they shall laugh and when
   and how loud and at whom and how long—
This is not covered in the vaudevillians saying
every audience is ninety per cent squirrels
and ten per cent nuts and the squirrels are
more to be considered than the nuts; almost
an axiom comes from the same vaudevillians:
what in one hour entertains and goes over big
in another hour starts a riot: the old reliable
jokes fail: hokum demands a new formula:
the query runs, "What are they laughing at this
year?"

"We got butter and we got the Kaiser," taunted the Dutch boy across
   the border.
"We got Hitler," argued the German lad from his side of the fence be-
   tween the two countries.
"We got butter, we got the Kaiser," repeated the Dutch boy, "and we're
   going to get Hitler."

"Have you a criminal lawyer in this burg?"
"We think so but we haven't been able to prove
it on him."

"What's become of your two boys that grew up
since I saw you last?"
"One is dead and the other is in the real estate
business in Wichita."

"Am I the first girl you ever kissed?"
"No, but I want you to know I am a lot more
particular than I used to be."

The Kansas City girl out of finishing school: "If you've got the right
   kind of a face and personality you don't need the education and if
   you haven't got the face and personality you can never get educa-
   tion enough."

"Yesterday," said the college boy home on vacation, "we autoed to the
country club, golfed till dark, bridged a while, and autoed home."
"Yesterday," said the father, "I muled to the cornfield and gee-hawed till
sundown, then I suppered till dark, piped till nine, bedsteaded till
five, breakfasted and went muling again."

A farmhand seeing the letters "P C" in a
dream asked if it meant "Preach Christ,"
his pastor counseling, "Perhaps it means
Plow Corn."

Even those who have read books on manners are sometimes a pain in the
neck.
If there is a bedbug in a hotel when I arrive he looks at the register for
my room number.
They invited themselves to the party: "If you are verandah then we are
ash can."
The fourth time they threw the unwelcome guest downstairs he dusted
himself off and called, "I know why you throw me out, you don't
want me up there."
At the third stop out of St. Louis where he was again kicked from the
vestibule platform, the traveler picked himself up and told an inquirer,
"It's nothing at all. I'm going to Cincinnati if my pants hold out."
He sat on a hot stove and didn't say a thing except, "Isn't there some-
thing burning?"
The joker who threw an egg into the electric fan soon was stood on his
tin ear.

One audience may wheeze like a calliope with sore tonsils and another
roar like a burning lumber yard.
Some of them, as you look closer, are slow as molasses in January—or
quick as greased lightning.
Some are noisy as a cook-stove falling downstairs, and others quiet as an
eel swimming in oil.
They have met salesmen and politicians low as a baboon's forehead, low
as a snake's belt-buckle.
Sure as a wild goose never laid a tame egg, they understand a crooked tree
throws only a crooked shadow.
They have heard of men trying to keep the sea back with a pitchfork.
They have seen cutups funny as a barrel of monkeys turn gloomy as a
graveyard on a wet Sunday.

They have seen one limber as an eelskin finally locked in like a fly in amber.

"Sometimes paying on the installment plan is for all the world like picking feathers out of molasses."
"Crooked as the letter Z, so crooked he could hide behind a corkscrew, so crooked he couldn't fall down a well, so crooked he can't lie straight in bed."
The poker party ran through Saturday night and Sunday and they came out with eyes like burnt holes in an army blanket.
Once in a blue moon something happens so they say it is rare as a snowbird in hell.
There's nothing to be scared of—unless you're afraid of a paper tiger.
The woman who'll kiss and tell is small as the little end of nothing.

In the daily labor of the people
by and through which life goes on
the people must laugh or go down.
The slippery roads, icy tools, stalled engines, snowdrifts, hot boxes, cold motors, wet matches, mixed signals, time schedules, washouts,
The punch-clock, the changes from decent foremen to snarling straw bosses, the sweltering July sun, the endless pounding of a blizzard, the sore muscles, the sudden backache and the holding on for all the backache,
The quick thinking in wrecks and breakdowns, the fingers and thumbs clipped off by machines, the machines that behave no better no worse no matter what you call them, the coaxing of a machine and fooling with it till all of a sudden she starts and you're not sure why,
A ladder rung breaking and a legbone or armbone with it, layoffs and no paycheck coming, the red diphtheria card on the front door, the price for a child's burial casket, hearse and cemetery lot,
The downrun from butter to oleo to lard to sorghum, the gas meter on the blink, the phone taken out, the bills and again bills, for each ten dollars due ten cents to pay with or nothing to pay with only debts and debts,
The human sardines of the rush hour car and bus, the gnawing fear of defeat till a workman never before licked says now-I'm-licked, the boy who says to-hell-with-work-you-never-got-anywhere-working-and-I'm-going-to-be-a-bum-good-by, the girl who doesn't know which way to go and has a wild look about it,

The pleasant surprises of changing weather when the saying passes it's-a-
    nice-day-isn't-it and they-can't-take-this-away-from-us, the shine of
    spring sunlight on a new planted onion patch after bright rain, the
    slow learning of what makes a good workman and the comfort of
    handling good tools, the joy of working with the right kind of a
    crew and a foreman who is "one of us," a foreman who understands,
The lurking treachery of machinery, good printers cursing "the innate
    cussedness of inanimate things," the pouring of molten ore at the
    right nick and the timing of the clutch of a crane or a lifting derrick
    or the dump of a steam shovel or the toss of a hawser from boatdeck
    to dockpost or the slowing to a stop for a red light or the eye on the
    clock for the deadline of a job marked rush,
The grades and lines of workmen, how one takes care and puts the job
    through with the least number of motions and another is careless and
    never sure what he is doing and another is careful and means well but
    the gang knows he belongs somewhere else and another is a slouch
    for work but they are glad to have him for his jokes and clowning.

The people laugh, yes, the people laugh.
They have to in order to live and survive under lying politicians, lying
    labor skates, lying racketeers of business, lying newspapers, lying ads.
The people laugh even at lies that cost them toil and bloody exactions.
For a long time the people may laugh, until a day when the laughter
    changes key and tone and has something it didn't have.
Then there is a scurrying and a noise of discussion and an asking of the
    question what is it the people want.
Then there is the pretense of giving the people what they want, with
    jokers, trick clauses, delays and continuances, with lawyers and fixers,
    playboys and ventriloquists, bigtime promises.
Time goes by and the gains are small for the years go slow, the people go
    slow, yet the gains can be counted and the laughter of the people
    foretokening revolt carries fear to those who wonder how far it will go
    and where to block it.

6 3

In a winter sunset near Springfield, Illinois
In the coming on of a winter gloaming,
A Negro miner with headlamp and dinner bucket,
A black man explained how it happens
In some of the mines only white men are hired,
Only white men can dig out the coal

Yet he would strike if the strike was right
And, "For a just cause I'd live in the fields
          on hard corn."

White man: "You take the crow and I'll take
the turkey or I'll take the turkey and you
take the crow."
Indian: "You don't talk turkey to me once."

In a corn-belt village after a Sunday game
a fan said to a farmhand second baseman:
"You play great ball, boy, a little more time
for practice and you could make the big
leagues."
"Sure, I know it, shoveling cow manure, that's
all that holds me back."

6 4

No matter how thick or how thin you slice it it's still baloney.
I would if I could and I could if I would but if I couldn't how could I,
          could you?
I never made a mistake in grammar but once in my life and as soon as
    I done it I seen it.
He was a good shoveler but I don't know as I would say he was a fancy
    shoveler.
"You're always talking about liberty, do you want liberty?" "I don't know
    as I do and I don't know as I do."
"The train is running easier now." "Yes, we're off the track now."
The chorus goes, "They take him by the hand, and they lead him to the
    land, and the farmer is the man who feeds them all."
"I hear a burglar in the house." "Wait, if he finds anything worth steal-
    ing we'll take it away from him."
"Did you say the sky is the limit?" "Yes, we won't go any higher than
    the sky."
"That dwarf ain't worth ten cents to see—he's five feet high if he's a
    foot." "Exactly, my good sir, he's the tallest dwarf in the world."

The sea rolls easy and smooth.
Or the sea roars and goes wild.

The smell of clams and fish comes
    out of the sea.
The sea is nothing to look at
    unless you want to know something
    unless you want to know
    where you came from.

The more things change the more they are the same.
The worse things are the better they are.
Things will not get better till they've been worse.
When everyone is wrong then everyone is right.
Everybody was wrong and nobody was to blame.

The windjammer drew into harbor after a long cruise
and they gathered around the captain for a good-by
and they understood exactly what he meant
and it seemed like old times to hear him roar:
    "You can all go to hell
    and I'm damned glad to be rid of you."
Why did they cheer him unless he was one of them?

The Mexicans give a toast:
salud pesetas tiempo para gastarse son,
health, money, time, what are they for but spending?

    The hoary English folk saying, "He'd skin a
        louse and send the hide to market," is sur-
        passed in gayety by the antique Persian
        proverb, "He snatches away a flea's hat,"
        meaning his calculations are very small,
        indeed, indeed. He could sit down and
        figure out how it might be possible to
        sneak up on a flea, snatch off its hat, and
        then by a circuitous route reach a market
        place where he would deliver the hat in
        exchange for what it might bring from
        someone who had a pet flea suffering
        for the want of a hat or from someone
        collecting flea hats who wished to add
        this particular specimen.

Who do you think you are
　　and where do you think you came from?
From toenails to the hair of your head you are
　　mixed of the earth, of the air,
Of compounds equal to the burning gold and ame-
　　thyst lights of the Mountains of the Blood of
　　Christ at Santa Fé.
Listen to the laboratory man tell what you are
　　made of, man, listen while he takes you apart.
Weighing 150 pounds you hold 3,500 cubic feet of
　　gas—oxygen, hydrogen, nitrogen.
From the 22 pounds and 10 ounces of carbon in
　　you is the filling for 9,000 lead pencils.
In your blood are 50 grains of iron and in the rest
　　of your frame enough iron to make a spike
　　that would hold your weight.
From your 50 ounces of phosphorus could be made
　　800,000 matches and elsewhere in your physical
　　premises are hidden 60 lumps of sugar, 20 tea-
　　spoons of salt, 38 quarts of water, two ounces
　　of lime, and scatterings of starch, chloride of
　　potash, magnesium, sulphur, hydrochloric acid.
You are a walking drug store and also a cosmos and
　　a phantasmagoria treading a lonesome valley,
　　one of the people, one of the minions and
　　myrmidons who would like an answer to the
　　question, "Who and what are you?"
One of the people seeing sun, fog, zero weather,
　　seeing fire, flood, famine, having meditations
　　　　On fish, birds, leaves, seeds,
　　　　Skins and shells emptied of living form,
　　　　The beautiful legs of Kentucky thoroughbreds
　　　　And the patience of army mules.

The sea holds colors in its own way:
below 55 fathoms no black,
below 300 fathoms no red, violet, white, gray,
below 600 fathoms no purple, green, orange:
　　"yellow and brown occur at all depths."

What have you above the ears?
Or are you dead from the neck up?
If you don't look out for yourself nobody else will.
What counts most is what you got under your own hat.
Your best friend is yourself.
Every man for himself and the devil take the hindmost.
I'm the only one of my friends I can count on.
I'm not in business for my health.
I'm a lone wolf; I work by myself.
I'm for me, myself and company.
Who said you could work this side of the street?

God loves the thief but he also loves the owner.
The big thieves hang the little thieves.
Set a thief to catch a thief.
Office without pay makes thieves.
The carpenters have sinned and the tailors are hanged.
He must have killed a few to get what he's got.
They'll sell you anything, even the blue sky.
Have you seen one man selling the ocean to another?
A farmer between two lawyers is a fish between two cats.

The rich own the land and the poor own the water.
The rich get richer and the poor get children.
The rich have baby napkins, the poor have diapers.
The big houses have small families and the small houses big families.
Why did Death take the poor man's cow and the rich man's child?

65

THE mazuma, the jack, the shekels, the kale,
The velvet, the you-know-what,
The what-it-takes, a roll, a wad,
Bring it home, boy.
Bring home the bacon.
Start on a shoestring if you have to.
Then get your first million.
The second million is always easier than the first.

And if you get more of them round iron men than you
    can use you can always throw them at the birds:
    it's been done.
Now take some men, everything they touch turns into money: they know
    how the land lays: they can smell where the dollars grow.
Money withers if you don't know how to nurse it along: money flies away
    if you don't know where to put it.
The first question is, Where do we raise the money, where is the cash
    coming from?
A little horse sense helps: an idea and horse sense
    take you far: if you got a scheme ask yourself,
    Will it work?
And let me put one bug in your ear: inside information helps: how many
    fortunes came from a tip, from being on the ground first, from hear-
    ing a piece of news, from fast riding, early buying, quick selling, or
    plain dumb luck?
Yes, get Lady Luck with you and you're made: some fortunes were tum-
    bled into and the tumblers at first said, Who would have believed it?
    and later, I knew just how to do it.
Yes, Lady Luck counts: before you're born pick the right papa and mama
    and the newsreel boys will be on the premises early for a shot of you
    with your big toe in your mouth.

        Money is power: so said one.
        Money is a cushion: so said another.
        Money is the root of evil: so said
            still another.
        Money means freedom: so runs an old
            saying.

        And money is all of these—and more.
        Money pays for whatever you want—if
            you have the money.
        Money buys food, clothes, houses, land,
            guns, jewels, men, women, time to be
            lazy and listen to music.
        Money buys everything except love,
            personality, freedom, immortality,
            silence, peace.

Therefore men fight for money.
Therefore men steal, kill, swindle,
    walk as hypocrites and whited
    sepulchers.
Therefore men speak softly carrying
    plans, poisons, weapons, each in the
    design: The words of his mouth were
    as butter but war was in his heart.
Therefore nations lay strange holds on
    each other; bombardments open, tanks
    advance, salients are seized, aviators
    walk on air; truckloads of amputated
    arms and legs are hauled away.

   Money is power, freedom, a cushion, the
    root of all evil, the sum of bless-
    ings.

   "Tell us what is money.
For we are ignorant of money, its ways and
    meanings,
Each a child in a dark storm where people
    cry for money."

Where the carcass is the buzzards gather.
Where the treasure is the heart is also.
    Money breeds money.
    Money runs the world.
Money talk is bigger than talk talk.
No ear is deaf to the song that gold sings.
Money is welcome even when it stinks.
Money is the sinew of love and of war.
Money breaks men and ruins women.
    Money is a great comfort.
    Every man has his price.
There are men who can't be bought.
There are women beyond purchase.
When you buy judges someone sells justice.
You can buy anything except day and night.

6 6

THE poobahs rise and hold their poobah sway
till their use is over
and other poobahs hitherto unheard of
step into their shoes and sit at the big tables
and have their say-so
till events order the gong for them:
and the fathers can never arrange for the sons
to be what the fathers were
in the days that used to be: not for long:
    both the people and the poobahs—
    life will not let them be.
A little bird flits to the window-sills
    morning by morning:
"Whither goest thou? whither and whither?"

They die at noon and midnight,
they are born in the morning, the afternoon,
and the river goes on
and the foamflecks of the river go on.
    The same great river carries along
    its foamflecks of poobahs and plain people.
    They and their houses go down the river,
    houses built for use or show
    down the crumbling stream they go—
cabins, frame lumber cottages, installment bungalows,
mail order residences picked from a catalogue,
mansions whose windows and gables laughed a rivalry,
    down the same river they all go.
A few stand, a few last longer than others
while time and the rain, water and air and time
    have their way,
morning by morning the little birds on the window-sills:
    "Whither goest thou? whither and whither?"

6 7

WAS he preaching or writing poetry or talking through his hat? He was
  a Chinaman saying, "The fishes though deep in the water may be

hooked. The birds though high in the air may be shot. Man's heart
only is out of reach. The heavens may be measured. The earth may
be surveyed. The heart of man alone is not to be known."

"Sleep softly, eagle forgotten," wrote an Illinois poet at the grave of the
only governor of Illinois sure to be named by remote generations.
"You have no ruins in America so I thought I would come and visit
you," said an English lord to a paralyzed hobo poet in Camden,
New Jersey.
"The fundamental weakness in every empire and every great civilization
was the weakness in the character of the upper classes," ventured a
Yale professor in a solemn moment.
"When historians of the future tell posterity what the World War was
about, they will agree upon a cause that nobody who fought it ever
suspected," said the chief of the high command of the Allied Armies.

"Bring me my liar," said a king calling for the historian of the realm.
"History is bunk," said a history-making motorcar king.
"Words," added this motorcar king, "are a camouflage for what is going
on in the mind."
"History is a fable agreed upon," said a shriveled smiling Frenchman.
"Even if you prove it, who cares?" demanded an Illinois state librarian.
"I shall arrange the facts and leave the interpretation to the reader," said
the hopeful biographer to the somber historian.
"The moment you begin to arrange you interpret," emitted the somber
historian.

"Do you make your newspaper for yourself or the public?" was asked a
New York founder who replied, "For the public, of course."
"Why isn't your newspaper more intelligent?" was asked a Chicago pub-
lisher who laughed, "We make our newspaper for boobs."

"Secret influence is the greatest evil of our time," testified a Harvard presi-
dent from a birthmarked anxious face.
"And," added another world-renowned educator, "the crookedest crooks
in the United States government have been well educated."
"Nevertheless," quoth an old-fashioned bibulous mayor of Milwaukee,
"this dying for principle is all rot."

"Put a dollar on the shelf thirty days and you have a dollar," said one
president of the Pennsylvania railroad. "Put a workingman on the
shelf thirty days and you have a skeleton."

"The struggle," said a delegate from the coal miners, "is between stock-holders who do not labor as against laborers who do not hold stock."

"The cry of 'Let us alone,'" urged a British commoner, "grows less resolute, more touched with frenzy."

"Thou shalt not steal," added another commoner, "assumes thou shalt not be stolen from."

"To cure the depression," said one adviser early in the depression, "you must put the patient on a rich, heavy diet because he is starving for nourishment and at the same time you must starve him because he is suffering and overstuffed with rich food."

"You make rifles," said an eagle-faced old railroad fireman to ten thousand Chicago workingmen at a summer picnic, "you make rifles—and you're always at the wrong end of them."

"The mystery of mysteries," contributed an engineer, "is to watch machinery making machinery."

"Art," offered an artist, "is something you can't put into words and when you do it isn't art."

"When I am not engaged in thought," said the possessor of one great mind, "I am employed in recovering from its effects."

"Millionaires," said one having two hundred millions, "millionaires who laugh are rare."

"War requires three things," urged a short commentator with a long head, "first, money; second, money; and third, money."

"Man," spoke up an anthropologist, "is a two-legged animal without feathers, the only one who cooks his food, uses an alphabet, carries fire-arms, drinks when he is not thirsty, and practices love with an eye on birth control."

"On the one hand an ignorant and arrogant government, and on the other hand a gang of ignorant and arrogant hoodlums—so often the voters must choose between these two," said a desperate registered voter in Philadelphia as he put a seidel of bock beer under his belt only two blocks from Independence Hall and the celebrated crack in the silent Liberty Bell.

"For what are we fighting?" inquired a Richmond editor in 1863. "An abstraction."

"Peace and amity," said a Georgian in the same year, "is obstructed by only two circumstances, the landing of the Pilgrim Fathers, and Original Sin."

"Sometimes," offered a Concord hermit building a hut for himself, "we

class those who are one-and-a-half-witted with the half-witted because
we appreciate only a third of their wit."
"Broadway is a street," typed the colyumist, "where people spend money
they haven't earned to buy things they don't need to impress people
they don't like."
"You ask me what is my theory of the universe," the physicist replied,
"when I haven't even a theory of magnetism."
"The great events of the world," submitted a historian, "take place in the
brain."
"In the last analysis," propounded a California wheat novelist, "the people
are always right—a literature which cannot be vulgarized is not litera-
ture at all and will perish."
"The durable culture of any nation," ventured another historian, "rests on
the mind and genius of its common folk, the masses of the people."

  In a hothouse room where sunlight never came
  hundreds of monster plants winding and twisting
  and by light and volume turned on and off
  you could make them grow fast or slow—
  you could see them trail in snake-vines,
  explode into mammoth elephant ears.
    They crept and reeled in processions
Of obedient giant clowns and dwarfs, grotesques,
Symbols of an underworld not yet organized by man,
Tokens of plenty and hunger in the controls of man
And the master of these dumb clumsy growths,
A dwarf and a hunchback, a deep believer
In the spirit of man mastering material environment,
Out of Schenectady a wizard loving mankind in peak and abyss,
Saying science and invention are the enemies of human want
And the world is organized to abolish poverty
Whenever the people of the world so will.

Mild and modest were the delegates meeting in
  Basel in 1912 and resolving:
"Let the governments remember . . . they cannot
  unleash a war without danger to themselves."
Mild and modest were the delegates meeting in
  Geneva in 1934 and resolving:
"Man is still, of all baggage, the most difficult to

transport, and so long as the occupational and
geographical mobility of labor and the effi-
ciency of its distribution among different ave-
nues and places of employment are not im-
proved at a rate corresponding to accelerated
technical change, there is reason to expect the
persistence of a higher volume of technolog-
ical unemployment."

"Listen to me,
     brother.
They'll hand yuh anything.
Look for the dirty work.
     Listen.
Never see nothin'.
Never know nothin'.
Never tell nothin'.
Then yuh'll get along.
If they want to frame on yuh,
     they will."

6 8

"THE drama of politics doesn't interest me," said a news rewrite man be-
    tween beers. "It's only the people running around trying to change
    one gang of bandits for another gang of bandits."
"I've written thousands of words about nothing," said rewrite number
    two, "and I can do it again."
"I don't know anything," chimed number three, "and come to think about
    it what I do know ain't so."
"What was it the doughboy wrote home?" a Sunday feature writer chipped
    in. "Pershing stood at the tomb of Napoleon and said, 'LaFollette,
    we are here!'"
"Next," burbled a city editor, "you'll be telling about the cub who wired
    from the town on fire, 'All is confusion can send nothing.'"
"Either that," he went on, "or the lad whose assignment was to interview
    God and be sure to get a picture."
"Or," not yet being interrupted, "the utilities chief who brushed by Saint
    Peter at the gate of heaven saying, 'I can't bother with you, where's
    God?'"

"I want money," said the editorial writer who knew where he got it, "in order to buy the time to get the things that money will not buy."

"If the utilities," the Sunday feature writer kicked in again, "could meter the moonlight the lovers would have to pay, pay, and pay."

"I love a few individuals," came a droll desk man, "but I've got a grudge in general against the human race."

"Me," came another desk man, "I hate a few individuals and outside of that I love the whole damn human family."

"Hell's bitches," a street man cut in, "are poverty, crime, ignorance and idleness. Disease and insanity are final breakdowns ending long periods of anxiety, fear, worry, and unrest."

"He's reading books, the sonofagun," interrupted the city editor. "He's going literary on us. And how are we going to get out a paper without poverty and crime?"

"I found out it takes a smart man to be a crook," said a new lad on the police run. "And then I got to asking why should a smart man want to be a crook? He doesn't have to."

"The way to be a big shot is don't know too much," a desk man offered. "What you don't know won't hurt you."

"Man," said a hitherto silent Sunday feature writer, "is infinitely more important than the property he creates. We cannot separate the individual from the work it produces. Property does not exist outside and above the men who jointly produce it."

"He'll be joining the guild soon if he hasn't already got a card," the editorial writer editorialized. "Bend thy neck, proud Sicambrian. Adore what thou hast burned. Burn what thou hast adored."

"May," a rewrite ended the session, "may the fair goddess, Fortune, fall deep in love with thee and prosperity be thy page."

"If you have nothing to do please don't do it here," said one of the rewrites opening the next day's session with a tall tankard.

"Nevertheless," rejoined a rewrite, "I can tell you I met a discouraged undertaker today saying his business was to bury the dead and it looked to him as though the dead have stopped dying."

"And I," put in a member of the art department, "met an intellectual who says to me why don't you draw the pelican and all I could hand him was why do I want to draw the pelican since it's all there when you look at it and any of the camera boys can do it quicker."

One camera boy saying, "I have found woman to be the same as man, with slight alterations," another burbled, "Thank God for those alterations."

"I don't see," put in the new college lad on the police run, "why any man wants to kill another. If he'll just wait the other man is going to die sometime anyhow."

"It's like men chasing after women," said a rewrite. "If they didn't the women would chase after them."

"We ought to have a series of interviews," offered a desk man, "on whether the man chases the woman or whether it's the woman that chases the man, columns and columns with pictures and snappy captions."

"They put on the wires today," said a unit from the telegraph desk, "an Irish poet saying when he's going to write a poem he has the same feeling a hen has when she's going to lay an egg."

"That's news," believed the city editor. "News is anything we think ought to be printed to gladden our readers' hearts or throw the fear of God into them."

"We describe the revels of the rich," interposed a slightly illuminated assistant Sunday editor, "so the poor may enjoy in imagination the pleasures their purses will not permit them in reality."

"Yet I notice," he went on, "my associates have considerable difficulty on various occasions in brightening and rendering readable the dull antics of the wives of the big advertisers."

"And," he continued, "if the big advertiser himself gets into difficulties so notorious that something must be printed we soften the blow to the fullest extent and this is as it should be for advertising is the life blood of a newspaper and who are we that we should bite the hand that feeds us?"

"You're a dirty radical bothered with a streak of the blessed Rotarian," put in a rewrite.

"In Moscow," interspersed one just back from Russia, "an English liberal tells me a bugler every morning steps out in front of the Kremlin and blows a long powerful blast and they ask him what for and he says, 'I am sounding the call for the international revolution of the united workers of the world who have nothing to lose but their chains and a world to gain,' and they ask him what he gets paid for this daily bugle call and he says, 'Not much—but it's a permanent job.' "

"For my part," an editorial writer ended his silence, "I begin each bright morning with praying: Lord, give me this day my daily opinion and forgive me the one I had yesterday."

"And I," rejoined the slightly illuminated one, "never quit dreaming of a time when every man is his own policeman, priest and editorial writer."

"You would wish yourself," the editorial writer had it, "out of your own job and me out of mine."

"Yes," as some of them prepared for the suburban trains, "one of these days science and invention will have rendered each one of us humble servants of the public a superfluous and unnecessary unit of labor and all we'll have to worry about is how to occupy our very valuable minds when there is nothing to do but nothing."

The city editor managed to have the final words.

"I'll take vanilla! horsefeathers!"

6 9

"A LAWYER," hiccuped a disbarred member of the bar, "is a man who gets two other men to take off their clothes and then he runs away with them."

"If the law is against you, talk about the evidence," said a battered barrister. "If the evidence is against you, talk about the law, and, since you ask me, if the law and the evidence are both against you, then pound on the table and yell like hell."

"The law," said the Acme Sucker Rod manufacturer who was an early Christian mayor of Toledo, Ohio, "the law is what the people will back up."

"You haven't climbed very high," said a Wall Street operator who was quoted in the press, "unless you own a judge or two."

> Lawyer: What was the distance between
>   the two towns?
> Witness: Two miles as the cry flows.
> Lawyer: You mean as the crow flies.
> Judge: No, he means as the fly crows.

> Between the Whig sheriff and the Demo-
>   cratic judge in Boone County, Mis-
>   souri, was a breach wide enough to
>   erect gallows.
> A visiting lawyer handed the judge a brief
>   spattered with large goose-quill pen-
>   manship.
> The judge turned the document crossways
>   and upside down scrutinizing it.

> "Can't that judge of yours read writin'?"
>   whispered the lawyer to the sheriff.
> "No," whispered the sheriff. "He can't
>   read readin', let alone writin'."

Who was the *twentieth* century lawyer who said of another lawyer, "He
has one of the most enlightened minds of the *eighteenth* century"?
and why did fate put both of them on the Supreme Court bench?

> The surgeon held his profession the oldest in
>   the world through the operation whereby
>   Eve was made of rib from Adam.
> The engineer held the world was once chaos
>   and its reorganization a matchless engineer-
>   ing feat.
> The politician put in, "Who made that chaos?"
>   And the laugh comes in there, a half a
>   laugh, and come to think about it, less
>   than half a laugh.

7 0

THE tumblers of the rapids go white, go green,
go changing over the gray, the brown, the rocks.
The fight of the water, the stones,
the fight makes a foam laughter
before the last look over the long slide
down the spread of a sheen in the straight fall.
    Then the growl, the chutter,
    down under the boom and the muffle,
    the hoo hoi deep,
    the hoo hoi down,
        this is Niagara.

The human race in misery snarls.
The writhing becomes a mob.
The mob is the beginning of something,
Perhaps the mournful beginning
Of a march out of darkness
Into a lesser darkness

And so on until
The domes of smooth shadows
Space themselves in tall triangles
And nations exchange oleanders
Instead of gas, loot and hot cargo.
The mob is a beginning, man lacking concert.
The hanging mob hangs more than its victim.
These seethings are a recoil and a downdrag.
Each debauch costs.
Fevers and rots run a course before growth.

> The mob is a beginning, man lacking concert.
> What is an army with banners and guns
> Other than a mob given form and orders to kill?
> And when will the nations exchange oleanders
> Instead of gas, loot and hot cargo?

  A train of soldiers passes.
The khaki lads cheer, laugh, sing, and the flag goes by.
They are young and the young time is the time to be gay, to sing, laugh,
    cheer, even out of car windows on the way to mine strike duty.
Some of these boys will be laid out stiff and flags will drape their coffins.
Some of the mine strikers will be laid out stiff and flags drape their coffins.
Faraway owners of the mines will read about it in morning papers along-
    side breakfast.

71

Who was that antique Chinese crook who put over his revolution and
    let out a rooster crow: "Burn all the books! history must begin
    with us!"
What burned so inside of him that he must burn all the books? and
    why do we all want to read those books just because he hated
    them so?
Yet we hand him this: He singled out no special lot of books for burn-
    ing: he hated books as such and wanted them all up in smoke.
"Let history begin with us," was his cry and maybe it began and what
    were its chapters and what was his name as its beginner?

> What is history but a few Big Names plus
>   People?

What is a Big Name unless the people love it
    or hate it
For what it did to them or for them while it
    was in the going?
And this Big Name means pretense and plunder,
    ashes and dung,
While another is armfuls of roses, enshrined
    beyond speech.

You may call spirits from the vasty deep,
Aye, you may—but will they come
When you call them?
You may sell an idea to the people
And sit back satisfied you have them your way
But will they stay sold on the idea?
Will they be easy to hold in line
Unless the idea has a promise of roots
Twisted deep in the heart of man
Being brought into play
As though justice between man and man
May yet breeze across the world with sea-smells
And a very old, a very plain homemade cry,
"Why didn't we think of this before?"

In the intimate circles of the dictator,
At the desk at the end of a long room
        where the imitation of God Almighty
        sits running the works,
In the speech and look of the main star
        and the lesser stars hovering in a
        cluster and an orbit,
They know in the pressure of their personal
        ego that this too shall pass away and be
        lost in the long mass shadow of the ever-
        living people
And down under the taboos and emblems, be-
        hind pomp and ritual, posture and strut,
        if the word justice is only one more word,
        if the talk about justice is merely window-
        dressing, if liberty is pushed too far in the

name of discipline, if the delicate lines
between personal freedom and requisite so-
cial performance are not every moment
a terrible load of care
There will be a payday and little bells lost in
the clang and boom of big bells.

People are what they are
because they have come out of what was.
Therefore they should bow down before what was
and take it and say it's good—or should they?

The advocates and exemplars of pride and gluttony
are forgotten or recalled with loathing.
The mouthpieces of dumb misery are remembered
for the bitter silences they broke with crying:
       "Look, see this!
       if it is alive or only half-alive
       what name does it go by,
       why is it what it is
       and how long shall it be?"

               Who can fight against the future?
               What is the decree of tomorrow?
               Haven't the people gone on and on
                   always taking more of their own?
               How can the orders of the day
                   be against the people in this time?
               What can stop them from taking
                   more and more of their own?

72

WHAT is a judge? A judge is a seated torso and head sworn before God
    never to sell justice nor play favorites while he umpires the disputes
    brought before him.
When you take the cigar out of your face and the fedora off your head in
    the presence of the court, you do it because it is required from those
    who are supposed to know they have come into a room where burns
    the white light of that priceless abstraction named justice.

What is a judge? The perfect judge is austere, impersonal, impartial, mark-
    ing the line of right or wrong by a hairsbreadth.
Before him, bow humbly, bow low, be a pilgrim, light a candle
For he is a rara avis, a rare bird, a white blackbird, a snowwhite crow.

What is a judge? A featherless human biped having bowels, glands, blad-
    ders, and intricate blood vessels of the brain,
One more frail mortal, one more candle a sudden change of wind might
    blow out as any common candle blows out in a wind change
So that never again does he sit in his black robes of solemn import before
    a crowded courtroom saying two-years ten-years twenty-years life for
    you or "hanged by the neck till you are dead dead dead."

What is a judge? One may be the owner of himself coming to his deci-
    sions often in a blur of hesitations knowing by what snarled courses
    and ropes of reason justice operates, with reservations, in twilight
    zones.
What is a judge? Another owns no more than the little finger of himself,
    others owning him, others having placed him where he is, others tell-
    ing him what they want and getting it, others referring to him as "our
    judge" as though he is measured and weighed beforehand the same as
    a stockyards hog, others holding him to decisions evasive of right or
    wrong, others writing his decisions for him, the atmosphere hushed
    and guarded, the atmosphere having a faint stockyards perfume.
What is a judge? Sometimes a mind giving one side the decision and the
    other side a lot of language and sympathy, sometimes washing his
    hands and rolling a pair of bones and leaving equity to a pair of gal-
    loping ivories.
What is a judge? A man picked for a job by politicians with an eye some-
    times on justice for the public, equal rights to all persons entering—
    or again with an eye on lucrative favors and special accommoda-
    tions—a man having bowels, glands, bladders, and intricate blood ves-
    sels of the brain.
Take that cigar out of your face. Take that hat off your head.
And why? why? Because here we are sworn never to sell justice and here
    burns the white light of that priceless abstraction named justice.

        What is a judge?
        He is a man.
     Yes, after all, and no matter what,

and beyond all procedures and investitures,
a judge is nothing more nor less than a man—
 one man having his one-man path, his one-
 man circle and orbit among other men
 each of whom is one man.
Therefore should any judge open his mouth
 and speak as though his words have an
 added light and weight beyond the speech
 of one man?
Of what is he the mouthpiece when he speaks?
Of any ideas or passions other than those gath-
 ered and met in the mesh of his own per-
 sonality? Can his words be measured forth
 in so special a realm of exact justice in-
 structed by tradition, that they do not re-
 late to the living transitory blood of his
 vitals and brain, the blood so soon to cool
 in evidence of his mortal kinship with all
 other men?

73

In the light of the cold glimmer of what everybody knows, why should the
 owners of the judges speak of respect for the law and the sanctity of
 the Constitution when they know so well how justice has been taken
 for a ride and thrown gagged and beaten into a ditch?
Why is it now a saying of the people, "You can't convict a million dol-
 lars"?
Why is the bribe-taker convicted so often and the bribe-giver so seldom?
Why does a hoary proverb live on its allegation that the nets of the law
 gather the petty thieves and let the big ones get away? what does this
 mean in the homes of the poor? how does it connect with crime and
 the poor?
Why should the propertyless depositors of wrecked banks be saying,
 "Wreck a bank from the outside and you get twenty years, wreck it
 from the inside and all you have to do is start another bank"?
What do the people say in their homes, in their churches, in their gather-
 ing places over coffee-and-doughnuts beer-and-pretzels? and how does
 the talk run about millionaire robbers, malefactors of great wealth,
 sitting easy with their loot while

One-two-three, five-six-seven every day the police seize and the courts order
    to jail
    this skulker who stole a bottle of milk,
    this shadow who ran off with a loaf of bread,
    this wanderer who purloined a baby sweater
    in a basement salesroom—
And the case is dismissed of the railroad yard plain-clothes detective who
    repeatedly called "Stop!" to a boy running with a sack of coal and
    the boy not stopping the dick let him have it. "It was dark and I
    couldn't see him clear and I aimed at his legs. My intention was to
    stop him running. I didn't mean for the bullet to go as high on him
    as it did."
Thieves? Yes. Little thieves? Yes. And they get it where the chicken gets
    the ax? Yes. And the big shots are something else? Yes. And you can't
    convict a million dollars? Not unless Tuesday is Saturday, neighbor.

What is a jury? Twelve men picked by chance and a couple of lawyers,
    twelve men good and true or not-so-good, six of one and a half dozen
    of the other.
A jury? A bundle of twelve fagots, a dozen human sticks light and dark
    with loves and hates, Protestant, Catholic, Jew, free-thinker, merchant,
    farmer, workingman, thief, wets and drys, union and scab, savers and
    spenders, tightwads and crapshooters, locked in a room to come out
    saying Yes in one voice, No in one voice, or else, "Don't ask us what
    is justice, we agree to disagree," all in one voice.
A jury? Twelve names out of a hat. Twelve picked blindfolded from a city
    directory or a polling list. The next twelve crossing Main Street, two
    blocks from the post office: Odd Fellows, Masons, Knights of Colum-
    bus, deacons, poker-players, Democrats, Republicans, Independents,
    Ku Klux and Anti-Ku Klux, ball fans, chippie chasers, teetotalers, con-
    verts and backsliders.
Now you got a jury. Add one judge. Add a few lawyers. Add newspapers,
    town gossip, "what everybody says." Add witnesses and evidence. Add
    it all. The jury verdict is guilty not-guilty or agree-to-disagree.

> "Do you solemnly swear before the ever-
>   living God that the testimony you
>   are about to give in this cause shall
>   be the truth, the whole truth, and
>   nothing but the truth?"

"No, I don't. I can tell you what I saw
and what I heard and I'll swear to
that by the everliving God but the
more I study about it the more sure
I am that nobody but the everliving
God knows the whole truth and if
you summoned Christ as a witness in
this case what He would tell you
would burn your insides with the
pity and the mystery of it."

74

WHAT other oaths are wanted now?
You can never make moon poems
for people who never see the moon.
Your moon poems are aimed
at people who look at the moon
and say, "Hello moon, good old moon,
"I knew you wouldn't forget me,
"Throw me a kiss, moon,
"I'll be seeing you, moon."
      And the sun? what of the sun?
      Can you make a sun poem
      For those having soot on the window-sill?
When smoke and smudge and building walls
      Stand between them and the sun
      How can they get to know the sun
And how would they know a sun poem if they
      Met one coming straight at them?
What use for them to hold a hand up against
the sun for the sake of seeing a silhouette
      of the blue frame of the handbones?
      In the slums overshadowed by smokestacks,
      In the tomato cans in the window-sills
      The geraniums have a low weeping song,
      "Not yet have we known the sun,
      not yet have we known the sun,"
      Modulated with a hoping song,
      "Some day we shall meet the sun

"And gather pieces of the sun into ourselves
"And be no longer stunted,
no longer runts of the slums."
          And babies? what of the babies?
Can you make baby poems
For those who love special babies
          clean antiseptic babies?
what of those Red Indian babies
fresh from the birthing-crotch?
For each of them the mystery-man raised
his right hand toward the sky and called:
"Hey you sun moon stars
          and you winds clouds rain mist,
          "Listen to me! listen!
"The news is another baby belonging
          has come to this earth of ours.
"Make its path smooth so it can reach
          the top of the first hill
          and the second hill.
"And hey you valleys rivers lakes trees grasses
you make its path smooth so it can reach
          the top of the third hill.
          "And listen you birds of the air,
          you animals of the tall timbers,
          you bugs and creepers,
          you too listen!
"All you of sky earth and air, I ask you, beg you
"Pass this baby on till it climbs up over
          and beyond the fourth hill.
"From then on this child will be strong enough
"To travel on its own and see what is beyond
          those four hills!"

7 5

HUNGER and only hunger changes worlds?
The dictate of the belly
that gnawing under the navel,
this alone is the builder and the pathfinder
sending man into danger and fire
and death by struggle?

Yes and no, no and yes.
The strong win against the weak.
The strong lose against the stronger.
And across the bitter years and the howling winters
    the deathless dream will be the stronger,
    the dream of equity will win.
There are shadows and bones shot with lights
    too strong to be lost.
    Can the wilderness be put behind?
    Shall man always go on dog-eat-dog?
    Who says so?
    The stronger?
    And who is the stronger?
And how long shall the stronger hold on
    as the stronger?
    What will tomorrow write?
    "Of the people by the people for the people?"
What mockers ever wrung a crop from a waiting soil
Or when did cold logic bring forth a child?
"What use is it?" they asked a kite-flying sky gazer
And he wished in return to know, "What use is a baby?"
The dreaming scholars who quested the useless,
who wanted to know merely for the sake of knowing,
they sought and harnessed electrodynamic volts
becoming in time thirty billion horses in one country
hauling with thirty-billion-horse-power
and this is an early glimpse, a dim beginning,
the first hill of a series of hills.

    What comes after the spectrum?
With what will the test-tubes be shaken tomorrow?
For what will the acetylene torch and pneumatic chisel be scrapped?
What will the international partnerships of the world laboratories track
    down next, what new fuels, amalgams, alloys, seeds, cross-breeds, un-
    foreseen short cuts to power?
Whose guess is better than anybody else's on whether the breed
    of fire-bringers is run out, whether light rays, death rays, laugh rays,
    are now for us only in a dim beginning?
Across the bitter years and the howling winters
    the deathless dream will be the stronger
    the dream of equity will win.

76

THE record is a scroll of many indecipherable scrawls,
telling the pay of the people for commencing action
toward redress of wrongs too heavy
to be longer borne.
                    "No strike is ever lost": an old cry
heard before the strike begins and heard long after, and
"No strike is ever lost": either a thought or an instinct
equivalent to "Give me liberty or give me death."
                    On the horizon a cloud no larger than
a man's hand rolls larger and darker when masses of people
begin saying, "Any kind of death is better than this kind
of life."

> The machine world of the insects
> individual spiders engineering exploits
> interwoven colonies of bees and ants
> clouds of grasshopper destroyers
> —they carry lessons and warnings
>   they do what they must
>   they are beyond argument.

The flowing of the stream clears it of pollution.
The refuse of humanity, the offscourings, the encumberings,
They are who?
They are those who have forgotten work and the price
At which life goes on.
They live in shambles overly foul and in mansions overly
Swept and garnished.
The flowing of the stream clears it of pollution.

77

THE bottom of the sea accommodates mountain ranges.
This is how deep the sea is
And the toss and drip of the mystery of the people
And the sting of sea-drip.
In the long catacombs of moss fish linger and move

Hearing the cries of dolphins while they too wander.
This is the depot of lost and unreclaimed baggage,
Colosseums of dead men's bones and the trunks of the
    dead men each with a lock of hair, a ringlet of
    somebody's hair in a locket, and a pack of love
    letters and a deck of cards and a testament and
    leather straps and brass buckles and brass locks
    holding their fasteners on the trunks.

7 8

WHAT did Hiamovi, the red man, Chief of
    the Cheyennes, have?
To a great chief at Washington and to a
    chief of peoples across the waters,
    Hiamovi spoke:
"There are birds of many colors—red, blue,
    green, yellow,
Yet it is all one bird.
There are horses of many colors—brown,
    black, yellow, white,
Yet it is all one horse.
So cattle, so all living things, animals,
    flowers, trees.
So men in this land, where once were only
    Indians, are now men of many colors—
    white, black, yellow, red.
Yet all one people.
That this should come to pass was in the
    heart of the Great Mystery.
It is right thus—and everywhere there
    shall be peace."
Thus Hiamovi, out of a tarnished and weather-
    worn heart of old gold, out of a living
    dawn gold.

What is the float of life that goes by us
in certain moods of autumn smoke
when tall trees seem in the possession of phantoms
carrying a scheme of haze

inevitably past changing sunsets
into a moist moonlight
and beyond into a baffling moonset
on a mist horizon?
These devices are made of what color and air?
And how far and in how does man make them himself?
    What is this pool of reverie
    this blur of contemplation
    wherein man is brother to mud and gold
    to bug and bird
    to behemoths and constellations?

In the evening twilight in the skyscraper office
and the hoom hoom of a big steamboat docking
and the auto horns and the corner newsboys
only half heard as far up as sixteen floors
the doctor meditated and spoke: "The rich come afraid to die, afraid
    to have their throats looked into, their intestines prodded. It hurts.
    Their power of resistance is gone. They can't stand pain. Things go
    wrong, they come into my office and ask what is the matter. I have
    to be careful how I say, 'You are growing old, that is all, everybody
    grows old, we all have to die.' That scares them. They don't want to
    grow old. They tell me I must find a way to keep them from growing
    old. They don't want to die. They tell me they will pay me to find
    a way so they won't have to die." Thus in the evening twilight, in
    the hoom hoom and the auto horns and the corner newsboys only
    half heard up sixteen floors.
        And he went on:
"I was in a hospital the other day. A man blind thirty-five years could see
    again. We walked out together. And up the street he saw a horse.
    He asked, 'What is that?' I said, 'It's a horse—didn't you ever see a
    horse before?' He answered, 'No, this is the first time I ever saw a
    horse.' "
        Thus in the evening twilight
        in the hoom hoom.

And the doctor went on: "A few weeks ago came a woman saying she
    had been to a great symphony concert, going out to walk miles, still
    hearing the grand crashes of that music, walking home on air, telling
    me, 'I went to bed and wept for three weeks—what is the matter

with me?' I had to tell her, 'Only a slight matter. You will be well
again when you learn to listen to the ticking of the clock.' "

To a lawyer who came saying he had undertaken more financial reorgani-
zations than there was time for and his nerves were shot the doctor
talked long about worry, gave the lawyer a box and 100 black beans:
"Each morning you drop a bean in the box and say, 'Worry is in the
bean and the bean is in the box.' "

In the hoom hoom of the big steamboat docking the doctor said, "Silence
is the great gratitude when bad music ends."

79

IN paper sacks the customers carry away millions of tons of goods daily
except Sunday.

And having used what they carry away in paper sacks they go back daily
except Sunday for more millions of tons of useable goods transferred
in paper sacks.

And the trade experts look on and call it consumption while the people
carrying the paper sacks have a way of alleging, "We have to eat,
don't we?"

And once there was a man who considered how he might make
a paper sack song and invent a paper sack dance. In the days
of his youth he had worked in the pulp. Joined with other
men and machines he had taken logs and cooked a mash
and dried and flattened it out and kept flattening it till it
was thin as paper and it was paper. And his sister in another
mill had watched a machine and tended it; daily except Sun-
day it spat forth its stint of millions of paper sacks.

And the brother and sister say to each other now, "We have made so many
millions of paper sacks we know exactly the feelings and ideas of any
one paper sack. One paper sack thinks just what another paper sack
thinks. And now when our jobs are gone because bigger and better
machines do what we used to do my sister and I say to each other:
Hello, old paper sack. And we talk about how we are a couple of
paper sacks thrown away and no longer wanted because there is no
answer to the question: Why are paper sacks so cheap?

"And we talk on and we decide we are something more than
paper sacks. We have a right to live and a right to work and
we have a right to say life ought to be good and life is more
than paper sacks. And we will go anywhere and listen to any

organizers and agitators who come to us saying: We speak
to you as people and not as paper sacks."

In Gloversville, New York, a woman daylong made mittens and the faster
she made the mittens the more the wages coming in for her and her
children.

And her hands became like mittens she said,
And in the winter when she looked out one night
Where the moon lighted a couple of evergreen trees:
"My God! I look at evergreens in the moonlight
and what are they? A pair of mittens.
And what am I myself? Just a mitten.
Only one more mitten, that's all.
My God! if I live a little longer in that mitten factory the whole world
will be just a lot of mittens to me
And at last I will be buried in a mitten and on my grave they will put up
a mitten as a sign one more mitten is gone."
This was why she listened to the organizer of the glove and mitten work-
ers' union; maybe the union could do something.
She would fight in the union ranks and see if somehow they could save
her from seeing two evergreens at night in the moon as just another
pair of mitts.

8 0

DEEP in the dusty chattels of the tombs,
Laden with luggage handed them
By departing ghosts saying, "It's yours, all yours,"
They give their ghost imprint to the time they live in.
They are to the people what they are to the sea,
To the harvest moon, to the living grassroots,
To the tides that wash them away babbling to some caretaker, "What
time is it?   where are we?"

And time, since you ask, time is the story-teller you can't shut up, he goes
on.
The king, like many a king, was a little coocoo, and hung up a challenge.
Whoever would tell him a story so long that he couldn't stand any
more of it would marry his princess daughter. Otherwise the story-
teller's neck would be blemished with a gleaming ax-blade. The story-
teller began on how grain elevators bulging with corn ran for miles
while the locusts spread out many more miles and there was only

one point of entry and egress for the crawling hordes of slithering
locusts, only one place for a locust to go in and out. And one locust
went in and brought out a grain of corn and another locust went in
and brought out another grain of corn. And another locust went in
and brought out another grain of corn. And another locust went in
and brought out another grain of corn. And so on and so on till the
king saw what he had let himself in for and speaking in the royal tone
customary to kings he told the story-teller, "You win, the girl is yours."
And this was back in the old days when kings were kings and wore
crowns and had crown jewels.

Time? The story-teller you can't shut up, he goes on.

> "Time is blind; man stupid."
> Thus one of the cynics.
> "Time is relentless; man shrewd."
> Thus one of the hopefuls.
>> Time passes; man laughs at it.
>> The sun-dial was one laugh.
>> The wrist-watch is another.
>> "Time? I can't stop it but I
>> can measure it."

8 1

CHICAGO seems all fox and swine,
Dreams interfused with smut, dung, hunger.
Yet Chicago is not all belly and mouth and
    overwrought sex and lies and greed
    and snobs.
Chicago has something over and beyond.
Sometime the seeds and cross-fertilizations
    now moving in Chicago may inaugurate
    a crossroads of great gladness.
The same goes for Omaha and points west,
    for Buffalo and points east.

Out of the shopping crowds at State and Madison, hot with bundles and
    bargains,
A humpty-dumpty runt of a man dived at high noon into a forest of rub-
    bernecks craning at a skywriting plane telling you what cigarette to
    smoke next, what cigarette to buy,

And he came up to say there was too much quick thinking and he would
　　offer a little slow thinking:

"From the museum mummies I came to these ghosts swirling around State
　　and Madison, Forty-second and Fifth Avenue, and about all I learned
　　was this, you can write it on a thumbnail:

"There is a dead past and a blank future and the same humanity is in
　　each and it's all ham and eggs, dog eat dog, the toughest guts have
　　their way, and they kill and kill to see who'll get the most marbles,
　　the most cocoanuts, the most little embossed pieces of paper."

And then he went on, wiping his chin with four fingers and a thumb,
　　screwing his eyes to a thin slit, and correcting himself:

"I take that back. Write it off as a loss. If the big arch of the sky were
　　paper and the violet depths of the sea were ink, I could never live
　　long enough to write the dreams of man and the dynamic drive of
　　those dreams.

"Who and what is man? He is Atlas and Thor and Yankee Doodle, an
　　eagle, a lion, a rooster, a bear that walks like a man, an elephant, a
　　moon-face, David and Goliath, Paul Bunyan and the Flying Dutch-
　　man, Shakespeare, Lincoln and Christ, the Equator and the Arctic
　　Poles, holding in one hand the Bank of England and the Roman
　　Catholic Church, in the other the Red Army and the Standard Oil
　　Company, holding in easy reach the dogs of war and the doves of
　　peace, the tigers of wrath and the horses of instruction.

"Let me sell you my dreams. Take these dreams for whatever you want to
　　pay me. You shall never be tired till the sea is tired. You shall never
　　go weary till the land and the wind go weary. You will be hard as nails,
　　soft as blue fog.

"Man is born with rainbows in his heart and you'll never read him unless
　　you consider rainbows. He is a trouble shooter with big promises. He
　　trades the Oklahoma roan mustang for a tub in the sky with wings
　　falling falling in Alaska. Hard as a rock his head is an egg and pon-
　　ders ponders. He is a phantasmagoria of crimson dawns and what it
　　takes to build his dreams."

So the finish. He ceased from wiping his chin with four fingers and a
　　thumb, ceased from screwing his eyes to a thin slit, ceased correcting
　　himself.

Then he vanished. In a wreath of blue smoke from a panatella seegar he
　　was gone, a scholar, a clown, and a dreambook seller who had said
　　enough for one day.

Turning a corner he talked to himself about the dust of the knuckles of

his great-grandfathers, how they once were hard as nails and could
pick a vest-button with a bullet, and how his own little knuckles
sometime would shiver into fine dust and how he wanted snowdrifts
piled over him and the inscription: HERE NO ONE LIES BURIED.

8 2

I PLEDGE my allegiance,
say the munitions makers and the international bankers,
I pledge my allegiance to this flag, that flag,
any flag at all, of any country anywhere
paying its bills and meeting interest on loans,
one and indivisible,
coming through with cash in payment as stipulated
with liberty and justice for all,
say the munitions makers and the international bankers.

> "Your million dollars, if you will pardon me,"
> said a polite shrimp, "came one of three
> ways. First, if you will pardon me, you
> took it somehow as profits within the law
> belonging to you, unless, second, you have
> it as a gift or bequest handed to you with-
> out your working for it, or unless, if you
> will pardon me, third and last, you took
> it, outside the law and yet beyond the
> reach of the law, as belonging to you
> rather than whoever had it before you
> got it from them."

What good is rain on a hard and sour soil?
Why put a driller and seeder
where the top soil is blown away?
Why put your headlights on in bright noon?
Why do favors where you know you get no thanks?

Some have their finger-nails pinked
a regular shade, according to custom.
Some, wearing pearls, have their finger-nails
tinted, enameled and polished

to match the precise color of their pearls.
Those with oyster pearls shade to a crystal,
others are touched with desert gray, sea green.
And cosmetics volume last year was over a billion.

8 3

WHO can make a poem of the depths of weariness
bringing meaning to those never in the depths?
Those who order what they please
when they choose to have it—
can they understand the many down under
who come home to their wives and children at night
and night after night as yet too brave and unbroken
to say, "I ache all over"?
How can a poem deal with production cost
and leave out definite misery paying
a permanent price in shattered health and early old age?
When will the efficiency engineers and the poets
get together on a program?
Will that be a cold day? will that be a special hour?
Will somebody be coocoo then?
And if so, who?
And what does the Christian Bible say?
And the Mohammedan Koran and Confucius and the Shintoists
and the Encyclicals of the Popes?
Will somebody be coocoo then?
And if so, who??

8 4

IN the chain store or the independent it is the people meeting the people:
"Would you like to be waited on? Could I wait on you? Could I be
of assistance? Is there something you would like? Is there something
for you? Could I help you? Anything I can help you to? What will
yours be? What can I get for you? What would you like? Is there
something?"

The rodeo hoss wrangler, the airplane stunter,
the living cannonball shot from a gun,
the animal tamer amid paws and fangs—

they use up their luck ahead of time,
they bet their necks and earn a living:
they play fair with their seen galleries
the same as lone hunters and explorers
aim to please unseen acres of fine faces,
aim to tell about it later maybe
if a public cares to hear.

   In this corner the spotlighted challenger,
   in this corner the world's heavyweight champ
   along with camera boys grinding,
   lads at the mikes giving round by round,
   they aim to please,
   to put it over big
   for the fish on the spot,
   for the many more fish beyond,
   one sports writer quizzing another,
   "How many of the fish are here?
   "What's your guess?"

The world series pitcher pets his arm,
prays he won't get a glass arm:
he too strives to please:
he would like to put smoke on the ball
and throw a hitless game:
when the big-boy home-run hitter
has an off day and fans the air,
at the umpire's cry "three strikes"
he may hear from the bleachers,
"Take the big bum out."

One movie star arches her eyebrows
and refers to "my public."
One soda-jerker arches his eyebrows,
curves malt-milk from shaker to glass
and speaks of "my public."
The dance marathon winning couple
bow sleepy thanks to their public.
The fire department ladder truck driver
sees his public at a standstill
on the sidewalk curbs.

The going-going-gone jewelry auctioneer
plays to another public.
And at every street intersection
these publics intersect.

Ringmasters in top hats, clowns on mules,
       circus riders in spangles,
little ladies doing somersaults on horses,
       acrobat families in pink tights
       sliding their own human toboggans—
the peanut, popcorn, and red lemonade sellers
they feel their crowds and read crowd moods.

"I know why I lost my crowd tonight,"
 said a flame of an actor.
"I never can do anything with them
 unless I love them."

The breezes of surface change blow lightly.
The people take what comes, hold on, let go.
       The high wheel bicycle was a whiz.
       Eskimo pie raked in a lot of jack.
       The tom thumb golf courses had a run.
       Yo yo charmed till yo yo checked out.
       The tree sitters climbed up, came down.
Sideburns, galways, handlebar mustaches, full beards,
they flitted away on winds whistling,
       "Where are the snows of yesteryear?"
meaning snow and stage-snow, the phony and the real
       gone to the second-hand bins, the rummage sales,
       the Salvation Army wagons.

       Stronger winds blow slow.
       Trial balloons are sent up.
       The public says yes, says no.
       The whim of the public rides.
       A hoarse cry carves events.

The platoon of police in uniform,
the drum-major with his baton
and a gold ball high in the air,

The silver cornet band, the fife-and-drum corps,
the Knights of Pythias in plume and gilt braid,
the speakers of the day with mounted escorts,
the fire department, the Odd Fellows, the Woodmen,
the civilian cohorts following the local militia,
American Legion, Veterans of Foreign Wars,
    they march between sidewalks
    heavy with a human heave,
    heavy with vox populi.

    "Me too, count me in.
    I want to belong.
    I do what's regular.
    I'll sign up.
    A trial package can't hurt me.
    Here's my name and dues.
    I'll try anything once."
This is the tune of today's razzle-dazzle.
Tomorrow the tune is never quite the same.
Tomorrow's children have it *their* own way.

    When the yes-men no longer yes
    or the no-men shift their no
    anything is in the cards.

Ask the public relations counsel.
He is a shortstop and a scavenger
smooth as a big league umpire
cool as a veteran horse race jockey
cool as a cube of cucumber on ice.
He will tell you there is a public
and this public has many relations
and you can't have too much counsel
when you're trying to handle it.
    Our ghost writers will ghost for you:
    they write it, you hand it out
    or you speak the speech written for you
    and nobody knows but the ghost
    and the ghost is paid
    for helping you with your public.

The cheer leader struts his stuff,
wigwags the swaying grand stand,
throws himself into alphabetical shapes
trying to orchestrate his crowd:
the fads and fashions innovators,
the halitosis and body odor frighteners,
the skin and complexion fixers,
the cigarette ads lying about relative values,
the nazi imitators, the fascisti imitators,
the ku klux klan and the konklave's wizard,
the makers of regalia, insignia, masks,
hoods, hats, nightshirts, skull-and-crossbones,
the spellbinder calling on all true patriots,
the soapboxer pleading for the proletariat,
the out-of-works marching marching
with demands and banners, "why? why?"
the strike leader telling why the men walked out,
the million-dollar-national-sales-campaign director,
the headache copy writer groping for one new idea,
the drive organizers planning their hoorah,
the neighborhood captains of tens and twenties,
the best-seller authors, the by-line correspondents,
the President at the White House microphone,
the Senators, Congressmen, spokesmen, at microphones—
　　Each and all have a target.
　　Each one aims for the ping ping
　　the bling bling of a sharpshooter.
　　　　Here is a moving colossal show,
a vast dazzling aggregation of stars and hams
selling things, selling ideas, selling faiths,
selling air, slogans, passions, selling history.
　　　　The target is who and what?
　　　　　　The people, yes—
　　sold and sold again
　　for losses and regrets,
　　for gains, for slow advances,
　　for a dignity of deepening roots.

8 5

ONE memorial stone reads:
"We, near whose bones you stand, were Iroquois.
The wide land which is now yours, was ours.
Friendly hands have given us back enough for a tomb."

      Breeds run out
      and shining names
      no longer shine.
Tribes, clans, nations, have their hour,
Hang up their records and leave.
Yet who could chisel on a gravestone:
        "Here lies John Doe," or,
"Here rest the mortal remains of Richard Roe"
And then step back and read the legend and say,
"Can this be so when I myself am John Doe,
        when I myself am Richard Roe"?

pack up your bundle now and go
be a seeker among voices and faces
on main street   in a bus station   at a union depot
this generation of eaters sleepers lovers toilers
flowing out of the last one now buried
flowing into the next one now unborn
short of cash and wondering where to?   what next?
jobs bosses paydays want-ads groceries soap
board and clothes and a corner to sleep in
just enough to get by
when its lamplighting time in the valley
where is my wandering boy tonight
in the beautiful isle of somewhere
the latest extra and another ax murder
he's forgotten by the girl he can't forget
she lives in a mansion of aching hearts
tickets?   where to?   round trip or one way?
room rent coffee and doughnuts   maybe a movie
suit-cases   packsacks   bandanas
names saved and kept careful

you mustn't lose the address
and what'll be your telephone number?
give me something to remember you by
be my easy rider
kiss me once before you go a long one
flash eyes   testaments in a rush
underhums of plain love with rye bread sandwiches
and grief and laughter: where to?   what next?

86

THE people, yes, the people,
Until the people are taken care of one way or another,
Until the people are solved somehow for the day and hour,
Until then one hears "Yes but the people what about the people?"
Sometimes as though the people is a child to be pleased or fed
Or again a hoodlum you have to be tough with
And seldom as though the people is a caldron and a reservoir
Of the human reserves that shape history,
The river of welcome wherein the broken First Families fade,
The great pool wherein wornout breeds and clans drop for restorative
    silence.

Fire, chaos, shadows,
Events trickling from a thin line of flame
On into cries and combustions never expected·
The people have the element of surprise.
    Where are the kings today?
What has become of their solid and fastened thrones?
Who are the temporary puppets holding sway while anything, "God
    only knows what," waits around a corner, sits in the shadows and
        holds an ax, waiting for the appointed hour?

    "The czar has eight million men with guns and bayonets.
    Nothing can happen to the czar.
    The czar is the voice of God and shall live forever.
    Turn and look at the forest of steel and cannon
    Where the czar is guarded by eight million soldiers.
    Nothing can happen to the czar."
They said that for years and in the summer of 1914

In the Year of Our Lord Nineteen Hundred and Fourteen
As a portent and an assurance they said with owl faces:
     "Nothing can happen to the czar."
Yet the czar and his bodyguard of eight million vanished
And the czar stood in a cellar before a little firing squad
And the command of fire was given
And the czar stepped into regions of mist and ice
The czar travelled into an ethereal uncharted siberia
While two kaisers also vanished from thrones
Ancient and established in blood and iron—
Two kaisers backed by ten million bayonets
Had their crowns in a gutter, their palaces mobbed.
     In fire, chaos, shadows,
In hurricanes beyond foretelling of probabilities,
In the shove and whirl of unforeseen combustions
     The people, yes, the people,
Move eternally in the elements of surprise,
Changing from hammer to bayonet and back to hammer,
The hallelujah chorus forever shifting its star soloists.

87

THE people learn, unlearn, learn,
a builder, a wrecker, a builder again,
a juggler of shifting puppets.
          In so few eyeblinks
          In transition lightning streaks,
the people project midgets into giants,
the people shrink titans into dwarfs.

          Faiths blow on the winds
          and become shibboleths
          and deep growths
          with men ready to die
for a living word on the tongue,
for a light alive in the bones,
for dreams fluttering in the wrists.

For liberty and authority they die
though one is fire and the other water

and the balances of freedom and discipline
are a moving target with changing decoys.

Revolt and terror pay a price.
Order and law have a cost.
What is this double use of fire and water?
Where are the rulers who know this riddle?
On the fingers of one hand you can number them.
How often has a governor of the people first
    learned to govern himself?

The free man willing to pay and struggle and die
    for the freedom for himself and others
Knowing how far to subject himself to discipline
    and obedience for the sake of an ordered so-
    ciety free from tyrants, exploiters and
    legalized frauds—
This free man is a rare bird and when you meet
    him take a good look at him and try
    to figure him out because
Some day when the United States of the Earth
    gets going and runs smooth and pretty there
    will be more of him than we have now.

8 8

THE response of wild birds
to a home on the way,
a stopping place of rest,
this and the wish of a child
to eat the moon
as a golden ginger cookie—
this is in the songs of the people.

The clods of the earth hold place
close to the whir of yellow hummingbird wings
and they divide into those hard of hearing
and those whose ears pick off
a smooth hush with a little wind whimper across it
and then again only the smooth hush.

What are these dialects deep under the bones
whereby the people of ages and races far apart
reach out and say the same clay is in all,
bringing out men whose eyes
search the earth and see no aliens anywhere,
pronouncing across the barriers the peculiar word:
    "Brother"?

Washing his shirt in a jungle near Omaha,
warming his java under a C.B.&Q. bridge,
a hobo mumbled to himself a mumbling poem
and said it was an outline of history
and you could take it or leave it,
you could ride the rods or hunt an empty
and he would mumble:
    "A hammering, a neverending hammering goes on.
    Suns and moons by platoons batter down
    the shovels and the clamps
    of other suns and moons.
    "By platoons always by platoons under a hammering,
    the cries of the tongs go kling klong
    to the bong bong of the hammers."

The bulls took him in.
The bulls gathered him.
In the lockup he thought it over.
In the cooler he was not so hot,
They said, and further they said,
He was nuts, he was dopey from white mule.
    Yet he kept on with his mumbling
    of the shovels and the clamps,
    of the tongs going kling klong
    and the bong bong of the hammers,
    of history and its awful anvils.

    "Listen," he cried,
"Kling klong go the mighty hammers,
kling klong on a mighty anvil,
steel on steel they clash and weld,
how long can you last? how long?

goes the clamor of the hammer and the anvil,
how long? goes the steel kling klong:
the gunmetal blue gives it and takes it:
in the fire and the pounding:
the hard old answer goes:
    let the works go on:
I will last a long time: yet a long time."

    A fly-by-night house, a shanty,
a ramshackle hut of tarpaper, tin cans,
body by fisher, frames from flivvers,
a shelter from rain and wind,
the home of a homeseeker having an alibi,
why did two hungers move across his face?
    One: when do we eat?
    The other: What is worth looking at?
        what is worth listening to?
        why do we live?
        when is a homeseeker
          just one more trespasser?
        and what is worth dying for?

8 9

MARSHALL FIELD THE FIRST was spick and span while alive
and wishing to be well kept and properly groomed
in the long afterward
he stipulated in a clause of his will
a fund of $25,000 be set aside and its income be devoted
to the upkeep of his tomb.
    The country editor of Stoughton, Wisconsin,
    was not so careful, less spick and span.
He left orders to the typesetters and they obeyed him.
    His obituary read: "Charlie Cross is dead."
    And that was all.
John Eastman died leaving the Chicago Journal to four men,
to four old friends who knew how to get out the paper.
And to make sure the obsequies would be correct and decent
    he instructed in his last will and testament:
    "Let no words of praise be spoken at my funeral."

What about that Chinese poet
traveling on a cart
with a jug of wine,
a shovel and a grave-digger?
    Each morning as they started
    he told the grave-digger:
    "Bury me when I am dead—
        anywhere, anytime."
He was afraid of a fancy funeral.
    What did he have?
He would be covered down like any coolie
    "anywhere, anytime," no music, no flowers.

What about that radio operator in the North Atlantic
on a stormlashed sinking Scandinavian ship
laughing the wireless message:
"God pity the poor sailors on a night like this"
adding word they were heading for Davy Jones' locker
and adding further:
"This is no night to be out without an umbrella!"
    What about him?
    And what did he have?
He went to a sea-tomb laughing an epitaph:
    "This is no night to be out without an umbrella."

Who was that professor at the University of Wisconsin working out a
    butter-fat milk tester
Good for a million dollars if he wanted a patent with sales and royalties
And he whistled softly and in dulcet tone: What in God's name do I
    want with a million dollars?
Whistling as though instead of his owning the million it would own him.

    Who was that South Dakota Norwegian who
        went to Siberia and brought back
    Wheat grains pushing the North American wheat
        area hundreds of miles northward?
    He could have had a million dollars and took
        instead a million thanks.

    Why did the two high wizards of applied
        electrodynamics say

All they wanted was board and clothes and time
    to think things over?
Why did they go along so careless about dollars,
    so forgetful about millions,
Letting others organize and gather the shekels
    and progress from boom to crash to boom
    to crash?
Why is the Schenectady hunchback dwarf one
    of the saints in shirtsleeves?
And why did the deaf mechanic in Orange, New
    Jersey, forget to eat unless his wife called
    him,
And why did he die saying: What is electricity?
    we don't know. What is heat? we don't know.
    We are beginners. "Look at the moon—it
    winks at the ignorance of the world."

What of the Wright boys in Dayton? Just around the corner they had
    a shop and did a bicycle business—and they wanted to fly for the
    sake of flying.
They were Man the Seeker, Man on a Quest. Money was their last
    thought, their final absent-minded idea.
They threw out a lot of old mistaken measurements and figured new ones
    that stood up when they took off and held the air and steered a
    course. They proved "the faster you go the less power you need."
One of them died and was laid away under blossoms dropped from zoom-
    ing planes. The other lived on to meditate: what is *attraction?* when
    will we learn *why* things go when they go?   what and where is the
    power?

Why is raggedy Johnny Appleseed half-man half-myth? From old cider
    mills he filled his sacks with apple-seeds and out of his plantings came
    orchards in Ohio and Indiana. "God ordained me a sower to sow that
    others might reap." Why will they remember the earthly shadow of
    Johnny with bronze figures tomorrow in Ohio and Indiana?

Was it true that Van Gogh cut off
one of his ears
and gave it to a daughter
of the streets,
to one who had pleasured him?

And if he did what did he mean by it?
And who could guess what Van Gogh
had in mind if anything in particular?
    In and out by thousands they went
    to see the Van Gogh exhibit
    of paintings touring America,
    in and out by thousands
    finding the color and line
    of a plain strange personality,
    something dear and rich
    out of the umber of the earth.
  Somewhere in what he flung from his brush
    was a missing ear
    and why it might be missed
    and a blunt gesture,
    "What of it?"

Why did the St. Louis Mirror editor name as his favorite Shakespeare
line: "I myself am but indifferent honest"? and how did he mean it
when in an owl-car dawn, ending a long night of talk, he blurted to
a poet, "God damn it, I tell you there are no bad people"?

Who was the St. Louis mathematician who figured it cost an average of
$37,000 to kill each soldier killed in the World War?
He figured too on a way of offering, in case of war, $1,000, one grand, to
every deserting soldier.
Each army, the idea ran, would buy off the other before the war could
get started.

Who was that Pittsburgh Scotchman terrorized by having a quarter bil-
lion dollars?
Why did he give it away before he died as though he could never take it
away with him?
Who was the Chicago Jew who threw millions of dollars into Negro
schools of the South?
Why did he once tell another Jew, "I'm ashamed to have so much
money"?

"There are no pockets in the shroud" may be carried farther:
"The dead hold in their clenched hands only that which they have given
away."

Who was that Roman: "I am a man and nothing on legs and human is
    a stranger to me"?
He could have met the first Negro who sang: "When you see me laugh-
    ing I'm laughing to keep from crying."

Did he give them a high and roaring laughter when he had his throne
    moved out into the sea,
When he sat in his sea-set throne and commanded the tide: "Go back!
    go back! it is I, King Knute who tell you so and I am putting you to
    this test because a circle of my advisers have told me over and again
    that I am beyond other plain people, I am made of no common clay
    and what I say goes and even the ocean will obey me and do what
    I say and therefore I give you the order to Go back! go back! and
    don't dare bring your stink of seawrack and salt water even to the foot-
    stool of this royal throne of mine"?
Did he give them a high and roaring laughter as the tide slowly and in-
    exorably rose over his footstool, to his knees, to his navel, to his neck,
When he rose, plunged and swam ashore and told them to let the throne
    be washed out to join the flotsam and jetsam of the immemorial sea?

Who was the young Nicodemus in Chicago so early in the twentieth cen-
    tury falling heir to a million dollars and writing a pamphlet of public
    inquiry titled The Confessions of a Drone and having one luminous
    and quivering question to ask:
Why was this money wished on me merely because I was born where I
    couldn't help being born so that I don't have to work while a lot of
    people work for me and I can follow the races, yacht, play horse polo,
    chase if I so choose any little international chippie that takes my eye,
    eat nightingale tongues, buy sea islands or herds of elephants or
    trained fleas, or go to Zanzibar, to Timbuctoo, to the mountains of
    the moon, and never work an hour or a day and when I come back
    I find a lot of people working for me because I was born where I
    couldn't help being born?

9 0

THE big fish eat the little fish,
    the little fish eat shrimps
    and the shrimps eat mud.
You don't know enough to come in when it rains.
You don't know beans when the bag is open.

You don't know enough to pound sand in a rat hole.
    All I know is what I hear.
    All I know is what I read in the papers.
    All I know you can put in a thimble.
    All I know I keep forgetting.

    We have to eat, don't we?
    You can't eat promises, can you?
    You can't eat the Constitution, can you?
I can eat crow but I don't hanker after it.
    Don't quarrel with your bread and butter.
    Some curse the hand that feeds them.
Many kiss the hands they wish to see cut off.
    You can't rob a naked man of his clothes.
He that makes himself an ass, men will ride him.
Stand like a good mule and you're soon harnessed.

    Be not rash with thy mouth.
    Praise no man before his death,
When pups bark old dogs go along doing whatever
    it was they were doing.
He who blackens others does not whiten himself.
The camel has his plans, the camel driver his plans.
The horse thinks one thing, he who saddles him another.
    Ask me no questions and I tell you no lies.
    The best witness is a written paper.
    Liars should have good memories.
    Some liars get monotonous.
    Hearsay is half lies.
    To say nothing is to say yes.
    Hold your tongue one second and
    a bundle of trouble is held off.
    Be careful what you say or
    you go out of the door
    and meet yourself coming in.
Hunger and cold deliver a man to his enemy.
    Hunger says to hell with the law.
    The empty belly instructs the tongue.
    Want changes men into wild animals.
Unless you say eat the hungry belly can't
    hear you.

91

WHO were those editors picking the most
detestable word in the English language
and deciding the one word just a little
worse than any other you can think of
is "Exclusive"?

The doorbells were many and the approaches screened and the corners
hushed in the care of frozen-faced butlers and footmen in livery,
London trained, chauffeurs, cooks, maids, twenty-two when counted,
for personal service in the Lake Shore Drive apartments overlooking
one blue of water meeting another blue of skyline.

And one young man yawned over his real estate and securities, his Chi-
cago and Manhattan skyscrapers, his silk mills in France, his woolen
mills in Scotland, his cotton mills north and south in the States,
yawned over the caretakers and trustees sober and dependable in cus-
tody of what had grown since he was a baby to whom accrued from
a dying father an estate beyond one hundred millions, one blue of
water meeting another blue of skyline then as now. Across the dust
and roar of Halsted Street he rode one afternoon into the seething
jungles and slums of the West Side, to yawn and smile, "This is No
Man's Land to me," never to go back, to sense it as a dull and alien
rabble, a polyglot of panhandlers mooching pig-stickers, structural
ironworkers after a day with rivets and bolts lifting schooners of beer
to laugh, "Here every man is as good as the next one and for the
matter of that a little better."

To a Long Island Sound country mansion he fled and in a scarlet English
hunting coat shot pheasants by the hundreds with retainers loading
the guns for him and his guests; to Buckingham Palace he flitted, to
the African gold coast, to the Riviera, to Biarritz, to nowhere among
multiplied nothings, from wife to wife and tweedledum to tweedledee,
in car, yacht and plane fleeing from No Man's Land, with a personal
service staff of twenty-two when counted, and always from the Lake
Shore Drive one blue of water meeting another blue of skyline.

And who are these others?

Why, they are the three tailors of Tooley Street, signing themselves, "We,
the people,"

Having an audacity easier to look at than three others, namely, one prime
   minister, one banker, one munitions maker, in the name of the people
   letting loose a war.
These others, you may have read, are "the great unwashed," "the hoi
   polloi," they are indicated with gestures:
"The rabble," "the peepul," "the mob with its herd instinct in its wild
   stampede," "the irresponsible ragtag and bobtail"—
Can they also be the multitude fed by a miracle on loaves and fishes, les
   misérables in a pit, in a policed abyss of want?
Was it this same miscellany heard the Sermon on the Mount, the Gettys-
   burg Speech, the Armistice Day news when confetti dotted the
   window-sills and white paper blew in snowdrifts on the city streets?
And in the Gettysburg speech was it written, "of the peepul, by the
   peepul, and for the peepul"?

When they gather the voices and prints from above what most often do
   they hear and read?
They are told to go north and south at once, for liberty, to go east and
   west at once, for liberty.
The advice is pounded in their ears, "Go up, go down, stand where you
   are, for liberty."
In one ear comes the clamor, "You are damned if you do," in the other
   ear, "You are damned if you don't."
And when liberty is all washed up the dictators say:
   "You are the greatest people on earth and we shall shoot only as
      many of you as necessary."

      Out of this mass are shaped
   Armies, navies, work gangs, wrecking crews.
      Here are the roars to shake walls
      and set roofs shuddering,
   Hecklers ready with hoots, howls, boos, meeouw,
   Bronx cheers, the razzberry, the bum's rush,
   Straw hats by thousands thrown from the bleachers,
   Pop bottles by hundreds aimed at an umpire,
   The units of the bargain sale crush, the subway jam,
   The office building emptying its rush hour stream,
   The millions at radio sets for an earful,
   The millions turning newspaper pages for an eyeful:
      This is the source and the headwater

Of tomorrow's Niagara of action, monotony, action,
    rapids, plungers, whirlpool and mist
    of the people and by the people,
    a long street and a vast field of faces,
    faces across an immeasurable mural,
    faces shifting on an incalculable panel,
    touched and dented with line and contrast,
    potatoes winking at cherry blossoms,
    roses here and ashes of roses there,
    thornapple branches hung with redhaws,
    hickory side by side with moss violets,
    the mangelwurzer elbowing the orchid.

    Here is a huggermugger becoming
    a cloud of witnesses, a juggernaut,
the Mississippi asking the peaks of the Rockies,
    "How goes it?"
a hallelujah chorus forever changing its star soloists,
    taking pyramid, pagoda and skyscraper in its stride,
    having survival elements and gifts in perpetuity,
    requiring neither funeral march, memorial nor epitaph.
    Why should the continuing generations
who replenish themselves in the everliving earth
need any tall symbol set up to be gazed at
as a sign they are gone, past, through,
when they are here yet,
so massively and chorally here yet
in a multitudinous trampling
of shoes and wheels, hands and tools, having heard:
    "The voice of the people is the voice of God,"
having heard, "Be ye comforted for your dreams shall come true on earth
    by your own works,"
having heard, "Ye shall know the truth and the truth shall make you
    free."

    The wheel turns.
    The wheel comes to a standstill.
    The wheel waits.
    The wheel turns.

"Something began me
and it had no beginning:
something will end me
and it has no end."

The people is a long shadow
trembling around the earth,
stepping out of fog gray into smoke red
and back from smoke red into fog gray
and lost on parallels and meridians
learning by shock and wrangling,
by heartbreak so often and loneliness so raw
the laugh comes at least half true,
"My heart was made to be broken."

"Man will never write,"
they said before the alphabet came
and man at last began to write.
"Man will never fly,"
they said before the planes and blimps
zoomed and purred in arcs
winding their circles around the globe.

"Man will never make the United States of Europe
nor later yet the United States of the World,
"No, you are going too far when you talk about one
world flag for the great Family of Nations,"
they say that now.

And man the stumbler and finder, goes on,
man the dreamer of deep dreams,
man the shaper and maker,
man the answerer.
The first wheel maker saw a wheel, carried
in his head a wheel, and one day found his
hands shaping a wheel, the first wheel.
The first wagon makers saw a wagon, joined
their hands and out of air, out of what
had lived in their minds, made the first
wagon.
One by one man alone and man joined

has made things with his hands
beginning in the fog wisp of a dim imagining
resulting in a tool, a plan, a working model,
    bones joined to breath being alive
in wheels within wheels, ignition, power,
transmission, reciprocals, beyond man alone,
alive only with man joined.
                Where to? what next?

Man the toolmaker, tooluser,
son of the burning quests
fixed with roaming forearms,
hands attached to the forearms,
fingers put on those hands,
a thumb to face any finger—
hands cunning with knives, leather, wood,
    hands for twisting, weaving, shaping—
Man the flint grinder, iron and bronze welder,
    smoothing mud into hut walls,
    smoothing reinforced concrete into
    bridges, breakwaters, office buildings—
two hands projected into vast claws, giant hammers,
    into diggers, haulers, lifters.
The clamps of the big steam shovel? man's two hands:
the motor hurling man into high air? man's two hands:
    the screws of his skulled head
    joining the screws of his hands,
pink convolutions transmitting to white knuckles
    waves, signals, buttons, sparks—
    man with hands for loving and strangling,
    man with the open palm of living handshakes,
man with the closed nails of the fist of combat—
    these hands of man—where to? what next?

9 2

THE breathing of the earth
may be heard along with
the music of the sea
in their joined belongings.

Consider the ears of a donkey
and the varied languages entering them.
Study the deep-sea squid
and see how he does only what he has to,
how the wild ducks of autumn
come flying in a shifting overhead scroll,
how rats earn a living and survive
and pass on their tough germ plasms
to children who can live where others die.
Mink are spotlessly clean for special reasons.
The face of a goat has profound contemplations.
Only a fish can do the autobiography of a fish.

93

AN aster, a farewell-summer flower, stays long in the last fall weeks,
Lingers in fence corners where others have shivered and departed.
The whites have mentioned it as the last-rose-of-summer, the red man
    saying, "It-brings-the-frost."
Late in the morning and only when sun-warmed does the flower-of-an-
    hour, the good-night-at-noon, open a while and then close its blossoms.
Even in the noon sun the scarlet pimpernel may shut its petals, as a storm
    sign, earning its ancient name of wink-a-peep and sometimes called
    the poor-man's-weather-glass.
John-go-to-bed-at-noon is the goat's beard plant shutting itself at twelve
    o'clock and showing again only when the next day's sun is out.
One looped vine of the hop-growers is a kiss-me-quick and more than one
    red flower blooming in rock corners is a love-lies-bleeding or a look-
    up-and-kiss-me.

The saskatoon is a shadblow looming white in the spring weeks when the
    shad are up the rivers and spawning,
And hanging its branches with the June berry, the Indian cherry, it is still
    the saskatoon fed by the melted snows of chinooks.

The toadflax, the ox-eye daisy, the pussy willow, rabbit bells, buffalo
    clover, swamp candles and wafer ash,
These with the windrose and the rockrose, lady slippers, loose-strife, thorn-
    apples, dragon's blood, old man's flannel,
And the horse gentian, dog laurel, cat-tails, snakeroot, spiderwort, pig

weed, sow thistle, skunk cabbage, goose grass, moonseed, poison
    hemlock,
These with the names on names between horse radish and the autumn-
    flowering orchid of a lavish harvest moon—
These are a few of the names clocked and pronounced by the people in
    the moving of the earth from season to season.

The red and white men traded plants and words back and forth.
The Shawnee haw and the Choctaw root, the paw paw, the potato, the
    cohosh and your choice of the yellow puccoon or white,
A cork elm or a western buckthorn or a burning bush, each a wahoo and
    all of the wahoo family
These from the tongues of name givers, from a restless name changer, the
    people.

9 4

THE sea only knows the bottom of the ship.
One grain of wheat holds all the stars.
The bosoms of the wise are the tombs of secrets.
When you must, walk as if on eggshells.
It looks good but is it foolproof?
Only a poor fisherman curses the river he fishes in.
I can read your writing but I can't read your mind.
      Threatened men live long.
      The glad hand became the icy mitt.
Applause is the beginning of abuse.
If born to be hanged you shall never be drowned.
Life without a friend is death without a witness.
      Sleep is the image of death.
Six feet of earth make us all of one size.
The oldest man that ever lived died at last.
The turnip looked big till the pumpkin walked in.
The dime looked different when the dollar arrived.
      Who said you are the superintendent?
      Spit on your hands and go to work.
Three generations from shirtsleeves to shirtsleeves.
We won't see it but our children will.

      Everything is in the books.
      Too many books overload the mind.

Who knows the answers?
Step by step one goes far.
The greatest cunning is to have none at all.
Sow wind and you reap whirlwind.
A hundred years is not much but never is a long while.
A good blacksmith likes a snootful of smoke.
Fire is a good servant and a bad master.
You can fight fire with fire.
The fireborn are at home in fire.

The stars make no noise.
You can't hinder the wind from blowing.
Who could live without hope?

9 5

SAYINGS, sentences, what of them?
Flashes, lullabies, are they worth remembering?
On the babbling tongues of the people have these been kept.
In the basic mulch of human culture are these grown.
Along with myths of rainbow gold where you shovel all you want and
take it away,
Along with hopes of a promised land, a homestead farm, and a stake in
the country,
Along with prayers for a steady job, a chicken in the pot and two cars in
the garage, the life insurance paid, and a home your own.

In sudden flash and in massive chaos
the tunes and cries of the people
rise in the scripts of Bach and Moussorgsky.
The people handle the food you eat, the clothes you wear,
and stick by stick and stone by stone
the houses you live in, roof and walls,
and wheel by wheel, tire by tire,
part by part your assembled car,
and the box car loadings of long and short hauls.

Those who have nothing stand in two pressures.
Either what they once had was taken away
Or they never had more than subsistence.

Long ago an easy category was provided for them:
    "They live from hand to mouth,"
Having the name of horny-handed sons of toil.
From these hands howsoever horny, from these sons,
Pours a living cargo of overwhelming plenty
From land and mill into the world markets.
    Their pay for this is what is handed them.
Or they take no pay at all if the labor market is glutted,
Losing out on pay if the word is: "NO HANDS WANTED
                         next month maybe
                         next year maybe
                         the works start."

96

BIG oil tanks squat next the railroad.
The shanties of the poor wear cinder coats.
The red and blue lights signal.
The control board tells the story.
Lights go on and off on a map.
Each light is a train gone by
Or a train soon heaving in.
      The big chutes grow cold.
      They stack up shadows.
      Their humps hold iron ore.
      This gang works hard.
      Some faces light up to hear:
      "We work today—
      what do you know about that?"

97

SOMEBODY has to make the tubs and pails.
Not yet do the tubs and pails grow on trees
    and all you do is pick 'em.
For tubs and pails we go first to the timber cruisers, to the loggers, hewers,
    sawyers, choppers, peelers, pilers, saw filers, skid greasers, slip tenders,
    teamsters, lumber shovers, tallymen, planers, bandsawmen, circular-
    saw-men, hoopers, matchers, nailers, painters, truckmen, packers,
    haulers,
For the sake of a tub or a pail to you.

And for the sake of a jack-knife in your pocket,
    or a scissors on your table,
The dynamite works get into production and deliver to the miners who
    blast, the mule drivers, engineers and firemen on the dinkies, the
    pumpmen, the rope riders, the sinkers and sorters, the carpenters,
    electricians and repairmen, the foremen and straw bosses,
They get out the ore and send it to the smelters, the converters where by
    the hands and craft of furnace crushers and hot blast handlers, ladlers,
    puddlers, the drag-out man, the hook-up man, the chipper, the span-
    nerman, the shearsman, the squeezer,
There is steel for the molders, the cutlers, buffers, finishers, forgers,
    grinders, polishers, temperers—
This for the sake of a jack-knife to your pocket or a shears on your table.
These are the people, with flaws and failings, with patience, sacrifice, de-
    votion, the people.

The people is a farmer, a tenant and a share-cropper, a plowman, a plow-
    grinder and a choreman, a churner, a chicken-picker and a combine
    driver, a threshing crew and an old settlers' picnic, a creamery co-
    operative, or a line of men on wagons selling tomatoes or sugar-beets
    on contract to a cannery, a refinery,
The people is a tall freight-handler and a tough longshoreman, a greasy
    fireman and a gambling oil-well shooter with a driller and tooler
    ready, a groping miner going underground with a headlamp, an engi-
    neer and a fireman with an eye for semaphores, a seaman, deckhand,
    pilot at the wheel in fog and stars.
The people? A weaver of steel-and-concrete floors and walls fifty floors up,
    a blueprint designer, an expert calculator and accountant, a carpenter
    with an eye for joists and elbows, a bricklayer with an ear for the pling
    of a trowel, a pile-driver crew pounding down the pier-posts.
The people? Harness bulls and narcotic dicks, multigraph girls and soda-
    jerkers, hat girls, bat boys, sports writers, ghost writers, popcorn and
    peanut squads, flatfeet, scavengers, mugs saying "Aw go button your
    nose," squirts hollering "Aw go kiss yourself outa dis game intuh
    anuddah," dead-heads, hops, cappers, come-ons, tin horns, small
    timers, the night club outfits helping the soup-and-fish who have to
    do something between midnight and bedtime.
The people? A puddler in the flaring splinters of newmade steel, a milk-
    wagon-driver getting the once-over from a milk inspector, a sand-hog
    with "the bends," a pack-rat, a snow-queen, janitors, jockeys, white

collar lads, pearl divers, peddlers, bundlestiffs, pants pressers, cleaners
and dyers, lice and rat exterminators.

So many forgotten, so many never remembered at all, yet there are well-
diggers, school-teachers, window washers who unless buckled proper
dance on air and go down down, coal heavers, roundhouse wipers,
hostlers, sweepers, samplers, weighers, sackers, carvers, bloom chippers,
kiln burners, cooks, bakers, beekeepers, goat raisers, goat hay growers,
slag-rollers, melters, solderers, track greasers, jiggermen, snow-plow
drivers, clamdiggers, stoolpigeons, the buck private, the gob, the leath-
erneck, the cop—

In uniform, in white collars, in overalls, in denim and gingham, a number
on an assembly line, a name on a polling list, a post office address, a
crime and sports page reader, a movie goer and radio listener, a stock-
market sucker, a sure thing for slick gamblers, a union man or non-
union, a job holder or a job hunter,

Always either employed, disemployed, unemployed and employable or
unemployable, a world series fan, a home buyer on a shoestring, a
down-and-out or a game fighter who will die fighting.

The people is the grand canyon of humanity
            and many many miles across.
The people is pandora's box, humpty dumpty,
            a clock of doom and an avalanche when it
            turns loose.
The people rest on land and weather, on time
            and the changing winds.
The people have come far and can look back
            and say, "We will go farther yet."
The people is a plucked goose and a shorn
            sheep of legalized fraud
And the people is one of those mountain slopes
            holding a volcano of retribution,
Slow in all things, slow in its gathered wrath,
            slow in its onward heave,
Slow in its asking: "Where are we now? what time
            is it?"

9 8

HOLD down the skylines now with your themes,
Proud marching oblongs of floodlighted walls.

Your bottom rocks and caissons rest
In money and dreams, in blood and wishes.

Stand on your tall haunches of checkered windows
    with your spikes of white light
Speaking across the cool blue of the night mist:
    Can we read our writing?
    What are we saying on the skyline?

Tell it to us, skyscrapers around Wacker Drive in Chicago,
Tall oblongs in orchestral confusion from Battery to Bronx,
Along Market Street to the Ferry flashing the Golden Gate sunset,
Steel-and-concrete witnesses gazing down in San Antonio on the little old
    Alamo,
Gazing down in Washington on the antiques of Pennsylvania Avenue:
    what are these so near my feet far down?
Blinking across old Quaker footpaths of the City of Brotherly Love: what
    have we here? shooting crossed lights on the old Boston Common:
    who goes there?
Rising in Duluth to flicker with windows over Lake Superior, standing up
    in Atlanta to face toward Kenesaw Mountain,
Tall with steel automotive roots in Detroit, with transport, coal and oil
    roots in Toledo, Cleveland, Buffalo, flickering afar to the ore barges
    on Lake Erie, to the looming chainstore trucks on the hard roads,
Wigwagging with air beacons on Los Angeles City Hall, telling the Mis-
    sissippi traffic it's night-time in St. Louis, New Orleans, Minneapolis
    and St. Paul—
Can we read our writing? what are we saying on the skyline?
Hold down your horizon spikes of light, proud marching oblongs.
Your bottom rocks and pilings rest in money and dreams, in blood and
    wishes.
The structural iron workers, the riveters and bolt catchers, know what you
    cost.

Yes, who are these on the harbor skyline,
With the sun gone down and the funnels and checkers of light talking?
Who are these tall witnesses? who these high phantoms?
What can they tell of a thousand years to come,
People and people rising and fading with the springs and autumns, people

like leaves out of the earth in spring, like leaves down the autumn
      wind—
What shall a thousand years tell a young tumultuous restless people?
They have made these steel skeletons like themselves—
Lean, tumultuous, restless:
> They have put up tall witnesses,
> to fade in a cool midnight blue,
> to rise in evening rainbow prints.

99

THE man in the street is fed
with lies in peace, gas in war,
and he may live now
just around the corner from you
trying to sell
the only thing he has to sell,
the power of his hand and brain
to labor for wages, for pay,
for cash of the realm.
And there are no takers, he can't connect.
Maybe he says, "Some pretty good men are on the street."
Maybe he says, "I'm just a palooka . . . all washed up."
Maybe he's a wild kid ready for his first stickup.
Maybe he's bummed a thousand miles and has a diploma.
Maybe he can take whatever the police can hand him,
Too many of him saying in their own wild way,
"The worst they can give you is lead in the guts."
Whatever the wild kids want to do they'll do
And whoever gives them ideas, faiths, slogans,
Whoever touches the bottom flares of them,
Connects with something prouder than all deaths
For they can live on hard corn and like it.
They are the original sons of the wild jackass
Crowned and clothed with what the Unknown Soldier had
If he went to his fate in a pride over all deaths.
Give them a cause and they are a living dynamite.
They are the game fighters who will die fighting.

Here and there a man in the street
is young, hard as nails,

cold with questions he asks
from his burning insides.

    Bred in a motorized world of trial and error
    He measures by millionths of an inch,
    Knows ball bearings from spiral gearings,
    Chain transmission, heat treatment of steel,
    Speeds and feeds of automatic screw machines,
    Having handled electric tools
    With pistol grip and trigger switch.
Yet he can't connect and he can name thousands
Like himself idle amid plants also idle.
He studies the matter of what is justice
And revises himself on money, comfort, good name.
He doesn't know what he wants
And says when he gets it he'll know it.
    He asks, "Why is this what it is?"
    He asks, "Who is paying for this propaganda?"
    He asks, "Who owns the earth and why?"
Here and there a wife or sweetheart sees with him
The pity of being sold down the river in a smoke
Of confusions taken from the mouths of the dead
And spoken as though those dead are alive now
And would say now what they said then.

"Let him go as far as he likes," says one lawyer who sits on several heavy
    directorates.
"What do we care? Is he any of our business? If he knew how he could
    manage.
"There are exceptional cases but where there is poverty you will generally
    find they were improvident and lacking in thrift and industry.
"The system of free competition we now have has made America the
    greatest and richest country on the face of the globe.
"You will seek in vain for any land where so large a number of people
    have had so many of the good things of life.
"The malcontents who stir up class feeling and engender class hatred are
    the foremost enemies of our republic and its constitutional govern·
    ment."
And so on and so on in further confusions taken from the mouths of the
    dead and spoken as though those dead are alive now and would say
    now what they said then.

Like the form of a seen and unheard prowler,
Like a slow and cruel violence,
is the known unspoken menace:
Do what we tell you or go hungry;
listen to us or you don't eat.

He walks and walks and walks
and wonders why the hell he built the road.

Once I built a railroad
. . . now . . .
brother, can you spare a dime?

To his dry well a man carried
all the water he could carry,
primed the pump, drew out the water,
and now
he has all the water he can carry.

We asked the cyclone
to go around our barn
but it didn't hear us.

100

THE Great Sphinx and the Pyramids say:
"Man passed this way and saw
a lot of ignorant besotted pharaohs."
The pink pagodas, jade rams and marble elephants
    of China say:
"Man came along here too
and met suave and cruel mandarins."
The temples and forums of Greece and Rome say:
"Man owned man here where man bought and sold
    man in the open slave auctions; by these chat-
    tels stone was piled on stone to make these now
    crumbled pavilions."
The medieval Gothic cathedrals allege:
"Mankind said prayers here for itself and for stiff-
    necked drunken robber barons."

And the skyscrapers of Manhattan, Detroit, Chi-
 cago, London, Paris, Berlin—what will they
 say when the hoarse and roaring years of
 their origin have sunk to a soft whispering?

Will the same fathoms come for the skyscrapers?
Will the years heave and the wind and rain haul
 and hover
Till sand and dust have picked the locks and blown
 the safes and smashed the windows and filled
 the elevator-shafts and packed the rooms and
 made ashes of the papers, the stocks and bonds,
 the embossed and attested securities?
Will it be colder and colder yet with ice on the
 ashes?
Even though the title-deeds read "forever and in
 perpetuity unto heirs and assigns for all time
 this deed is executed"?
Will it be all smoothed over into a hush where no
 one pleads
"Who were they? where did they come from? and
 why were they in such a hurry when they
 knew so little where they were going?"

As between the rulers and the ruled-over what
 does the record say?
Name the empires and republics with rulers wise
 beyond their people.
When have they read the signs and recognized a
 bridge generation?
When have the overlords and their paid liars and
 strumpets
Held as a first question, "What do the people want
 besides what we tell them they ought for their
 own good to want?"?
And second, "How much of living fact is under
 these cries and revolts, these claims that ex-
 ploiters ride the people?"?
And third, "What do they do to themselves who
 sell out the people?"?

When hush money is paid
to whom does it go
and by whom is it paid
and why should there be a hush?

When aldermen and legislative members say,
"We can put this through for you but it will take a
     little grease,"
What is the grease they mean and from whom
     comes this grease?
Let this be spoken of softly. Let sleeping dogs lie.
     What you don't know won't hurt you.
The trail leads straight to those in the possession of
     grease, the big shots of bespoken and anointed
     interests.

When violence is hired
and murder is paid for
and tear gas, clubs, automatics,
and blam blam machine guns
join in the hoarse mandate,
"Get the hell out of here,"
why then reserve a Sabbath
and call it a holiness day
for the mention of Jesus Christ
and why drag in the old quote,
"Thou shalt love thy neighbor
     as thyself"?

Said a lady wearing orchids
for a finality they betoken
distinct from cabbages
aloof from potatoes
and speaking with a white finality
from a face molded in half-secrets:
"Some things go unspoken in our circle:
no one has the bad grace to bring them up:
they exist and they don't:
when you belong you don't mention them."

Between highballs at the club amid the commodious leather chairs, only
    the souse, the fool, would lift a glass with the toast:
"Here's to the poor! let 'em suffer, they're used to it."
And if a boy fresh from college and the classics offers the point, "Money
    sometimes rots people,"
He'll hear from someone: "Maybe so but you can't have too big a surplus
    to take care of the future."

        "There are men who can be hired
        for work that must be done
        and I would rather hire them
        than do the work myself."
        Thus in the front office
        the big fellow in charge,
        hired by absentee owners,
        hired for work that must be done,
        has an alibi and good reasons:
        unless he keeps out of the red
        he too goes: he hires and fires:
        he is the overseer: in his ears
        one droning iron murmur:
        "We want results, re-sults.
        "You'll show results or else."
        So he hires and fires:
        new names go on the payroll,
        old names are dropped:
        personnel, production, outlet, sales,
        each has its own heebie-jeebies,
        each brings its special jitters:
        the picture always changes:
        one little innocent new idea
        one harmless looking patent
        can wreck the works, the payrolls,
        the mahogany front office,
        the absentee owners:
        unless the competitor is watched
        and met and handled,
        either killed off or satisfied,
        the works go to rust,

to the weavers of cobwebs
weaving in iron and mahogany:
Thus in the front office amid the desk buttons
and the switchboard phone and the private line,
amid slips holding safe-combination-numbers,
amid the keys to safe-deposit-vaults
and the documents known to associates and attorneys
besides other documents held in reserve,
written communications private and confidential,
spoken messages not to be put in writing,
memoranda in low tone to Jones for immediate attention
and withheld from Abernathy for definite reasons
Abernathy having plenty enough to do as it is,
items touching rivals real and potential,
competitors ruthless with a jungle cunning,
competitors fighting in the open with a decent code,
competitors in the red and dazed by the graph
of volume and sales sliding down always down,
telegrams to be sent in cipher strictly and see to it,
telegrams for the press, for Congress, for the public,
quarterly earnings report for investors,
fully detailed report for the Chairman of the Board,
information sheets to be scanned and torn up,
other notations to be read closely and filed
in a fireproof private vault with a time-lock,
signed agreements hardly worth the public eye,
schedules, rebates, allowances, working arrangements—
        amid these props
        of time and circumstance
        a big shot executive sits
with an eye on the board of directors first of all,
next the stockholders owning control,
next the vast eggheaded investing public,
and after these the men who run the works
from the engineers, chemists, geologists, intelligentsia
on to the white collar clerks and bookkeepers
and the overall crews who take whatever weather comes,
        in fumes and dust, in smoke, slag and cinders
        meeting production and delivery demands—
and finally the buyers, the consumers, the customers,

the people, yes, what will we let them have?
> Around a big table—decisions—
> wages up, wages down, wages as is—
> prices up, prices down, prices as is—
> this is the room and the big table
> of the high decisions.

They may consider lower prices
for the benefit of the consumer
or again to wreck a competitor.
They may hold prices down
because it's worth something to have
the good will of the public, the mass buyers.
Or they may raise prices and get all they can
while the getting is good, explaining,
"We are not in business for our health,
what we lose or win is our business."
Some of them trail with Marshall Field:
"The customer is always right," others with
Cornelius Vanderbilt: "The public be damned."
Others say one thing and do another.
And what have we here? what is this huddle?
Shall we call them scabs on their class?
Or are they talking to hear themselves talk?
They say Yes to Ford, to Filene, to Johnson,
to the Brookings Institution: one little idea:
After allowing for items to protect future operation
every cut in production cost should be shared
with the consumers in lower prices
with the workers in higher wages
thus stabilizing buying power
and guarding against recurrent collapses.
"What is this? Is it economics, poetry or what?
"Do you think you can run my business?
> "Are you trying to fly the flag
> of Soviet Russia over my office?"
> You're in a room now where you hear
> anything you want to hear
> and the advice often runs:
>> You can do anything you want to
>> unless they stop you.

Sometimes they fight among themselves
in a dog-eat-dog struggle
for control and domination,
sending an opponent to the Isles of Greece,
leaving him not even a shirt,
or letting him leap from a tenth-floor fire-escape.

What is to be said
of those rare and suave swine
who pay themselves a fat swag of higher salaries
in the same year they pay stockholders nothing,
cutting payrolls in wage reductions and layoffs?

What of those payday patriots
who took three hundred millions of profit dollars
from powder and supply contracts
in the same years other men by thousands
died with valor or took red wounds in a gray rain
for the sake of a country, a flag?

Lincoln had a word for one crew: "respectable scoundrels."
They reaped their profits from the government's necessity in money,
blankets, guns, contracts,
And when they gambled on defeat in May of '64 and sent gold prices to
new peaks
Lincoln groaned, "I wish every one of them had his devilish head shot off."

One by one they will pass
and be laid in numbered graves,
one by one lights out
and candles of remembrance
and rest amid silver handles and heavy roses
and forgotten hymns sung to their forgotten names.

1 0 1

THE unemployed
without a stake in the country
without jobs or nest eggs
marching they don't know where

marching north south west—
    and the deserts
marching east with dust
deserts out of howling dust-bowls
deserts with winds moving them
    marching toward Omaha toward Tulsa—
these lead to no easy pleasant conversation
they fall into a dusty disordered poetry.

"What was good for our fathers is good enough
for us—let us hold to the past and keep it
all and change it as little as we have to."
    Since when has this been a counsel and light
    of pioneers? of discoverers? of inventors?
    of builders? of makers?

        Who should be saying,
    "We can buy anything, we always have,
    we can fix anything, we always have,
    we're not in the habit of losing,
    on the main points we have our way,
    we always have"?
        who should be saying that and why?

As though yesterday is here today
and tomorrow too will be yesterday
and change on change is never hammered
on the deep anvils of transition
    the words may be heard:
"Every so often these sons of the wild jackass
    have to be handled. Let them come.
We've got the arguments, the propaganda machinery,
    the money and the guns. Let them come.
What was good for our fathers is good enough for
    us. We fight with the founding fathers."

What is the story of the railroads and banks,
of oil, steel, copper, aluminum, tin?
of the utilities of light, heat, power, transport?
what are the balances of pride and shame?

who took hold of the wilderness and changed it?
who paid the cost in blood and struggle?
what will the grave and considerate historian
loving humanity and hating no one dead or alive
have to write of wolves and people?
what are the names to be remembered with thanks?

Now they justify themselves to themselves:
we took things as we found them:
we never tried to shoot the moon:
we never pretended to be angels:
industry and science are slowly
making the world a better place to live in:
the weak must go under before the strong:
we'll always have the poor and the incompetent.

What then of those odd numbers
who have pretended to be angels
while using the fangs of wolves?
and what of the strong ones
who sat high and handsome
till they met stronger ones
till they were torn asunder
and outwolfed by bigger wolves?

And who plucked marvels
of industry and science
out of unexpected corners
unless it was the moon shooters
taking their chances
out in the great sky of the unknown?
who but they have held to a hope
poverty and the poor shall go
and the struggle of man for possessions
of music and craft and personal worth
lifted above the hog-trough level
above the animal dictate:
                    "Do this or go hungry"?

1 0 2

"*Accordingly, they commenced by an insidious
debauching of the public mind . . . they have
been drugging the public mind.*"
What was this debauchery? what this drugging?
and how did Abraham Lincoln mean it July 4, 1861?

> The public *has* a mind?
> Yes.
> And men can follow a method
> and a calculated procedure
> for drugging and debauching it?
> Yes.
> And the whirlwind comes later?
> Yes.

Can you bewilder men by the millions
with transfusions of your own passions,
mixed with lies and half-lies,
texts torn from contexts,
and then look for peace, quiet, good will
between nation and nation, race and race,
between class and class?

Who are these so ready
with a hate they are sure of,
with a prepared and considered hate?
who are these forehanded ones?

> Before the boys in blue and gray
> took the filth and gangrene
> along with the glory,
> Little Aleck Stephens, hazel-eyed
> and shrunken, saw it coming:
"When I am on one of two trains coming in
opposite directions on a single track,
both engines at high speed—and both
engineers drunk—I get off at the first
station."

  Is there a time to counsel,
"Be sober and patient while yet saying Yes
to freedom for cockeyed liars and bigots"?
  Is there a time to say,
"The facts and guide measurements are yet
to be found and put to work: there are
dawns and false dawns read in a ball of
revolving crystals"?
  Is there a time to repeat,
"The living passion of millions can rise
into a whirlwind: the storm once loose
who can ride it? you? or you? or you?
   only history, only tomorrow, knows
   for every revolution breaks
as a child of its own convulsive hour
shooting patterns never told of beforehand"?

1 0 3

THE wind in the corn leaves among the naked stalks
and the assurances of the October cornhuskers
throwing the yellow and gold ears into wagons
and the weatherworn boards of the oblong corncribs
and the heavy boots of winter roaring
around the barn doors
and the cows drowsing in peace at the feed-boxes—
while sheet steel is riveted into ships and bridges
and the hangar night shift meets the air mail
and the steam shovels scoop gravel by the ton
and the interstate trucks parade on the hard roads
and the bread-line silhouettes stand in a drizzle
and in Iowa the state fair prize hog crunches corn
and on the truck farms this year's scarecrows
lose the clothes they wore this summer
and stand next year in a change of rags—
these are chapters interwoven of the people.

   When a slow dim light moves
   on the face of vast waters
   and in its slow dim changing

baffles keen old captains
the reading of the light
in its shifting resolves
is the same as trying to read
the hosts of circumstance
deepening the paths of action
with a decree for the people:
    "Tomorrow you do this because
    you can do nothing else."

    What is it now
in the hosts of circumstance
where plainspoken men multiply,
what is it now the people are saying
near enough to the ribs of life
and the flowing face of vast waters
so they will go on saying it
in deepening paths of action
running toward a slow dim decree:
    "You do this because
    you can do nothing else"?

1 0 4

WHEN was it long ago the murmurings began
and the joined murmurings
became a moving wall
moving with the authority of a great sea
whose Yes and No
stood in an awful script
in a new unheard-of handwriting?
"No longer," began the murmurings,
"shall the king be king
"nor the son of the king become king.
"Their authority shall go
"and their thrones be swept away.
"They are too far from us, the people.
"They listen too little to us, the people.
"They hold their counsels
"without men from the people given a word.

"Their ears are so far from us,
"so far from our wants and small belongings,
"we must trim the kings
"into something less than kings."
And the joined murmurings became a moving wall
with Yes and No in an awful script.
And the kings became less.
The kings shrank.

What is it now
the people are beginning
to say—
is it this?
and if so
whither away and
where do we go
from here?
"What about the munitions and money kings,
the war lords and international bankers?
the transportation and credit kings?
the coal, the oil, and the mining kings?
the price-fixing monopoly control kings?
Why are they so far from us?
why do they hold their counsels
without men from the people given a word?
Shall we keep these kings and let their sons
in time become the same manner of kings?
Are their results equal to their authority?
Why are these interests too sacred for discussion?
What documents now call for holy daylight?
what costs, prices, values, are we forbidden to ask?
Are we slowly coming to understand
the distinction between a demagogue squawking
and the presentation of tragic plainspoken fact?
Shall a robber be named a robber when he is one
even though bespoken and anointed he is?
Shall a shame and a crime be mentioned
when it is so plainly there,
when day by day it draws toil, blood, and hunger,
enough of slow death and personal tragedy to certify

the kings who sit today as entrenched kings
are far too far from their people?
What does justice say?
or if justice is become an abstraction or a harlot
what does her harder sister, necessity, say?
Their ears are so far from us,
so far from our wants and small belongings
we must trim these kings of our time
into something less than kings.
Of these too it will be written:
    these kings shrank."
        What is it now
        the people are beginning
        to say—
        is it this?
        and if so
        whither away and
        where do we go from here?

1 0 5

ALWAYS the storm of propaganda blows.
Buy a paper. Read a book. Start the radio.
Listen in the railroad car, in the bus,
Go to church, to a movie, to a saloon.
And always the breezes of personal opinion
are blowing mixed with the doctrines
of propaganda or the chatter of selling spiels.
Believe this, believe that. Buy these, buy them.
Love one-two-three, hate four-five-six.
Remember 7-8-9, forget 10-11-12.
Go now, don't wait, go now at once and buy
Dada Salts Incorporated, Crazy Horse Crystals,
for whatever ails you and if nothing ails you
it is good for that and we are telling you
for your own good. Whatever you are told,
you are told it is for your own good and not
for the special interest of those telling you.
Planned economy is forethought and care.

Planned economy is regimentation and tyranny.
What do you know about planned economy
and how did this argument get started and why?
Let the argument go on.

The storm of propaganda blows always.
In every air of today the germs float and hover.
The shock and contact of ideas goes on.
Planned economy will arrive, stand up,
and stay a long time—or planned economy will
take a beating and be smothered.
The people have the say-so.
Let the argument go on.
Let the people listen.
Tomorrow the people say Yes or No by one question:
    "What else can be done?"
In the drive of faiths on the wind today the people know:
"We have come far and we are going farther yet."

Who was the quiet silver-toned agitator who
said he loved every stone of the streets of
Boston, who was a believer in sidewalks, and
had it, "The talk of the sidewalk today is
the law of the land tomorrow"?

"The people," said a farmer's wife in a Minnesota country store while
    her husband was buying a new post-hole digger,
"The people," she went on, "will stick around a long time.
"The people run the works, only they don't know it yet—you wait and see."

    Who knows the answers, the cold inviolable truth?
And when have the paid and professional liars done else than bring wrath
    and fire, wreck and doom?
And how few they are who search and hesitate and say:
"I stand in this whirlpool and tell you I don't know and if I did know I
    would tell you and all I am doing now is to guess and I give you
    my guess for what it is worth as one man's guess.
"Yet I have worked out this guess for myself as nobody's yes-man and
    when it happens I no longer own the priceless little piece of territory

under my own hat, so far gone that I can't even do my own guessing
for myself,
"Then I will know I am one of the unburied dead, one of the moving
walking stalking talking unburied dead."

1 0 6

SLEEP is a suspension midway
and a conundrum of shadows
lost in meadows of the moon.
    The people sleep.
    Ai! ai! the people sleep.
Yet the sleepers toss in sleep
and an end comes of sleep
and the sleepers wake.
    Ai! ai! the sleepers wake!

1 0 7

    THE people will live on.
The learning and blundering people will live on.
    They will be tricked and sold and again sold
And go back to the nourishing earth for rootholds,
    The people so peculiar in renewal and comeback,
    You can't laugh off their capacity to take it.
The mammoth rests between his cyclonic dramas.

The people so often sleepy, weary, enigmatic,
is a vast huddle with many units saying:
    "I earn my living.
    I make enough to get by
    and it takes all my time.
    If I had more time
    I could do more for myself
    and maybe for others.
    I could read and study
    and talk things over
    and find out about things.
    It takes time.
    I wish I had the time."

The people is a tragic and comic two-face:
hero and hoodlum: phantom and gorilla twist-
ing to moan with a gargoyle mouth: "They
buy me and sell me . . . it's a game . . .
sometime I'll break loose . . ."

    Once having marched
Over the margins of animal necessity,
Over the grim line of sheer subsistence
    Then man came
To the deeper rituals of his bones,
To the lights lighter than any bones,
To the time for thinking things over,
To the dance, the song, the story,
Or the hours given over to dreaming,
    Once having so marched.

Between the finite limitations of the five senses
and the endless yearnings of man for the beyond
the people hold to the humdrum bidding of work and food
while reaching out when it comes their way
for lights beyond the prisms of the five senses,
for keepsakes lasting beyond any hunger or death.
    This reaching is alive.
The panderers and liars have violated and smutted it.
    Yet this reaching is alive yet
    for lights and keepsakes.

    The people know the salt of the sea
    and the strength of the winds
    lashing the corners of the earth.
    The people take the earth
    as a tomb of rest and a cradle of hope.
    Who else speaks for the Family of Man?
    They are in tune and step
    with constellations of universal law.

    The people is a polychrome,
    a spectrum and a prism
    held in a moving monolith,

a console organ of changing themes,
a clavilux of color poems
wherein the sea offers fog
and the fog moves off in rain
and the labrador sunset shortens
to a nocturne of clear stars
serene over the shot spray
of northern lights.

The steel mill sky is alive.
The fire breaks white and zigzag
shot on a gun-metal gloaming.
Man is a long time coming.
Man will yet win.
Brother may yet line up with brother:

This old anvil laughs at many broken hammers.
There are men who can't be bought.
The fireborn are at home in fire.
The stars make no noise.
You can't hinder the wind from blowing.
Time is a great teacher.
Who can live without hope?

In the darkness with a great bundle of grief
the people march.
In the night, and overhead a shovel of stars for
keeps, the people march:
"Where to? what next?"

NEW SECTION

FOR

KENNETH AND LETHA DODSON

STORMS BEGIN FAR BACK

STORMS begin far back.

You can't have a storm offhand
like somebody took a notion and
decided a storm would be right
handy to come off now and here.

> The moan and lash of the winds
> came out of a place nice for
> them, nice for their growing.

> The anger of the waters lay
> breeding, spawning, pent up
> and ready to go.

>> The blaze of the prongs,
>> the zigzags of forked fire,
>> they had a long seed-time
>> in a womb of unborn flame
>> before they went to town
>> and came howling, "You don't
>> know what goes on here but
>>> we'll tell you."

This storm now didn't come out of nowhere
—it had a starting place, a home and womb
—far back it began, brother, sister,
—far back, sweetheart.

[Voices]

BOOKS MEN DIE FOR

LIGHTS or no lights,
so they stand waiting
. . . books men die for.

For this a man was hanged.
For this a man was burned.
For this two million candles
    snuffed their finish.
For this a man was shot.

Open the covers, they speak,
they cry, they come out as from
open doors with voices, heartbeats.

    Fools: I say hats off.
    Fools: I say, who did better?
    Fools: I say with you:
                  What of it?

You books in the dark now with the lights off,
You books now with the lights on,
    What is the drip, drip, from your covers?
    What is the lip murmur, the lost winds wandering
                  from your covers?
Books men die for—
           I say with you: what of it?

OPEN LETTER TO THE POET ARCHIBALD MacLEISH WHO HAS FORSAKEN HIS MASSACHUSETTS FARM TO MAKE PROPAGANDA FOR FREEDOM

THOMAS JEFFERSON had red hair and a violin
and he loved life and people and music
and books and writing and quiet thoughts—
a lover of peace, decency, good order,

summer corn ripening for the bins of winter,
cows in green pastures, colts sucking at mares,
apple trees waiting to laugh with pippins—
Jefferson loved peace like a good farmer.
And yet—for eight years he fought in a war—
writing with his own hand the war announcement
named The Declaration of Independence
making The Fourth of July a sacred calendar date.
And there was his friend and comrade
Ben Franklin, the printer, bookman, diplomat:
all Franklin asked was they let him alone
so he could do his work as lover of peace and work—
Franklin too made war for eight years—
the same Franklin who said two nations
would better throw dice than go to war—
he threw in with fighters for freedom—
for eight years he threw in all he had:
the books, the printshop, fun with electricity,
searches and researches in science pure and applied—
these had to wait while he joined himself
to eight long years of war for freedom, independence.

Now, of course, these two odd fellows
stand as only two among many:
the list runs long of these fellows,
lovers of peace, decency, good order,
who throw in with all they've got
for the abstractions "freedom," "independence."
Strictly they were gentle men, not hunting trouble.
Strictly they wanted quiet, the good life, freedom.
They would rather have had the horses of instruction
those eight years they gave to the tigers of wrath.
The record runs they were both dreamers
at the same time they refused imitations of the real thing
at the same time they stood up and talked back
at the same time they met the speech of steel and cunning with their
    own relentless steel and cunning.

[1940]

MR. ATTILA

THEY made a myth of you, professor,
    you of the gentle voice,
    the books, the specs,
    the furtive rabbit manners
    in the mortar-board cap
    and the medieval gown.

They didn't think it, eh professor?
On account of you're so absent-minded,
you bumping into the tree and saying,
"Excuse me, I thought you were a tree,"
passing on again blank and absent-minded.

Now it's "Mr. Attila, *how* do you do?"
Do you pack wallops of wholesale death?
Are you the practical dynamic son-of-a-gun?
Have you come through with a few abstractions?
Is it you Mr. Attila we hear saying,
"I beg your pardon but we believe we have made some degree of progress
    on the residual qualities of the atom"?

                                   [August, 1945]

IS THERE ANY EASY ROAD TO FREEDOM?

A RELENTLESS man loved France
Long before she came to shame
And the eating of bitter dust,
Loving her as mother and torch,
As bone of his kith and kin
And he spoke passion, warning:
"*Rest is not a word of free peoples—
rest is a monarchical word.*"

A relentless Russian loved Russia
Long before she came to bare agony

And valor amid rivers of blood,
Loving her as mother and torch,
As bone of his kith and kin:
He remembered an old Swedish saying:
"The fireborn are at home in fire."

A Kentucky-born Illinoisan found himself
By journey through shadows and prayer
The Chief Magistrate of the American people
Pleading in words close to low whispers:
"Fellow citizens . . . we cannot escape history.
The fiery trial through which we pass
Will light us down in honor or dishonor
To the latest generation . . .
We shall nobly save or meanly lose
                the last best hope of earth."
Four little words came worth studying over:
        "We must disenthrall ourselves."
And what is a thrall? And who are thralls?
Men tied down or men doped, or men drowsy?
        He hoped to see them
        shake themselves loose
        and so be disenthralled.

There are freedom shouters.
There are freedom whisperers.
Both may serve.
Have I, have you, been too silent?
Is there an easy crime of silence?
Is there any easy road to freedom?

                        [*December, 1941*]

THE MAN WITH THE BROKEN FINGERS

(When this tale of methodically inflicted agony was published in The Chicago Times
Syndicate newspapers August 23, 1942, it brought inquiries whether it was war propa-
ganda or based on an actual incident. My informant was a Norwegian ski champion
known as Lieutenant "Andreas" for the safety of his home kinfolk. He gave the inci-
dent as he had it from the son of the main tragic figure. Among many other related
points was one of German soldiers whose minds began to crack under the strain of the
inhuman acts required of them by their superiors, such soldiers being returned to Ger-
many as "mental cases" needing therapeutic treatment. "Andreas," a sober and modest
hero, was killed in a bomber flight over Berlin. Friends of "Andreas" say the story below
had translation into other languages and circulation by undergrounds.)

THE Man with the Broken Fingers throws a shadow.
Down from the spruce and evergreen mountain timbers of Norway—
And across Europe and the Mediterranean to the oasis palms of Libya—
He lives and speaks a sign language of lost fingers.
From a son of Norway who slipped the Gestapo nets, the Nazi patrols,
The story comes as told among those now in Norway.

Shrines in their hearts they have for this nameless man
Who refused to remember names names names the Gestapo wanted.
"Tell us these names. Who are they? Talk! We want those names!"
And the man faced them, looked them in the eye, and hours passed and
     no names came—hours on hours and no names for the Gestapo.
They told him they would break him as they had broken others.
The rubber hose slammed around face and neck,
The truncheon handing pain with no telltale marks,
Or the distinction of the firing squad and death in a split second—
The Gestapo considered these and decided for him something else again.
"Tell us those names. Who were they? Talk! Names now—or else!"
And no names came—over and over and no names.

So they broke the little finger of the left hand.
Three fingers came next and the left thumb bent till it broke.
Still no names and there was a day and night for rest and thinking it over.
Then again the demand for names and he gave them the same silence.
And the little finger of the right hand felt itself twisted,
Back and back twisted till it hung loose from a bleeding socket.
Then three more fingers crashed and splintered one by one
And the right thumb back and back into shattered bone.

Did he think about violins or accordions he would never touch again?
Did he think of baby or woman hair he would never again play with?
Or of hammers or pencils no good to him any more?
Or of gloves and mittens that would always be misfits?
He may have laughed half a moment over a Gestapo job
So now for a while he would handle neither knife nor fork
Nor lift to his lips any drinking-cup handle
Nor sign his name with a pen between thumb and fingers.

And all this was halfway—there was more to come.
The Gestapo wit and craft had an aim.
They wanted it known in Norway the Gestapo can be terrible.
They wanted a wide whispering of fear
Of how the Nazis handle those who won't talk or tell names.
"We give you one more chance to co-operate."
Yet he had no names for them.
His locked tongue, his Norwegian will pitted against Nazi will,
His pride and faith in a free man's way,
His welcoming death rather than do what they wanted—
They brought against this their last act of fury,
Breaking the left arm at the elbow,
Breaking it again at the shoulder socket—
And when he came to in a flicker of opening eyes
They broke the right arm first at the elbow, then the shoulder.
By now of course he had lost all memory of names, even his own.
And there are those like you and me and many many others
Who can never forget the Man with the Broken Fingers.
His will, his pride as a free man, shall go on.
His shadow moves and his sacred fingers speak.
He tells men there are a thousand writhing shattering deaths
Better to die one by one than to say yes yes yes
When the answer is no no no and death is welcome and death comes soon
And death is a quiet step into a sweet clean midnight.

[*August 23, 1942*]

FREEDOM IS A HABIT

Freedom is a habit
and a coat worn
some born to wear it

some never to know it.
Freedom is cheap
or again as a garment
is so costly
men pay their lives
rather than not have it.
Freedom is baffling:
men having it often
know not they have it
till it is gone and
they no longer have it.
What does this mean?
Is it a riddle?
Yes, it is first of all
in the primers of riddles.
To be free is so-so:
you can and you can't:
walkers can have freedom
only by never walking
away their freedom:
runners too have freedom
unless they overrun:
eaters have often outeaten
their freedom to eat
and drinkers overdrank
their fine drinking freedom.

[*June 13, 1943*]

ELEPHANTS ARE DIFFERENT TO DIFFERENT PEOPLE

Wilson and Pilcer and Snack stood before the zoo elephant.

Wilson said, "What is its name? Is it from Asia or Africa? Who feeds it? Is it a he or a she? How old is it? Do they have twins? How much does it cost to feed? How much does it weigh? If it dies, how much will another one cost? If it dies, what will they use the bones, the fat, and the hide for? What use is it besides to look at?"

Pilcer didn't have any questions; he was murmuring to himself, "It's a house by itself, walls and windows, the ears came from tall corn-fields, by God; the architect of those legs was a workman, by God; he stands like a bridge out across deep water; the face is sad and the eyes are kind; I know elephants are good to babies."

Snack looked up and down and at last said to himself, "He's a tough son-of-a-gun outside and I'll bet he's got a strong heart, I'll bet he's strong as a copper-riveted boiler inside."

They didn't put up any arguments.
They didn't throw anything in each other's faces.
Three men saw the elephant three ways
And let it go at that.
They didn't spoil a sunny Sunday afternoon;
"Sunday comes only once a week," they told each other.

ON A FLIMMERING FLOOM YOU SHALL RIDE

Summary and footnote of and on the testimony of the poet MacLeish under appointment as Assistant Secretary of State, under oath before a Congressional examining committee pressing him to divulge the portents and meanings of his poems.

> Nobody noogers the shaff of a sloo.
> Nobody slimbers a wench with a winch
> Nor higgles armed each with a niggle
> and each the flimdrat of a smee,
> each the inbiddy hum of a smoo.
>
> Then slong me dorst with the flagdarsh.
> Then creep me deep with the crawbright.
> Let idle winds ploodaddle the dorshes.
> And you in the gold of the gloaming
> You shall be sloam with the hoolriffs.
>
> On a flimmering floom you shall ride.
> They shall tell you bedish and desist.
> On a flimmering floom you shall ride.
>
> > [Poetry]

SCROLL

> MEMORY is when you look back
> and the answers float in
> to who? what? when? where?

The members who were there then
are repeated on a screen
are recalled on a scroll
are moved in a miniature drama,
are collected and recollected
for actions, speeches, silences,
set forth by images of the mind
and made in a mingling mist
to do again and to do over
precisely what they did do once—
this is memory—
sometimes slurred and blurred—
this is remembering—
sometimes wrecking the images
and proceeding again to reconstruct
what happened and how,
the many little involved answers
to who? what? when? where?
and more involved than any
      how? how?

THE FIREBORN ARE AT HOME IN FIRE

Luck is a star.
Money is a plaything.
Time is a storyteller.
The sky goes high, big.
The sky goes wide and blue.
And the fireborn—they go far—
      being at home in fire.

Can you compose yourself
The same as a bright bandana,
A bandana folded blue and cool,
Whatever the high howling,
The accents of blam blam?
Can I, can John Smith, John Doe,
Whatever the awful accents,
Whatever the horst wessel hiss,

Whatever books be burnt and crisp,
Whatever hangmen bring their hemp,
Whatever horsemen sweep the sunsets,
Whatever hidden hovering candle
Sways as a wafer of light?

Can you compose yourself
The same as a bright bandana,
A bandana folded blue and cool?
Can I, too, drop deep down
In a pool of cool remembers,
In a float of fine smoke blue,
In a keeping of one pale moon,
Weaving our wrath in a pattern
Woven of wrath gone down,
Crossing our scarlet zigzags
With pools of cool blue,
With floats of smoke blue?

Can you, can I, compose ourselves
In wraps of personal cool blue,
In sheets of personal smoke blue?
        Bach did it, Johann Sebastian.
So did the one and only John Milton.
        And the old slave Epictetus
        And the other slave Spartacus
        And Brother Francis of Assisi.
So did General George Washington
        On a horse, in a saddle,
        On a boat, in heavy snow,
        In a loose cape overcoat
        And snow on his shoulders.
So did John Adams, Jackson, Jefferson.
So did Lincoln on a cavalry horse
At the Chancellorsville review
        With platoons right, platoons left,
In a wind nearly blowing the words away
        Asking the next man on a horse:
"What's going to become of all these
        boys when the war is over?"

The shape of your shadow
Comes from you—and you only?
Your personal fixed decisions
Out of you—and your mouth only?
                Your No, your Yes, your own?

Bronze old timers belong here.
Yes, they might be saying:
                Shade the flame
Back to final points
Of all sun and fog
In the moving frame
Of your personal eyes.
Then stand to the points.
Let hunger and hell come.
Or ashes and shame poured
On your personal head.
Let death shake its bones.
The teaching goes back far:
                Compose yourself.

        Luck is a star.
        Money is a plaything.
        Time is a storyteller.
And the sky goes blue with mornings.
And the sky goes bronze with sunsets.
And the fireborn—they go far—
                being at home in fire.

                        [*Collier's, September 4, 1943*]

MR. LONGFELLOW AND HIS BOY
(*An old-fashioned recitation to be read aloud*)

Mr. Longfellow, Henry Wadsworth Longfellow,
    the Harvard Professor,
    the poet whose pieces you see in all the schoolbooks,
"Tell me not in mournful numbers
    life is but an empty dream . . ."

Mr. Longfellow sits in his Boston library writing,
Mr. Longfellow looks across the room
    and sees his nineteen-year-old boy
propped up in a chair at a window,
home from the war,
a rifle ball through right and left shoulders.

In his diary the father writes about his boy:
    "He has a wound through him a foot long.
     He pretends it does not hurt him."
And the father if he had known
would have told the boy propped up in a chair
how one of the poems written in that room
    made President Lincoln cry.
And both the father and the boy
would have smiled to each other and felt good
about why the President had tears over that poem.

Noah Brooks, the California newspaperman,
could have told the Longfellows how one day
Brooks heard the President saying two lines:
    "Thou, too, sail on, O Ship of State!
    Sail on, O Union, strong and great!"
Noah Brooks, remembering more of the poem, speaks:
    "Thou, too, sail on, O Ship of State!
    Sail on, O Union, strong and great!
    Humanity with all its fears,
    With all the hopes of future years,
    Is hanging breathless on thy fate!
    We know what Master laid thy keel,
    What workmen wrought thy ribs of steel,
    Who made each mast, and sail, and rope,
    What anvils rang, what hammers beat,
    In what a forge and what a heat
    Were shaped the anchors of thy hope!
    Fear not each sudden sound and shock,
    'Tis of the wave and not the rock;
    'Tis but the flapping of the sail,
    And not a rent made by the gale!
    In spite of rock and tempest's roar,

In spite of false lights on the shore,
Sail on, nor fear to breast the sea!
Our hearts, our hopes, are all with thee,
Our hearts, our hopes, our prayers, our tears,
Our faith triumphant o'er our fears,
Are all with thee—are all with thee!"

Noah Brooks sees Lincoln's eyes filled with tears,
        the cheeks wet.
They sit quiet a little while, then Lincoln saying:
"It is a wonderful gift to be able to stir men like that."
Mr. Longfellow—and his boy sitting propped up in a chair—
with a bullet wound a foot long in his shoulders—
would have liked to hear President Lincoln saying
        those words.

Now Mr. Longfellow is gone far away, his boy, too,
        gone far away,
and they never dreamed how seventy-eight years later
the living President of the United States, in the White House at Wash-
        ington,
takes a pen, writes with his own hand on a sheet of paper
about the Union Ship of State sailing on and on—
        never going down—
how the President hands that sheet of paper
to a citizen soon riding high in the air, high over salt water,
high in the rain and the sun and the mist over
        the Atlantic Ocean,
riding, pounding, flying, everything under control,
crossing the deep, wide Atlantic in a day and a night,
coming to London on the Thames in England,
standing before the First Minister of the United Kingdom
so the whole English-language world
from England across North America to Australia and
        New Zealand
can never forget Mr. Longfellow's lines:
        "Thou, too, sail on, O Ship of State!
        Sail on, O Union, strong and great!"

[Collier's, June 14, 1941]

THE LONG SHADOW OF LINCOLN: A LITANY

(We can succeed only by concert. . . . The dogmas of the quiet past are inadequate
to the stormy present. The occasion is piled high with difficulty, and we must rise with
the occasion. As our case is new so we must think anew and act anew. We must dis-
enthrall ourselves. . . . DECEMBER 1, 1862. *The President's Message to Congress.*)

BE sad, be cool, be kind,
remembering those now dreamdust
hallowed in the ruts and gullies,
solemn bones under the smooth blue sea,
faces warblown in a falling rain.

Be a brother, if so can be,
to those beyond battle fatigue
each in his own corner of earth
 or forty fathoms undersea
 beyond all boom of guns,
 beyond any bong of a great bell,
 each with a bosom and number,
 each with a pack of secrets,
each with a personal dream and doorway
and over them now the long endless winds
 with the low healing song of time,
 the hush and sleep murmur of time.

Make your wit a guard and cover.
Sing low, sing high, sing wide.
Let your laughter come free
remembering looking toward peace:
"We must disenthrall ourselves."

Be a brother, if so can be,
to those thrown forward
for taking hardwon lines,
for holding hardwon points
 and their reward so-so,
little they care to talk about,
their pay held in a mute calm,
highspot memories going unspoken,

what they did being past words,
what they took being hardwon.
Be sad, be kind, be cool.
Weep if you must
And weep open and shameless
before these altars.

There are wounds past words.
There are cripples less broken
than many who walk whole.
There are dead youths
with wrists of silence
who keep a vast music
under their shut lips,
what they did being past words,
their dreams like their deaths
beyond any smooth and easy telling,
having given till no more to give.

There is dust alive
with dreams of The Republic,
with dreams of the Family of Man
flung wide on a shrinking globe
with old timetables,
old maps, old guide-posts
torn into shreds,
shot into tatters,
burnt in a firewind,
lost in the shambles,
faded in rubble and ashes.

There is dust alive.
Out of a granite tomb,
Out of a bronze sarcophagus,
Loose from the stone and copper
Steps a whitesmoke ghost
Lifting an authoritative hand
In the name of dreams worth dying for,
In the name of men whose dust breathes
of those dreams so worth dying for,

what they did being past words,
beyond all smooth and easy telling.

Be sad, be kind, be cool,
remembering, under God, a dreamdust
hallowed in the ruts and gullies,
solemn bones under the smooth blue sea,
faces warblown in a falling rain.

Sing low, sing high, sing wide.
Make your wit a guard and cover.
Let your laughter come free
like a help and a brace of comfort.

The earth laughs, the sun laughs
over every wise harvest of man,
over man looking toward peace
by the light of the hard old teaching:
    "We must disenthrall ourselves."

Read as the Phi Beta Kappa poem at the Mother Chapter of William and Mary College, Williamsburg, Virginia, December, 1944. Published in the *Saturday Evening Post*, February, 1945.

WHEN DEATH CAME APRIL TWELVE 1945

CAN a bell ring in the heart
telling the time, telling a moment,
telling off a stillness come,
in the afternoon a stillness come
and now never come morning?

Now never again come morning,
say the tolling bells repeating it,
now on the earth in blossom days,
in earthy days and potato planting,
now to the stillness of the earth,
to the music of dust to dust
and the drop of ashes to ashes
he returns and it is the time,

the afternoon time and never come morning,
the voice never again, the face never again.

A bell rings in the heart telling it
and the bell rings again and again
remembering what the first bell told,
the going away, the great heart still—
and they will go on remembering
and they is you and you and me and me.

And there will be roses and spring blooms
flung on the moving oblong box, emblems endless
flung from nearby, from faraway earth corners,
from frontline tanks nearing Berlin
        unseen flowers of regard to The Commander,
from battle stations over the South Pacific
        silent tokens saluting The Commander.

And the whitening bones of men at sea bottoms
or huddled and mouldering men at Aachen,
        they may be murmuring,
        "Now he is one of us,"
        one answering muffled drums
in the realm and sphere of the shadow battalions.

Can a bell ring proud in the heart
        over a voice yet lingering,
        over a face past any forgetting,
        over a shadow alive and speaking,
over echoes and lights come keener, come deeper?

Can a bell ring in the heart
in time with the tall headlines,
the high fidelity transmitters,
the somber consoles rolling sorrow,
the choirs in ancient laments—chanting:
        "Dreamer, sleep deep,
        Toiler, sleep long,
        Fighter, be rested now,
        Commander, sweet good night."

[*Woman's Home Companion*, June, 1945]

Present Hour

JAN, THE SON OF THOMAS

As I said before one Saturday night
when the moon hung a curve of flame,
in the east a baby-shoe of silver:
    I must forget the last war,
    never remember the war before,
    nor the wars on wars far back:
    I must put them away
    in a black sack filled
    and packed high with forgettings
    and then by one marvel of oblivion
    forget the next war
    putting the war to come
    in the same black sack of forgettings.

This could be a subtle trick
learned out of patient practice,
an act of will and humor
often performed beforehand
in repeated images of the mind—
a device of double contemplations
    looking to the east, to the west,
    hearing the voices of the next war.

Was I not always a laughing man?
Did I ever fail of ready jests?
Have I added a final supreme jest?
They may write where my ashes quiver:
    "He loved mankind for its very faults.
    He knew how to forget all wars past.
        He so acted
        as to forget the next war."

PEACE BETWEEN WARS

BETWEEN the long wars
there has always been peace
and likewise
between the short wars.

The longer the wars
the less was the peace
while the wars went on
and the shorter the wars
the sooner the peace came.

Whenever the peace
came to an end
the resulting war
always ran
either short or long.

Whenever a war ended
the resulting peace
ran till the next war.

Thus each peace
had its punctuation
by a war short or long
and each war at its end
ushered in an era
of peace short or long.

Therefore we know
absolutely,
incontestably,
the peace we now see
will run
till the next war begins
whereupon peace
will be ushered in
at the end of the next war.

Beyond this
we know little
absolutely, incontestably.

SCRIPTSMITH

I GIVE you the cosmos, freely the whole works.
Go to it, take the works and run it.
Or let it run itself.
Maybe if you stand off by yourself
You'll see the entire intricate farflung
           shebang of the universe
      the whole complicated sidereal affair
running itself like a watch God made
       and God will see to winding it
       so you dont have to get up in the night
       saying you forgot to wind it—
Hi bud—I give you the cosmos, the whole works—
Freely I hand it to you to keep.
Freely you can hand it to whoever you think
         might want it to keep.
. . . And now a few words from our sponsor.
    He is a rat, a louse, a lobscouse,
       a mismash slicker,
       a loudmouth liblab.

ENEMY NUMBER ONE

"I WRITE for antiquity,"
said a handsome mournful galoot
thereby cancelling every last other one
who might be saying,
"I write for posterity,"
as though antiquity was never posterity
to its preceding antiquities
and as though nevertheless
our posterity will never be an antiquity
to its successive posterities,

as though each posterity has not said
to several precessive antiquities,
"Kiss my posterior and forget about it."

He never had no fun, is that it?
All around him animals
        eating each other,
        eating themselves,
snarling slithering conniving animals.
Each citizen, except himself and his elite,
        nothing less than a heel.
No grand designs, no high hopes, no banners
        nor slogans nor shibboleths
        worth any man's following.
You could summarize his row of books:
        Humanity is a mess of eels and heels.
        The human race is its own Enemy Number One.
        For him the Family of Man stinks now
                and if you look back
                for him it always has stunk.

WORMS AND THE WIND

WORMS would rather be worms.
Ask a worm and he says, "Who knows what a worm knows?"
Worms go down and up and over and under.
Worms like tunnels.
When worms talk they talk about the worm world.
Worms like it in the dark.
Neither the sun nor the moon interests a worm.
Zigzag worms hate circle worms.
Curve worms never trust square worms.
Worms know what worms want.
Slide worms are suspicious of crawl worms.
One worm asks another, "How does your belly drag today?"
The shape of a crooked worm satisfies a crooked worm.
A straight worm says, "Why not be straight?"
Worms tired of crawling begin to slither.
Long worms slither farther than short worms.
Middle-sized worms say, "It is nice to be neither long nor short."

Old worms teach young worms to say, "Don't be sorry for me unless you
have been a worm and lived in worm places and read worm books."
When worms go to war they dig in, come out and fight, dig in again,
come out and fight again, dig in again, and so on.
Worms underground never hear the wind overground and sometimes they
ask, "What is this wind we hear of?"

THE ABRACADABRA BOYS

The abracadabra boys—have they been in the stacks and cloisters? Have
they picked up languages for throwing into chow mein poems?
Have they been to a sea of jargons and brought back jargons? Their salu-
tations go: Who cometh? and, It ith I cometh.
They know postures from impostures, pistils from pustules, to hear them
tell it. They foregather and make pitty pat with each other in Latin
and in their private pig Latin, very ofay.
They give with passwords. "Who cometh?" "A kumquat cometh." "And
how cometh the kumquat?" "On an abbadabba, ancient and honor-
able sire, ever and ever on an abbadabba."
Do they have fun? Sure—their fun is being what they are, like our fun
is being what we are—only they are more sorry for us being what we
are than we are for them being what they are.
Pointing at you, at us, at the rabble, they sigh and say, these abracadabra
boys, "They lack jargons. They fail to distinguish between pustules
and pistils. They knoweth not how the kumquat cometh."

SHOES OF TRAVEL

After overwhelming filth and amazing betrayals Odd Nansen looked at
the concentration camp and was reminded of Norse folk-lore. "What is
the white layer in chicken dung?" "Oh, that's chicken dung too." This
comes bitter as an Arabic, "The shadow of the hunchback? That too is
hunched."

"I had no shoes, and I murmured, till I met a man who had no feet."
And what did they say? What words passed between the barefoot and the
footless? If Barefoot spoke thanks with overmuch of pity did he get
curses, laughter or silence from Footless?

"Look under your hat—it may tell you something." The Armenians pass this along and further allege, "A man from hell is not afraid of hot ashes." And what woman of them weaving a shadowed tapestry first began asking, "What can the rose do in the sea or a violet before the fire?"?

"A good heart always does a little extra." The Chinese give it. "The people's heart is heaven's will," they have been saying for long, and "Cleanse your heart as you would cleanse a dish. Vast chasms can be filled but the heart of man never. Emptiness of a heart prepares it for good news. The emptiness of a valley makes it yield an echo."

"When a Jew has a boil he has no onion and when he has an onion he has no boil." The Jews tell it with laughter. And somberly they say, "It will not be any lighter until it is first quite dark." Yet why should the Swiss be saying, "Night, love, and women give wrong ideas"? What then becomes of ten thousand poems written to night, to love, to women?

Freedom is everybody's job. Everybody is freedom's job. Jobs are everybody's freedom. When freedom shrieks everybody should listen. And everybody should be free to do what? When freedom flits then what? And should the question be asked continuously, oh constantly, like this: "Who paid for my freedom and what the price and am I somehow beholden?"?

TURN OF THE WHEEL

THEY are old over there, older than we are.
They fathered our speech and mothered many a document we hold dear.
We came from there in the seeds of our forefathers.
We are in debt to them, we owe them much.
Yet we came away from them because we wanted no more of what they
    held out to us.
We are the same as they and yet not the same.
And in the turn of the wheel of time we shall not be the same nor shall
    they.

Never did the map of Europe stay put.
Wave on wave swept over it in change on change.
What one time belonged here in another time belonged there
And the shift of the belongings had always a cost of strife and cunning.
This river once ours no longer is ours and those mountains once we owned
    we no longer own

And there are plains and rich valleys we took back and lost again and won
and once more lost.

Geography costs—why does the map of Europe never stay put?

Why do these cries go ringing so endless over land and its boundary
claims, over who shall own land and make it pay?

MANY HANDLES

BEWARE writing of freedom: the idea is political.

Beware too writing of discipline: there too is politics.

Be careful of abstractions: they become bright moths.

When images come test them by trial and error: let them vanish should
they choose exits.

Would you accept a thesis in governance of the writing of poems?

Why not listen to these poets on how those ones fall into categories the
same as eggs or potatoes?

Your personal choice has high validity and fidelity—for you Bruddah
Bones—for you—alone—by yourself—in the dust—in the wing whirr
of midges morning-born and noon-demised.

Light rose-candles and contemplate yourselves, gentlemen all—speak lofty
praise of each other—form cliques or claques and wear mandarin
queues taking your cues from each other—it has been done.

Let the cubes go by themselves in declarations they have the answers
while likewise the globes foregather and rate the globes as having the
finalities of the exquisite far-flung verities.

Have we not heard conversations between cube and globe and neither of
them enjoying the shape of the other?

Has not the square stood up and publicly called the circle a sonofabitch
because of animosities induced by the inevitable mutual contradic-
tions of form?

Now the rats—there we may have something—the rats make war on all
forms non-rat—wherefrom and howcome the enduring plasm of the
rat—the ageless and timeless unity and fraternity of the rats?

> Many the handles whereby to take hold,
> many the dishes to choose and eat therefrom,
> many the faces never chosen
> yet worn by many as though chosen
> as though saying, "This one on me my choice was."

In the Dark Ages many there and then
had fun and took love and made visions
and listened when Voices came.
Then as now were the Unafraid.
Then as now, "What if I am dropped into levels
          of ambiguous dust and covered
          over and forgotten? Have I in my
          time taken worse?"
Then as now, "What if I am poured into numbers
          of the multitudinous sea and sunk
          in massive swarming fathoms? Have
          I gone through this last year
          and the year before?"
In either Dark Ages or Renascence have there
been ever the Immeasurable Men, the Incalculable
Women, their outlooks timeless?
Of Rabelais, is it admissible he threw an excel-
lent laughter and his flagons and ovens made
him a name?
Of Piers Plowman, is it permissible he made sad
lovable songs out of stubborn land, straw and
hoe-handles, barefoot folk treading dirt floors?
Should it be the Dark Ages recur, will there be
again the Immeasurable Men, the Incalculable
Women?

THE UNKNOWN WAR

Be calm, collected, easy.
In the face of the next war to come, be calm.
In the faint light and smoke of the flash and the mushroom of the first
bomb blast of the Third World War, keep your wits collected.
At the information to be given out, after the few days of the fast moving
next war, take it easy, be calm and collected, and say to yourself, First
things come first and after this world comes another.
     Beware of the matters not to be spoken of.
     Beware of such matters as must be spoken of.
          Watch your ears as to things heard often.
          Watch your ears as to things seldom heard.

Pick and choose of what comes to your ears.
Select and sift, believe or disbelieve.
And on stated occasions, feeling a little high,
Believe perfectly in the completely unbelievable,
Thus making, under the tilt and feel of your hat,
Myths your own, miracles beheld of your eyes alone.

"Introducing," said a spieler, winking at a shill, "introducing Miss Nuclear
Fission, a wild gal in her time and she's gonna be wilder yet, and you
notice I don't dare touch her she's that wild."
"Introducing," said a spieler with a cock-eye at a shill, "introducing Mr.
Chain Reaction, her pal and dancing partner, a hairy brute, ten bil-
lion gorillas in one and when he tickles you, what gives? Nothin—only
you die laughin."
So what? So we must be calm, collected, easy, facing the next war,
And we can remember the man sitting on a red hot stove as he sniffed the
air, "Is something burning?"
Or the Kansas farmer, "We asked the cyclone to go around our barn but
it didn't hear us."
Or we can turn to the Books and take a looksee and then take a cry or
a laugh, as it pleases.
They say, do the Books: Begin your war and it becomes something else
than you saw before it began—it runs longer or shorter than planned,
it comes out like nobody running it expected, ending with both sides
saying, "We are surprised at what happened!"
A Marshal of France spoke like a gambler flipping a card or throwing
ivory cubes, saying as though he had finished what might be said:
"The controlling factor in war is the Unknown."
Wherefore we take a deep look into the unfathomable and come out with
a fingerhold on wriggling deductions fished from a barrel of conniving
and fructifying eels:
The bombs of the next war, if they control, hold the Unknown blasts—
the bacterial spreads of the next war, if they control, reek with the
Unknown—the round-the-curve-of-the-earth guided missiles of the
next war, should they control, will have the slide and hiss of the Un-
known—the cosmic rays or light beams carrying a moonshine kiss of
death, if and when they control, will have the mercy of the sudden
Unknown.
        We shall do the necessary.
        We shall meet the inevitable.

We shall be prepared.
We shall stand before the Unknown,
aware of the controlling factor
    the controlling factor
    the controlling factor
           —the Unknown

Packsack

1. Early Period

NOCTURN IV

THE claims of the sea, of the tide, move out.
The moon comes in with a claim its own.
Painters on the beach paint their claims.
    The chains drip with smears of this mystery.
    The brushes chase the smear over canvas.
    Preliminary sketches are baffled by claims.
The brass mist holds a long arm over the molten sea-moon gold, the
    changing sea-mist brass.
Tall sea winds come with their claims and make the picture something else
    again.
Memories of sea mist may be voices, faces, with melting brass lights gone
    before tall winds.

           [1908]

BRIM

BRIM's hammer hit a wheelbarrow; a sliver of iron sent itself through the lens of the eye into the eyeball.

Brim in the white sheets wonders if he will lose an eye and if a wedding is put off when a woman says a one-eyed man won't do.

The doc says maybe the eye will last; the doc X-rays, goes in with a knife, holds the slit with wires, pulls the sliver out with a magnet, stitches the eyeball, and says a week later the eye is saved.

Brim knows now the wedding comes off; among the white sheets with one eye dark he knows his sweetheart will not face a one-eyed man at the breakfasts of life's years.

A month; the doc knows the eye is lost; the doc is thinking; it is not so easy to tell a man one eye is lost; still more it is not so easy to tell a man what must be told again to a woman who wonders whether it will pay her to have a one-eyed man to eat breakfast with all along life's years.

Brim is in the white sheets thinking; the doc is in his office thinking; the woman . . . the woman. . . .

[1928]

FRANÇOIS VILLON FORGOTTEN

THE women of the city where I was forgotten,
The dark-eyed women who forgot me heard me singing
And it helped them the more to be forgetting
And I sang and sang on helping them to forget
In the city where I sang to be forgotten.

I slept with a woman ten men had forgotten.
She said I'd forget her and she'd forget me.
She said the two of us could sing one song
      On how bitter yesterday was
And another on tomorrow more bitter yet.
The two of us sang these songs.

Five women said they would forget me,
Since I sang with a heart half-broken,
Since I sang like a man expecting nothing.
Five women have forgotten me.
Ask them and they answer:
He's dim as mist to remember
        and oh he's long gone.

[1920]

BROKEN SONNET

MAY the weather next week be good to us.
    The strong fighting birds, so often ugly,
Jab the songsters and bleed them
And send them away; the wranglers rule,
The fast breeders, the winter sparrows,
The crows. The weeds, the quack grass,
The tough wire-grass, they have it all
Their way. May the weather next week
Be good to us.

[1920]

THE HAMMER

I HAVE seen
The old gods go
And the new gods come.

Day by day
And year by year
The idols fall
And the idols rise.

Today
I worship the hammer.

[1910]

HAMMERS POUNDING

GRANT had a sledgehammer pounding and pounding and Lee had a sledge-
hammer pounding and pounding
And the two hammers gnashed their ends against each other and broke
holes and splintered and withered
And nobody knew how the war would end and everybody prayed God his
hammer would last longer than the other hammer
Because the whole war hung on the big guess of who had the hardest
hammer
And in the end one side won the war because it had a harder hammer than
the other side.
Give us a hard enough hammer, a long enough hammer, and we will
break any nation,
Crush any star you name or smash the sun and the moon into small
flinders.

[1915]

SEE THE TREES

SEE the trees lean to the wind's way of learning.
See the dirt of the hills shape to the water's way of learning.
See the lift of it all go the way the biggest wind and the strongest water
want it.

[1928]

THE WIND ON THE WAY

EVERY day is the last day.
I have waited for tomorrow
And it has never come.

A wash of sand on the beaches
And we handle it soft and write
Our names on it.
    The sand goes out, comes in,
And there is no tomorrow, no yesterday.
    Everything is now.

I have heard sopranos in great cathedrals
Sing these high and low spokes of light.

And I have heard lonesome accordion players
Ring the changes on it hi-hi and lo-lo.

Every day is the last day.
       Tomorrow is the wind on the way.

          [1920]

ALOOF

FIRE of winter sunset,
   Your talk is red and gold
      In smoldering shadow.

Monolog of day and night
    between sun and stars,
You are an old man
       who chooses few words.

          [1913]

DUST

HERE is dust remembers it was a rose
   one time and lay in a woman's hair.
Here is dust remembers it was a woman
   one time and in her hair lay a rose.
Oh things one time dust, what else now is it
   you dream and remember of old days?

          [1913]

2. Little People

SWEEPING WENDY: STUDY IN FUGUE

WENDY put her black eyes on me
and swept me with her black eyes—
sweep on sweep she swept me.
>   Have you ever seen Wendy?
>   Have you ever seen her sweep
>   Keeping her black eyes on you
>   keeping you eyeswept?

PAPER I

PAPER is two kinds, to write on, to wrap with.
If you like to write, you write.
If you like to wrap, you wrap.
Some papers like writers, some like wrappers.
Are you a writer or a wrapper?

PAPER II

I WRITE what I know on one side of the paper
    and what I don't know on the other.
Fire likes dry paper and wet paper laughs at
    fire.
Empty paper sacks say, "Put something in me,
    what are we waiting for?"
Paper sacks packed to the limit say, "We hope
    we don't bust."
Paper people like to meet other paper people.

DOORS

An open door says, "Come in."
A shut door says, "Who are you?"
Shadows and ghosts go through shut doors.
If a door is shut and you want it shut,
    why open it?
If a door is open and you want it open,
    why shut it?
Doors forget but only doors know what it is
    doors forget.

BOXES AND BAGS

The bigger the box the more it holds.
Empty boxes hold the same as empty heads.
Enough small empty boxes thrown into a big empty box fill it full.
A half-empty box says, "Put more in."
A big enough box could hold the world.
Elephants need big boxes to hold a dozen elephant handkerchiefs.
Fleas fold little handkerchiefs and fix them nice and neat in flea handker-
    chief-boxes.
Bags lean against each other and boxes stand independent.
Boxes are square with corners unless round with circles.
Box can be piled on box till the whole works comes tumbling.
Pile box on box and the bottom box says, "If you will kindly take notice
    you will see it all rests on me."
Pile box on box and the top one says, "Who falls farthest if or when we
    fall? I ask you."
Box people go looking for boxes and bag people go looking for bags.

WE MUST BE POLITE
(Lessons for children on how to behave under peculiar circumstances)

1

If we meet a gorilla
what shall we do?

Two things we may do
if we so wish to do.

Speak to the gorilla,
very, very respectfully,
"How do you do, sir?"

Or, speak to him with less
distinction of manner,
"Hey, why don't you go back
where you came from?"

2

If an elephant knocks on your door
and asks for something to eat,
there are two things to say:

Tell him there are nothing but cold
victuals in the house and he will do
better next door.

Or say: We have nothing but six bushels
of potatoes—will that be enough for
your breakfast, sir?

ARITHMETIC

ARITHMETIC is where numbers fly like pigeons in and out of your head.

Arithmetic tells you how many you lose or win if you know how many you
had before you lost or won.

Arithmetic is seven eleven all good children go to heaven—or five six
bundle of sticks.

Arithmetic is numbers you squeeze from your head to your hand to your
pencil to your paper till you get the answer.

Arithmetic is where the answer is right and everything is nice and you can
look out of the window and see the blue sky—or the answer is wrong
and you have to start all over and try again and see how it comes out
this time.

If you take a number and double it and double it again and then double
it a few more times, the number gets bigger and bigger and goes

higher and higher and only arithmetic can tell you what the number
is when you decide to quit doubling.

Arithmetic is where you have to multiply—and you carry the multiplica-
tion table in your head and hope you won't lose it.

If you have two animal crackers, one good and one bad, and you eat one
and a striped zebra with streaks all over him eats the other, how many
animal crackers will you have if somebody offers you five six seven
and you say No no no and you say Nay nay nay and you say Nix
nix nix?

If you ask your mother for one fried egg for breakfast and she gives you
two fried eggs and you eat both of them, who is better in arithmetic,
you or your mother?

LITTLE GIRL, BE CAREFUL WHAT YOU SAY

LITTLE girl, be careful what you say
when you make talk with words, words—
for words are made of syllables
and syllables, child, are made of air—
and air is so thin—air is the breath of God—
air is finer than fire or mist,
finer than water or moonlight,
finer than spider-webs in the moon,
finer than water-flowers in the morning:
    and words are strong, too,
    stronger than rocks or steel
stronger than potatoes, corn, fish, cattle,
and soft, too, soft as little pigeon-eggs,
soft as the music of hummingbird wings.
    So, little girl, when you speak greetings,
when you tell jokes, make wishes or prayers,
    be careful, be careless, be careful,
    be what you wish to be.

3. Sky Talk

SKY TALK

Wool white horses and their heads sag and roll,
Snow white sheep and their tails drag far,
Impossible animals ever more impossible—
    They walk on the sky to say How do you do?
    Or Good-by or Back-soon-maybe.

Or would you say any white flowers come
    more lovely than certain white clouds?
Or would you say any tall mountains beckon,
rise and beckon beyond certain tall walking clouds?

Is there any roll of white sea-horses equal to
    the sky-horse white of certain clouds rolling?

Now we may summon buyers and sellers
and tell them go buy certain clouds today,
        go sell other clouds tomorrow,
        and we may hear them report
Ups and downs, brisk buying, brisk selling,
    Market unsteady, never so many fluctuations.

Can there be any veering white fluctuations,
    any moving incalculable fluctuations
    quite so incalculable as certain clouds?

                                    [Voices]

RIDDLES AND WHIMS
(for Lloyd and Kathryn Lewis)

What flies forever and rests never? The Wind. So say Senegalese. Maybe
they know. Forever is a long time—it is beyond time. And it rests never?
Could be. I'll work on it.

Who are the comrades that always fight, and never hurt each other? The Teeth. Here are the Senegalese again. I let 'em have it.

What runs faster than a horse, crosses water, and is not wet? The Sun. This is the French or, you might say, Early Frog.

What man stands between two ravenous fishes? The tongue between the teeth. Samoans tell that one—a puppet play for chillern.

Twenty brothers, each with a hat on his head, who are they? Fingers and toes, with nails for hats. Samoans again. I like Samoans.

The Irish farmer's wife in Derry, after he died she killed his horse. To the wailing landlord she cried, "Would ye have my man go about on foot in the next world?" I like her. She believed. That next world was real to her.

Wabash Avenue, a cold winter night, and an old Irishwoman selling pink-sheet newspapers reporting on ponies in Florida that afternoon. As she handed me a paper for my two cents she wished me to know, "My hat was on every horse!" This idea warmed her. Down the home stretch came the pounding hoofs. And on every horse she had a hat. I like her too.

BRIGHT CONVERSATION WITH SAINT-EX

1

THERE is a desperate loveliness to be seen
in certain flowers and bright weeds on certain planets.
    With the weeds I have held long conversations
    and I found them intelligent
    even though desperate and lovely.
    The flowers however met me shortspoken.
    "Yes" and "No" and "Why?" were their favorite words.
    And they had other slow monosyllables.
    They seemed even to have practiced their monosyllables.
    They seemed to find it more difficult
    Than the gaudy garrulous bright weeds
        to be intelligent, desperate and lovely.
Take a far journey now, my friend, to certain planets.

Meet then certain flowers and bright weeds and ask them
What are the dark winding roots of their desperate loveliness.
    See whether you bring back the same report as mine.
    See whether certain long conversations
        and certain slow practiced monosyllables
        haunt you and keep coming back to haunt you.
For myself, my friend, I have come to believe on certain planets
                    anything can happen.

2

There was a ring of gold
kept its circle around the moon
five hours one Tuesday night.
    When the ring went away
    it was gone in an eyeblink
    and the moon stood alone.
And I folded away in a little album
a pattern of moving gold haze
ready to fade in an eyeblink.

3

When the smoke of the clouds parted
there came on the night blue of sky
the brighter blue of a little star
tremulous with hazards of travel.
And why should I have been saying,
    "Go forth, little star.
    Be not afraid, small traveller.
    Remember it holds importance
    for you to be what you are
    and be seen where you are
    by random gazers like me"?
And I am asking why I should tell a star
    to go on being a star.

MEADOW IN SUMMER

THE north summer wind swept the hay.
The hay bowed howdy to the sun.
The long hay meadow ran a flag of brown
To the skyline blue, a light sweet blue.
Buy me a shirt of blue like that.
Bury my daughters in blue like that.

[Voices]

GUARANTEED ANTIQUE

LIFE is just a bowl of cherries.
Death is a kiss and an ashtray.

Suppose Judas Iscariot
had written Mary Magdalene:
"I love you, I love you."
    Would Mary have answered:
    "You . . . you? Since when?"

Life is just a bowl of cherries.
Death is a kiss and an ashtray.

[Voices]

YOU SHALL HAVE HOMES

THESE are the fields I called for.
These are the miles of the long night beginning.
These are the open ways of summer corn.
These are the grass and the moon changing.
Let the riddles of the yellow harvest come.

You shall have homes
out and away in the blue mist,
off and gone in the gray haze;
you shall have homes.

Go, birds, eat the last of the corn.
Pick it up now in the harvest clean-ups.
Then go, birds.

The time of the gardens is come,
The time of the bold last blazes,
The time of the old slow burnings.
Name over their names, bees, goldenrods,
Blues so much deeper than the earlier blues,
Yellows running out changes of yellow,
Purple putting out new strips of purple.
The crisp of a weaving, dropping time is here.

> You shall have homes.
> Out and away, off and gone,
> In a blue mist, in a gray haze—
> You shall all have homes.

[1920]

TWO MOON FANTASIES

1

SHE bade the moon stand still.
And the moon stood still for her,
At her request came to a stillstand.
"I am in love," she was saying.
She reached up with a single finger,
Pushed the moon with one little finger
And put the moon where she wanted it.
"I am in love," she was saying.
> On a later day, far later,
> She found her magic lacking.
> The moon was the same
> And her one finger the same
> Yet nothing happened.
And her laughter rang glad as she cried:
> "It was a good trick while it lasted."

2

The moon is a bucket of suds
yellow and smooth suds.
The horses of the moon dip their heads
into this bucket and drink.
The cats of the moon, the dogs, the rats,
they too go to this bucket for drink.
Thus an apparition told it.
To him the moon meant drink and drinkers.

The moon is a disc of hidden books.
Reach an arm into it
and feel around with your hands
and you bring out books already written
and many books yet to be written
for the moon holds past, present, future.
Thus an apparition related the matter.
To him the disc meant print and printers.

DROWSY

Sleep is the gift of many spiders
The webs tie down the sleepers easy.

OUR HELLS

Milton unlocked hell for us
and let us have a look.
Dante did the same.
Each of these hells is special.
One is Milton's, one Dante's.
Milton put in all that for him
was hell on earth.
Dante put in all that for him
was hell on earth.

If you unlock your hell for me
And I unlock my hell for you

They will be two special hells,
Each of us showing what for us
is hell on earth.
Yours is one hell, mine another.

THIS STREET NEVER SLEEPS

At the corner
of Forty-second and Broadway
it is feet and wheels
wheels and feet
far in the morning.

"Let us give Tomorrow nothing,"
is the cry down under.

"What has Tomorrow done for us?"
is the asking,
feet and wheels
wheels and feet
far in the morning.

There is a Fool sleeps
at Forty-second and Broadway.
He knows so little
He knows almost nothing.
He knows only the Wilderness waits
He knows the Wilderness comes:
feet and wheels
wheels and feet
far in the morning
at Forty-second and Broadway.

NEW SONG FOR INDIANA OPHELIAS

Twist your fingers, cheery.
Hum-ho on a jig in your head.
Hum-ho fee-fi-fo and a rum-tum-tiddle-dee-oo. Twist your apron, cheery.

Whistle what the fiddler hissed when he rosined the bow: It's hell on the
  Wabash in blossom time.
So wash the dishes, so pick up the room, put a thornapple branch in a
  pitcher of water, listen twice to the bobwhite call.
So go on singing hum-ho tiddle-de-oo, twist your fingers in your apron,
  cheery.
Sing, "Blossoms O blossoms lay my head in tub of blossoms, bring me an
  arm of blossoms, take 'em away, they kill me— No nah nah nah,
  bring me back blossoms, lay my head in a tub of blossoms."

[1922]

MOONLIGHT AND MAGGOTS

The moonlight filters on the prairie.
The land takes back an old companion.
The young corn seems pleased with a visit.
In Illinois, in Iowa, this moontime is on.
A bongo looks out and talks about the look of the moon
As if always a bongo must talk somewhat so in moontime—
  The moon is a milk-white love promise,
  A present for the young corn to remember,
  A caress for silk-brown tassels to come.
  Spring moon to autumn moon measures one harvest.
  All almanacs are merely so many moon numbers.
  A house dizzy with decimal points and trick figures
  And a belfry at the top of the world for sleep songs
  And a home for lonesome goats to go to—
Like now, like always, the bongo takes up a moon theme—
There is no end to the ancient kit-kats inhabiting the moon:
Jack and the beanstalk and Jacob's ladder helped them up,
Cats and sheep, the albatross, the phoenix and the dodo-bird,
They are all living on the moon for the sake of the bongo—
Castles on the moon, mansions, shacks and shanties, ramshackle
Huts of tarpaper and tincans, grand real estate properties
Where magnificent rats eat tunnels in colossal cheeses,
Where the rainbow chasers take the seven prisms apart
And put them together again and are paid in moon money—
The flying dutchman, paul bunyan, saint paul, john bunyan,

The little jackass who coughs gold pieces when you say bricklebrit—
They are all there on the moon and the rent not paid
And the roof leaking and the taxes delinquent—
Like now, like always, the bongo jabbers of the moon,
Of cowsheds, railroad tracks, corn rows and cornfield corners
Finding the filter of the moon an old friend—
Look at it—cries the bongo—have a look! have a look!

Well, what of it? comes the poohpooh—
Always the bongo is a little loony—comes the poohpooh,
The bongo is a poor fish and a long ways from home.
Be like me; be an egg, a hardboiled egg, a pachyderm
Practical as a buzzsaw and a hippopotamus put together.
Get the facts and no monkeybusiness what I mean.
The moon is a dead cinder, a ball of death, a globe of doom.
Long ago it died of lost motion, maggots masticated the surface of it
And the maggots languished, turned ice, froze on and took a free ride.
Now the sun shines on the maggots and the maggots make the moonlight.
The moon is a cadaver and a dusty mummy and a damned rotten investment.
The moon is a liability loaded up with frozen assets and worthless paper.
Only the lamb, the sucker, the come-on, the little lost boy, has time for the moon.

Well—says the bongo—you got a good argument.
I am a little lost boy and a long ways from home.
I am a sap, a pathetic fish, a nitwit and a lot more and worse you couldn't think of.
Nevertheless and notwithstanding and letting all you say be granted and acknowledged
The moon is a silver silhouette and a singing stalactite.
The moon is a bringer of fool's gold and fine phantoms.
On the heaving restless sea or the fixed and fastened land
The moon is a friend for the lonesome to talk with.
The moon is at once easy and costly, cheap and priceless.
The price of the moon runs beyond all adding machine numbers
Summer moonmusic drops down adagio sostenuto whathaveyou.
Winter moonmusic practices the mind of man for a long trip.
The price of the moon is an orange and a few kind words.

Nobody on the moon says, I been thrown out of better places than this.
No one on the moon has ever died of arithmetic and hard words.
No one on the moon would skin a louse to sell the hide.
The moon is a pocket luckpiece for circus riders, for acrobats on the flying
    rings, for wild animal tamers.
I can look up at the moon and take it or leave it.
The moon coaxes me: Be at home wherever you are.
I can let the moon laugh me to sleep for nothing.
I can put a piece of the moon in my pocket for tomorrow.
I can holler my name at the moon and the moon hollers back my name.
When I get confidential with the moon and tell secrets
The moon is a sphinx and a repository under oath.

    Yes Mister poohpooh
I am a poor nut, just another of God's mistakes.
You are a tough bimbo, hard as nails, yeah.
You know enough to come in when it rains.
You know the way to the post office and I have to ask.
They might fool you the first time but never the second.
Thrown into the river you always come up with a fish.
You are a diller a dollar, I am a ten o'clock scholar.
You know the portent of the axiom: Them as has gits.
You devised that abracadabra: Get all you can keep all you get.

  We shall always be interfering with each other, forever be arguing—
    you for the maggots, me for the moon.
Over our bones, cleaned by the final maggots as we lie recumbent, per-
    fectly forgetful, beautifully ignorant—
        There will settle over our grave illustrious tombs
        On nights when the air is clear as a bell
        And the dust and fog are shovelled off on the wind—
        There will sink over our empty epitaphs
            a shiver of moonshafts
            a line of moonslants.

SPECIAL STARLIGHT

THE Creator of night and of birth
was the Maker of the stars.

Shall we look up now at stars in Winter
And call them always sweeter friends
Because this story of a Mother and a Child
Never is told with the stars left out?

Is it a Holy Night now when a child issues
Out of the dark and the unknown
Into the starlight?

> Down a Winter evening sky
> when a woman hovers
> between two great doorways,
> between entry and exit,
> between pain to be laughed at,
> joy to be wept over—
> do the silver-white lines
> then come from holy stars?
> shall the Newcomer, the Newborn,
> be given soft flannels,
> swaddling-cloths called Holy?

Shall all wanderers over the earth, all homeless ones,
All against whom doors are shut and words spoken—
Shall these find the earth less strange tonight?
Shall they hear news, a whisper on the night wind?
"A Child is born." "The meek shall inherit the earth."

"And they crucified Him . . . they spat upon Him.
And He rose from the dead."

Shall a quiet dome of stars high over
Make signs and a friendly language
Among all nations?

Shall they yet gather with no clenched fists at all,
And look into each other's faces and see eye to eye,
And find ever new testaments of man as a sojourner
And a toiler and a brother of fresh understandings?

> Shall there be now always
> believers and more believers

of sunset and moonrise,
of moonset and dawn,
of wheeling numbers of stars,
and wheels within wheels?

Shall plain habitations off the well-known roads
Count now for a little more than they used to?

Shall plain ways and people held close to earth
Be reckoned among things to be written about?
Shall tumult, grandeur, fanfare, panoply, prepared loud noises
Stand equal to a quiet heart, thoughts, vast dreams
Of men conquering the earth by conquering themselves?
Is there a time for ancient genius of man
To be set for comparison with the latest generations?
Is there a time for stripping to simple, childish questions?

On a Holy Night we may say:
The Creator of night and of birth
was the Maker of the stars.

THE PRESS IS PECULIAR

THE morning newspaper is useful,
Likewise the evening pink sheet
For the service of these anonymous
Hopefuls who go forth and seek
The reward from whosoever
May be so good as to hand them,
Any anonymous one of them,
The boon and bestowal of a job.
First of all the newspaper
Passed the time for them,
Told them of dead and living fools,
Of follies and enterprises,
Of men dead as doornails,
Of women soft as pity and mist,
Of bank wrecks, wage cuts,

Tomatoes, potatoes, cheaper,
Better times ahead.
Just around the corner
Happy days here again,
Headlines, want ads, comic strips,
Kaleidoscopic phantasmagoria—
It passed the time for them.
And when night came with mercy,
Night and the sleep time of proud man,
Either on a crummy flophouse floor
Or else on the chilly park grass,
They had a bed and a blanket to order;
The morning paper, the evening pink sheet.
It is neither a boast nor a conjecture.
The press is peculiar.
The press serves the public.

[1933]

GLASS HOUSE CANTICLE

Bless Thee, O Lord, for the living arc of the sky over me this morning.

Bless Thee, O Lord, for the companionship of night mist far above the skyscraper peaks I saw when I woke once during the night.

Bless Thee, O Lord, for the miracle of light to my eyes and the mystery of it ever changing.

Bless Thee, O Lord, for the laws Thou hast ordained holding fast these tall oblongs of stone and steel, holding fast the planet Earth in its course and farther beyond the cycle of the Sun.

SWELL PEOPLE

There will always be monkeys and peacocks;
The monkeys for melancholy, the peacocks for pride;
The monkeys for chatter and crying out loud;

The peacocks for showing their tails and a fan of feathers.
Either they will be at your door soon
Or you will meet them the next time you travel.
 Who can get away from them?
 And they always say they are well met.

PUBLIC LETTER TO EMILY DICKINSON

FIVE little roses spoke
for God to be near them,
for God to be witness.

Flame and thorn were there
in and around five roses,
winding flame, speaking thorn.

Pour from the sea
one hand of salt.
Take from a star
one finger of mist.
Pick from a heart
one cry of silver.

Let be, give over
to the moving blue
of the chosen shadow.

Let be, give over
to the ease of gongs,
to the might of gongs.

Share with the flamewon,
choose from your thorns,
for God to be near you,
for God to be witness.

SCRIPTURE

WILLIE HENDERSON, Massachusetts-born, painted and dreamed in Chicago, ending in The City of the Holy Faith of Francis of Assisi, on the maps written as Santa Fé,
Where Willie paints, dreams, whistles, and sings offkey, where Willie on a day meets Alfonzo and the father of Alfonzo.
"It is a hard year, let me pay you for the alfalfa you let me feed my pony," said Willie to the father of Alfonzo at the pueblo of San Ildefonso.
"We have it together now," said the father of Alfonzo, "and when it is gone we go without it together," said the father of Alfonzo.

[1925]

WALL SHADOWS

THESE walls they knew those shadows
Who moved then as shadows holding bones,
Lights and tongues spread over bones.
Now with those shadows gone from these walls
Do these walls ever say, "When we try, we can remember those shadows"?

ONE MODERN POET

HAVING heard the instruction:
"Be thou no swine,"
He belabored himself and wrote:
"Beware of the semblance
of lard at thy flanks."

LIGHT AND MOONBELLS

THEY could bend low
and be to each other
a blue beam of molten light.
They wrought together keepsakes
thin as the air of five moonbells.

CORNUCOPIA

The naked cornucopia of autumn fields
bids us look for the harvest moon
and many buttons of green become gold,
tawny spun mist of haze hung hither
and many leaves blown thither, shaken,
change on change of russet and umber,
floats foretelling snow maybe soon;
in huts of thought, in witness rooms,
        snowfalls, long white snowfalls often.

LITTLE CANDLE

Light may be had for nothing
or the low cost of looking, seeing;
and the secrets of light come high.
Light knows more than it tells.
Does it happen the sun, the moon
choose to be dazzling, baffling?
They do demand deep loyal communions.
So do the angles of moving stars.
So do the seven sprays of the rainbow.
So does any little candle
speaking for itself in its personal corner.

MOMENTS OF DAWN RIDERS

Those who straddle foaming sea-horses and ride into the sunrise
do so with no instrument board, no timetables.
Those who watch one rainbow after another dissolve in seven prisms
they seem to gather reputations for being rainbow chasers—
they also choose bright mornings of clear weather and fading daystars
to study the organization of the sprockets of the bursting dawn.
They go out of their way to contemplate either a forty-eight-hour blizzard
or a short light snowfall and the bigger the flakes the shorter—

and the slow shadows of a summer moondown they wouldn't try to make
   over
nor any significant bushels of potatoes nor baskets of corn running over
nor poignant orchids ready to perish at a wrong breath or accent
nor any single scarlet moss-rose piteous in a wild raindrench
nor a boy of brown hair and eyes at Saipan, "It's hard to go,"
nor a blue-eyed boy at Arnhem with a wry smile, "Good-by chum this
   is it."

CROSSED NUMBERS

DELPHINIUMS are born
and why is a why
and when is a when.

Folded and kept for unfolding
one in a series of leaves
moves in a cunning of numbers
and numbers are never and now
and why is a why.

One is a two is a number.
Join them and cross them
and see them be numbers
be numbers beyond numbers.

Toss them in wanton spirals.
Weave them in grave communions.
Frame them with lighted eyelashes.
Let them have opening closing lips.
The wind is a when and a how
and a giver of laughing numbers
and a thrower of crying numbers.

One delphinium by itself
   is a who and a who.
A stalk of blue from a weaving earth
A sheaf skyblue from a waltzing sun
And one is a two is a number
And a spoke of light is a why
And one yes one is a who and a who.

[UMPAWAUG FARM, *Connecticut, 1933*]

NIGHT BELLS

Two bells   six bells   two bells   six bells
On a blue pavilion
Out across a smooth blue pavilion
And between each bell
One clear cry of a woman
"Lord God you made the night too long too long."

HARMONICA HUMDRUMS

AND so the days pass
and so we drift and dawdle.
Bright stood the mountains,
brighter loomed the sea.
And so the nights go on
and so we flash and fade.
Green lay the hills,
greener a river evening.
Stones wore gray lichen
and trees a morn mist.
And so the gold be gone.
And so the harm be ashes.
First moved the moonrise.
Later dropped the moondown.
Handy shoved the dawn.
Handydandy shone the sun.

[*Poetry*]

CHANGING LIGHT WINDS

CHANGING light winds
blew over the sea,
came blue, came gold,
came silver with spray,
came white in dreamsnow
with long foam feathers,

long sleepy snowfalls,
then gray over the flats
an overcast of monotone—
night and stars a while
then night and no stars.

NUMBER MAN
(for the ghost of Johann Sebastian Bach)

HE was born to wonder about numbers.

He balanced fives against tens
and made them sleep together
and love each other.

He took sixes and sevens
and set them wrangling and fighting
over raw bones.

He woke up twos and fours
out of baby sleep
and touched them back to sleep.

He managed eights and nines,
gave them prophet beards,
marched them into mists and mountains.

He added all the numbers he knew,
multiplied them by new-found numbers
and called it a prayer of Numbers.

For each of a million cipher silences
he dug up a mate number
for a candle light in the dark.

He knew love numbers, luck numbers,
how the sea and the stars
are made and held by numbers.

He died from the wonder of numbering.
He said good-by as if good-by is a number.

[*Poetry*]

ANYWHERE AND EVERYWHERE PEOPLE

THERE are people so near nothing
    they are everywhere without being seen.
There are people so eager to be seen
    they nearly always manage to be seen.
There are people who want to be everywhere at once
    and they seem to get nowhere.
There are people who have never been anywhere
    and they are less anxious about it than those
    who have been everywhere.
Could it be there are people so near to nothing
    they might be so humble as to say, "We go
    everywhere without being seen and it comes
    right easy on us"?
Could it be there are people who have never been seen
    anywhere and they ask people who have been seen
    everywhere, "How does it feel to be seen everywhere?"